The Silk Weavers of Kyoto

Nishijin weaver Mrs. Shibagaki Kimie peering through the warp. Photograph by Matsuo Hiroko.

The Silk Weavers of Kyoto

Family and Work in a Changing
Traditional Industry

Tamara K. Hareven

UNIVERSITY OF CALIFORNIA PRESS

Berkeley / Los Angeles / London

University of California Press
Berkeley and Los Angeles, California

University of California Press, Ltd.
London, England

© 2002 by
The Regents of the University of California

Library of Congress Cataloging-in-Publication Data

Hareven, Tamara K.
    The silk weavers of Kyoto : family and work in a changing traditional
industry / by Tamara K. Hareven.
        p.   cm.
    Includes bibliographical references and index.
    ISBN 0-520-22817-0 (cloth : alk. paper) — ISBN 0-520-22818-9 (alk.
paper)
    1. Weavers—Japan—Kyoto. 2. Silk weaving—Japan—Kyoto. 3. Silk—
industry—Japan—Kyoto. 4. Work and family—Japan—Kyoto.
5. Nishijin (Kyoto, Japan) I. Title.

HD8039.T42 J314 2002
331.7'677391242'09521864—dc21   2002068457

Printed in Canada
10 09 08 07 06 05 04 03 02
10 9 8 7 6 5 4 3 2 1

This book is dedicated to
the people of Nishijin — past and present,
Professor Morioka Kiyomi,
Irene and Richard Brown,
the memory of Yamamoto Ichiro,
and the memory of my parents, Mirjam and Saul Kern.

Contents

Illustrations and Tables

Maps

Figures

Tables

Preface

This book addresses key issues that have preoccupied historians, anthropologists, and sociologists over several decades concerning the interrelationships between family and work. As a case study, it examines the lives of the craftspeople and manufacturers who produce a luxury silk textile—the *obi* (sash) worn over *kimono*—in Kyoto's traditional weaving district, named Nishijin. As a social historian whose work is interdisciplinary, I have pursued questions relating to this topic since the late 1960s. Over the past three decades, while endeavoring to develop the historical study of the family as a new field of scholarship, I have also conducted research on the family's interaction with the process of industrialization in the United States.

My initial research on this topic examined family and work patterns over the twentieth century in what was the world's largest textile factory before World War II, the Amoskeag Mills in Manchester, New Hampshire. The key questions I pursued involved the family's adaptation to industrial life and its interaction with the factory system. I reconstructed the Amoskeag workers' careers, family patterns, and kinship networks from a variety of rich sources, such as company employee files, vital records, and company records, as well as from intensive oral history interviews. As part of this study, between 1971 and 1981 I interviewed the former workers of the Amoskeag Mills, and their adult children. Most members of the parent generation were immigrants, including a large proportion of French Canadians. I described the interview process and my findings in *Amoskeag: Life and*

Work in an American Factory City (1978) and *Family Time and Industrial Time* (1982).[1]

Due to the richness of the sources and the methods I developed, I was able to document the roles of the family and of the larger kinship group both in the home and on the factory floor. The two books resulting from this study contributed to the reversal of prevailing sociological and historical myths that viewed the family as a passive agent in response to industrial life.

In contrast to these myths, the textile workers in the Amoskeag Mills, in the emergent as well as the mature factory system, depended on kin to recruit workers, to organize and assist migration for relatives, to train young workers or newly arrived immigrants in the factory's workrooms, and to supervise or discipline younger relatives. While exercising job controls within the factory, kin disciplined new workers not to exceed implicitly agreed-upon production quotas when they were pushed to do so by management, and they protected their younger and new-immigrant members on the factory floor. Workers thus carried their kinship ties and their traditions of reciprocity into the factory, modified them in response to the pressures of industrial work, and addressed the industrial system on its own terms (Hareven 1978, 1982). Once these findings reversed the stereotype of social breakdown, my primary questions had to be restated as: Under what circumstances was the family an active agent, and under what circumstances did the family succumb to the vagaries of the industrial system?

The family's relationships to the world of work—to technological and economic changes, to shifting opportunities and constraints, and to the decline and disappearance of the industries that employed its members—were guided by the family's own strategies. These strategies changed in relation to the different circumstances the family encountered. Family strategies were only partly governed by economic choices. They were also driven by cultural considerations (Hareven 1990). In order to understand differences in the family's response to changing circumstances and constraints in relation to its own culture, it became important to compare family and work patterns in the United States with those in other cultures.

---

1. I conducted interviews of former workers and managers of the Amoskeag Mills in Manchester, New Hampshire, from 1972 to 1977. During this period, I interviewed about four hundred people in several lengthy interview sessions (three to four hours each). From 1978 to 1983, Kathleen Adams and I conducted interviews of the children of the former Amoskeag workers, who were then in their sixties and seventies.

To address these issues comparatively, between 1982 and 1996 I conducted life history interviews with Japanese manufacturers, weavers, and other craftspeople involved in the production of specialized textiles, the *obi* mentioned earlier, in a highly traditional industry established in Kyoto more than five hundred years ago. Since 1995, I have continued comparative research by also conducting life history interviews of current and former manufacturers and silk weavers in Lyon, France, and Vienna, Austria. I decided to interview directly in these other cultures because I believe that in cross-cultural comparisons there is no substitute for researchers immersing themselves in the societies studied.

Aside from the cultural differences between Japan and the United States, the Amoskeag Mills and the Kyoto silk-weaving enterprises differed dramatically in the organization of production, in scale, in structure, and in the product itself. At the Amoskeag Mills, the workers wove cloth on mechanical looms for mass consumption, while the Nishijin weavers were working in a household production system, employing their own family members, and making a highly valued luxury textile. Nevertheless, as this book will show, I found many similarities between Amoskeag and Nishijin in the interaction of families with the production of textiles and in the laborers' and craftspeople's perceptions of their roles and identities.

This book examines patterns of family and work in Nishijin as they have changed over this past century. It also presents the testimonies of the people involved about their lives in relation to the changes in the industry; their family histories; their self-perceptions as craftspeople; their relationships with their employers; their coping with insecurities and crises; and their frustrations, sorrows, and joys. These extensive life history interviews of weavers, artisans in auxiliary crafts related to weaving, and manufacturers — which I conducted over an eleven-year period, while visiting Kyoto twice a year during the university's summer and winter vacations and during one entire sabbatical year — present the Nishijin people's own stories. When reading these interviews, it is important to remember that the interviews express people's own perceptions of their lives and the worlds and events surrounding them; they do not necessarily present "objective truth" (see appendix).

The major strength of oral history lies not in the accuracy or objectivity of the account. Instead, its strength lies in its ability to reveal an essence of past lives that allows isolated events to be connected into a sequence that permits some interpretation. A uniquely valuable historical experience in itself, oral history offers almost the only feasible route for the retrieval of perceptions and experiences of whole groups who did not leave written records.

This book is organized in two parts. The first presents descriptive and analytical chapters about the transformation of the work process, the organization of production in relation to family and gender roles, and the Nishijin craftspeople's mentality and relationship to their work and product. The second provides translated and edited narratives of the Nishijin people in their own words. A final chapter addresses comparative strands between the Nishijin experience and that of the West.

This is the only book that brings the voices of Japanese craftspeople and manufacturers to English-language readers through extensive interview narratives. Several other books on Japanese laborers, such as Edward Fowler's *San'ya Blues* (1996), provide brief testimonies by individuals who were interviewed, but none contains English narratives like those presented here. While the Nishijin people's testimonies are included as sources for the reconstruction of their life and work patterns as discussed in the first part of this book, they are also here in their own right. The edited interview narratives provide insight into how these people interpreted their lives, how they viewed the world around them, and how they coped with adversity and change. These rich testimonies capture a way of life that is rapidly disappearing; they present images of a vanishing world.

Because the topics addressed by these narratives are not limited to the central issues discussed in this book, readers will be able to gain firsthand knowledge of and insights into a great variety of experiences and ways of thinking of Japanese craftspeople and manufacturers. A recurring natural development in the historians' craft, and in that of other social scientists, is the emergence of new interests in research issues that have not been previously explored. For example, historians have recently become intensely interested in life history and oral history testimonies, not merely as data sources for analysis and interpretation but also in what the process of the reconstruction of life history entails. As new questions addressed to the past arise in the future, searchlights cast on these narratives from different directions will reveal new dimensions of these vanishing personal and historical experiences.

Getting to know Japanese people and interviewing them intensively within their own culture has profoundly influenced me as a historian and as a human being. The long period during which I conducted this research in Japan exposed me to what Alexis de Tocqueville described as turning the mirror onto ourselves. The interview experience in Kyoto, which started as a comparative project, emerged as an endeavor important in its own right. This is why it took so long to complete this project. Trying to understand another culture is a formidable and humbling task.

In 1991, when my parents, who lived in Israel, were staying with me in Delaware during the Gulf War, my father asked me, "When are you going to finish your book on Japan? You have been going back and forth to Japan so many times, and there is still no book." I responded by saying, "Maybe I will never finish this book, because I have to learn so much about Japan, and I need to keep going back there." After some moments of silence, my father turned to my mother and said, "She is right. It takes a long time to understand another culture." Indeed, I am still learning.

As a social science historian, it is my goal to be as objective as possible. In this case, however, it is important for me to mention that this is also a book of compassion and passion. I feel a deep compassion for the Nishijin people, whose world is vanishing before their eyes, and I have a great passion for the city of Kyoto.

Acknowledgments

Over the many years of researching and writing this book, I have become enormously indebted to numerous individuals and institutions in Japan, the United States, and Europe for their interest in this project, for their support, and for their friendship. These individuals and institutions have invested their interest, support, and good will. Many people have taken time out of their personal and professional lives to help this project materialize.

First and foremost are the people of Nishijin, to whom this book is dedicated, and others in Kyoto, outside Nishijin, who generously shared their time and became partners in this long project. My deep gratitude and admiration go to the Nishijin people, who generously allowed me to interview them repeatedly over many years; who shared their life stories and thoughts with me; who introduced me to their relatives, friends, and fellow workers; and who opened their homes to me.

I am indebted to the Japan Society for the Promotion of Science, the Japan Foundation, the Joint Committee on Japanese Studies co-sponsored by the Social Science Research Council, the American Council of Learned Societies, and to the Japan-U.S. Educational Commission for their support of the early stages of research for this project. I am also grateful to Seijo University for an initial grant for starting exploratory interviews in Nishijin in 1982; to Doshisha University's Institute for the Humanities and the Social Sciences, where my research project was

All names of Japanese people in this volume follow the Japanese convention of listing a person's last name first.

based while I was a visiting professor in 1984, 1985, and 1986–87; and to Keio University, where I was the Harvard Yen Ching Exchange Professor in 1986–87.

I am also very grateful for support and assistance from Clark University, where I started this project; the Center for Population Studies at Harvard University; and the University of Delaware.

The Nishijin Textile Industrial Association [Nishijin Ori Kōgyō Kumiai] provided me with valuable information and bibliographic materials. The association introduced me to its key demonstration weavers (Mrs. Fujiwara, Mrs. Fuwa, and Mrs. Shibagaki), whose life stories form a crucial part of this book and with whom I have enjoyed a close association over eleven years. Mr. Takahashi Kozo, director of the association, was always helpful and provided me with valuable information. Ms. Matsuo Hiroko, who was the main photographer of the Nishijin Textile Industrial Association, generously shared her photographs with me and gave me permission to include the ones I requested in this book. She also taught me a great deal about Nishijin. I would also like to thank the Nishijin Textile Industrial Association and the Nishijin Foundation for permission to publish some of their photographs.

I am very grateful to Professors Kamiko Takeji, David Plath, and the late Professor Masuda Kokichi for their help and encouragement when I started this project in 1982. Professor Hayami Akira provided continuing encouragement, support, and guidance, and shared his expertise in the economic history and historical demography of Japan. At Doshisha University, the late Professor Nakamura Ken was extremely helpful in introducing me to several Nishijin manufacturers and wholesalers at the very beginning of my research. Professor Tanaka Masato, then director of Doshisha University's Institute for the Humanities and Social Sciences, acted generously as my academic sponsor while I was a visiting professor and provided his continuing support, guidance, and friendship. Professor Matsumoto Michiharu, at Doshisha University, generously shared his findings from his research in Nishijin from the 1960s and provided me with the original questionnaires of the survey he and his interdisciplinary team had conducted in Nishijin in 1962. Professor Hashimoto Mitsuru and his father, Professor Hashimoto Makoto, generously shared with me their interest in Nishijin and encouraged my research, and Professor Hashimoto Mitzuru collaborated on computer analysis of older surveys taken in Nishijin.

Professor Morioka Kiyomi, to whom this book is dedicated, has been my greatly valued friend over two decades and a continuing supporter of this research. He has provided his valuable guidance and friendship all these years and has been my tutor in my efforts to understand Japanese society and culture. I greatly appreciated traveling with him and his research team, as well as with him and his wife to remote villages in Japan. This afforded me a great opportunity to learn about Japanese culture and folklore. Professor Morioka has read the entire manuscript of this book and has provided invaluable suggestions on every level of detail. Professor Sakakibara Yasuo, of Doshisha University, and Professor Sakakibara Masako have provided guidance and information on the life of Nishijin and generously extended their hospitality and friendship over many years. In the most recent stages of finalizing the manuscript, Professor Sakakibara Yasuo took a great deal of trouble to answer my questions and help me fill in gaps in the economic history of Japan and Nishijin. Their daughter, Richie, has been an invaluable interpreter during interviews and in the translation of Japanese scholarly works and documents on Nishijin over several years. Professor Kitazawa Yasuo first introduced me to the traditional craftspeople of Kyoto, including a great variety of crafts in addition to textiles.

Mr. Nishiguchi Mitsuhiro, then director of the Division of Traditional Industries in Kyoto's municipal government, provided me with invaluable information and introductions to people for interviewing. I particularly enjoyed our "Nishijin walks," where he kindly shared with me his expertise and passion for this traditional textile industry. Mr. Nonaka Akira, one of the most creative Nishijin manufacturers, has been a great friend and supporter, has shared with me many aspects of Nishijin I would have been unable to discover on my own, and has been frank and open with me in his interpretations of the Nishijin world. Mr. Nonaka and his wife have also often provided me with gracious hospitality in their home. My gratitude for generous gifts of time and hospitality also goes to the late Mr. Maizuru Masajiro, former president of the Nishijin Maizuru Company; to Mrs. Maizuru Michiko, his daughter; and to Mr. Maizuru Kazuo, her son—the current president of the company. Mrs. Maizuru, in particular, has been my inside guide in the Nishijin world and in some other wonderful areas of Kyoto.

I have been extremely fortunate to have excellent, dedicated interpreters, who helped arrange the interviews and then facilitated the process with skill and grace. Among these, Dr. Ochiai Emiko and Dr. Himeoka Toshiko were outstanding in their expertise and dedication. Both were doctoral students when they kindly agreed to act as my interpreters at the first phase of my interviews in the 1980s. Now they are established and well-known scholars and I continue to appreciate our long-time friendship. I have benefited from many other interpreters, too numerous to mention, but all of whom were dedicated, helpful, and thoughtful. Their contributions made it possible for me to come in contact with inner experiences of Japanese people I would have never been able to reach on my own. My interpreters were my cultural guides and teachers. They taught me how to behave in various situations unknown in my experience in Western culture and how to conform to Japanese rules of human relations. I am also very grateful to Dr. Chimoto Akiko, who translated for me important documents on the economic history of Nishijin.

The two interpreters who consistently supported my research over all these years were Mrs. Kasakura Kiku and Mrs. Sotobayashi Kimie. I am deeply grateful for the persistent help, support, and friendship of these two women. Both acted as very effective interpreters, served as "ambassadors" in scheduling interviews and visits, and graciously assisted me in developing continuing relationships with the people I interviewed. They provided sustaining support for over a decade, and I appreciate the privilege of their friendship, as much as their research help. Mrs. Sotobayashi also helped me in many aspects of managing daily life in Kyoto. She shared with me the beauty of Kyoto's gardens, temples, and traditional crafts, and year after year we enjoyed together investigating the preparations for the Gion Festival and the procession. More recently, during the final period of preparation of this book, both Mrs. Kasakura and Mrs. Sotobayashi provided enormous assistance in my efforts to contact the people interviewed and the various organizations in order to secure permission for publication of these interviews and photographs. Mrs. Kasakura, in particular, embarked on extensive correspondence and visits with individuals and organizations and invested a great deal of energy, acting as an intermediary in Kyoto for securing these permissions and for further clarifications for the text.

I was fortunate to have excellent transcribers in Cambridge, Massachusetts, who translated the interviews from the tapes directly into English. The transcribers were graduate students from Kansai (western Japan, where Kyoto is located) or Japanese wives of American graduate students. The chief transcribers were Mr. Hirazawa Yasu and Mr. Machida Toho. I am very grateful to them for their thoughtful and precise translation, as well as to Ms. Yoshie Gordon and Ms. Mariko Marceau.

Over the many years of preparation and editing, I have benefited from the effective help of my research assistants at the University of Delaware, most notably Margie Kiter, Liz Park, and Brooke Bollinger. This last year, I have been privileged to benefit from the thoughtful and precise editing by Elizabeth Feather and Loren Marks at the University of Delaware. Loren Marks has been extremely helpful with his incisive suggestions for the painful but necessary reduction in length of the interview narratives. Elizabeth Feather has invested a great deal of effort in achieving consistency in terminology and style throughout the manuscript. Both have provided outstanding support in the difficult process of revising the manuscript, and have cheerfully handled tedious work. Ms. Feather has grappled with the awesome task of developing the glossary of Japanese words, and in assuring consistency in the English translation of these words throughout the manuscript.

Fumi Kumatani, a student at the University of Delaware, provided very effective help in the translation of Japanese documents and scholarly articles on Nishijin that have come to light since the completion of the original draft of the manuscript. Her valuable translation made it possible to expand and clarify important source material. Stephanie Fiedor, then at the University of Delaware, conducted valuable quantitative analysis of a survey of households of the Nishijin weaving district, and Saul Hoffman, her mentor and my colleague, offered generous guidance for coding and for analysis.

Thanks to Linda Parrish, cartographer at the University of Delaware, who drew the original drafts of the maps. Thanks are also owed to cartographer Bill Nelson, who prepared the final versions. Photo expert George Freeman of the Art History Department has provided his skills and discerning eye in preparing the photographs for publication. He invested a great deal of effort and good will in dealing with various problems in order to present the most accurate images. Professor Lawrence Marceau has been very helpful in clarifying terminologies and historical aspects of Japanese culture. During the final stages of dealing with the copyedited manuscript, Janice Thompson at the University of Delaware provided a great deal of help and support in answering queries from a distance.

This type of sustained research in another culture depends on local hospitality and friendship. In addition to the scholars, craftspeople, and experts in Japan mentioned earlier, many friends, hosts, and hostesses generously enabled me to feel at home in Japan. Through their kind hospitality, Ann and Yoshio Tsuda in Kobe helped me and many other Americans feel particularly welcome. Mrs. Ishii Toshiko provided friendship and hospitality, and she also introduced me to the Kurama Fire Festival in the mountains north of Kyoto, which became an important part of my research. The owners of the Yo-Sa-So Inn, in Ine Chō on the Tango Peninsula, provided generous hospitality in their wonderful inn while I was interviewing repeatedly in the Ine Chō villages. They did everything to facilitate my research in the surrounding areas.

I am grateful for the sustaining and supportive friendship in Kyoto for over a decade with Mr. Yamamoto Ichiro, owner of the Menami Restaurant. Mr. Yamamoto, who ran a wonderful small counter restaurant, provided me with hospitality and warm friendship. It was a very special experience to return to Menami in the evenings after long interviews, to share my observations with him and to learn from Mr. Yamamoto's observations of Kyoto life. He and his wife, Noriko, generously made me part of their family. Unfortunately, Mr. Yamamoto died at a young age in 1992 after a tragic illness. This book is also dedicated to his memory.

Many of my colleagues and friends in the United States and Europe provided continuing advice and support, along with valuable critiques. Among them, James Lee stands out as someone who provided expert advice on the manuscript and was always there to help, in the midst of his own busy schedule. Kathleen Adams read several versions of the manuscript and provided invaluable suggestions as well as her support in numerous ways through our very long friendship. Deborah Andrews read parts of the manuscript and made valuable suggestions. The long-term support and friendship of Kathleen Adams, Irene and Richard Brown, Glen Elder, Andrejs Plakans, Maris Vinovskis, Ron Walters, and Judy Wilson greatly helped me sustain my scholarly endeavors over these years, especially during difficult times. I am also very grateful for the friendship and support of Robin Palkovitz, my friend and colleague at the University of Delaware, and for that of Perry and Sheila Goldlust, in Wilmington, Delaware. Thanks also to George and Susan Cicala and to Sam and Shelly Gaertner at the University of Delaware. In Europe, I am grateful for support and encouragement from my friends Patrice Bourdelais, Rolande Bonaine, Antoinette Fauve-Chamoux, Bengt and Greta Ankarloo, Jean Paul Lehners, Michael Mitterauer, and Martine and Olivier Zeller. Professor Sepp Linhart kindly enabled me to use the library of the Institute for Japanese Studies at the University of Vienna.

Stanley Holwitz, editor and assistant director at the University of California Press, has been a great source of inspiration and help over many years. I greatly appreciate his encouragement and his support for this book. I owe thanks to Laura Pasquale and Cindy Fulton, project editor, also at the press, for their valuable editorial guidance and help. Lynn Withey, director of the press, has also encouraged this project for many years, and I am grateful for her help during the last stages of production.

Since interviewing in Nishijin, several people I was close to have passed away. Over the past few years, Mr. Yamamoto Ichiro, Mr. Konishi, Mr. Nagahama senior, Mr. Nishitani, Mr. and Mrs. Shibagaki senior, Mrs. Yasuda, Mr. Maizuru, and Professor Watanabe Kazuko (my friend and a great source of help and hospitality) have died. I would like to honor their memory through this book, and I hope the book does justice to their contributions.

While checking the page proofs for this book, I had the privilege of returning to Kyoto and of visiting again most of the people I had interviewed and who had become part of my life. I was thus able to update the information about changes in their lives and in Nishijin. During this stay, I was a fellow at the Nichibunken, the International Research Center for Japanese Studies. I am very grateful for the Center's hospitality and support, especially from Ms. Okuno Yukiko, who takes care of foreign scholars in a remarkable way. During the elaborate process of checking the page proofs, I also benefitted from the help of my interpreters and friends, Mrs. Kasakura and Mrs. Sotobayashi, who have helped me all these years. I also greatly appreciate the help of two doctoral students at Kyoto University—Sandra Schaal and Carly Toplis—who have helped me with the page proofs while taking time out from their important schedules. Professor Patricia Fister was a great help with the Latin rendering of Japanese words. While working on the page proofs, I was staying as a long-term resident in the Kyoto Palace Side Hotel. I would like to thank the staff of the hotel for making me feel at home and for all the support they gave me.

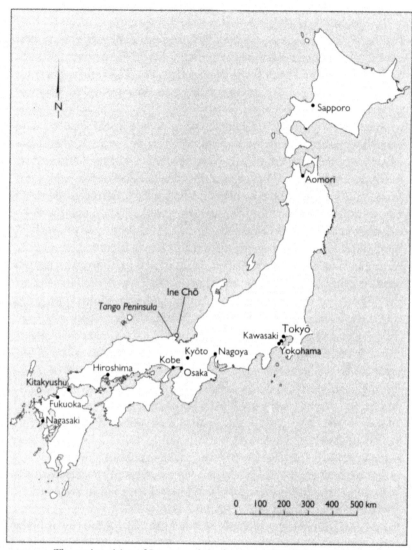

MAP 1. The major cities of Japan, and the location of the Tango Peninsula and Ine Chō

MAP 2. The prefectures of Japan

PART ONE

Family, Work, and the Division of Labor in Nishijin

A Historical Analysis

CHAPTER I

From Amoskeag to Nishijin

In January 1981, I visited Kyoto for the first time and went immediately to see the historic Nishijin weaving district. At that time, I had no intention of carrying out research in Nishijin. Having written about family and work in the textile industry in New England, my main purpose was to see the weaving enterprises and work processes and to talk with some of the weavers. With the help of an interpreter, I visited several highly skilled weavers who were operating traditional handlooms *[tebata]* in the Nishijin Textile Center *[Nishijin Ori Kaikan]*, which is run by the Nishijin Textile Industrial Association *[Nishijin Ori Kōgyō Kumiai]*. I was startled when some of the older weavers said, "Mine is the last generation to weave on traditional handlooms." Shocked by this revelation, I wanted to examine the Nishijin situation in depth and find out why these highly skilled craftspeople had a sense of impending doom. My own research as an American social historian focused on the relationship between the family and work in a declining textile industry in New England (Hareven 1978, 1982). The visit to Nishijin evoked many memories and images of a decade of interviewing the former workers of the Amoskeag Mills and their children. The Amoskeag workers and the Nishijin craftspeople had a great deal in common. They shared a strong attachment to their work and to the high quality and fame of their product. In both Amoskeag and Nishijin, the workers developed

This chapter has been adapted from my article, "From Amoskeag to Nishijin: Reflections on Life History Interviewing in Two Cultures," which was published in International Annual of Oral History for 1990: Subjectivity and Multiculturalism in Oral History, ed. Ronald J. Grele (Westport, Connecticut: Greenwood Press, 1992).

a deep loyalty to the companies for whom they worked and strongly identified with their products. Both the American and the Japanese workers experienced a sense of loss and betrayal as the world of work in which they had invested their best years was crumbling before their eyes, leaving them stranded. I wanted to understand what Nishijin's weavers were experiencing in a comparative context, and I was determined to return and research the situation.

Nishijin textiles are nationally famous for *obi*, the sash worn over the *kimono*, which has become a cultural property of Japan. An essential component of the *kimono* costume, the Nishijin *obi* is an elaborate piece of craftsmanship. It is worn only for highly festive rituals, such as weddings, special celebrations, flower arrangement, tea ceremonies, the Noh and Kabuki plays, and traditional Japanese dance. While both men's and women's *kimono* require *obi*, Nishijin *obi* is worn almost entirely by women, except for Noh players and Kabuki actors. In addition to being used in the fashioning of *obi*, the artistic Nishijin textiles are also used to make brides' wedding coats *[uchi-kake]*, garments for the crown prince's adulthood ceremony, and tapestries for wall hangings, traditional screens, and, more recently, table covers. Nishijin *obi* is made from a brocade in which colorful silk, gold, and silver threads are interwoven. The specific characteristic of this textile is that the silk threads are dyed prior to the weaving *[saki-zome]*. The brilliant weavings are textured, with some of the motifs raised in relief *[mon-ori]*. The sculptured texture of a Nishijin brocade, which resembles embroidery, is a product of the complex weaving of colorful threads, rather than dyeing or painting on a monochromatic cloth.

Nishijin designs incorporate the traditional symbols of Japanese culture, especially those related to the scenery around Kyoto, including this historic city's temples and festivals. The motifs and colors of the *obi* also harmonize with the seasons. The designs and colors are adjusted to each ceremonial occasion on which the *obi* is worn and to the season of the year. They display maple leaves and chrysanthemums in autumn; snow-covered pagodas and plum blossoms in winter; and cherry blossoms, irises, and peonies in spring. Mr. Yamaguchi, one of Nishijin's most artistic manufacturers who reproduces paintings depicting *The Tale of Genji* in weavings observed: "Most of the weaving techniques in the world converge in the weaving techniques of Nishijin. I wanted to use those techniques, as much as possible, to their utmost perfection. . . ." Design and weaving take place in the historic Nishijin district, close to the center of Kyoto, where the production of this textile has become a way of life (see maps 3 and 4).

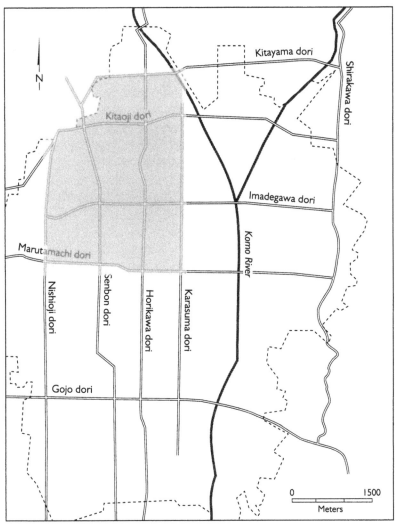

MAP 3. Kyoto City with the Nishijin area highlighted. *Dori* means "street."

This chapter discusses my interview experiences in Nishijin as they emerged and developed in the context of my changing relationship with the Nishijin people. Under a fellowship from the Japan Society for the Promotion of Science, I returned to Kyoto in fall 1982 and spent three months interviewing manufacturers and weavers in Nishijin. My first contacts were with manufacturers *[orimoto]*, to whom I was introduced by colleagues at Doshisha University, and with several demonstration weavers in the Nishijin Textile Center. The first people I interviewed

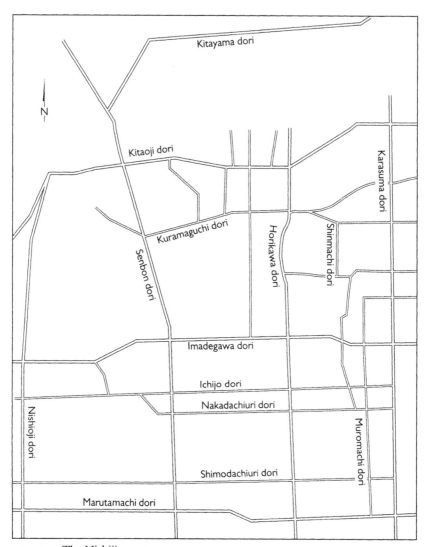

MAP 4. The Nishijin area

introduced me to their fellow manufacturers, weavers, relatives, and friends. Pursuing prospective people who would agree to be interviewed through these networks, I was fortunate to have access to an increasing number of weavers and manufacturers. These people were engaged in various forms of production of Nishijin *obi*, using handloom or powerloom weaving. I interviewed weavers working in small factories as well as in household production. In the beginning, I interviewed individuals.

Whenever a person had a spouse or another relative who was also a weaver, I interviewed that person as well. Sometimes I conducted the additional interview in tandem with the original person, and other times I interviewed the people separately (see appendix on interview method).

Some of my questions, which were derived from my research on the Amoskeag Mills, surprised the Japanese weavers whom I interviewed. Assuming that my questions were based on privileged inside information in Nishijin, they asked me: "How do you know to ask these questions?" I showed them my book, *Amoskeag: Life and Work in an American Factory City*. Looking at the historic photographs in the book, the Nishijin weavers were struck by the similarities between their work situation and that of fellow textile workers in distant America, even though the Amoskeag Mills had been the world's largest textile factory and produced commercial cloth on mechanical looms. They were also impressed by the differences between their traditional, small-scale enterprises and the giant textile factories in the United States.

Over a twelve-year period, I returned to Kyoto each year and spent three to four summer months and periodically two winter months, as well as a sabbatical year in 1986–87, conducting interviews in Nishijin. Over these years, I repeatedly interviewed some of the same people and their relatives, as well as new people I met. I interviewed a total of 200 people, including 110 women and 90 men. Early in the interview process, I discovered that over one half of Nishijin *obi* were woven in the cottages of farmers and fishermen in the Tango Peninsula, on the Japan Sea, about three hours from Kyoto City by train. Hence, in 1983, with the help of local community leaders, I also started interviewing the cottage weavers in Tango, in order to compare their experiences with those of the urban artisans in Kyoto.

The interviews, which lasted two to three hours each, were typically open-ended, following free-form questions that I posed as the conversation progressed. I conducted all of the interviews with the help of interpreters, and I recorded the entire interviews and conversations in their entirety with the permission of the people interviewed.[1] As my

---

1. In all cases, I was accompanied by an interpreter who translated the conversation back and forth. In order not to hamper the smooth flow of the conversation, I asked the interpreter to translate lengthy replies in summary only. I recorded the entire interview. Each tape was subsequently translated and transcribed by other interpreters in its entirety. This provided an additional check on the translation during the interview. To assure accuracy of translation, colleagues at Doshisha University and at other universities in western Japan checked the tapes.

friendships with the Nishijin people grew, the interviews gained greater depth. In addition to answering my questions about their family histories and work relations and about their sense of themselves as craftspeople [shokunin], the people interviewed talked about their deep concerns over Nishijin's impending decline. The formal sessions extended into longer social occasions that often continued in the weavers' homes late into the night.

"What's My Life to You?"

Like the former workers in the Amoskeag Mills, Nishijin weavers were initially puzzled as to why I should want to interview them about their lives and families rather than talk to more "famous" and "important" people. Similar to the Amoskeag workers, the Nishijin weavers initially felt that their lives were of no relevance for understanding the historical process. In both Manchester, New Hampshire in the 1970s and Nishijin in the 1980s, the people I approached graciously agreed to participate in the interviews, even though they were initially skeptical of their centrality to the history of their industry and communities. In both cases, their acceptance of the interview was guided by their work ethic. Many of them independently said, "If it is really necessary, I will help you do your job."

Work ethic and attachment to their craft served as important bridges with the people I interviewed, both in Nishijin and in Amoskeag. In my initial encounters with Nishijin weavers, my questions focused on their work. In most cases, during the first visit I asked weavers to describe their work process while they were sitting at their looms. After several visits, as I was asking weaver after weaver to describe his or her work, my interpreter asked me with irritation: "Dr. Hareven, why are you asking this woman to describe what she is doing? The other weavers already told you all about it." I had to point out to him that once weavers became immersed in sharing the intricacies of their work, their self-consciousness and shyness about the interview disappeared. The strong relationship between the weaver, the loom, and the textile product took over, just as it had in the Amoskeag interviews.

In Nishijin, weavers described their work with a sense of immediacy because weaving still formed the focus of their daily existence. The former Amoskeag workers, on the other hand, had not done any weaving for forty years. Yet they became animated when asked to describe their past work. Even frail, elderly men and women got up from their chairs and demonstrated, as if they were operating machinery. In both Nishijin and Amoskeag, the relationship of these men and women to the weaving process and to their product had become a central mark of their identities. "Textile language" served as a powerful means of communication.

As the interviews progressed, the Nishijin weavers and manufacturers gradually became absorbed in the interview process and began to share information about their lives with frankness. This was partly in response to my deep interest in the details of their life histories and their past and present experiences. Most of them had never before been in close quarters with a westerner; they had not even been in an interview situation with a Japanese person. My regular return visits to see the people I was interviewing each year, or several times a year, increased their confidence in my deep commitment to seeing them again and to continuing to explore their situation. In the fall of 1982, the night before my departure from Kyoto after my first round of interviews, Mr. Fujiwara, a weaver who had spoken to me openly at great length, urged me: "Now be sure to return to Kyoto soon, because you are taking part of our lives with you."

Another major reason for the Nishijin weavers' increasing responsiveness derived from anger and frustration over the decline of their industry. Nishijin was in the midst of a depression following the so-called Oil Shock. At the time I was interviewing these weavers, they were feeling a deep sense of betrayal by their employers, for whom they and their ancestors had worked loyally for generations. The Nishijin weavers saw these interviews as an opportunity to discuss the meaning of the crises and discontinuities they were experiencing in their work lives with a foreigner who was deeply interested in their lives, as well as with each other.

Weaving Relationships

When I started to interview in Nishijin, I approached weavers primarily in their workplaces—the Nishijin Textile Center and small factories—during their lunch and tea breaks or after work. I was introduced to various manufacturers by officials of the Nishijin Textile Industrial Association. I visited the manufacturers' offices and, after I interviewed the manufacturers, they usually introduced me to the weavers working for them. Initially I talked to the weavers in small groups. I then made appointments with individual weavers for separate interviews. I made it a point, however, to meet other weavers directly and individually, in case my being introduced by the manufacturer carried certain biases or was intimidating.

I was not at first invited into the weavers' homes, and I did not dare request to visit them at home. In Japan, the separation between "inside" and "outside" is strict, and I respected this boundary. As my relationships with various weavers developed over several interview sessions, I inquired about visiting them in their homes to interview them at greater length and to meet their families. I first asked two demonstration weavers from the Nishijin Textile Center—Mrs. Fujiwara and Mrs. Shibagaki—whether I could visit their homes and interview their husbands and parents. Mrs. Shibagaki immediately invited me to her home, which was located in a middle-class area with relatively small modern houses, in a recently developed district northwest of Nishijin, near Ryoanji Temple. Mr. and Mrs. Shibagaki used their home as a residence only, since Mrs. Shibagaki was working as a highly skilled demonstration weaver on a traditional handloom at the Nishijin Textile Center and her husband was a highly skilled handloom weaver making brocade in a high-class handloom weaving factory. Mrs. Shibagaki also invited Mr. Matsushita, a native of Kyushu, to the interview. Mr. Matsushita, a younger weaver who worked with Mrs. Shibagaki's husband, was one of the outspoken, energetic leaders of his factory's company union and of the Greater Nishijin Textile Labor Union [Nishijin Ori Rōdō Kumiai].[2]

While we huddled around the low table at which Mrs. Shibagaki usually entertained (even though she had a Western dining table and high-back chairs), she served refreshments and dinner. Mr. Shibagaki and Mr. Matsushita talked about the grave situation in Nishijin and about its impact on the factory where they worked. As the evening progressed, they expressed their bitterness and sense of betrayal over Nishijin's impending decline in production. Mr. Matsushita, who had migrated as a young man from his native town in Kyushu to work in Nishijin, was free of the web of formality that enmeshed Kyoto natives and spoke his mind frankly and passionately. Both Mr. Shibagaki and Mr. Matsushita complained about the weakness of the Greater Nishijin Textile Labor Union and its inadequacy in protecting the weavers' interests.

---

2. The Nishijin Ori Rōdō Kumiai—the Greater Nishijin Textile Labor Union—consisted of members who worked in small factories, as well as cottage weavers. Because of the difficulty in organizing cottage weavers, the union's membership was small. Mr. Shibagaki and Mr. Matsushita were the leaders of their company union, which was affiliated with the Greater Nishijin Textile Labor Union.

The next day, Mr. Shibagaki and Mr. Matsushita arranged for me to visit the factory where they worked. When I arrived, I was received by the production manager, to whom I was introduced by Mr. Shibagaki and Mr. Matsushita. The manager led me into the weaving room, where about thirty weavers were sitting at traditional handlooms in close proximity to each other. Mr. Shibagaki and Mr. Matsushita were working side by side at their respective looms, each weaving a magnificent stretch of *obi*. Their style of weaving produced a figured brocade with a sculptured effect, called Ming *tsuzure*. The technique, which originally came from China, requires a great deal of physical strength. The weavers had to manipulate the wooden handlooms with their feet by putting pressure on the foot pedals in order to batch the warp threads according to the punch cards on the jacquard mechanism.[3] I was surprised to see how physically demanding this job was, and how different Mr. Shibagaki and Mr. Matsushita looked in their work pants with sweat pouring down their faces and bare chests.

Following my visit to the factory, Mr. Shibagaki and Mr. Matsushita scheduled a meeting with the general secretary and several other leading officials of the Greater Nishijin Textile Labor Union at their headquarters. After the meeting with the union officials, I again visited Mr. and Mrs. Shibagaki in their home, and Mr. Matsushita was also present. Mrs. Shibagaki was one of the very few women weavers in Nishijin who was an active union member. She participated in all of our meetings with the union members, and often brought up important questions and issues for discussion during the interviews. For the next meeting, in order to reciprocate and free Mrs. Shibagaki from the elaborate rituals of hospitality, I invited her, her husband, and Mr. Matsushita to dinner in the modest traditional inn where I was staying. Dinners are typically served in private dining rooms, where guests sit at low tables on the *tatami* floor. Dining in this traditional setting facilitated uninterrupted conversations with my guests and the interpreter. Mr. Matsushita's wife did not work outside the home and, in typical Japanese fashion, she did not accompany him on social occasions.

Mrs. Shibagaki's participation in public activities and the fact that she accompanied her husband to restaurants and various social events were

---

3. The jacquard mechanism enables the weaver to manipulate the warp by batching its threads in accordance with the design pattern. The weaver pushes a pedal and then puts the shuttle through the opening in the warp made between these batched threads. The jacquard mechanism uses hundreds of punched cards for each obi. These punched cards were the precursors to the floppy disk now used by many manufacturers.

exceptional in Nishijin. Mrs. Shibagaki participated in these social activities in the company of male artisans and officials because she was a highly respected and skilled handloom weaver, holding the status of a professional in the Nishijin Textile Center. She was accustomed to public relations because hundreds of visitors surrounded her every day in the Textile Center, where she demonstrated and explained her technique to the public. In April 1990, when the Emperor and the Empress came to visit Nishijin, they closely observed Mrs. Shibagaki's unique technique of *tsuzure* weaving and asked her questions about her work in front of national television cameras. Mrs. Shibagaki showed the imperial couple her fingernails, the ends of which are filed like saws, so she can pull the weft through the warp in this particular type of weaving. This encounter was immortalized in a photograph of Mrs. Shibagaki sitting at her loom while the Emperor and Empress were intently looking over her shoulder and were conversing with her.

During all of our meetings with Mrs. Shibagaki's colleagues, her husband, and her parents-in-law, she was always recognized by her fellow weavers and relatives as my primary contact. She arranged the appointments and was present at all of the interviews with her friends, associates, and relatives. When I requested to interview her husband's parents (both of whom were retired weavers, still working part-time), she first arranged a meeting with them in her home. After I became acquainted with the older couple, she finally agreed to bring me to their modest house, despite their recurring protests that their house was too small.

Unlike their son and daughter-in-law, the older Shibagaki couple lived in a tiny Nishijin house facing the wall of the Kitano Shrine, a major shrine in the western part of Kyoto on the edge of Nishijin. The house was a typical Nishijin weaver's residence. These narrow wooden houses are nicknamed *unagi-no-ne-doko*, the "sleeping place of the eel," because of their long, tunnel-like shape. Mrs. Shibagaki and her husband joined us at the interview in the older couple's house. In order to keep the flow of my conversation with her parents-in-law uninterrupted, Mrs. Shibagaki served tea, refreshments, and evening snacks. Moving back and forth between the small cooking alcove and the sitting area where we were talking, Mrs. Shibagaki helped clarify my questions or jog the memories of her parents-in-law.

In contrast to Mrs. Shibagaki, Mrs. Fujiwara, also a highly skilled demonstration weaver who worked side by side with Mrs. Shibagaki in the Nishijin Textile Center, was initially reluctant to let me visit her home. She brought Noriko, her nineteen-year-old daughter who was studying English, to participate in my interviews of her, which I con-

ducted in the employees' cafeteria at the Nishijin Textile Center. During
these early interviews, Mrs. Fujiwara and her daughter sketched a complicated portrait of Mrs. Fujiwara's husband, a highly skilled handloom
weaver who worked in one of the famous Nishijin weaving factories.
Mrs. Fujiwara and her daughter eagerly described Mr. Fujiwara in affectionate but critical language. Mrs. Fujiwara criticized her husband's
unstable career as a weaver, since he had been forced numerous times
to change the manufacturer for whom he worked. She told us that he
was repeatedly penalized for his efforts to organize a company union
and for criticizing his employers' working conditions and labor relations.

I asked Mrs. Fujiwara if I could visit her home and meet her husband
and her father, who was a retired weaver but was still working secretly
[yami].[4] Mrs. Fujiwara tried to avoid my request in various ways by
using a great deal of indirect language. A week later, I once again
brought up the question of visiting Mrs. Fujiwara's house. Mrs. Fujiwara said that she was too embarrassed for me to see her small, old,
wooden house. I impressed upon her how people in the United States
value old houses. I showed her a picture of the interior of my house, a
restored three-decker in Cambridge, Massachusetts. After seeing the
photograph, Mrs. Fujiwara agreed to the visit.

Unlike Mrs. Shibagaki's middle-class home, Mrs. Fujiwara's house
was a small, narrow, wooden structure in the northwestern section of
Nishijin, near Daitokuji Temple. The manufacturers built many of these
houses as an investment in the 1920s, when they expanded the Nishijin
weaving district by constructing new weavers' cottages and enticing
workers to move there. Mr. Nishitani, Mrs. Fujiwara's father, made that
move with his parents when he was still in grade school. He continued
to live and weave in the same cottage into his old age. Mrs. Fujiwara
was born and grew up in that house, and later returned to live there
with her husband and children. Normally the oldest son would continue
to reside with his parents and bring his wife into the parental household;
in Mr. Nishitani's case, however, the movements and transitions of his
children were more complicated. The Fujiwara family's house was indeed tiny. It was so small that when five of us sat around the *kotatsu*
[the low sunken table with a foot-warming heater underneath], there
was no room for anyone to pass through the room to the outdoor toilet.

During our first visit, my interpreter and I talked with Mrs. Fujiwara,

---

4. Officially retired weavers continued to work "secretly" in their own homes for
specific manufacturers. The arrangement is illegal because of income tax and social security
regulations.

her daughter (Noriko), and her father (Mr. Nishitani). Her husband was nowhere in sight. Mrs. Fujiwara said with a tolerant smile that her husband was playing *pachinko* or mah-jongg with his friends, as was usual for him at that time of night. Mr. Nishitani, a highly skilled hand-loom weaver in his seventies, told us his life story with modesty but without hesitation. During the long evening, we sat comfortably with our feet under the *kotatsu* while Mrs. Fujiwara served various Japanese teas, sweets, and fruit. She occasionally interfered with her father's narrative, clarified old-fashioned concepts, or corrected the chronology. Mr. Nishitani talked primarily about Nishijin in the old days and about his life as a weaver. He did not yet touch on his family's history, so we were at first unaware of Mrs. Fujiwara's resentment of her father's earlier liaison with a *geisha* and his "betrayal" of her mother. We learned in a subsequent interview that shortly after the death of Mrs. Fujiwara's mother, Mr. Nishitani married the *geisha* with whom he had had a long affair. On the following visit to Mrs. Fujiwara's house, we also met her son, who worked as a low-ranking manager at McDonald's, and his wife, who was a stewardess for Japan Air Lines. The son's wife was fluent in English. The young couple resided separately from the parents. We had not yet met Mrs. Fujiwara's husband.

I finally met Mr. Fujiwara two days before my return to the United States. I visited the Fujiwara house in the late afternoon. It was Mrs. Fujiwara's day off, and she suggested that it would be a good time to interview her father. At about 5:30 P.M., she interrupted the interview and asked the interpreter and me to stay for dinner. She said that since she was not working that day, she had a chance to prepare *suki-yaki*, a special luxury beef dish served to guests or during celebrations. By then I had been sufficiently briefed by Japanese friends to know that while visiting someone's house in Kyoto in the afternoon, one should refuse a spontaneous invitation to stay for dinner. I was warned that such invitations were made only out of politeness and were not meant to be sincere; if one accepted them, it would be considered improper. I declined the invitation. Mrs. Fujiwara insisted, however, that we stay, because her husband had instructed her to ask me to stay for the evening. He also requested that she summon him from the *pachinko* parlor if I agreed to stay. I accepted the invitation.

Mr. Fujiwara arrived at 6:00 P.M., after his daughter fetched him from the *pachinko* parlor. He told me that upon realizing that this was my last visit to his house during this trip, he wanted to be sure to have a chance to talk with me. He wanted me to "understand Nishijin the way it really is," from his perspective. He said solemnly that he had never had a conversation with a foreigner before, and certainly not with a professor from a "famous" university. Sitting at the *kotatsu* with his wife and daughter, Mr. Fujiwara told his story for three hours without interruption. He told me what "Nishijin was really about." He recounted in great detail his employment history, his frequent job changes, and the various conflicts preceding each encounter that led to his being fired again and again. His wife and daughter were listening attentively— his daughter with amusement and his wife with a bantering that masked her anger and frustration. In the course of the evening, it gradually became clear that Mr. Fujiwara's story was intended as much for the benefit of his wife and daughter as for me. He definitely hoped to receive affirmation from me.

Mr. Fujiwara's career was atypical for Nishijin because he changed employers numerous times. As one of the most outspoken weavers in Nishijin, he was frequently fired because he spoke his mind to the manufacturer or because he insisted on the rights of the union. He had also been blacklisted several times and was able to obtain employment again only because of the manufacturer's recognition of his exceptional skills. During this period of labor surplus in Nishijin, he became more subdued, but he still spoke his mind despite his wife's anxiety that he might lose his job again:

The employer does not like what I say, and I feel that I am discriminated against by him. The way of thinking in Nishijin is old. The manufacturers speak about fairness, but we have our own pride as *shokunin* [craftsmen]. When they pay so little and take our jobs away, we feel that they do not appreciate our skill. . . . Where I work, the union amounts to almost nothing. Everything is the way the *oyakata* [antiquated paternalistic term for manufacturer] says. . . . They prevent us from having a union.

As Mr. Fujiwara was reciting his bitter account, Mrs. Fujiwara burst angrily into the conversation: "How many times do you think that you will continue to change jobs? Remember! This is not America!"[5] Mr. Fujiwara turned to me and said: "You know me by now. Can you imagine me not speaking my mind?"

During my subsequent visits to Kyoto twice a year, I often visited

5. Mrs. Fujiwara's comparison with labor turnover in America was prompted by my earlier statement that in the United States it was common for workers to change jobs and employers.

Mr. and Mrs. Fujiwara's home and continued my conversations with them, their daughter, and Mr. Nishitani. Following that first evening of self-revelation, Mr. Fujiwara was always present at the interviews. The Fujiwara family and I developed a mutual understanding about the tensions surrounding Mr. Fujiwara's "disorderly" career and his continuing determination to speak his mind to his employers. His wife frequently teased him about his repeated job changes. She always referred contemptuously to his obsessions with *pachinko* and mah-jongg, which at times led him to skip or interrupt his work. The entire family joked about it, and I had become part of the family's private joking circle.

Unlike the Shibagaki and Fujiwara families, whom I met on my own, I was introduced to another key couple, Mr. and Mrs. Konishi, by the manufacturer who employed them. At my request, the manufacturer took me to a weaver's cottage in Nishijin during work hours. He said that he chose Mr. and Mrs. Konishi because of the high quality of their weaving and because of their typical Nishijin house. He escorted me to a small wooden house situated on a narrow lane off Nishijin's main thoroughfare, where Mr. and Mrs. Konishi both worked and lived. When we entered, husband and wife were working in the small weaving shed, which was the first space as one entered the house. They were each sitting at a wooden handloom, weaving. Following the manufacturer's introduction, I asked Mr. and Mrs. Konishi a question about their weaving. I was surprised that Mrs. Konishi replied before her husband had a chance to do so. Later, as I continued to interview in Nishijin, I noticed again and again that Nishijin women weavers were outspoken and shared the conversation equally with their husbands. The manufacturer left and we continued to talk with Mr. and Mrs. Konishi for about an hour. I then made an appointment for a future interview.

Mr. and Mrs. Konishi were frank from the outset, even though we had been introduced by the manufacturer. Throughout our nine-year relationship, they never hesitated to criticize their manufacturer or the policies he followed in trying to curtail production at the expense of the weavers. They were among the most vocal and insightful critics of their manufacturer and the Nishijin system in general. Following our first conversation in their weaving shed, I visited Mr. and Mrs. Konishi on repeated evenings in their narrow sitting room. Husband and wife always spoke in tandem, taking turns to finish each other's sentences. They spoke about Nishijin with passion, but also had enough detachment to joke about it occasionally. They also humorously recounted various episodes in their personal lives, especially those concerning their courtship and marriage. Their marriage was one of love, unlike the typical arranged marriages of their age group. They remained close to each other in a way that I rarely observed among Japanese couples their age. Mr. Konishi did not go out drinking with his friends. He and his wife usually spent their evenings and Sundays together as a couple or with their children. Their closeness was also reflected in their interactions with each other during the interviews, in their comfortable style of discourse, and in their affectionate bantering. Only Mrs. Konishi, however, served the tea and refreshments.

During my repeated visits to the Nishijin weavers' houses, a "culture" of the interview clearly emerged. This culture was expressed in the assumptions that Mr. and Mrs. Konishi, the Fujiwara family, and other weavers I interviewed had about my involvement with their lives. After my second visit to Nishijin, they expected me to follow a regular pattern: to arrive once or twice a year (depending on whether I was able to come during my winter holidays) and to visit them. They never demanded it, but in the fashion of many other Japanese communications, they conveyed their wishes implicitly. My regular return visits to Kyoto provided the continuity in our relationships. The weavers and their family members began to count on these visits as a kind of affirmation of our relationships. In short, we had become partners in a mutual process of creation that assumed a life of its own.

Some of the people I was close to, such as the Fujiwara, Shibagaki, and Konishi families, began to take it for granted that I would be staying until late in the evenings. Each time when I felt it would be polite to pack up the tape recorder and leave, they encouraged me to stay, saying, "We have not told you yet about" this or that. They also became accustomed to my interview style—using the tape recorder and communicating with them through interpreters. My late sessions definitely stretched Japanese hospitality codes, but my hosts encouraged me and seemed to enjoy the conversations. It became important for them to affirm the routines that we shared in the interview: "You always do this," or, "We always do this together." An emphasis on such interview routines became significant to them as an established custom, a kind of signal that all was going well. One time when I was preparing to leave at 10:00 P.M. because I had to make an overseas call, Mrs. Fujiwara asked if something was wrong. She said, "You always leave after 11:00 P.M."

My partnership with the people in Nishijin extended beyond the exciting experiences and rituals of the interviews. As time went on, the

Nishijin weavers and manufacturers developed a real understanding of the issues I was interested in and began to supply me, of their own initiative, with new information in areas related to our conversational themes. Since employment conditions and work relations in Nishijin were changing rapidly as the depression in its industry progressed, each time I visited, the people I interviewed offered me updates about developments in Nishijin, as well as in their own lives. They also saved newspaper clippings and reports for me. As our ties deepened, they began to treat me as a distant relative. While I was in Kyoto, some of them included me in wedding celebrations and in funerals. They reported illnesses and deaths, marriages and births, and other personal or family events in the New Year's cards they sent to me in America. The people I interviewed closely in Nishijin were as much interested in me and in my interpreters as I was in them. They usually asked me questions indirectly, through the interpreter, because they were too shy to ask me personal questions directly. I showed them pictures of my house, family, and work environment in Massachusetts. I also frequently brought them gifts that were representative of American crafts and folk art, or of American scenes related to textiles.

By coincidence, I discovered an additional significant tie that helped cement our relationships: I was the same age as Mrs. Shibagaki, Mrs. Fujiwara, and Mrs. Konishi. In Japan, "same age" evokes a much stronger bond than it would in western society. It implies a capacity for empathy and mutual understanding on a level that Japanese people would not expect from those even one year older or younger than themselves. "Same age" was particularly helpful in my development of a relationship with this group of Nishijin weavers, because they were still working and were therefore more self-conscious and concerned with their privacy than the older generation, who were more accessible and eager to talk about the past. The sense of closeness that derived from being the same age helped me gain access to and win the trust of the middle-aged weavers. In Manchester, New Hampshire, the life stages of the people interviewed also considerably affected the degrees of their openness to the interviewer. However, the exact ages of the people interviewed did not carry such significance.

Even though I was close in age to those particular Nishijin people, I represented to them, especially to the women, a very different model of work and personal life—one that, in their culture, was characteristic of men. The women weavers exaggerated what they considered to be major accomplishments in my career: to be a university professor, an author of several books, and a world traveler. They juxtaposed these to their own careers. When some of them characterized their careers as inferior to mine, I reminded them that my work had required far less training time than the nine years expected to complete an apprenticeship as a Nishijin weaver. I also pointed out that the products of my work were more modest than theirs. I did not make products that were used as hangings in temples and public buildings or worn by the Crown Prince in his adulthood ceremony.

The Role of Interpreters

The interpreters' lives and social status were also topics of great interest to the people interviewed. Nishijin people are very selective about whom they let into their homes. Even though I had been accepted into their homes, they wanted to know about the Japanese interpreters. They were interested in their backgrounds, what they were doing, and how we had met. These questions were never posed as conditions for admittance; rather, they were asked during casual conversations when tea or coffee was served. The people we interviewed had enormous admiration for any Japanese person who was fluent in English, as most of my interpreters were (or at least appeared to be to my Japanese hosts). Being fluent in a foreign language was considered to be a sign of exceptional talent. Some of the people I interviewed wanted to know how and where the interpreters had been able to learn English because they wanted to find similar instruction for their own children.

The interpreters were indispensable to my interaction with the Nishijin people. Since my interpreters were not from Nishijin, I familiarized them in advance with the Japanese terms related to textiles, weaving, and the organization of production in Nishijin. I instructed them to use these terms in Japanese rather than run the risk of mistranslation. When the interpreters were unfamiliar with a new term, they often asked the person interviewed to clarify their statements related to Nishijin modes of production before they translated for me. In addition to translating, some interpreters acted as my cultural guides. They taught me, for example, how to bow and greet people, where to sit in a room, and what special words to say when served food or drink. Early on, one interpreter, an undergraduate student majoring in English literature who had studied in an American university, taught me the significance of extended farewells. When leaving someone's house, it is customary for the host or hostess to stand outside the front door and to keep bowing as long as the departing guest is visible. After my first visit to Mr. and Mrs. Konishi's house, I said my goodbyes and left at 11:00 P.M. As I started walking down the narrow lane, the interpreter kept prodding me, "Dr. Hareven, turn around and bow!" I turned around and saw Mr. and Mrs. Konishi still standing in front of their house. I bowed, walked, turned around, and bowed again. The lane was long, and the strap of my bag containing the tape recorder, camera, and books cut into my shoulder each time I bowed. As we reached the turn to the main cross street, I looked back and could still see my hosts standing in front of their house. Once more, the interpreter urged, "Dr. Hareven, bow again!"

The interpreters also facilitated communication by refining or adjusting the tone of questions that they felt might be perceived as intrusive or offensive. Most of these questions related to conditions of poverty and insecurity in the past, and to kin assistance. While I was grateful for this refinement of my questions, I requested that the interpreters not change the meaning or contents of my questions. I asked them to tell me whenever they perceived a problem in translating a question. On some occasions, my middle-class women interpreters tried to shield me from asking questions they considered too intrusive. After I became close to the Nishijin people and asked these questions again and again, I found that none of the people I interviewed was offended by my questions. The problem resulted from the interpreters' middle-class propriety, rather than from the people interviewed. I had encountered a similar situation when interviewing former workers in the Amoskeag Mills. The young Franco-American man who helped me with the French-language interviews, a Manchester, New Hampshire, native, found it difficult to ask women who were the age of his grandmother questions about birth control. Actually, many of the older women he interviewed about this issue were outspoken and eager to share their memories about how they had managed the Catholic Church's prohibition of birth control.

While my interpreters in Kyoto were educating me in the intricacies of Japanese manners and customs, I also had to teach some of them to overcome their class and cultural biases. My first interpreter in 1982, an undergraduate student, had studied for two years in a southern university in the United States and was fluent in English. The son of an upper-class Kyoto family, he was extremely conservative in his attitudes and seemed untouched by his American experience. When he accompanied me in Nishijin, I was unaware of his biases. After several interview sessions, he said to me with surprise: "Dr. Hareven, I could have never imagined that Nishijin *shokunin* [craftspeople] would be so articulate and so refined!"

Another interpreter was a middle-aged woman who had lived the sheltered existence of an affluent, suburban housewife. She was shocked when she saw the living conditions of the Nishijin weavers, especially the close overlapping of work space and living space. She was also indignant about the stories that Mrs. Fujiwara told about her father's affair with a *geisha*. She insisted that in her circles "such things would never happen!" Whenever I discovered such biases in an interpreter, I did not bring that person into Nishijin again. Over time, I was able to find sensitive interpreters who became personally interested in the ways of life and people of Nishijin. These interpreters appreciated the opportunity to discover an important dimension of Kyoto's life, one with which they had not been familiar. They subsequently continued to maintain ties with the people whom we interviewed by accompanying me to various events in Nishijin, such as festivals and exhibitions.

I deliberately avoided employing interpreters who were from Nishijin, because of the strong atmosphere of conformity within the Nishijin village *[mura]*. Many of the Nishijin people themselves viewed Nishijin as a narrow village. I was concerned that the people interviewed might consider my bringing Nishijin natives or residents as interpreters as an intrusion into their privacy. Also, if an interpreter knew too much about Nishijin, the people interviewed would take for granted a great deal of the information about Nishijin life and would fail to explain in detail. This happened in Manchester, where the people interviewed described their world in great detail to someone from outside the community, but the same people responded to an interview assistant from Manchester by saying: "You know, my dear, what this is about. Why do I need to repeat it?" (Hareven 1978, 1982).

Turning Points in the Relationship

An important turning point in my interview relationship with the Nishijin people occurred when my research became publicly known through newspaper interviews and the publication of some of my statements about Nishijin's crisis. Beginning in 1985, the *Kyoto Shimbun* (Kyoto's leading newspaper) and journals published by the Nishijin Textile Industrial Association and by the Kyoto municipal and prefectural governments began to print articles about me and my research. In 1987, a local television station did a brief documentary film on my research and accompanied me to some of the weavers' houses in Nishijin. The Nishijin people felt that I was becoming "famous" in Kyoto, and this meant a great deal to the people I interviewed. They were proud that the professor [sensei] with whom they had a close relationship was turning into a public figure. They also delighted in the publicity for Nishijin's cause expressed in my articles in the popular press and in government publications.

When news reporters first approached me, I deliberated for some time before I agreed to be interviewed. I was concerned that my statements in the press might bias the sources for my study in two ways. First, once the Nishijin people knew my interpretation, they might cater their statements to fit my point of view. Second, I was concerned that my advocacy of the preservation of Nishijin's architecture might antagonize the manufacturers who disagreed with me. On the other hand, I felt moved to give something back to the community that had been so helpful to me—a commitment historians, anthropologists, and sociologists who study communities often bear.

In the interviews for newspapers, I described the purpose of my research in Nishijin and the topics of concern. I did not share my scholarly interpretations, because my study was still in progress. I did, however, strongly advocate the need to save Nishijin's traditional industry and the sources of livelihood of its artisans and manufacturers in the face of the crisis that threatened to engulf them. I emphasized the need to keep Nishijin weaving in its historic location, rather than permit it to become a "brain center" where *obi* are planned and designed but not woven. I also stressed the significance of saving Nishijin's traditional architecture and streetscapes, which were in danger of being destroyed.

My advocacy attracted the attention of government officials on the municipal and prefectural levels. Some of them identified with my point of view but felt incapable of forging any major changes. They wanted to provide me with a forum for voicing my opinions, in the hope that my recommendations, coming from what they considered a well-qualified outsider, would have a better chance of attracting the attention of city planning officials and community members. Kyoto Prefecture's magazine on labor economics invited me to write an article. When they published "The Nishijin Dilemma" in Japanese in 1985, it attracted a great deal of attention in government circles and in Nishijin (Hareven 1985). The weavers and other craftsmen who read it agreed with my analysis and advocacy. While the Nishijin manufacturers with whom I was close generally agreed with my interpretation of the Nishijin crisis, some opposed my plea for the preservation of Nishijin's architecture and streetscapes. They were afraid that my article might stimulate the municipal or prefectural government to issue preservation ordinances that would interfere with real estate development in Nishijin. They debated the preservation issue with me, but continued to be friendly and helpful in facilitating my research.

In November 1987, I was invited to give a lecture at the World Conference on Historic Cities, hosted by the mayor of Kyoto. In a lecture entitled "The Nishijin Problem in World Perspective," I advocated for the preservation of Nishijin's industry and streetscapes. I brought examples from many other parts of the world where such preservation projects were being accomplished, including India, Indonesia, Thailand, and the United States. I pointed out the irony in the fact that the techniques and designs of Nishijin weaving were first brought to Japan from China. Those techniques were later lost in China because of wars and revolutions. Paradoxically, they were currently being revived in China by Nishijin manufacturers with the cooperation of the Chinese government, while they were at risk of becoming extinct in Japan. Kyoto's municipal government published the Japanese translation of my lecture in its economics journal. The Nishijin people began to read about themselves and about the struggles of their industry and community. As a result, Nishijin weavers, like the former workers in the Amoskeag Mills, began to see more clearly the links between their individual lives and the history that they had helped make. The publicity for my views about Nishijin did not alter the substance of my communications with the people I interviewed; rather, it deepened our relationship, as Nishijin people began to view me as a permanent friend and ally.

The opportunity to spend a whole sabbatical year in Kyoto in 1986–87 led to my immersion in Nishijin in a way that far exceeded my earlier two-to-three-month encounters. I was able to follow life in Nishijin over an entire year's cycle, including its various festivals, fairs, and celebrations. At their invitation, I attended many of these events with Nishijin people. During that year, I also began to take Japanese-language classes at the YMCA in Kyoto. The lessons, combined with the opportunity for daily interaction in Japanese, enabled me to communicate in Japanese to a limited extent. I began to feel closer to the people with whom I had spoken previously only through interpreters. While I continued to conduct formal interviews with the help of interpreters, I could at least have casual conversations in Japanese. I began to understand what Nishijin people were saying, and I was able to express my feelings to them in Japanese. Nishijin people were tolerant of my linguistic clumsiness and appreciated the sincerity of the feelings conveyed. Most important, my new limited language skills provided me with the ability to use certain characteristic terms that expressed gratitude or sympathy or that requested certain people to do things for which there are no real equivalent terms in English.

My relationship with the Nishijin people was transformed into a partnership and friendship that has grown over time. Of course, this affected the nature of the data gathered. When analyzing and interpreting the interview materials collected in Nishijin, I am conscious of the impact that the changes in my relationship with the community may have had on the nature of the evidence. This is true, however, of all research projects utilizing interviews and fieldwork. (See appendix.)

CHAPTER 2

A World within a World

It is hard to tell the real situation of Nishijin from the
outside. We have a saying in Kyoto that Honganji [the head
temple of Pureland Buddhism], the Gion entertainment
district, and Nishijin cannot be penetrated by outsiders.

Mr. Yamaguchi

As Mr. Yamaguchi pointed out, residents of Kyoto believe that the
world of Nishijin, like that of the temples or teahouses, is rooted in a
long, complex tradition, with a sense of mystery that cannot be easily
unraveled by outsiders. The Kyoto people have generated a stereotype
of Nishijin as an antiquated and, at times, almost sinister setting — a sort
of hidden world. This image is one that Nishijin weavers and manufacturers would like to erase. In reality, some aspects of Nishijin life remain
hidden but are hardly sinister (except as they are sometimes exploited
on Japanese television and in soap operas).

Nishijin is the name for three interrelated entities: the district of
Kyoto west of the Imperial Palace, in which silk-brocade weaving has
been carried out for five centuries; the production process, which is
complicated and requires the finest weaving skills in Japan; and the
unique product — the brocade used for priestly garments and for *obi*
[sash for the kimono] that are worn on the highest ceremonial occasions,
such as weddings, the tea ceremony, Noh plays, and traditional festivals.
Although its importance has not been officially declared, Nishijin cloth
is considered informally a cultural property of Japan. For the weavers,

FIGURE 1. Rooftops of the core of Nishijin, around 1970. Photograph by Matsuo Hiroko.

artisans, manufacturers, and tradesmen who work and live there, Nishijin, which has been nicknamed *mura* [village], represents a way of life — a tradition of family-based craftsmanship and industry that has been embedded in the community for centuries. Over many generations, Nishijin manufacturers, craftspeople, and shopkeepers have developed a strong identity as "Nishijin people."

The Nishijin weaving district was established in 1477, following the Onin Civil Wars, which lasted for a decade. When Kyoto, the capital at that time, was torn by war, a group of weavers took refuge in the merchant city of Sakai, near Osaka. At the end of the war, they returned and settled outside the western city walls in a former military camp (*Nishijin* means "western camp"). These weavers developed Nishijin into a thriving community of textile craftspeople and merchants who were appointed purveyors to the Emperor and to feudal lords. Over the

FIGURE 2. Street scene in Nishijin, near the Kitano shrine, about 1945. Courtesy of Matsuo Hiroko.

FIGURE 3. Typical street in Nishijin quarter. Photograph by Tamara Hareven.

centuries, Nishijin survived political upheavals and economic crises resulting from the wars among feudal lords, major fires and earthquakes that destroyed Kyoto neighborhoods, and, finally, the transfer of the capital from Kyoto to Edo (the early name for Tokyo).

Since the designs and techniques of Nishijin textiles were imported from China, Nishijin weaving initially resembled Chinese textiles. The originality of Japanese designs in various crafts began to emerge during the sixteenth century and Nishijin's luxury brocade assumed patterns and styles that have become more typically associated with an original Japanese design. The characteristic "sculptured" weave of Nishijin brocade emerged during that period, and the *obi* was developed as an integral part of the *kimono* costume. The use of the luxury silk cloth woven in Nishijin was at first restricted to the imperial court and the nobility. It was, however, difficult to enforce these restrictions. In the fifteenth and sixteenth centuries, *samurai* warriors, wealthy merchants, and courtesans of the pleasure quarters also began to wear Nishijin silk *kimono*. *Samurai* wore glamorous Nishijin textiles even during periods of thrift, when the shogunate and feudal lords ordered that *samurai*, who by then had become bureaucrats rather than warriors, wear modest garments. In the Edo Period (1600–1867), as a result of its unification under the Tokugawa Shogunate, Japan experienced a long period of peace, stability, and prosperity, during which the demand for luxurious Nishijin cloth increased among the wealthy city dwellers *[chōnin]*. These urban middle classes, who promoted the flowering of literature and of various forms of entertainment, including Kabuki theater, became important consumers of Nishijin's gorgeous textiles and of other products of craftsmanship produced in Kyoto (Reischauer 1989).

Support from the Tokugawa Shogunate for the development of luxury textiles led to the diversification of production of silk weavings in other parts of Japan, particularly in Kiryu in the north. Nishijin suffered from this competition and responded by organizing guilds aimed at improving and controlling the quality of its products. Late in the Tokugawa Period, Nishijin also suffered a major blow from the decline in demand for luxury fabrics resulting from a series of crop failures in Japan. Its economic problems were intensified by the Meiji Emperor's transfer of the capital from Kyoto to Tokyo in 1869, and the decline in the availability of quality silk threads, because of competition from Western markets. Following the Meiji Restoration, as part of a general effort by various prefectural and municipal governments to revitalize and encourage local, traditional industries, the governor of Kyoto Prefecture took important steps to introduce new technology into Nishijin weaving. In 1872, he dispatched three textile experts from Kyoto to Lyon, France, with instructions to acquire the techniques and machinery of the jacquard. One of the three emissaries, who stayed in Lyon longer in order to acquire greater knowledge, died in a shipwreck just before reaching the shores of Japan. The other two experts introduced the jacquard mechanism into Nishijin. The Hall of Weaving, established by the mayor of Kyoto in 1887, became an important workshop for dissemination of the new technology (Morris-Suzuki 1994).

The introduction of the jacquard, followed by the spread of the powerloom, revitalized Nishijin's industry and made it supreme in Japan. These technological changes coincided with the further expansion of an affluent middle class, able to purchase Nishijin *kimono* and *obi*. This considerably broadened the market for Nishijin fabrics at the very time when the manufacturers transformed the organization of weaving in Nishijin into a household production system.

The Nishijin industry attracted highly skilled craftspeople and merchants, as well as impoverished *samurai* and apprentices from other parts of Japan, who joined various aspects of its production. These newcomers received special permits to apprentice and later join the Nishijin guilds of manufacturers, weavers, and wholesalers. The purpose of the guilds was to restrict competition and maintain a monopoly on high-quality production of silk. Following the Meiji Modernization, after the apprenticeship and guild system became less formal, Nishijin continued to attract young men and women from the countryside of western Japan to apprentice in weaving and related crafts and then to settle as independent craftspeople. As will be detailed, introduction of the jacquard and subsequently of the powerloom early in the twentieth century led to a major transformation of Nishijin's production system during the first decades of the twentieth century. The most significant change was in the emergence of the household production system, discussed in chapter 3.

The Nishijin industry continued to experience ups and downs throughout the twentieth century, in response to changing business cycles and the Japan-China War (1894–95). Its worst period was, however, during World War II. Since Nishijin silk cloth was considered a luxury product, its weaving was stopped completely by government orders during the war. The powerlooms were broken up and used for the production of weapons. Only 5 percent of the Nishijin weavers were designated by the government to keep weaving Nishijin products for the sake of "the preservation of skills." Nishijin production was shut down for al-most a decade. During the post-war recovery, Nishijin weaving was reestablished, first secretly in the black market and then officially in the 1950s, after the restrictions were revoked. Following the post-war rebirth of the industry, Nishijin experienced a boom in the early 1950s. Bene-fiting from this recovery, Nishijin textiles began to sell all over Japan, and Kyoto residents nicknamed Nishijin weavers *gachaman*. This re-ferred to the idea that each time the shuttle clicked when it moved across the warp, a weaver earned a *man* [ten thousand *yen*]. The boom period resulted in overproduction, which then made the manufacturers vul-nerable during Nishijin's ensuing depression in 1955, caused by the Ko-rean War. Following its recovery after the Korean War, Nishijin enjoyed a decade of prosperity until dwindling markets, resulting from the Oil Shock of the early 1970s, caused its continuing decline.

Continuity and Change

In many respects, Nishijin represents the complexities of contemporary Japan. While Western literature praising the success of modern Japan has extolled harmony, conformity, and efficiency as the secrets of Japan's being "number one," Nishijin represents another side of Japan—one too frequently overlooked by Western commentators (Vogel 1979). Nishijin's current problems highlight the contradictions hidden beneath the surface of a "streamlined" modern Japanese society. The tensions between lingering tradition and rapid modernization have been played out within Nishijin since World War II. Despite its traditional character, Nishijin has been affected by the complexities characteristic of contem-porary Japan. Its craftspeople and manufacturers are caught in the cross-currents of new and old, between modern technology and traditional culture, and between bureaucratic organizations and persistent family traditions.

Nishijin remains, however, an enclave of traditional craftsmanship and aesthetics in the world of Sony and Mitsubishi. Nishijin weavers and manufacturers participate in most aspects of modern Japanese life, but the product, the weaving methods, the internal organization and division of labor, and the weavers' aesthetic values and view of them-selves as *shokunin* [craftspeople] all demonstrate the survival of their traditions, even in modified form. The Japanese term for Nishijin pro-duction is significant in itself. It is called *dentō sangyō*, a traditional in-dustry. Although the term may appear to be internally contradictory, it is used in Japan to define the production of various traditional items, such as pottery, lacquerware, metal, and paper, in addition to textiles. The term designates the traditional character of these crafts, while acknowledging changes in production methods and in the division of labor.

Nishijin should not be considered, however, a monolith. Its technology, modes of production, and division of labor have changed significantly over time (as will be shown). Changing tastes and fashions have affected the style and colors of Nishijin *obi*, yet the product has retained its basic motifs and designs. A Nishijin *obi* is still instantly recognizable. Nishijin has maintained its traditions and high standards of craftsmanship, even though the introduction of modern technology has transformed the craft into a partly mechanized industry. Some historians and anthropologists have recently criticized scholars' designation of the dichotomy between "traditional" and "modern" in Japan, and have claimed that Japanese people who present themselves as "traditional," may have actually "reinvented" traditions (Vlastos 1998). The Nishijin case is somewhat different, because its manufacturers and weavers use modern technology to produce a traditional product. The survival of their craft depends on making this product as consistent as possible with its historic antecedents in design and in motifs. The loyalty of Nishijin manufacturers and weavers to traditional images and designs is an essential condition for their survival, rather than a reinvention. On the other hand, the "traditional" designs and motifs that go into an *obi* have also undergone important adaptations to changing fashions and tastes over Nishijin's existence. A Taisho-period *obi* looks very different from a Meiji-period *obi* or from a contemporary one.

In Nishijin's narrow streets, the planning and production of cloth have been integrated within this traditional neighborhood, characterized by traditional *machi-ya* [townhouse] architecture. In this setting, the manufacturers' and craftpeople's work and family lives have been almost inseparable for centuries. As previously mentioned, many weavers still live and weave inside small, typically wooden houses, which are nicknamed the "sleeping place of the eel." The tiny rooms are arranged in a sequence, and one passes through from one room into the next. The weaving workshop that is attached to the house has a packed-earth floor, into which the looms are sunk to facilitate maintenance of sufficient humidity for the silk. Some houses have a skylight in the roof, similar to those in nineteenth-century weavers' cottages in Lancashire, England.

The tightly integrated houses flanking the narrow streets and lanes form a textured urban landscape. The unique sense of place is most striking in the northwestern parts of Nishijin, between Horikawa Street and Daitokuji Temple, and in the Kashiwano area, with its narrow streets behind the Kitano Shrine. When walking in Nishijin's streets in the 1980s, one would get caught up in the hustle and bustle of the community's historic industry. Almost every house carried a sign or a *noren* [split curtain hanging over the entrance as a shop sign] denoting its particular craft or the name of the "house," meaning the firm. Glimpses through the semi-open screen doors revealed the array of activities related to weaving, such as dyeing and winding of the thread, tying of the warp, pattern-making, and the production of the punch cards for the jacquard, as well as weaving. In some of Nishijin's narrow streets, the sound of clicking looms filled the air into the early evening.

Following the decline and depression of Nishijin's industry since the 1980s, the texture of the Nishijin "village" and its atmosphere have changed considerably. As increasing numbers of manufacturers closed their companies, the intensity of activity in Nishijin declined precipitously. Because of high land values, the area has become a hunting ground for real estate developers, who have been transforming Nishijin's historical streetscapes into a hodgepodge of poorly designed, modern, commercial buildings. Multi-story concrete buildings, some with imitation Spanish Colonial façades, stand out like false teeth amid the rows of traditional wooden buildings. Some of these modern buildings are manufacturers' new headquarters, built to express pride and modernity, but most of them are "mansions" (meaning "apartment buildings" in "Japanese English") built for investment by manufacturers who took advantage of the high land values and liquidated their weaving companies because of Nishijin's decline.

Ms. Matsuo Hiroko—outstanding, long-time photographer for the Nishijin Textile Industrial Association—recently published a book of her magnificent photographs of Nishijin. A statement in her introduction obviously suggests that the devastation of Nishijin's architecture has continued: "Today, the traditional townhouses of the artisans are being pulled down, creating such a desert of vacant lots in which it is now rare to hear a child's voice" (Matsuo 1999).

Family Business and Division of Labor

Nishijin weaving is fundamentally a family industry on the level of manufacturers, weavers, and other craftspeople in auxiliary processes, such as designers, pattern-makers, dyers, warpers, yarn-twisters, and harness makers. All these stages of production are closely integrated and family-based. The manufacturer's family business has historically been the backbone of the industry (see fig. 4). On the weavers' level, family-based production has been the predominant form since the beginning of the twentieth century. Today, Nishijin families still view the work of individual members as part of the family's collective effort. In many cases, the wives and daughters-in-law of manufacturers work in their company's office, train young weavers, process orders, and receive the public. For example, Mrs. Maizuru, widow of one company's president, who was working with her father and husband, and later with her son, described her work as follows:

When I got married, I was shocked to see the antiquated financial notebooks that our company used. I went to management school for one year to help my husband as his secretary and bookkeeper. Eventually I changed the record keeping to something more rational. . . . When the clerk reached retirement age, we got the computer. The computer and I share the tasks she used to do.

As Mrs. Yasuda, mother of the president of the Yasuda Company and grandmother of his successor, put it:

The men mainly work in public areas, such as sales and management, whereas other family members look after the weavers. This is what you find in most of the Nishijin family companies wherever you go.

Among the weavers, almost all members participate in the family's production effort. Even weavers who worked individually in factories usually belonged to families in which most members were engaged in the cottage industry. As Mr. Nishitani, a highly skilled handloom weaver, put it: "When I was a child, we were three brothers and sisters and my parents, all weaving together. . . . I learned weaving from my parents." Some weavers and their descendants have worked for the same manufacturers' families over several generations.

In addition to weaving, the manufacturers subcontract services from other craftspeople as part of the preparatory and auxiliary stages required prior to weaving. Unlike the weavers, the craftspeople who carry out these auxiliary operations are not the manufacturers' employees. They maintain their own small family businesses and subcontract [shita-uke] their services to different manufacturers. Similarly to the manufacturers, some of them have also functioned in Nishijin as family businesses for generations. The manufacturer is at the center of the planning and pro-

FIGURE 4. The Nagashima Manufacturing Company's office and design room. Photograph courtesy of the Nagashima Weaving Company.

duction process. He plans the type of *obi* he would like to produce and commissions the design from artists on the basis of a sketch (see fig. 5). If he is satisfied, he orders the pattern-makers to translate the design into precise diagrams on graph paper, which are used for punching the cards for the jacquard mechanism. (As will be seen, the computer has been increasingly used for this part of the process.) These punch cards, which are attached to the loom through the jacquard mechanism, determine the design (see fig. 6). The manufacturer buys the silk thread, sends it to the dyer, and then sends the dyed thread to the warp-maker and the harness-maker. Finally he sends the warp, the harnesses, the yarn, and the punched cards to the weavers, who weave the *obi* in their homes. At each stage, the auxiliary craftsmen deliver the thread, the warp, and the other parts back to the manufacturer, who then sends them on to the next craftsperson, and finally to the weaver. The weavers return the finished *obi* to the manufacturer. Specialists in the manufacturer's office then inspect the quality. If they find defects, they send the *obi* back to the weaver. If the weaver is able to correct the imperfections, he has to repair them; if not, he is charged for the imperfections and ordered to weave anew. If there are no defects, after proper examination and labeling, the manufacturer sends the *obi* to the wholesaler.

Even though a manufacturer could save time and money by having the dyed threads sent to the warp-maker, who in turn would send them on to the weaver, the manufacturer prefers to have the materials returned to him at each stage for quality control and centralization. In addition, there are also issues of trust. As Mr. Aioi, the head of a family warping business, explained, the manufacturer deliberately avoids having the various auxiliary subcontractors interact with each other, because of his mistrust of them:

In dealing with us and with subcontractors, the manufacturer likes to stay at the center of the process. After sending the product to be dyed, he wants to check the colors himself. Dye is something very subtle. He also wants to limit contacts among various craftspeople with whom he has subcontracts, in order to keep their business attached to him. He does not want the subcontractors of dyeing, warping, or harness making to contact each other. This is a traditional strategy of Nishijin manufacturers. Even though my brother deals with several manufacturers, each manufacturer guards his business secrets and protects his business from any leakage. We know what colors the manufacturers use, but we do not know how they use them in their designs. Some weavers make use of secret information from their manufacturer in order to get better positions with other manufacturers.

FIGURE 5. Drawing the design on graph paper in preparation for punching the cards for the jacquard. The image is of the floats of the Gion Festival in Kyoto. This is one of the three most nationally recognized festivals of Japan. Photograph by Matsuo Hiroko.

FIGURE 6. Punching the design on the cards for the jacquard. Photograph by Matsuo Hiroko.

FIGURE 7. Winding the weft onto the bobbins *[nuki-maki]*, 1946. Photograph courtesy of Matsuo Hiroko.

FIGURE 8. Twisting the thread *[ito-kuri]*. Photograph by Matsuo Hiroko.

Looking at this issue from the point of view of the manufacturer, Mr. Yamaguchi emphasized a relationship of trust:

In Nishijin, there are interdependent relationships between weavers and dyers. The relationships between the manufacturer and the different specialists, such as dyers, are very important. We are allowed to change our subcontracts *[shita-uke]* with these specialists as we like, but we are related to each other in sincerity. If they do something insincere, we may switch to another dyer. We could start a business without capital only if we had trust from other craftspeople to whom we subcontract the preparatory work. We could ask them to do some work without cash payments, if they had trust in us.

The smooth running of the manufacturer's enterprise and his economic survival depend on the wholesalers, whose businesses are also family-based. The manufacturer buys the silk yarn from the wholesaler of silk thread *[ito-ya]* and has to pay him cash. Yet he markets his *obi* through wholesalers for *kimono* wear *[ton'ya]* on consignment. The manufacturer's economic stability thus rests on the availability and price of silk thread and on the quick sale of his *obi* by his wholesalers for *kimono* wear. Nishijin manufacturers have traditionally dealt with two types of wholesalers for *kimono* and *obi*: the local, intermediate wholesalers based in Nishijin *[sanchi don'ya]* and the Muromachi wholesalers [Muromachi *don'ya*], who distribute the product nationally. The Muromachi wholesalers have long been concentrated in the district by this name, southeast of Nishijin along Muromachi Street above Shijo Street, in the center of Kyoto. This district also happens to be in the heart of the Gion Festival's precinct. The Muromachi wholesalers sell the *obi* to regional wholesalers for nationwide distribution to retail stores. Similarly to the manufacturers, weavers, and other craftspeople, the wholesalers also operate in family businesses. In recent years, Nishijin manufacturers have been bypassing the intermediate wholesalers located in Nishijin and have been dealing more and more directly with the Muromachi wholesalers. As will be explained, the persistence of the traditional dependence of manufacturers on wholesalers is one of the sources of Nishijin's demise. Most wholesalers wait nine months to a year before they pay the manufacturers, instead of making direct payment, and pay only when the *obi* is sold. Initially the manufacturer receives only a promissory note *[tegata]*. On the other hand, while he waits to be paid by the wholesaler, the manufacturer has to pay cash for silk thread at the time of purchase, as well as for the services of other craftspeople.

Following the post–World War II recovery, the manufacturers have continued to maintain family businesses, but the larger family concerns have been incorporated into companies. Family members who work in the company are considered employees and are paid salaries. Even such "modern" corporations with many employees are, at their core, family businesses in which several family members work together and where the oldest son is usually the successor. In the Yasuda Tsuzure Company, which made the most traditional handwoven *obi*, three generations worked together: the father (president), son (vice president), and grandson (who was being groomed for succession at the time of the interview).[1] The president's mother, wife, and son's wife worked with them in the family enterprise. (See interview of Yasuda family.)

The weavers who form the essential base of Nishijin's industry work predominantly as cottage weavers *[debata]* in their own homes. (The earlier term for cottage weaver was *chinbata*. The main difference between the two is that the *debata* owns his own loom, while the *chinbata* used to rent his from the manufacturer. Currently most cottage weavers own their own looms.[2]) Small numbers of the weavers work in factories *[uchibata]*. Nishijin factories are small workshops employing from ten to twenty workers on the premises (Chujo 1984). Most manufacturers run one or several small factories but rely primarily on a large network of cottage weavers. As will be detailed, all cottage weavers were historically located in Kyoto City, but now only about 40 percent of the weavers are in Nishijin. The remainder live and work in the countryside along the Japan Sea west of Kyoto, and in China and Korea.

Since the late Meiji Period, the bulk of Nishijin weaving has been increasingly produced in a cottage industry system *[kanai kōgyō]*. This system gained momentum as the dominant form of production beginning in the early 1920s, and is still the most characteristic organization of production in Nishijin. The cottage weavers are employees of the manufacturer, even though they own their looms, employ their own family members, and weave in their own homes. The manufacturer supplies the raw materials and the designs. The cottage weaver delivers the finished *obi* to the manufacturer and receives payment for the piece.

An Uneasy Relationship

Each weaving household is permitted to work for only one manufacturer, because of the manufacturers' fear of having their designs stolen.

---

1. Mr. Yasuda's son became president after his father's retirement.
2. The interview texts employ the terms *debata* and *chinbata* interchangeably.

The weavers' livelihood depends on an even flow of orders from the manufacturer. During boom periods, the weavers rush to the manufacturer's house (or send their wives or children) to deliver a finished *obi* as soon as it is ready, so that they can obtain the next order. During periods of low demand, the manufacturer slows down production by curtailing the orders. This renders the weavers vulnerable to market fluctuations. The pay system in Nishijin is based on piece rates. The weaver is paid for the finished *obi* at a rate set by the manufacturer. Regardless of how many family members weave together, the payment is not made to each individual but to the head of the weaving household or his wife for each *obi* that they produce. The manufacturer sets the rates through separate negotiations with each weaver. As a consequence, the weavers do not know what others are getting. This increases the atmosphere of competitiveness and secrecy in Nishijin. This system also partly accounts for the weakness of the Nishijin Labor Union. During good times, weavers had some leverage for negotiating, because they were able to change manufacturers. Ronald Haak (1975), who interviewed in Nishijin from 1968 to 1970, emphasized that being able to bargain individually with the manufacturers was an important source of morale for the weavers. By the 1980s, when I was interviewing during Nishijin's decline, the weavers had lost their leverage. In a declining market, they felt trapped with their manufacturers and had to accept their pay rates and tolerate the cuts in production. In the entire period, the Nishijin Labor Union was helpless in protecting the weavers' rights. During good times, cottage weavers did not support the union, because they preferred to bargain individually. During bad times, the union was too weak to protect the weavers' rights. As Mr. Fujiwara, a highly skilled handloom weaver put it: "If you don't complain, you get less. . . . [I]t's also the weavers' fault that we don't have a union."

Insecurity and Vulnerability

Contrary to the stereotype of the streamlined, permanent work lives often cited as typical of careers in modern Japan, the careers of Nishijin weavers have been fluid and fragile under the impact of various forces. Weavers' economic security declined and rose in relation to war and peace, business cycles, world markets, changing fashions, new technology, and Japanese government tariffs imposed on imported silk thread from China. Since silk *obi* was a luxury product, the Nishijin industry was the first to suffer curtailment or complete production stoppages during depressions or wars. Nishijin weavers thus experienced uneven and insecure employment patterns over generations. Even the most highly skilled weavers, for whose services manufacturers competed during good times, characterized their work lives as "hand-to-mouth." For Nishijin weavers, "disorderly" work careers, in terms of irregular orders from the manufacturers, were the norm rather than the exception. There has thus been continuity in the Nishijin weavers' uneven, cross-stitched careers from one generation to the next. As Mr. Nishitani (seventy-five years old at the time of the interview) put it:

Only old persons like me can tell the deep personal history of the Nishijin industry since the Meiji Period. My life was full of ups and downs.[3] The present is quite calm. . . . So many changes have happened, I tell you. Every time we had a war, business became brisk all of a sudden and then it became dull again. Such things happened so many times in my life that I can't count them all. After the war [World War II], the business gradually stabilized and is balanced now. . . . The hardest times I remember in Nishijin were in my childhood when I was about fourteen or fifteen years old . . . about sixty years ago. Around that time, we couldn't have days off. We had off only twice a month, on the fifteenth and the first, but if we rested on these days, we couldn't eat. Rice was our main food [shushoku]. . . . On the way back home, after delivering the product to the manufacturer, I could only buy one or two shō of rice.[4] It was really a hand-to-mouth existence [sonohi-gurashi].

Within the context of this hand-to-mouth existence caused by the fickleness of the industry, Nishijin men and women organized their careers and charted their family strategies to maximize opportunities for work in good times, adapt to constraints in bad times, and tide over depressions and disasters. They strove to maintain their craft and their family's livelihood in the unpredictable world of industry and trade on which they depended.

Technological Change

Since the late nineteenth century, Nishijin has experienced dramatic technological changes that have altered the character of the weavers'

---

3. Because of thematic emphasis, the order of the narrative in this quote is different than in the appearance of these statements in the text of the interview.

4. A shō of rice is approximately 1.4 kilograms.

craft. Nishijin's system of production underwent several transformations in the late nineteenth and early twentieth centuries, following the introduction of the jacquard mechanism and the powerloom. These technological innovations provided the opportunity for women to become weavers and made possible the emergence of the weavers' family-based household production system, which continues to the present. The introduction of the jacquard system from Lyon in the 1870s and 1880s revolutionized traditional weaving.[5] In the original "human jacquard" system, the weaver's wife or child sat on the second tier of the wooden drawloom and manipulated the warp by hand, selecting and batching the strands of the warp that had to be clustered in various configurations in order to determine the design (see fig. 9). Since the introduction of the jacquard, the weaver has been manipulating the punch cards with the design *[mongami]*, which are attached to the warp with a foot pedal (see fig. 10). This innovation freed the women who worked as "human jacquards" and made them available as potential weavers, just at the time when the use of powerlooms began to spread in Nishijin. In the early 1980s, manufacturers started to replace the old punch-card system with the computerized jacquard. The designs for the jacquard are now entered onto a floppy disk, which is placed in a disk drive attached to the loom. Contrary to a common misunderstanding, this direct jacquard method does not replace the weaver. It only substitutes a floppy disk for thousands of punch cards bound together on a bulky chain, which posed a serious storage problem in Nishijin's cramped quarters; but the old-fashioned "piano method" of punching the cards by hand and foot, similarly to earlier methods of punching computer cards, has become obsolete.

In addition to the jacquard, the major technological innovation that has revolutionized the division of labor and redefined the craft has been the powerloom, which first appeared in Nishijin in the late Meiji Period (in the 1880s). The number of powerlooms has increased gradually since the Taishō Period (the 1920s) and has risen dramatically since World War II. Since 1980, powerlooms have replaced a major portion of the handlooms. In 1984, Nishijin manufacturers used some twenty thou-

5. The jacquard system uses punch cards, like a player piano, or as computers used to. The cards are bound together into a large roll, and are attached to the warp. When the weaver pushes a pedal, the next card in the sequence is activated, thus changing the batching of the threads to follow the design, while the weaver pulls the weft through. The jacquard mechanism can be attached either to a *tebata* [handloom] or to a *riki-shokki* [powerloom]. It is not a loom by itself.

FIGURE 9. Edo-period painting of *takahata* [handlooms with double tiers for the "human jacquard"]. Photograph courtesy of the Nishijin Foundation [*Zaidan*].

FIGURE 10. Punched jacquard cards [*mongami*]. Photograph by Matsuo Hiroko.

sand powerlooms and only about five thousand handlooms. The Nishijin powerloom, however, differs from industrial mechanical looms. The type of brocade woven in Nishijin requires much greater skill and craftsmanship than ordinary industrial weaving. In Nishijin, even powerloom weavers must manipulate the shuttles by hand in order to achieve the intricate designs. Weavers on industrial powerlooms usually operate several looms at the same time. In Nishijin, a weaver works on only one powerloom at a time. Technological improvements in the powerloom enable weavers to produce color and texture effects that are similar or even superior to those of the handloom. For example, on the power-loom one can weave a much more complicated *bokashi* design [a complex weaving design with a gradation of colors shading off into each other, like in an impressionistic painting] that encompasses a larger range of colors. Similarly, an attachment to the loom that uses a robot-like hand to pull the gold threads through the warp automatically *[hikibaku]* con-siderably speeds up the weaving of gold brocade. This device is also easier on the weaver. In the traditional system, the weaver has to pull the gold threads through by hand. Because the mechanical *hikibaku* im-plement is very expensive, the hand method for pulling gold threads still predominates.

While powerloom weaving has become the dominant form of tech-nology in Nishijin since World War II, traditional handlooms have per-sisted. Unlike in the process of industrialization in Western Europe, powerloom weaving in Nishijin did not totally replace handloom weav-ing, nor did a factory system replace the cottage industry. A significant characteristic of Nishijin has been the coexistence of various forms of production and of old and new technology. Despite technological in-novations occurring over time, Nishijin weaving has continued to be a traditional industry *[dentō sangyō]*. Powerlooms and handlooms have coexisted side by side, sometimes within the same household or work-shop. This has considerably intensified the complexity of production in Nishijin.

Nishijin in Crisis

In 1962, Sosuke Otomo, the Nishijin handloom weaver in Kawabata Yasunari's novel *The Old Capital*, predicted the doom of small, home-based Nishijin handloom weaving: "Small home businesses like mine with hand looms will probably disappear within twenty or thirty years. . . . If one survived, wouldn't it have to be under government sponsor-ship as an 'Intangible Cultural Treasure'?" (Kawabata 1962, 40). The scenario Otomo described is now close to becoming reality. Handloom weaving is at risk of vanishing from Nishijin, but neither the national nor the prefectural government has made an effort to save this tradi-tional industry or to protect it as an Intangible Cultural Treasure.

Since 1980, Nishijin has started to face an unprecedented crisis and has experienced a depression that threatens its survival. The decline of

Nishijin is primarily due to the vanishing consumer markets for *kimono*, resulting from women's preference for Western fashions. This has led to curtailment of production and consequently to increasing unemployment and insecurity for Nishijin weavers. The causes of the decline, however, are far more complex than this single factor. The decline has been intensified by internal problems in production and marketing.

Economic decline in Nishijin started in the early 1970s with the energy crisis (Oil Shock) that affected the whole Japanese economy, but a steadier, more severe decline became apparent in the early 1980s. Nishijin manufacturers were particularly vulnerable to the Oil Shock because many had overproduced during the preceding boom period and some had even expanded beyond capacity. "A Nishijin company is like a pimple," goes one saying. "When it gets too big, it bursts." An average of forty-five to fifty manufacturers have shut down in Nishijin each year since 1984. Most surviving firms have severely curtailed production.

In addition to shrinking markets and the Oil Shock, Nishijin's crisis has been intensified by several other factors. The price of silk thread in Japan has been artificially high because the Japanese government, in its effort to protect domestic silk growers, has imposed a high tariff on imported Chinese silk thread. Nishijin manufacturers must, therefore, pay the same price for otherwise cheap Chinese silk as for Japanese-grown silk, despite several attempts by the Nishijin Textile Industrial Association to lobby with the national government. In 1989, the association of silk necktie weavers in Nishijin sued the government for damages resulting from this interference with free trade, but the association lost.

The social and economic consequences of the current crisis are complicated by Nishijin's traditional production and marketing system. Most importantly, Nishijin's decline is exacerbated by the traditional power still wielded by the Muromachi wholesalers. Because the wholesalers control the communication channels with consumers, many manufacturers are not attuned to changing tastes. The manufacturers' exclusive dependency on these wholesalers has made them vulnerable to the wholesalers' power as well as to their failure. The wholesalers drive up the profit on *kimono* and *obi* to a level that, in certain cases, prices Nishijin products out of the consumers' reach. Even people who would like to buy a luxurious *obi* often cannot afford it. The department store price of a high-quality handwoven *obi*, produced by a famous manufacturer, might be the equivalent of ten thousand dollars.

In turn, the fortunes of the manufacturer are tied to those of the wholesalers. Manufacturers' dependency on wholesalers reaches far back into Nishijin's long history. If a wholesaler goes bankrupt, the manufacturers who are heavily invested with that wholesaler sink with him. Many manufacturers who have stock tied up with certain large wholesalers go bankrupt in the wake of the wholesalers' collapse. In 1985, for example, a wholesaler escaped to Hawaii and committed suicide after his company went bankrupt. Manufacturers depending on him also went bankrupt. Even when confronting the crisis of the 1980s, most Nishijin manufacturers were unable to circumvent the wholesaler because they lacked the know-how to develop independent distribution routes and direct communication with retail markets. Some younger Nishijin manufacturers are now circumventing the wholesalers.

Nishijin manufacturers' efforts to deal with shrinking markets have led them to hire cottage weavers in the farming and fishing villages in the Tango Peninsula along the Japan Sea, and in China and Korea. The manufacturers feel that they have to employ the weavers in these places in order to survive economically. The wives and daughters of farmers and fishermen in the Tango villages form a cheap labor force. About 50 percent of all Nishijin *obi* are now produced in the Tango Peninsula, about four hours north of Kyoto by car. (Another 10 percent of Nishijin *obi* are woven in China and Korea.) Tango had its own traditional cottage industry, weaving plain white silk crepe for *kimono* [Tango *chirimen*], which was used for dyeing and hand-painting. When the demand for *chirimen* declined in the 1970s, Tango weavers began to weave Nishijin *obi*. In addition, Tango fishermen's and farmers' wives who had not woven previously were taught Nishijin weaving techniques by agents of Kyoto manufacturers and began to weave in their homes. This has provided an important supplement to the family income of Tango fishermen and farmers. Cottage weavers in Tango who produce *obi* commissioned by Nishijin manufacturers use Nishijin designs and raw materials. Their product is sold under a Nishijin label, although they generally have no direct contact with the manufacturer in Nishijin. The manufacturers prefer to communicate with the Tango weavers through a local middleman [*daikō-ten*], who instructs the weavers, supplies the designs and raw materials, delivers the finished *obi* to the manufacturer, and transmits the pay to the weavers (see interview of Mrs. Uebayashi).

The weaving of Nishijin *obi* in cottages outside Kyoto City and Japan has had a devastating impact on Nishijin weavers, who are painfully aware that they are gradually losing their work to low-skilled and low-paid weavers in the countryside. "I think that by sending products to be made in the countryside or in Korea, the manufacturers in this Nishijin business are choking their own necks like suicide," observed Mr. Konishi with bitterness. In reality, both Nishijin and Tango weavers are vulnerable to the declining market; it is simply a matter of time before the crisis will affect Tango weavers as well. Nishijin manufacturers avoid forming direct relationships with the weavers in the countryside, because sooner or later they will have to curtail production in Tango. They feel less responsibility toward an unknown rural labor force than toward the Nishijin weavers whom they have known for generations and with whom they have always interacted directly. Until recently, the squeeze resulting from the decline was felt much more acutely in Nishijin than in Tango. In the late 1980s, the Tango weavers also began to experience the impact of the depression. First powerloom weavers in Nishijin began replacing handloom weavers; then Tango weavers began replacing both Nishijin handloom and powerloom weavers; now the depression is threatening the survival of all weavers in Nishijin and Tango.

The crisis threatens the traditional relationship between the family and weaving, which has been the foundation of this historic industry. The manufacturers' and the weavers' family businesses have become increasingly insecure, rendering entire families vulnerable to economic depression. This has discouraged sons of manufacturers and sons and daughters of weavers from continuing the family business and household industry. The double bind in Nishijin is the absence of successors. Although both manufacturers and weavers acknowledge the importance of having young successors, they do not encourage their own children to succeed them. Both groups feel that without successors the industry will not survive, yet neither manufacturers nor weavers feel that they are able to attract successors with a promise for the future.

Nishijin's decline has undermined the weavers' security more dramatically than that of the manufacturers. The weavers have begun to experience increasing unemployment and insecurity. Most manufacturers have not fired the weavers outright. They have encouraged early retirement for older weavers, have avoided hiring replacements for retiring weavers, and have curtailed the workloads for the remaining weavers. Some manufacturers have been deliberately slowing down the weavers' pace by imposing a long waiting period before providing them with a new order. Each time the weavers deliver a completed *obi*, the manufacturers delay the weavers by an interval just long enough to curtail the weaver's production, but not long enough for them to qualify for unemployment compensation. As Mrs. Konishi put it:

The way the manufacturers deal with the decline is not really to tell us that they are reducing production. But they are reducing our work time by changing the orders, or asking us to wait for just a short while because they "are now having the threads dyed." They do this to us from time to time, but they don't ask us to stop weaving completely or anything like that.

Mr. Konishi added, "This is the characteristic of Nishijin. . . . This sort of thing is unthinkable in other businesses. There lies the peculiarity of Nishijin [laugh]." For Nishijin weavers, the gradual loss of their livelihood and craft represents a tragic betrayal by the manufacturers to whom they and their ancestors have been loyal for generations. Nishijin became famous over centuries because of the skill and pride of its weavers. Many of them retain this pride, but they feel it is being undermined by the uncertainty of their futures. (See Mr. Fujiwara's interview.)

Other traditional textile industries all over Japan have also experienced some decline related to the *kimono* market. The situation in Nishijin, however, is more severe than in other areas. For example, by contrast to Kurume *kasuri* [hand-dyed indigo cloth with a splashed pattern, from Kurume City in Kyushu], Nishijin brocade is produced almost exclusively for *kimono*. The use of Nishijin fabric for interior decorating has not been sufficiently explored. Kurume *kasuri* and other types of dyed cloth, especially indigo-dyed *[aizome]* textiles, have long been popular in Japan and abroad for tablecloths, cushion covers, wall decorations, split entrance curtains *[noren]*, and restaurant furnishings, as well as clothing. Indigo-dyed cottons appeal to Western fashion markets because of their simple textures and colors. Nishijin textiles in their current form, on the other hand, fail to sell easily in the European and American markets because they are too ornate, complex, and heavy and too expensive to use in garments.

Nishijin's crisis does not represent the classic situation of a traditional craft being displaced by industrialization, as was the case in nineteenth-century Europe and the United States. Nishijin has mechanized some aspects of its production but has not developed large-scale factories. Even with the use of the powerloom, Nishijin weaving is a traditional industry. Nishijin's decline results from larger economic and social factors and from changing tastes, not from mechanization. This point is extremely important for our understanding of Nishijin's future. If it were strictly a case of industrialization, the process would be essentially irreversible. Because the problems lie mainly in the realms of economics and social structure, Nishijin could still be saved.

Most Nishijin weavers and manufacturers have expressed the belief that there will continue to be a market for their very specialized, expensive *obi*. The disturbing question is how many of the current manufacturers will be able to survive in such a limited market. As Mr. Konishi put it:

Everybody in this business wants to survive, no matter what happens. Even if some people go bankrupt, others want to survive at their expense. No matter how hard the economic depression might be, on the surface people pretend with smiles that everyone is getting along well with each other, and yet they are very competitive at the bottoms of their hearts.

During the 1980s, some manufacturers revised their strategies. Using the typical Nishijin weaving techniques, they began to make other products, such as handbags, neckties, or textiles for interior decoration, such as curtains and upholstery. For other manufacturers, such a change seems unbearable because their very identity has been tied for generations to the production of high-quality Nishijin cloth intended for ceremonial purposes. These manufacturers cling to the belief that there will always be a market for first-class Nishijin *obi*. A major problem that has stood in the way of the manufacturers finding a way to deal with the crisis has been their own competitiveness and distrust of each other. Because of the manufacturers' historic fear of having their designs stolen, the Nishijiin Textile Industrial Association has failed in its attempts to establish cooperation and sharing in the organization of such centralized money-saving facilities as a communal computer center for designs and pattern-making.

Over the centuries, Nishijin has experienced numerous business cycles involving periods of curtailed production and unemployment. Many older people who have lived through recessions in Nishijin view the current one as the most serious and irreversible in their experience. Even if *kimono* makes a comeback and the market recovers, what would that mean for Nishijin? More than half of Nishijin *obi* are now woven outside Kyoto. The new generation is not continuing the traditional family industries. As Mr. Fujiwara expressed in frustration:

Nishijin is strong even in the depression. They said it would go bankrupt a thousand times, but it has not yet. What I am concerned about is the lack of young labor power. They should prepare something for the future, but they do nothing.

CHAPTER 3

Family Business, Cottage Industry

My family was a weaving family and I was urged to weave
against my will. I grew up with the weaving sounds. I was
seventeen years old when I started weaving. Even before that,
while I was still in school, I helped my parents twist and
spool the thread. I did many errands for them. My mother
died early and I had to help my father. My father is still
weaving *tsuzure* at age seventy-five. I was ten years old when
my mother passed away. I had one older sister and three
younger brothers. My grandmother took care of us. She was
living with us. She was like a mother to us. She brought us
up—five children. We also took care of her. She lived to age
ninety-six. She was also a weaver, but she said that she did
not like it very much, and finally gave it up. I resisted
weaving, but my grandmother persuaded me to acquire
weaving skills in order to survive.

Mrs. Fujiwara

The Interweaving of Family and Work

Mrs. Fujiwara (forty-five years old at the time of the interview) pointed
out that prior to World War II, Nishijin cottage weavers engaged the
entire family in the weaving enterprise. Husband and wife, older sons,
and older daughters worked side by side. Before the introduction of
powerlooms, men did most of the weaving, and their wives, daughters,

See an earlier discussion of these developments in Hareven 1988 and Hareven 1992.

and aging parents carried out subsidiary tasks involving preparation and clean-up *[shita-shigoto]*. Mrs. Fujiwara's father, Mr. Nishitani, remembered the intensive involvement of all his family members in household production:

Sixty years ago, all of us, my father and I also, all of us worked together. . . . We worked in the night until 9:00 P.M. or 10:00 P.M. We worked until late, even after the war. . . . We could not eat unless we worked. So I had to quit elementary school in the second semester of the sixth grade. . . .

Following the introduction of the powerloom, wives became weavers as well, but they still continued to help with their husbands' preparatory tasks and with the clean-up. Children were initiated into the craft by assisting their parents with such menial tasks as winding the thread or changing bobbins, cleaning, and running errands. Mr. Koyama (eighty years old at the time of the interview) recalled:

Young people today don't know about life in Nishijin. We couldn't even receive compulsory education. If we didn't stop going to school in the sixth grade and didn't have work, parents and children couldn't eat. Even before we entered the sixth grade, we had to wind the weft.

Following the introduction of compulsory junior high school attendance and child labor laws after World War II, children ceased to be important in household production, but husbands and wives, young adult children, and aging parents continued to work together in the cottage industry.[1] Parents tried to maintain continuity in their household production by pressuring their sons to become weavers, even when some children preferred to leave home and learn other occupations. Parents' expectations for their children to follow after them as weavers have since changed. Heads of weaving households also trained young migrants from the countryside who came to live in their households as apprentices. After completion of the apprenticeship, the heads of these

1. Nishijin families maximized their household labor force in periods of high demand for *obi* and, conversely, divested themselves of "extra mouths to feed" during slow periods by sending children out for apprenticeships or for adoption. In Japan, the adoption system was used by manufacturing, crafts, and farm families as a way to secure and train a family worker and heir. Poorer families tended to send children for adoption, usually with families they knew. Even well-to-do families sometimes sent a son out for adoption to another family who had no male heir. In some cases, apprenticeships were followed by adoption by the master.

households helped launch the apprentices, enabling them to establish their own weaving households.

Before World War II, children aged ten or older learned initial tasks by helping at home and then apprenticed with their parents, other relatives, or unrelated individuals. In the Meiji and early Taishō Periods, children were sent out to apprentice at an even younger age, and were often placed in the homes of nonrelatives. At the conclusion of the apprenticeship, young weavers could either stay on to work for their masters, return to work for their parents or relatives, or find jobs with other weavers. As Mr. Koyama observed, "Second and third sons were kicked out [from their parents' farms] to be apprenticed." He recalled how his father sent him to apprentice in Kyoto during the early Shōwa Period:

One day, my father said, "What about my son?" He decided without asking me, because at that time we obeyed our parents. Without thinking anything, when my father told me to leave home, I went to Kyoto. I learned to weave with a relative. He was a cottage weaver. Based on a contract, they promised me some money after ten years. So I stayed at his house for ten years. After the term was up, the master said I could somehow earn a living by working independently. I went out to rent a house; I found a small house where I worked on a loom that my former master gave me. That was when I was twenty-four. When I was twenty-five, I got married.

Very poor parents sent their children to apprentice in other people's houses in exchange for money they received in advance. In this system, the children were working to pay their parents' debt. The children were often treated as servants, instead of being taught a trade. This type of indentured apprenticeship was called *nenki-bōkō*. Mr. Konishi explained this practice with bitterness:

In the old days, the kids had an education only up to the fourth grade. After that, they were forced to leave for *nenki-bōkō* [indentured apprenticeship] for three or five years. . . . During the *nenki-bōkō*, they did not receive any pay and they could not leave their master by any means, because the parents borrowed money in advance from the master [in exchange for their child's service]. . . . It's like selling a human being. You know how young people won't listen to parents now? Nowadays, if they were sent for *nenki-bōkō*, the kids would say it's illegal. In those days, they must have been so impoverished!

Following World War II, legislation based on the American Fair Labor Standards Act prohibited child labor and children started to apprentice at age fourteen or later. The collective family character of Nishijin weaving, especially its predominance as a cottage industry, had serious implications for marriage and the relations between the generations. Men preferred to marry women with weaving backgrounds in order to maximize their family's labor force and to benefit from the backup their wives provided by performing preparatory and maintenance tasks. Mr. Shibagaki (eighty years old at the time of the interview), in a joint interview with his wife, noted, "It was a common thing, especially in Nishijin, to meet your future husband or wife in the factory, because both men and women worked there." Weavers usually referred to marriages resulting from factory courtship as love marriages in contrast to arranged marriages *[miai]*. Mr. Shibagaki revealed, however, that underlying these love marriages were strategic calculations:

It is to the advantage of a Nishijin weaver to marry a wife who is a weaver, because she can help at home in weaving when we need help. My wife is helping right now. Women continued to work in the factory after their marriage, usually until they got pregnant and their babies were born. After they had babies, they couldn't go out to work.

His wife (seventy-five years old at the time of the interview) added: "After our first baby was born, I continued to weave at home."

Nishijin mothers tried to discourage their daughters from marrying weavers because they knew how difficult the life of a Nishijin wife was. As young Mrs. Shibagaki put it: "In my generation, more women are working, since our parents told us to learn weaving. Young people growing up in Nishijin now do not want to work here, because they have seen their parents weaving at home and they know how hard it is." Families who had no connection with Nishijin work were particularly wary about their daughters taking on the demanding tasks of a Nishijin wife, which involved being a full-time weaver as well as handling all of the domestic chores and child care. Mrs. Konishi (forty-six years old at the time of the interview), who was the daughter of a salary man and a housewife, claimed that Mr. Konishi "deceived" her during their courtship. When she met him in a dance hall twenty-two years earlier than the interview, he initially disguised his occupation: "We didn't know at the beginning that my husband was a weaver," recalled Mrs. Konishi laughingly. In her mind, Mr. Konishi did not fit the stereotype that Kyoto people had of Nishijin residents: "He didn't reveal this to us. I myself didn't know exactly what weavers do. My parents didn't, either." Mr. Konishi (fifty-one years old at the time of the interview) explained, apologetically: "You see, some people have looked only at the bad aspects of Nishijin. Women in Nishijin have to work from morning to night; this is the tradition, so to speak." His wife added:

He thought that I wouldn't go out with him any more, so he didn't mention that he was a weaver in Nishijin. When we went out, he would be properly dressed. . . . [H]e looked neat when we would go out, so my parents and I couldn't tell where he was from. He was very relaxed about such matters as time, too. He would ask me in midday, for example, if I wanted to go to the movies or something in the early evening. So I was impressed that he was so free, and also that he seemed to have a lot of money. In fact, he had a lot of money. He used to buy me all sorts of things, like shoes. If I said I wanted a dress, he would buy me one right away; so I really liked that [laugh]. He had a lot of money before our marriage.

Emergence of the Nishijin Cottage Industry

The family-based cottage industry has emerged as the characteristic system of Nishijin since the beginning of the twentieth century. Nishijin silk weaving was transformed into a household production system *[kanai kōgyō]* during the late nineteenth and early twentieth centuries. By the beginning of the Taishō Period, cottage weaving had become the dominant form of production in Nishijin. Under this system, called *chinbata* ["hiring of the loom"], the weavers wove textiles in their own households following orders from a manufacturer. They received the designs, the warp, and the raw materials from the manufacturer and they were paid by the piece. Before World War II, the weavers used looms rented from the manufacturer. *Chinbata* is the term for both the system and for the type of household weaver who rented looms from the manufacturer.[2] The emergence of Kyoto's cottage industry involved new technology and changes in the organization of production within the family. The role of the family, particularly the emergence of women as weavers, was crucial in helping bring about this transformation.

The cottage industry gained momentum as Nishijin's dominant form of production in the early 1920s. It was accompanied by the ex-

---

2. *Chinbata* literally means "hire" *[chin]* "loom" *[bata]*, because originally the cottage weaver rented the loom from the manufacturer. After World War II, the term was changed to *debata* — "weaving for the outside" — because by then most cottage weavers owned their looms. In this discussion, the terms *chinbata*, *debata*, and "cottage weavers" will be used interchangeably.

pansion of the weaving district into new, previously unsettled neighborhoods. Increasing numbers of weavers started to produce for the manufacturers in their own homes, rather than in the manufacturer's house. Migrants from outside Kyoto came to train with the heads of weaving households, hoping to acquire skills and eventually establish their own *chinbata* households rather than continue to work as employees of other cottage weavers. In the manufacturing of *obi*, household weaving gradually replaced the historic employment system *[totei]*, which had prevailed in Nishijin since the Edo Period (Honjo 1930; Yasuoka 1977).

In the earlier *totei* system, weaving had been limited to men. A weaver worked for the manufacturer as a hired live-in employee *[shokkō]* in the manufacturer's house. He started his apprenticeship in the manufacturer's house in his early teens, sometimes as early as age ten. After completing his apprenticeship, he stayed to work in the manufacturer's house as a journeyman. The average length of the apprenticeship period was nine years — three years to learn the basic skills, three years to perfect the skills, and three years to "thank" the master *[o-rei bōkō]*. In those last three years, the apprentice was expected to use his newly acquired skills to work for the master at a pay rate lower than that of a journeyman. The apprentices and the journeymen lived and worked in the master's house and ate their meals with the master's family, but often at separate tables. In many cases, they were fed food inferior to that of the master's family. Engaged in a paternalistic relationship with the master and his family, journeymen had to remain single as long as they worked and lived in the master's house. If they decided to become independent, the master bestowed on them the status of an affiliate shop *[noren wake]* and assisted them in establishing their own weaving house, but one that was under his aegis: the new shop carried the insignia of the master's house on the *noren* — the split curtain hanging over the entrance that serves as a shop sign (Honjo 1930).

By contrast to the weaver in the *totei* system, the *chinbata* lived and wove in his own household, using looms rented from the manufacturer. The *chinbata* was the employee of the manufacturer and produced Nishijin cloth for a national market. The *chinbata* and his household members usually worked for one manufacturer at a time. *Chinbata* were free to change manufacturers, but in reality they could secure new employment only during periods of labor shortage. They received the silk threads, the warp, and the designs for each *obi* from the manufacturer, delivered the finished product to the manufacturer, and were paid by the piece. During periods of high demand for *obi*, the *chinbata* also employed occasional weavers from outside their household to help them fill the manufacturer's orders. Since Nishijin's reconstruction after World War II, most cottage weavers have owned their own looms. The name of the system has changed, therefore, from *chinbata* [hired loom] to *debata* [household weaver producing for outside orders]. Both the *chinbata* and the *debata* usually engaged most of their family members in household production. The earlier *totei* system differed considerably from the *chinbata* system in its stable employment practices. Because of the manufacturer's paternalistic responsibility toward the employees working and living in his house, the *totei* system provided young men with continuity of employment following their apprenticeship, even during periods of economic depression. The *chinbata*, however, had a more precarious relationship with the manufacturer, more prone to fluctuation depending on the amount and frequency of orders they received.

The emergence of the *chinbata* system, as noted in chapter 1, was accomplished by two technological developments in the late Meiji Period, both of which had a significant impact on women's work and on the family's organization of production. The first was the introduction of the jacquard system into Nishijin in the 1880s; the second was the spread of the powerloom *[riki-shokki]*, which appeared in Nishijin early in the twentieth century. The jacquard mechanism made it unnecessary for women to serve as "human jacquard." It released women to be potential weavers. Prior to the introduction of the jacquard, women were sitting on the second tier of the loom, batching the threads of the warp for the design. The jacquard has often been confused with the mechanization of weaving, which led to the displacement of traditional craftsmen. Actually, in both Europe and Japan the jacquard was used for both handlooms and powerlooms to produce the desired designs. The weaver was still doing the weaving.

Another major development early in the twentieth century—the introduction of the powerloom—made it possible for women to become weavers, because its manipulation did not require thrusting from the hip (see fig. 11). The powerloom was used for weaving the same type of cloth as the handloom but required less physical strength and, to some extent, less skill. The use of powerlooms spread in Nishijin during the Taishō Period, even though the handloom *[tebata]* still predominated. The attraction of the powerloom was obvious. It took one-third less time to weave the same piece by powerloom than by handloom. The training period was also far shorter. The spread of the powerloom further increased the demand for household weavers and enabled larger numbers of women to weave. As Mr. Koyama stated:

FIGURE II. A powerloom weaver. Photograph by Matsuo Hiroko.

In the case of the handloom, almost all the weavers were men. When the powerloom was introduced, women replaced men, as if they had been waiting for this. After all, the handloom requires hands and feet. It requires physical strength. The powerloom does not; just watching. They have to use their hands only. Weaving is not men's work any more; to tell the truth, it is work for women. I cannot imagine weaving as men's work. . . . Ordinary things such as *obi* are not men's work here. After all, women are patient with their work. Men soon get tired. Women do more detailed work. I think so.

Mr. Koyama may have exaggerated this last point, since many men also weave on powerlooms. Without a doubt, however, the powerloom had a dramatic impact on the division of labor in Nishijin. It now takes two to three years to train a handloom weaver and only one year to train a powerloom weaver. In addition to its being physically more manageable, the shorter training period made powerloom weaving more accessible to women, since women were reluctant to embark on a long training period that would delay marriage.

The opportunity for women to take on powerloom weaving was a main factor in the spread of cottage weaving as the dominant form of production in Nishijin. Having the female members of the household weave along with male members enabled a cottage weaver to maximize household production and justify his investment in buying and maintaining looms. Similar to proto-industrial production in eighteenth- and nineteenth-century Europe, the powerloom increases employment opportunities for all of the cottage weaver's family members. From the *chinbata*'s point of view, household production could increase the family's income by employing all able family members under his own supervision. The earlier *totei* system led to the dispersal of the family labor force, because individual family members had to work and live in different manufacturers' houses. The household weaving system, on the other hand, depended on the contributions of as many family members as possible to collective family production. By employing their family members as weavers in their own households, many cottage weavers actually aspired to own several looms and eventually become independent, small-scale manufacturers *[jimae]*.

For manufacturers, the use of powerlooms facilitated the employment of larger numbers of weavers, including wives and daughters who had previously been engaged in preparatory work rather than actual weaving. The *chinbata* system also worked to the manufacturers' advantage, because it relieved them from maintaining workers and machinery on their own premises. Manufacturers were able to save on space, light, and heat, and were less bound by their traditional paternalistic obligations toward the apprentices and weavers who were working and living in their own households. Vestiges of the paternalistic system remained, in that manufacturers retained some sense of obligation toward the cottage weavers working for them, but these protective relationships have eroded since World War II. The *chinbata* system also provided manufacturers with a labor force through the *chinbata*'s family. Instead of training their own apprentices and employing their own weavers, the manufacturers could leave these tasks to the *chinbata* head of household.

As the powerloom spread in Nishijin during the 1920s and 1930s, some *chinbata* expanded their operations and hired unrelated weavers to work for them, in addition to their family members, during periods of high demand. These employees often lived and worked in their own homes, but some young employees, especially those who came from the countryside, worked and lived in the *chinbata*'s house. Some young workers came to Nishijin as apprentices and then continued to weave as wage workers for the *chinbata*. Their relationship to the head of the *chinbata* household was, however, far less formal than that of the apprentices and journeymen in the *totei* system.

The cottage industry that emerged at the beginning of the century was not an entirely new phenomenon in Japan. Household production for an outside manufacturer had existed in various traditional crafts since the Tokugawa Period (Saito 1983). However, in Nishijin, until the end of the Meiji Period, the *totei* system was the main form of production for weaving. The transition to household weaving in Nishijin began in the late Meiji Period. In Meiji 39 [1906], cottage weavers *[chinbata]* constituted 68 percent of Nishijin weavers. By the beginning of the Taishō Period, their proportion had risen to 76 percent, peaking at 80 percent in the middle of the Taishō Period (Hattori 1948). By developing new neighborhoods for the weavers in the northern and western outlying districts of Nishijin during the Taishō Period, the manufacturers demonstrated their commitment to the cottage industry as the preferred form of employment and production. Cottage weaving emerged as the dominant form of production among Nishijin weavers and has persisted to the present. It has coexisted with small factories, which emerged in the early Shōwa Period (Honjo 1930). The majority of Nishijin *obi*, however, has continued to be produced in the cottage industry.

Since the origins of the *chinbata* system, the status of the cottage weavers has been subject to ambiguous perceptions. On the surface, the *chinbata* appear to be self-employed, because they produce in their own homes. In reality, they are employees of the manufacturers. Exploiting these ambiguities in the post–World War II period, the manufacturers often perpetuated the image of the *chinbata* as small, self-employed entrepreneurs, because they did not want the cottage weavers to come under the regulation, protection, and rights stipulated in the Fair Labor Standards Act, which was modeled on its United States predecessor. Finally, in 1957, after a long struggle, the Committee on Labor Relations of the central government, consisting of business and labor representatives, ruled that the *chinbata*'s status qualified as "labor" *[rōdō-sha]* and was therefore entitled to protection under the law setting maximum hours and minimum wages. (This holds true for Kyoto City, but not for the Tango villages.)

Both the *chinbata* and their employees generally ignored these labor standards. The piece-rate system made a minimum wage impossible to enforce, and the cottage weavers themselves did not adhere to the ruling on maximum hours. Explaining that a limit on working hours is incompatible with a cottage weaver's work habits and needs, Mr. Hiraoka, the production manager in one of the Nishijin firms, compared the mentality of cottage weavers to that of a housewife: "Does a housewife stop her work after eight hours, if her tasks are not finished?" (See Mr. Hiraoka's interview.) The ambiguity in the status of the *chinbata* has also been reinforced by the self-image of those *chinbata* who aspired to become independent small manufacturers eventually.

Even though they worked in their own homes, the *chinbata* were actually employees of capitalist manufacturers. Their status and mode of production were similar to those of proto-industrial workers in Western Europe during the first part of the nineteenth century, who were engaged in household production in a putting-out system, such as spinning and weaving or making gloves or lace. The *chinbata* did not own the looms, the raw materials, or the designs. They received the designs and raw materials from the manufacturer, wove only to the manufacturer's orders, and were paid for each finished piece.

The status of *chinbata* and *debata* has continued to be ambiguous to the present. Japanese economic historians have debated whether Nishijin *chinbata* should be considered as "labor" or as "self-employed." Some historians have viewed the *chinbata* as a transitional group "at risk" of becoming self-employed and, therefore, as potentially moving into the capitalist class. Economic historian Hattori Shiso (1948) stressed that the distinguishing feature between *chinbata* and *jimae* was whether or not they owned looms. He claimed that those *chinbata* who owned looms had actually declined from *jimae* status, while those who rented looms had started as *chinbata* and were therefore "proletarian." Hattori viewed the emergence of the *chinbata* system as the culmination of a historical trend leading to the weakening of an industrial, proletarian class in Nishijin.

While it is true that many *chinbata* were originally *jimae* who had declined to *chinbata* status, owning the looms was not the major distinguishing feature between *chinbata* and *jimae*, as Hattori claimed. Like a manufacturer, the *jimae* planned and designed his product, purchased the silk thread, and commissioned from the appropriate craftspeople the preparatory operations, such as dyeing the thread, drawing the design, making the patterns, and preparing the warp. The *jimae*, along with his family members, then wove the *obi* in his own household or hired additional *chinbata* weavers. Like the manufacturer, the *jimae* also marketed the finished product to the wholesaler *[ton'ya]*. The difference between the *jimae* and the manufacturer involved the number of employees and capital each had. The *jimae* employed mainly his own family members and owned several looms; the manufacturer had a larger enterprise, hired many cottage weavers, and had access to capital.

The image of the *chinbata* as a self-employed small entrepreneur stemmed partly from the experience of some *chinbata* who aspired to own several looms and produce cloth independently as *jimae*. These *chinbata* — Mr. Nishitani, for example — moved up to the *jimae* rank and then slid back down to the *chinbata* level as a result of market fluctuations or personal misfortune. Some of these "fallen" *jimae* recovered their status later, while others remained *chinbata* for the rest of their work lives. The *jimae* who were most prone to this failure were those who had risen from the *chinbata* ranks. The proportion of *chinbata* in Nishijin increased considerably following a severe economic depression in Meiji 40 [1907], when many independent small manufacturers collapsed. During that crisis, these small entrepreneurs reverted back to *chinbata* status and rented looms from manufacturers (Hattori 1948). *Jimae* were particularly susceptible to collapse during periods of depression, because they had virtually no capital. Like the manufacturers, they had to pay for silk thread in cash, but failed to receive instant cash from the wholesaler for their finished product. They were vulnerable to the slightest market swings, especially to changes in the prices of silk thread. Cottage weavers were not directly vulnerable to the same risks that *jimae* faced, but were subject to exploitation by the manufacturer. They were affected by the manufacturers' insecurities during periods necessitating decline in production, which led to unstable employment. These conditions drove the *chinbata* to a "hand-to-mouth" existence (see Mr. Nishitani's interview).

Consolidation of the Chinbata System in Kyoto

The *chinbata* system continued to spread in Kyoto through the 1930s and became the major production system for Nishijin *obi* and *kimono*. *Chinbata* households recruited rural migrants to Kyoto and absorbed them into an urban industry. In 1933, non-family employees in *chinbata* households constituted only about 7 percent. A comparison of *chinbata* heads of household with their employees in the early 1930s suggests important differences in their origins. The majority (about 63 percent) of the *chinbata* heads in the Kamigyo-ku district, which is geographically almost identical to the historic Nishijin weaving district, were natives of Kyoto City, while 10 percent had come from the rural regions of Kyoto Prefecture, mostly from the Tango Peninsula. Twenty-one percent came from rural areas in neighboring prefectures (Shiga, Ishikawa, and others), 1 percent came from Korea, and the remaining 5 percent came from other areas of Japan (Kyoto-fu, Gakumu-bu, Shakai-ka 1934, 6–9). A major portion of *chinbata* household heads thus had stable roots in Kyoto.

Nonrelative weavers employed in *chinbata* households came predominantly from the countryside. Of these workers in *chinbata* households, only 33 percent were natives of Kyoto City. The remainder were weavers who came from the outside *[yojin]:* 11 percent had migrated from the rural districts of Kyoto Prefecture and 34 percent had come from other rural districts, generally from the same districts of origin as their employers. In addition to Japanese employees working for the *chinbata* household who were unrelated to the heads of household, 21 percent were from Korea (Kyoto-fu, Gakumu-bu, Shakai-ka 1934, 7). Many *chinbata* who migrated from outside Kyoto City initially came to Nishijin as temporary laborers or apprentices and worked their way up to found their own *chinbata* households. In turn, they employed new migrants who came to Nishijin to apprentice as weavers. The *chinbata* system in Nishijin thus served as an important stabilizer of rural-urban migration. In addition to providing employment opportunities for its own members, the *chinbata* household attracted migrants into a stable production system, as the manufacturers' households had previously done under the *totei* system. This historical function of absorbing migrants into a household industry can be found in other Japanese traditional crafts and household industries that were established since the Tokugawa Period (Saito 1983).

Consolidation and progression of the *chinbata* system is evident in the changes in family origins of *chinbata* household heads. In 1934, these heads were predominantly the first generation to engage in this kind of production, but the picture had changed considerably by 1968, when 65 percent of *chinbata* household heads were descendants of *chinbata*. Among the sons of *chinbata* household heads, 32.3 percent succeeded to their fathers' *chinbata* businesses and 33.5 percent had declined to *chinbata* status from *jimae* (see table 1). While the *chinbata* system continued to depend on labor recruitment from outside Kyoto, the Nishijin base of the craft is evident in the fact that by 1967 a higher proportion of *chinbata* (approximately 56 percent of female *chinbata* and 78 percent of male *chinbata*) were natives of Nishijin (see table 2). This perpetuation of the *chinbata* system from one generation to the next is even more dramatic considering the disruptive impact of World War II, which paralyzed production in Nishijin for almost an entire decade. The stabilization of the Nishijin *chinbata* population is also reflected in the increased number of *chinbata* household heads who were the third generation in Nishijin. In a 1962 survey, Matsumoto (1968, 12) found that 20 percent of the families in his sample engaged in Nishijin weaving were the third generation born in Nishijin, and 30 percent were the second generation born in Nishijin. About 17 percent were the first generation born in Nishijin, and about 30 percent were newcomers from outside Kyoto.

Entrenchment of the *chinbata* system in Nishijin is also reflected in my further analysis of Matsumoto's original 1962 questionaires. Of 377 *chinbata* heads of household, about 59 percent reported Nishijin weaving as their first job and 9 percent reported Nishijin-related jobs as their previous employment. Of 243 *chinbata* heads of household, 44.5 percent were the first generation of *chinbata* who had founded their household production, while 36.6 percent inherited the business from their fathers and 19 percent from their grandfathers. Patterns of succession followed the usual custom in Japan. Of the 243 *chinbata* heads of household who had been in this occupation for more than one generation, 48 percent were the first son and about 33 percent were the second son of the previous owner. The reasons successors cited for taking over the business were overwhelmingly retirement, death, or illness of the former owner.[3]

The increasing rootedness of Nishijin weavers in Kyoto was reflected in their marriage patterns as well. In his sample of 316 male *chinbata* weavers in Nishijin, Matsumoto (1968, 12–13) found that 51.6 percent married women who were born in Nishijin and 49 percent of the men were sons of women native to Nishijin. About 39 percent of the sample were descendants of two Nishijin-born parents. Matsumoto concluded that the stabilization and integration of migrants into the Nishijin community occurred, however, through apprenticeship and work in *chinbata* households rather than through marriage. Nishijin men and women tended to marry partners from Nishijin or from greater Kyoto rather

---

3. Professor Matsumoto very kindly turned over his original 1962 questionnaires to me and I reanalyzed them, applying new questions.

TABLE 1. Occupations of the Fathers of *Chinbata*, 1967

	Male *Chinbata*		Female *Chinbata*	
	N	%	N	%
Chinbata	52	32.30	39	26.71
Jiei[a]				
Weaving	54	33.54	33	22.60
Nishijin-related	7	4.35	1	0.69
Others	27	16.77	55	37.67
Employed				
Nishijin-related	3	1.86	4	2.74
Others	11	6.83	6	4.11
Unknown	7	4.35	8	5.48
Total	161	100	146	100

SOURCE: Mitsuka Takeo, "Nishijin Kigyō ni Okeru Chinbata Rōdōsha no Seikatsu to Sono Jittai" (Characteristics of *Chinbata* Workers in Nishijin Today), *Jinbun-gaku* (1968): 61.

[a]*Jiei* means "independent business" or "self-employed."

TABLE 2. Birthplaces of *Chinbata* by Gender, 1967

	Male		Female	
	N	%	N	%
Nishijin	126	78.26	86	55.84
Kyoto City	7	4.35	7	4.55
Kyoto Prefecture	9	5.59	23	14.93
Other prefectures	19	11.80	31	20.13
Unknown	0	0.00	7	4.55
Total	161	100	154	100

SOURCE: Mitsuka Takeo, "Nishijin Kigyō ni Okeru Chinbata Rōdōsha no Seikatsu to Sono Jittai" (Characteristics of *Chinbata* Workers in Nishijin Today), *Jinbun-gaku* (1968): 60.

than migrants, while migrants tended to marry people from their own hometown or region (Matsumoto 1968). This differs from the later testimonies of Nishijin weavers, whom I interviewed in the 1980s, who claimed that they did not want their daughters to marry Nishijin weavers.

Thus, at the peak of Japan's post-war modernization, the Nishijin industry continued to consolidate and advance its traditional character as a household-based production system with time-honored designs and techniques. In the 1950s, by contrast to the 1930s, a large number of *chinbata* household heads were Kyoto natives who had inherited the cottage industry from their fathers. A shift in the recruitment patterns of Nishijin weavers occurred after World War II. While earlier, the Nishijin *chinbata* system had recruited considerable proportions of its workers from outside Kyoto City, after the war it experienced a localization of the labor force. This decline in the recruitment of migrants into an urban craft was not limited to Nishijin. It was typical of Kyoto in general. In the 1960s, Kyoto boasted the highest proportion of its population to be born in the same city, by contrast to other Japanese cities that listed high proportions of migrants (see table 3).[4]

By 1960, the former Kamigyo-ku district (now divided into two districts—Kita-ku and Kamigyo-ku) was still Kyoto's major traditional silk-weaving area. About 90 percent of the silk-weaving businesses, 80 percent of the workers employed, and almost 74 percent of the products in Kita-ku still revolved around Nishijin weaving. Similarly, about 80 percent of the businesses, 72 percent of the workers, and 73 percent of the products in Kamigyo-ku were Nishijin-based. The production of Nishijin silk in the 1960s continued to be carried out in the manufacturers' small family businesses and in the weavers' households, as it had been in the 1930s, following the traditional division of labor but with some major modifications (Matsumoto 1968). The industry had experienced significant changes following World War II. In compliance with the Fair Labor Standards Act, children were prohibited from working full-time, even in household production. Although children continued to help with the family's production effort on a part-time basis, they ceased to be regular working members of the *chinbata* household. School attendance became compulsory for children up to age fourteen. Subsequent increases in high school attendance age removed more teenagers from Nishijin's household labor force.

Although the internal division of labor in Nishijin's household production has changed, the basic reliance on the *chinbata* system has persisted. In the 1960s, *chinbata* occupied about 60 percent of the entire Nishijin labor force. *Obi* was still their major product, with about 70 percent of the Kamigyo-ku *chinbata* engaged in weaving *obi*. The Nishijin industry has continued to be composed predominantly of small-

---

4. This calculation, presented by Matsumoto (1968), does not include Tokyo, which apparently had an even higher proportion of a stable population than Kyoto.

TABLE 3. Percentage of Urban Population Born in the City
Where They Live Now, 1965

Kyoto	46.9
Nagoya	37.2
Yokohama	33.6
Osaka	32.5
Kobe	29.9
Kitakyushu	27.0

SOURCE: Matsumoto Michiharu, "Nishijin Kigyōsha no Chiiki Sei-katsu: Toku-ni Nishijin Kigyō o Kiteisuru Chiiki Seikatsu no Takushitsu ni Tsuite" (Lifestyle of Nishijin Workers: Especially about Characteristics of Lifestyle, Which Regulates Nishijin Industry). *Jinbun-gaku* 109 (1968): 11.

The original table does not include Tokyo. Apparently Tokyo contained a larger number of locally born residents than the cities that were included in the table.

scale, family-based enterprises. In 1962, 5,458 of the 6,918 (78.9 percent) Nishijin manufacturing businesses used just one to four looms. Among *chinbata*, 93.5 percent of the *obi* weavers employed one to four family members, and 83 percent of the weavers of plain *kimono* cloth *[ki-jaku]* employed a similar number of family members. Labor recruitment patterns in Nishijin also suggested that even larger companies, employing between thirty and ninety-nine workers, still tended to rely most heavily on personal connections for hiring their weavers (see table 4).

Nishijin's weaving industry has continued to depend on small family firms on the manufacturers' side and on a family-intensive labor force in household production on the weavers' side. In the 1970s, as Nishijin manufacturers began to seek low-wage weavers in the countryside, they introduced a household production system into the villages in the Tango Peninsula. The *chinbata* (now *debata*) system replicated itself in the cottages of farmers and fishermen with one major difference. While the urban household production system in Nishijin engaged husbands, wives, and other family members, in the countryside the wife has generally been the only weaver in the family. With some exceptions, the husband continued to work in agriculture and fishing. In rare cases (like Mr. Nagahama; see interview), the husband quit fishing and also became a weaver.

The case of Nishijin provides an unusual example of the complexities inherent in a traditional industry's interaction with technological change. The introduction of new technology did not lead to the emer-

TABLE 4. Recruitment Sources of Nishijin Employees, 1962 (in percentages)

Number of Employees in Firm	Employment Agency	School	Personal Connection	Other	Unknown
1–29	2.5	1.2	52.1	42.6	1.6
30–99	3.9	10.4	58.6	27.1	
Over 100	30.8	9.3	11.3	48.6	

SOURCE: Furumai Toshio, "Nishijin Kigyō no Daiyoji Chōsa ni Motozuku Rōdō Tōkei Shiryō" (Statistics of Labor Conditions in Nishijin Industry). *Dōshisha Keizaigaku Ronsō* 14, no. 5 (1965).

gence of a factory system. Instead, a flexible household production system joined forces with modern technology to create a new form of household industry based on a traditional, collective family economy. The *chinbata* and the manufacturers for whom they worked used modern technology to develop and consolidate a household industry that utilized progressively modern machinery for the making of a highly traditional product.

CHAPTER 4

Family Work
in Household Production

Nishijin is such a place where family members work together.
All textile families are busy. Everyone in the family helps each
other.

Mrs. Yasuda

The relationship between family and work patterns among Nishijin
weavers and manufacturers in the development of the cottage industry
has undergone a sequence of changes since the beginning of the twentieth century. As explained earlier, the new household production system
peaked in the 1930s, after major transformations that began earlier in the
twentieth century. These include the widespread use of powerlooms
[riki-shokki], the increasing number of women weavers, and the expansion of weaving households [chinbata] into previously unsettled rural
districts north and west of historical Nishijin. The manufacturers developed these neighborhoods to accommodate the growing industry's
needs for new space and the expanding population of chinbata households.

One neighborhood, the Taiho school district, was settled in bamboo
groves owned by Daitokuji Temple. The manufacturers leased land from
the temple, built small houses, and offered the poorer chinbata an opportunity to move there from the crowded and older, but more expensive, Nishijin quarters. Mr. Nishitani, who still lived in one of the original houses at the time of the interview, recalled:

We moved to the Taiho district around 1920. My parents were very poor, and
we lived in crowded quarters in Nishijin. When the orimoto [manufacturer] of-

fered them the opportunity to move, they decided, "Let's go ahead and have a new start." We were so poor at that time we could not even afford to pay the movers. We sold our chest of drawers [*tansu*] and sideboard so that my father could buy a cart. We then loaded all our possessions on the cart and we started our walk, pulling the cart. It took several years before we had electricity there, and my parents were weaving by the light of the kerosene lamp. We were far from Nishijin, so I had to keep running back and forth to deliver the *obi* and pick up the threads. I was happy most of the time. Sometimes they would give me a bowl of rice or a sweet in the *orimoto*'s house. During my long run from Daitokuji [temple] to Nishijin, I kept wondering what they would give me this time.

These new neighborhoods outside historical Nishijin enabled manufacturers to expand production and place looms in their weavers' newly built homes. Weavers who moved there escaped the cramped quarters of old Nishijin and obtained the additional space necessary to maintain one or two looms. The new space was particularly attractive to young household heads who were unable to establish production in their fathers' crowded houses.

In addition to the interviews, prefectural and municipal investigations of household production and living conditions in Kyoto's Kamigyo-ku district — the center of the silk-weaving area of Nishijin and its related industries — reveal some of the household arrangements and internal division of labor in the old and new Nishijin neighborhoods. During the early 1930s, the Kyoto prefectural government investigated the living and working conditions, health status, and household economy of Nishijin cottage weavers [*chinbata*]. The 1933 prefectural survey and a 1948 municipal investigation are the only surviving government surveys of the household characteristics of Nishijin's cottage industry. The reports based on these surveys, although uniquely rich in their coverage of economic conditions, are limited in the demographic information they offer. They contain no direct information on family structure or on community patterns. Two additional surveys, using much smaller samples and asking different types of questions, were conducted in 1962 and 1969. The first was directed by sociology professor Matsumoto Michiharu with his interdisciplinary team at Doshisha University in 1962 (Matsumoto 1968), and the second, on the work and quality of life of Nishijin wives, was conducted by an association of volunteer researchers, the Kyoto Women's Problems Research Committee (Kyoto Women's Problems Research Committee 1969).

The prefectural survey showed that in the early 1930s more than half of Nishijin's labor force was engaged in the cottage industry. The 1933

survey covered all 4,937 *chinbata* households in Kamigyo-ku; this constituted a little more than half of the households in the entire Kamigyo-
ku district. The majority of Kyoto manufacturers and cottage weavers
who were producing plain cloth for *kimono [ki-jaku]* and *obi* were concentrated there. Out of the 20,541 household members living in the
district, 8,160 were *chinbata* (Kyoto-fu, Gakumu-bu, Shakai-ka 1934, 7,
11). The majority of the remaining *chinbata* household members who
were not weavers were also engaged in occupations related to the Nishijin industry. They worked either as weavers in factories or as artisans
in related crafts, such as dyeing and winding the thread, tying the warp,
pattern-making for the design, and punching cards for the jacquard.
These auxiliary crafts, which were carried out by separate small family
businesses, made all the essential preliminaries to weaving. The non-
chinbata families also included manufacturers *[orimoto]* and small-scale
independent manufacturers *[jimae]* (Kyoto-fu, Gakumu-bu, Shakai-ka
1934, 6–7).

The 1933 perfectural survey divided the Kamigyo-ku district into six
units, each consisting of a cluster of adjacent administrative primary
school districts. Although the administrative division of urban neighborhoods into school districts is an arbitrary bureaucratic one, the clusters defined for the 1933 investigation represent stages in the expansion
of Nishijin's weaving households into new peripheral areas. The districts
in south and central Kamigyo-ku encompass the older historical Nishijin
area, while the north and west districts represent neighborhoods developed since the 1920s. These new districts had high concentrations of
chinbata weavers who settled there with the encouragement of manufacturers.[1]

By the early 1930s, these new neighborhoods — with narrow streets
typical of Nishijin, wooden houses wedged closely together, and
thousands of looms clicking away from dawn into the late evening —
had become densely populated. While the residents in the new districts
were the poorest among Nishijin weavers during the 1920s, the 1933
survey reveals only minor income differences among the various school

1. These newer districts also contained the Taiho school district to the north of Nishijin
(including adjacent clusters) with a population of 7,340 (1,192 households), and the Nina
and Shoran school districts to the west with a population of 5,543 (1,366 households).
These areas, which outnumbered the original Nishijin district, were settled in the 1920s
as part of an expansion of the Nishijin cottage industry into the newly developed weaving
districts in the outlying neighborhoods. The remaining four clusters of school districts
(containing populations of 2,897, 2,463, 1,462, and 782, respectively) constituted the traditional historic districts of Nishijin.

districts. Kamigyo-ku's new "suburban" districts, including the Taiho school districts on one side and the Nina and Shoran school districts on the other, had become mature manufacturing neighborhoods. They re-created the traditional modes of Nishijin production with several dif-ferences. They relied more heavily on *chinbata* than the historic Nishijin district had; they used a greater number of powerlooms; and they were more likely than the older districts to employ migrants from the coun-tryside (Kyoto-fu, Gakumu-bu, Shakai-ka 1934).[2]

The *chinbata* system was the major source of income for the weaving households in all these newly developed districts. It also provided the opportunity for training and employment for migrants. The historic Nishijin district within Kamigyo-ku continued to serve as the head-quarters for manufacturers who functioned as planners, managers, and producers of the various operations, such as design, warping *[seikei]*, tying harnesses *[soko]*, repair of finished products, storage of raw ma-terials and stock, management of production, and marketing of Nishijin *obi* to wholesalers. Some manufacturers employed weavers in small fac-tories *[uchibata]* on their premises, in addition to their *chinbata* weavers. Before World War II, all planning took place in the manufacturer's house, which served as the business headquarters as well as the family residence. Some manufacturers also continued to use sections of their own houses to board factory workers and apprentices, or they built additional boarding houses for young workers whom they recruited from the countryside. (See interviews of Mrs. Yasuda and Mr. and Mrs. Konishi.)

Characteristics of the *Chinbata* Population

Some historians studying proto-industrialization in Western and Cen-tral Europe have linked changes in the age and sex structures and in demographic behavior of people engaged in cottage production to this new system (Medick 1981; Mendels 1972). The changes they identified included an earlier age at marriage and earlier commencement of child-bearing, as well as an increase in marital fertility, both reflecting a strat-egy common among weaving families to speed up family formation in order to maximize the number of family members available for house-

2. As will be seen later, the districts differed little in age of population, gender struc-ture, family size, and income.

hold production (Mendels 1972; Medick 1976). These generalizations have subsequently come under criticism. Later studies questioned the uniformity of the impact of proto-industrialization on such changes in demographic behavior and found that such changes differed according to region, interaction with the local agricultural structure, and the type of cottage industry involved (Gutmann and Leboutte 1984; Mitterauer 1992).

Following his investigation of the demographic consequences of proto-industrialization for Japan, Saito (1983) concluded that during the Tokugawa Period rural districts had already experienced substantial proto-industrial development. Unlike the situation in Europe, proto-industrialization in Japan produced no major demographic changes. It is important, though, to note the difference in context and time period. Saito focused exclusively on rural areas primarily involving food production in the nineteenth century. The *chinbata* system in twentieth-century Nishijin, on the other hand, developed in the late Meiji and early Taishō Periods and involved an urban-based craft that required advanced skills. Nevertheless, the emergence of the cottage industry in Nishijin was also unaccompanied by demographic change. The age and sex distribution of Kamigyo-ku's *chinbata* population was similar to that of the rest of Kyoto and of Japan in general. In addition, the average age at marriage remained unchanged with the emergence of the Nishijin *chinbata* system.[3] In Nishijin, demographic behavior was unaffected by participation of *chinbata* women in household production or in work outside the household. The average age at marriage and number of children of Nishijin women weavers were consistent with the overall pattern in Japanese urban areas at the time.[4]

3. The low ratio of males to females in the 15–25 age group in Kamigyo-ku was also typical of Kyoto in general. The absence from the *chinbata* population of young men in this age group can be explained either as a result of their military recruitment for the Japan-China War or because they moved from Kyoto to work elsewhere. A similar high proportion of male absence in the 30–45 age group is evident in the 1948 investigation of Nishijin. This may suggest a cohort phenomenon: members of these same age cohorts were still absent from Kyoto ten years later, and absent again after World War II. Some may have died in the war. Others might have sought employment elsewhere, since in 1948 Nishijin's industry was just beginning to recover from the war. Information on age at marriage is available only from the 1948 report; comparable figures for 1933 are unavailable.

4. Since the 1933 survey does not provide this type of demographic information, one has to rely here on the 1948 report and assume that no dramatic changes in demographic behavior had occurred since the 1930s.

Despite its function as a production unit, the average size of the *chinbata* household (4.3 members) was surprisingly small. Most households had between three and five members and household size remained consistently small. It was 5.35 in the 1940s (Kyoto-shi, Shakai-ka 1948) and 4.38 in the 1960s (Mitsuka 1968).[5] Actual family size would have been even smaller, since some households also included employees who were nonrelatives. The small household size may also have been life-course–related. For example, young couples might still be having children at home, while older couples' children may have left home. This pattern may also reflect the custom of low-income families sending children to other households because they had "too many mouths to feed." These families usually sent one or two children to be raised in another household, sometimes in a relative's home. These children had the ambiguous status of apprentice *[hōkō]*, which may have actually entailed learning a trade or being a servant, similar to young apprentices and servants in colonial New England (Demos 1970). In Japan, many of these children were eventually adopted by the family with whom they apprenticed. In other cases, children were sent directly for adoption by other families, instead of passing through a stage of apprenticeship.

Even when taking these explanations into account, the relatively small size of *chinbata* households suggests that the dominant form of household structure in Kamigyo-ku was nuclear. With an average household size of 4.3, one could hardly assume that a high number of *chinbata* families co-resided with the older generation. Former weavers who had lived in Kamigyo-ku all their lives confirmed in interviews that co-residence of the oldest married son with his parents—a pattern still modal in Kyoto and many other parts of Japan—was not always the dominant practice among Nishijin *chinbata*. The tendency of these *chinbata* to live in nuclear households during this time differed from that of craftsmen in other traditional Kyoto industries, such as the Kiyomizu potters, where the successor to the craft, usually the oldest son and his family, co-resided with the parents.

There are two possible explanations for the tendency toward living

---

5. The mean household size in Nishijin did not differ dramatically from that of the rest of Japan. It was 4.98 in 1930 and 4.99 in 1940. Carl Mosk (2001) found that the mean household size for Osaka in 1930 was 4.9 in the old core of the city and 4.9 in the industrial periphery. I am grateful to Carl Mosk for information on this issue. I am also indebted to Ochiai Emiko for valuable demographic information. (See also Japan Statistics Bureau, Management and Coordination Bureau 1920 and Ochiai 1997.)

in nuclear households in Nishijin. One is the weavers' need for household space for their looms. In the small, crowded Nishijin houses, little space was available for the older generation. About 58 percent of old Nishijin houses contained an average of two rooms (see table 5); the workspace occupied one-third of the household space. Since the older generation was still weaving on a part-time basis, it would have been very difficult for three generations to reside and work together. Another explanation for the nuclearity and small household size of the *chinbata* was the younger generation's migration to new neighborhoods in the 1920s. When a young *chinbata* family relocated to a newly developed area, the older generation stayed behind in old Nishijin. If their parents joined them later, they lived in an adjacent house rather than in the same one. Thus the settlement of younger *chinbata* families in the new districts might also have contributed to the increase in the proportion of nuclear households. In the 1962 survey of Nishijin weaving households, Matsumoto and his team (1968) also found a low rate of co-residence of *chinbata* couples with the older generation. Only 9.5 percent of the individuals interviewed by Matsumoto were listed as either father or mother of the head of the household co-residing with him (see table 6); (Matsumoto 1968).

The high proportion of *chinbata* household heads who were natives of Kyoto City suggests, however, that the presence of nuclear households resulted not only from migration to Kyoto, but was also present among native Kyoto *chinbata*. This residential separation between the generations in the early 1930s may also have been a function of the patterns of *chinbata* sons' succession to their parents' household production. Since the Nishijin *chinbata* system was a relatively new development in the 1920s and 1930s, many *chinbata* may have been the first generation to embark on household weaving (see table 1). The high incidence of *chinbata* household heads who were the first generation in Nishijin and of their separate residence from the older generation may be explained by the fact that more than half of the *chinbata* families in Kamigyo-ku lived in newly settled neighborhoods.

Separate households in old Nishijin did not entail, however, a complete separation among the generations. The interviews confirm that, in most cases, parents of the household heads were living in the same district and often in the same neighborhood, even if not in the same household. It was common for aging parents to work together with their *chinbata* children, even if they resided apart. Aging parents tended to help in the weaving process by doing the preparatory work [shita-

TABLE 5. Housing Conditions for *Chinbata*, 1933

		N	%
Housing	Own	148	3.0
	Rent	4,789	97.0
	Total	4,937	100.0
Number of rooms	1	695	14.1
	2	2,854	57.8
	3	553	11.2
	4	720	14.6
	5	114	2.3
	6	1	0.0
	Total	4,937	100.0

SOURCE: Kyoto-fu, Gakumu-bu, Shakai-ka, *Nishijin Chin'ori Gyōsha ni Kansuru Chōsa* (Research on Nishijin Pieceworkers), (Kyoto: Kyoto-fu, Gakumu-bu, Shakai-ka, 1934), 138–9, table 24.

TABLE 6. Relationship of *Chinbata* to Head of Household

Relationship	Frequency	Percentage	Cumulative Percentage
Wife	306	22.7	22.7
Husband	15	1.1	23.8
First son	214	15.9	39.7
Daughter	294	21.8	61.5
Other sons	212	15.7	77.2
Father	49	3.6	80.8
Mother	79	5.9	86.7
Brother	27	2.0	88.7
Sister	29	2.2	90.9
Son's wife	27	2.0	92.9
Grandchild	38	2.8	95.7
Servant	6	0.4	96.1
Other	11	0.8	96.9
Grandparents	13	1.0	97.9
Son-in-law	1	0.1	98.0
Daughter's husband	2	0.1	98.1
Child	25	1.9	100
Total	1,348	100	

SOURCE: Calculated from original survey questionnaires for 1962 Nishijin survey by Matsumoto Michiharu.

shigoto].[6] Grandmothers usually took care of young children in order to give mothers more time for weaving.

The *chinbata*'s relatively small household size persisted over time. The 1948 Kyoto municipal investigation of the Nishijin weaving district reveals little, if any, change in the average *chinbata* household size. It also shows little difference between the household sizes of *chinbata* and of small, independent manufacturers *[jimae],* even in the case of *jimae* who owned more than ten looms. The major distinction in household size, as would be expected, was between *chinbata* and *jimae* on the one hand, and manufacturers on the other. The absence of a major difference in household size between *chinbata* and *jimae* is largely due to the fact that *jimae* came generally from *chinbata* backgrounds, and vice versa. As suggested above, most *jimae* had not yet achieved the necessary stability to continue their entrepreneurial status from generation to generation. Manufacturers had slightly larger families but lived in dramatically bigger houses than *chinbata* or *jimae*. A later report found that manufacturers' houses averaged twelve rooms while *chinbata* houses averaged 2.74 rooms. Only 3 percent of *chinbata* and *jimae* owned their houses. The size of the manufacturers' houses, of course, reflected greater affluence and higher status. The manufacturers' houses were also constructed to function as business headquarters, and, at times, as the site of small factories, in cases where manufacturers employed both factory workers and *chinbata* (Kyoto-shi, Shakai-ka 1948).

The Division of Labor in the Household Industry

The Nishijin cottage industry was family-intensive and depended on a collective family economy. Work in the *chinbata* household converged around a family effort. Production took place in the home, and most *chinbata* relied heavily on their family members' labor. The economic dependence of the *chinbata* household on family labor is reflected in the 1933 survey. About 85 percent of *chinbata* households in Kamigyo-ku relied on weaving as their major source of income. This dependence is also expressed in the high proportion of women who participated in household weaving. Weavers who were unrelated to the head constituted a small portion of the *chinbata* labor force: In 1933, non-family members made up only about 7 percent of the working population in

6. *Shita* means "low" and *shigoto* means "work."

chinbata households. The male-female ratio for *chinbata* workers was four to three (Kyoto-fu, Gakumu-bu, Shakai-ka 1934, 11).

As would be expected, the majority of the *chinbata* heads of household were male and most wove at home (the survey reported 3,566 male and 245 female heads of household). Most of the female heads of household also wove at home (see table 7). The high rate of women's participation in weaving is dramatically reflected in the proportion of family members other than household heads listed as weaving in *chinbata* households. More than twice as many female non-heads than male non-heads participated in household production (1,237 males and 3,112 females). Female family members other than heads included wives, daughters, and other relatives. The male family members other than heads included sons and other relatives of the household head; the other males constituted a smaller proportion than the other females, because the overwhelming majority of household heads were male. Three-quarters of all male heads of household and other male family members were also engaged in household weaving. Similarly, three-quarters of all female family members worked in the *chinbata*'s family production. Handloom *[tebata]* weavers were predominantly men because this work was physically demanding and because men had traditionally been handloom weavers. As explained earlier, following the spread of powerloom weaving, increasing numbers of women became weavers. It is no coincidence that the school districts in Kamigyo-ku with high concentrations of powerlooms (Taiho and Nina) also contained a higher proportion of women weavers.

The age and sex structure of the Kamigyo-ku population in 1933 suggests that the higher involvement of women than men in household weaving occurred only among the younger age groups. Since women in the 15–20 age group outnumbered men, one would assume that more women than men were weaving, or at least were engaged in preparatory work related to weaving in the household. The male-female ratios in the 15–20 and 21–25 age groups were 0.76 and 0.81, respectively (Kyoto-fu, Gakumu-bu, Shakai-ka 1934, tables section, 3). The absence of young men in this age group may have necessitated greater involvement of young women.

Was women's high participation rate in cottage weaving matched by a time investment similar to that of the men? According to the 1933 Kyoto prefectural investigation, women *chinbata* weavers carried time loads quite similar to those of men, but the distribution of working hours was very different. The majority of women (about 75 percent) worked more than twenty days a month, and a sizeable number of

TABLE 7. Number of Household Heads and Household Members in *Chinbata* Households by Gender, 1933

	Male	Female	Total
Chinbata			
Household head	3,566	245	3,811
Family members other than head	1,237	3,112	4,349
Total	4,803	3,357	8,160
Weaving-related industries			
Household head	155	5	160
Family members other than head	118	670	788
Total	273	675	948

SOURCE: Kyoto-fu, Gakumu-bu, Shakai-ka, *Nishijin Chin'ori Gyōsha ni Kansuru Chōsa* (Research on Nishijin Pieceworkers), (Kyoto: Kyoto-fu, Gakumu-bu, Shakai-ka, 1934), 99.

women worked between ten and twenty days a month. Women working less than ten days a month constituted only 2 percent of the entire female *chinbata* labor force. An examination of workloads in terms of average number of hours worked each week, however, modifies the picture of women's full-time participation. Compared with men, a higher proportion of women worked five to ten hours a day, while a much higher proportion of men worked ten to fifteen hours a day. Women constituted a small minority among those working over fifteen hours a day and a vast majority among those working less than five hours a day (see table 8). This pattern suggests a greater tendency toward part-time work and long interruptions for women.

The majority of part-time *chinbata* weavers were women, because wives carried the additional burdens of child care and housework. The interviews provide ample evidence of how women juggled their schedules. Mrs. Konishi, a highly skilled weaver who worked side by side with her husband in a weave shed attached to their small house, explained: "I begin cooking supper and taking care of my children a little bit around 4:00 or 5:00 P.M. So I can't really get absorbed in the weaving. The children come home and tell me one after another that they are hungry." Mrs. Konishi's children were in high school when she made this statement. She said that while her children were younger she had no time to weave. She started weaving just a short time before her son entered junior high school, and when her daughter was already in high school.

TABLE 8. Average Working Days per Month and Working Hours per Day of *Chinbata* Household Members by Gender, 1933

| | | Household Heads | | | | Family Members | | | |
| | Total | Male | | Female | | Male | | Female | |
		N	%	N	%	N	%	N	%
1–10 days	93	20	0.56	1	0.41	3	0.24	69	2.22
11–20 days	1,303	418	11.72	80	32.65	129	10.37	676	21.77
More than 20 days	6,764	3,128	87.72	164	66.94	1,112	89.39	2,360	76.01
Total	8,160	3,566	100	245	100	1,244	100	3,105	100

Average Working Hours per Day of *Chinbata* Household Members by Gender, 1933

| | | Household Heads | | | | Family Members | | | |
| | Total | Male | | Female | | Male | | Female | |
		N	%	N	%	N	%	N	%
1–5 hours	192	19	0.53	1	0.41	5	0.40	167	5.38
6–10 hours	3,200	1,135	31.83	135	55.10	395	31.75	1,535	49.44
11–15 hours	4,380	2,193	61.50	94	38.37	772	62.06	1,321	42.54
More than 15 hours	388	219	6.14	15	6.12	72	5.79	82	2.64
Total	8,160	3,566	100	245	100	1,244	100	3,105	100

SOURCE: Kyoto-fu, Gakumu-bu, Shakai-ka, *Nishijin Chin'ori Gyōsha ni Kansuru Chōsa* (Research on Nishijin Pieceworkers), (Kyoto-fu, Gakumu-bu, Shakai-ka, 1934), 118, table 19.

Even highly skilled women weavers viewed their weaving as supplemental to their husbands' work, and perceived little distinction between their overall contributions to the family through child rearing and housework and their work as weavers. "My husband is the major breadwinner in the family!" exclaimed Mrs. Konishi. "Oh, it couldn't be me." Her husband was laughing as she said this. Mrs. Konishi earned only about one-third of the income her husband did, even though the pay rate per unit of the *obi* she wove was higher than that of her husband's product.[7] That was because she wove at a much slower pace, due to the complicated process required, and because of the many interruptions she experienced.

A survey of the life and labor of Nishijin housewives, conducted in 1969 by the Kyoto Women's Problems Research Committee, found overwhelming evidence for the multiplicity of stresses on Nishijin wives, resulting from the combination of weaving, preparatory work, child care, and housework. Although women were paid the same rates as men for their piecework, women's income was much lower than men's, because women were weaving fewer hours than men. While men wove for an average of 9 hours exclusively, women wove for an average of 7.5 hours. This figure for women did not account for interruptions for housework and child care. On the average, women spent an additional 6 hours during weekdays and 6 hours on the weekend on domestic chores and family needs outside these 7.5 hours. By comparison to salary men's wives, who were typically full-time homemakers, Nishijin wives spent less time on housework, although they spent more time on housework than women employed outside the home. Housework was made difficult by the fact that Nishijin houses were old, small, and crowded, and that dust and fiber remnants generated by weaving spread through the rooms.

To carry out their numerous tasks, women started their workdays much earlier in the morning than men, and some stayed up until midnight. These time pressures were intensified for mothers with young children who had no grandmother living in the household or nearby. Child care was particularly difficult because of the absence of play spaces both inside and outside the house. The houses were crowded together and close to the road, while parks and playgrounds were too distant (Kyoto Women's Problem Research Committee 1969).

7. Even though cottage weavers are normally paid as a household unit, in this case Mr. and Mrs. Konishi's pay rates were calculated separately, because they wove two different kinds of *obi*.

The survey also found that Nishijin wives' recreational activities were minimal. They spent only ten minutes reading the newspaper each day, mostly the family and society columns. Their main recreation was watching television. Unlike salary men's wives, most Nishijin wives did not attend *kimono* shows. Because of their stressful workloads, 87 percent of the Nishijin wives surveyed reported health problems, which doctors named "the Nishijin syndrome." The symptoms included backache, numb and swollen legs, arthritis, eye-fatigue, nearsightedness, constipation, anemia, nettle rash, stiff shoulders, headaches, sleeplessness, and fatigue in the mornings. All these symptoms, except for anemia and constipation, are directly related to weaving and the environment in which the looms are set. The report pointed out that Nishijin manufacturers were more concerned with having sufficient humidity for the fibers than with adequate lighting and air. As the women advanced in age, these diseases and fatigue became chronic and the women suffered from rheumatism. In addition, Nishijin women had a high rate of miscarriage. They usually continued to weave until the day before giving birth (Kyoto Women's Problem Research Committee 1969).

My interviews with Nishijin weavers also suggest repeatedly that beginning in the 1930s, the wives and daughters of *chinbata* were increasingly employed in weaving. At the same time, they assisted their male relatives in preparatory work, took care of children, and did household chores. As Mrs. Konishi put it:

In Nishijin there are many weavers, regardless of whether they are men or women, who are earning money. But the women cannot take care of the household if they are weaving as rigorously as their husbands. There aren't many who weave at home, you see—not even one out of ten women who weave make additional income for the family as I do. Women who weave are usually weaving along with their husbands. Some women are even better than their husbands. Sometimes the husband goes to the supermarket to buy food [amazed]! My husband never goes into a supermarket. He waits outside around the corner all the time until I finish shopping. There are many households like this in Nishijin.

Once again, the interviews reveal that even when women were full-time weavers, other family members interrupted the women's weaving for child care and domestic chores and the women stopped their own work to assist the men in preparatory tasks. Mrs. Konishi took for granted the interruptions in her weaving in order to run errands:

Also, I usually go to the manufacturer to deliver the finished *obi* and pick up the new orders, because it is more profitable this way. When we go on errands, we don't earn much. It is better for my husband to continue weaving while I run the errands, because I don't earn as much as my husband, due to housework. It is very common for women to go over to the manufacturer and deliver all their husbands' finished products, because men work more efficiently.

Because of the low rates of co-residence with the older generation in Nishijin, few mothers had access to consistent help from grandmothers for housework and child care. Help from grandparents was more available in the villages in Tango, because co-residence with the older generation was more common. As Mrs. Nagahama, a weaver of wedding coats *[uchi-kake]* in a Tango fishing village, put it:

After my marriage, I was weaving all day. The grandparents [Mr. Nagahama's parents] took care of our children a great deal. Grandmother did the household work, including cooking. When we began weaving, I used to work from 6:00 A.M. to 7:00 P.M. No matter how small the children were, I worked all those hours. Nowadays, I go to weave after all the children leave for school. I even work after supper till 8:30 P.M. I have very little time to be with our children. I talk with them before they leave for school or over dinner.

The part-time character of cottage weaving in terms of hours invested, particularly for *chinbata* women (even when they reported it as their full-time occupation), reflects the uneven rhythm of the industry. Regular, continuous employment is rare in the production of luxury textiles, which is frequently subject to the ups and downs under fickle business cycles. This cross-stitched pattern of employment has also required the flexibility of members' contributions to the *chinbata* families' collective economies. Flexibility was essential for survival. Since 85 percent of *chinbata* income derived from weaving and related tasks, and since 96 percent of weavers engaged in the household enterprise were family members, the *chinbata* had to marshall the labor of most household members in order to survive. At the same time, they had to secure other sources of income as backup for slump periods in their industry. In 1933, the average *chinbata* household income was about fifty *yen* a month, of which eleven *yen* were spent for rent (see table 9). With this type of balance sheet, the *chinbata* were able to save about twenty-one *yen* a year and were usually in debt for about seventy *yen* a year. *Chinbata* were even more vulnerable to economic problems under the impact of the depression in the early 1930s. The family budgets recorded in the 1933 survey reveal that in order to pay rent, *chinbata* families had to reduce their food expenses drastically. Many had to borrow money from

TABLE 9. Average Household Budget of *Chinbata*
Households, 1933

Total income per month (*yen*)	49.65
Income from *chinbata* per month	42.16[a]
Total expenditures per month	53.03
House rent per month	11.05
Total savings per year	21.33
Total debt per year	69.15

SOURCE: Kyoto-fu, Gakumu-bu, Shakai-ka, *Nishijin Chin'ori Gyōsha ni Kansuru Chōsa* (Research on Nishijin Pieceworkers), (Kyoto: Kyoto-fu, Gakumu-bu, Shakai-ka, 1934), 34–98, tables 12–16.

[a]These households derived 84.9 percent of their income from *chinbata* work.

their manufacturers *[orimoto]* in order to survive. Since the manufacturers set a loan limit of thirty *yen* per family, the weavers were eventually forced to turn to the pawnshops to supplement their decreased wages (Kyoto-fu, Gakumu-bu, Shakai-ka 1934).

One form of escape from their dependence on a fickle industry was for *chinbata* wives to weave elsewhere. During the 1930s, as the use of the powerloom spread even further in Nishijin, some *chinbata* wives worked as powerloom weavers in factories. Women weavers whom I interviewed insisted that they actually preferred factory weaving to working at home, because the factory provided them with steady wages and sociability in the workrooms. During periods of curtailment of production in recessions or depressions, factory weavers became vulnerable as well. Some Nishijin weavers' households tried to avert such situations by sending at least one family member to seek work outside Nishijin textile production. However, such households were caught in the double-bind of needing their entire household labor force during periods of high demand, while trying to find alternative employment in order to protect themselves during slow periods. Nishijin weavers' economy was, by definition, a flexible household economy that required continuing revision of family strategies in response to the ups and downs in the industry. The remarkable paradox in the lives of Nishijin weavers was the contrast between the continuity of the craft from one generation to the next on the one hand, and the precariousness and instability of the weavers' work lives and income on the other.

CHAPTER 5

The Mentality and Identity of the Nishijin Craftspeople

My mother was already weaving when she had me in her womb. Yes! I was born a weaver. I was listening to the weaving sound when I was born.

Mr. Shibagaki

Nishijin craftspeople *[shokunin]* see their main identity in weaving, a feeling reinforced by the continuity of their craft over several generations in their families. Their identity rests on their sense of competence and skill, on their commitment to making a special textile famous for its unique quality and design, and on their membership in a community in which all aspects of life are deeply interwoven with the production of this textile. As Mr. Nishitani, a highly skilled handloom weaver, put it: "My family lived here. I was born here. If you work on Nishijin weaving for forty or fifty years, you can't do anything else besides Nishijin. . . ." Even though many of the Nishijin people did not initially choose to be weavers, they have come to identify with weaving as their way of life. They are acutely aware of themselves as "Nishijin men and women" and as members of the Nishijin "village" *[mura]*, where daily life and interaction are governed by the community's internal, unspoken code of behavior. Even their language differs in some respects from the standard Kyoto dialect. At times, Nishijin people describe feelings or situations in metaphors borrowed from the world of spinning and weaving. The Nishijin word for "confusion," for example, is "the threads are all tangled up." It is important to realize, however, that Nishijin is not an isolated village. It is centrally located in Kyoto City, only blocks away from the Imperial Palace. These craftspeople's sense of place in the Nishijin "village" is inseparable from their work and way of life. They have a strong sense of themselves not only as practitioners of a particular craft engaged in making a nationally famous product, but also as members of a community famous over five centuries for the production of magnificent ceremonial cloth. Ironically, their strong identification with Nishijin has also become a source of tension and ambivalence, especially since the traditional industry they have served so loyally has been experiencing a severe decline.

In the closed world of Nishijin, conformity to its unspoken codes of behavior governs all aspects of life, including the regulation of production. Because of the proximity of weavers' houses to one another, little escapes the neighbors' attention along Nishijin's narrow lanes. The pressure for conformity extends to weavers' attempts to control each other's work schedules in the neighborhood. Conformity in Nishijin is so powerful that it penetrates private life and family relations. Nishijin wives have often felt subtle, and sometimes overt, pressure from neighbors to keep the wooden slats on the front walls of their houses shiny. Despite their heavy workloads as weavers, housewives, and mothers, some women, like Mrs. Konishi, still rise at dawn to polish the slats with soybean oil in order to avoid criticisms from neighbors. Likewise, Mr. Konishi did not dare be seen on his narrow Nishijin lane helping his wife carry grocery bags from the bus, thus conforming externally to the community pressure on men not to engage in what are considered women's tasks. When the couple shopped at a market in another district, Mr. Konishi helped carry the bags outside their neighborhood. But once they entered their neighborhood, Mrs. Konishi took all of the bags. As she observed: "When we go to the market, my husband helps me carry the bags to the bus. But when we get off the bus and turn into our lane, only I carry the bags."

Residents who were born and raised in Nishijin have occasionally lost their sense of perspective on whether the behavior and attitudes they describe were peculiar to Nishijin "village." When describing their world, they identified certain behaviors as unique to Nishijin, even though these could also be found among other traditional craftspeople, as well as among other industries in Kyoto and in other areas of Japan. For example, Nishijin weavers I interviewed attributed their fathers' past conduct, such as gambling, "playing around" with *geisha*, or having a "second wife" (mistress), to Nishijin's peculiar ways of life, rather than to a more widespread style of male comportment in Japan. Nishijin weavers also thought that their quest for quality and perfection was unique to Nishijin, when this attitude and a strong identification with the fame of the product characterize other traditional Japanese industries, such as pottery, papermaking, and metal work. Nishijin craftsmen have accepted the common stereotype to which they have been subjected in areas outside Nishijin that they were gambling and drinking away their earnings.

Disgruntled weavers attributed their being treated unfairly by their employers to Nishijin's unique atmosphere, rather than to general problems in labor relations in Japan. Some of the behaviors they described were, indeed, specifically rooted in Nishijin's paternalistic traditions of the relationships between manufacturer and weaver, and particularly to the erosion of these patterns. Using the antiquated paternalistic terms *oyakata* [father] and *kokata* [child] to describe manufacturers and weavers, they emphasized the "feudal" character of employer/employee relations that they felt still survived in Nishijin. Other strategies that the manufacturers followed in response to their industry's decline—such as wage cuts, curtailment of production, layoffs, and pressure for early retirement—were by no means unique to Nishijin, though many weavers perceived them to be. The repeated characterization of the relations between manufacturers and craftspeople in Nishijin runs like a thread through many interviews, especially in Mr. and Mrs. Konishi's and Mr. Fujiwara's accounts. Nishijin craftspeople are disgruntled over the dead hand of the "feudal past" that renders them submissive to their employers without the benefits of paternalism that were typical of Nishijin's "feudal" relations before World War II. This is why Nishijin weavers feel that the manufacturers take advantage of their loyalty and commitment to perfection in their craft.

The Spiritual Exercise

Nishijin weavers' quest for perfection is a key element in their self-perception as craftspeople. To them, weaving is not simply a job or a source of livelihood. It is a way of life. (See interview of Mr. Nishitani.) Weavers spend their entire lives improving their skills and perfecting their product. In addition to learning from one another, they frequently visit museums and temples to study the surviving fragments of ancient Japanese and Chinese textiles. The most highly skilled weavers in Nishijin, whom I interviewed, often expressed their regrets that some older techniques had already been forgotten and lost to their generation. Some lamented the occurrence of these losses in their fathers' and grandfathers' generations.

The weavers' sense of perfection is rooted in their understanding of the larger context of Japanese culture in which their craft, their products, and the aesthetic symbols they use are embedded. Even weavers with limited schooling know the meanings, origins, and significance of the design symbols woven into Nishijin fabrics. Even the older weavers who have only a primary school education are familiar with the intricacies of the tea ceremony, flower arrangement, Noh play, and religious rituals in which the cloth they weave has a central role.

Mr. Nishitani, an accomplished handloom weaver (seventy-five years old at the time of the interview), described his lifelong quest for perfection as a continuing "spiritual exercise":

I cannot weave easily. I have been doing this for sixty years, but still it is impossible to be perfect. I still enjoy weaving. Although I have been weaving for sixty years, I really don't know everything. Weaving this cloth requires deep knowledge. I still study weaving, and I haven't done anything so perfect that I can say, "This has been done without any mistake." There is always some part I don't really like. So that is the spiritual exercise: I want to make a perfect weaving without any mistake. This is what keeps me going.

His son-in-law, Mr. Fujiwara, a highly skilled weaver (forty-eight years old at the time of the interview), explained the difficulty in maintaining such high standards:

And this spiritual condition is not easy. We can't measure our product in meters. I'm hardly able to say I really like all of it from the beginning to the end. I can't be completely satisfied, even if there is no flaw. I don't make any flaws, but still the design cannot come out perfectly. This always happens [laugh]. I set my own standards. Even if I don't make an actual mistake, I still wish this part could be done more perfectly. So it is difficult. Honestly, I say now that I cannot easily achieve a perfect score.

As can be seen in his interview, Mr. Fujiwara is proud of maintaining a high quality of production, despite his bitterness against his employers. This is an important feature of Nishijin weavers' attitudes. Their commitment to making a perfect product is so profound that they separate it from their sense of alienation toward the way their employers treat them. Mr. Shibagaki, a handloom weaver (eighty years old at the time of the interview), elaborated on the importance of a continuous quest for perfection:

Nishijin people have said repeatedly that our work requires practice all the way until we die. We deal with different designs all the time, and we make samples whenever we get them. We examine our products and seek reactions to our samples. At this age, I can take orders for any type of weaving. When a weaver feels confident about his product, he cannot say that he is unable to make something. Production in Nishijin changes and designs change. Even at this age, we still face some difficulties that laymen wouldn't recognize, but we accept almost any order.

Like many other accomplished Nishijin craftspeople of his generation, Mr. Shibagaki regretted the recent decline in the quality of the products and in the standards by which they were judged:

I think you may say that the quality of Nishijin products has declined in certain respects that laymen wouldn't recognize. In the past, people could criticize us just by spreading the cloth and feeling its surface. They could tell which part was hard or soft. But now you will rarely see such a response. Even if you think you have woven a very fine cloth, you feel somewhat sad when others treat it without much care. In the past, people cared for the quality of products more than for efficiency in production. Nowadays, the treatment of quality products is the same as of non-quality products. Now the manufacturer seeks profit by asking weavers to produce more and faster, and we elderly weavers cannot compete with younger people in terms of efficiency. So younger weavers, who may lack in advanced techniques and quality but who weave faster, are more welcome. This is the tendency of today. In this respect, you may well talk about the decline in quality.

Mr. Konishi explained that weavers who have a strong commitment to perfecting their product are never free from this quest. Even on vacations and holidays, they constantly think of ways to improve their product.

The Dual Identity of Women

Identification with the quality of the product and with its long tradition is not limited to men. Women weavers also have a strong identity as craftspeople, but there is a duality inherent in their self-characterization. As weavers, Nishijin women express the same sense of expertise and standards of perfection articulated by male weavers. On the other hand, as dutiful wives, the women acknowledge that their role as weavers is secondary and auxiliary to that of their husbands and to the family's collective enterprise. Whether they weave on the handloom or the powerloom, women also express a deep consciousness as craftspeople and work with the same meticulousness and expertise as men. Like the men, the women are dedicated to making a perfect product and view their work lives as a continuous search for perfection. Even though they spoke in the interviews in the characteristic "female" Japanese language, one that is more modest and understated than that of men, women weavers described the actual weaving process and the techniques in great detail and talked about their work with pride. As Mrs. Shibagaki, a highly skilled handloom weaver (forty-seven years old at the time of the interview), put it:

Weaving is still difficult for me now, but after ten years I came to enjoy the work. I like the idea of creating. I can hardly be satisfied; I always want to create better products. Whenever I look at things in nature, I want to recreate them in a weaving. . . . And when I look at the product that I successfully made, I feel really happy.

The complexity of women weavers' relationships to their work, however, is greater than that of men, because of the women's orientation to their domestic responsibilities and their position within the family. Like women textile workers in nineteenth- and twentieth-century Europe and the United States, Japanese women weavers view their husbands as the main breadwinners. Describing their own roles as weavers as ancillary to that of their husbands, they perceive their work as a contribution to the collective family economy and as inseparable from child-rearing and homemaking.

As Mrs. Fujiwara, an expert handloom weaver (fifty years old at the time of the interview), who was initially reluctant to take on weaving, related:

I am proud of my job now. I love it and I can see many people while working here. . . . My husband does the same type of weaving I do. He also weaves on a handloom. . . . Some wives do the preparatory work for their husbands. I prefer using my own skills. This way I can make more money. Also, I wanted to accomplish something for myself but I also love housework. I never use instant food and I knit and sew for my family with my own hands. I never depend on anybody else. I even educated my children in that way. It is all right for women to work outside the home, but they should also take care of their families.

Her husband, on the other hand, emphasized the importance of a work career for women's lives: "Women who have skills cannot be satisfied with the housework only." There was, however, a difference between Mrs. Fujiwara's approach to her husband's involvement in housework and that of her daughter:

My husband does not help me, not at all. I do not want him to do housework. He has his own job outside. . . . He works longer hours than I do. But my daughter tells me that I should educate him to help me.

Since they view their textile work as ancillary to that of their husbands, wives who weave at home tolerate the interruptions in their work, annoying as they may be, as an inevitable aspect of their domestic role. Even highly skilled women weavers run errands in order to protect their husbands' weaving schedules. Mrs. Konishi, recognized as a fine weaver in her own right, accepted all of the interruptions in order to facilitate her husband's weaving. Women weavers help their husbands with preparation, such as winding the yarn, tying the warp, and cleaning up. They carry out all these tasks in addition to housework and child care. Even when some of them receive assistance with these domestic tasks from their mothers-in-law, the wives still interrupt their weaving to run errands, shop, and handle various needs of family members and more distant kin.

Nishijin women view their life paths as interwoven strands of work and family obligations, with little separation between the two. Even though they worked intermittently during the early years of child-rearing, they still perceived their weaving careers as continuous throughout their lives. When they were too old to weave, they worked on subsidiary tasks [shita-shigoto], which literally means "under work" or low-status work, by helping their fathers, brothers, or husbands who were full-time weavers at home. A survey of a sample of Nishijin housewives, conducted in 1969 by the Kyoto Women's Problems Research Committee, identified the dilemma inherent in Nishijin women weavers' perception of their work as being secondary to that of their men. The report concluded that their view of their work as part-time makes women tolerate lower income and lower status, and prevents them from asserting themselves (Kyoto Women's Problems Research Committee 1969).

Most wives deliver the finished obi to the manufacturer and pick up new orders and raw materials. By acting as their weaving households' external agents, however, wives are directly in touch with the manufacturers' world and are familiar with the broader context in which Nishijin *obi* is produced. They thus serve as important liaisons between their households and the outside world. Women often bring home news about changes in the marketplace, production methods, and wage policies. They find out about impending curtailments in production and about other problems concerning the weaving of *obi*. Despite these repeated encounters with the manufacturers' world, women do not negotiate wage rates, or the nature or number of orders. Men, on the other hand, obtain news about prices and work relations in the evenings while drinking, playing mah-jongg, and gambling with other men, or at the Greater Nishijin Textile Labor Union meetings, though very few Nishijin cottage weavers belong to the union.

In the interviews, Nishijin husbands frequently acknowledged their wives' multiple roles as homemakers, mothers, contributors to the family economy, and highly skilled weavers. The older Mr. Shibagaki, for example, first glorified his wife's domestic role: "Women have to do many miscellaneous things in housework, when compared to men. And that kind of work is more worthwhile than weaving. For instance, the wife has to clean around the house, go shopping; everything depends on her. That's why we can concentrate on our jobs." His wife (seventy-five years old at the time of the interview), on the other hand, insisted on her significant contribution to the family's economy as a weaver: "Well, unless I worked, we couldn't have eaten." Her husband agreed: "Our livelihood depended on that, so to speak." Their daughter-in-law (forty-seven years old), who was present at the interview, claimed that she personally was weaving "for both joy and money," but the older woman humbly insisted: "I just follow what is necessary—nothing special." At that point, Mr. Shibagaki felt that his wife had gone too far in understating her role as a weaver. He countered, "My wife has acquired sophisticated skills, and when she looks at her product, I think she likes it the more for her commitment to weaving."

Young Mrs. Shibagaki, who had a stronger sense of herself as a craftsperson and artist than her mother-in-law and than most Nishijin women, expressed anger about her husband's unwillingness to help with housework:

I often insist that my husband should share the housework, but he will not move. Since he was brought up that way, he cannot change now. I am angry because I do not have time for myself. I wanted to weave at home. I like working here [Nishijin Textile Center], but I also have to do all the shopping and the housework. Japanese men, including my husband, cannot do housework. I will make my grandson into a person who can do everything. He is just two months old. It may be the fault of women that men behave this way.

Mrs. Fuwa, who is also a highly artistic handloom weaver but who married late (at age thirty-seven) and had a baby shortly thereafter, was also disappointed that her husband was not helping with housework. Since her husband is not a Nishijin weaver, she negotiated with him prior to her marriage to assure that he would not stop her from working as a weaver:

My husband does not object to my work, because I like the work, and he promised before marriage that I could continue working. That was my condition to marriage. And he has not changed his mind yet. No, not yet [laugh]. He works in construction. He is a builder. My husband does not take care of the child. He says, "It's a woman's job to do child care" [laugh]. Yes, I sort of knew this in advance. But he takes care of her more than I had expected. Because normally he is the kind of person who doesn't even stretch his hand out to pick up an ashtray or a newspaper.

Expertise, skill, and fine reputations as weavers bestow on women a special status in the community, one that they could not have attained solely as housewives. Even some women who are too old to sustain weaving all day, but who still have sharp eyes and nimble fingers, work as *tate-tsunagi* — tying the threads of the new warp to the loom's frame. As on-call experts, these women go in pairs from house to house carrying the tools of their trade: delicate bamboo rods that are used to separate the rows of threads when tying the knots. They are paid well by the weavers and are served tea, sweets, and sometimes a meal in each weaver's house where they come to tie the warp. Weavers treat these women with awe, because the continuity in their production depends on the *tate-tsunagi* women's timely arrival. The weavers also fear these women, because they are notorious for carrying gossip from house to house. "Watch out! The *tate-tsunagi* women are coming!" is a common warning neighbors utter to each other in Nishijin. Anxious that rumors might spread in the community, Nishijin wives quickly straighten out the sandals *[geta]* that are piled at the entrance to the house and arrange them in neat rows — an important symbol of orderliness in Japanese homes.

Wives of other traditional craftsmen, such as potters, also view their supportive tasks as integral aspects of their family responsibilities (Kleinberg 1983). There is, however, a fundamental difference between the division of labor in potters' and weavers' families. The wives and daughters of traditional potters rarely participate in actual production. They help with procuring raw materials, some preparatory work, cleaning up, packing and shipping, and handling the sales. The only exception is in industrial potteries, such as in Arita in Kyushu, where women do skilled work similar to that of men, in painting and glazing, for example. In contrast to the potters' wives, Nishijin women weavers often possess skills equal to or greater than those of their husbands. These skills and participation in the production process affect Nishijin women's comportment.

Nishijin women weavers' sense of competence and understanding of their craft were expressed in the style of their participation in the interviews. Unlike the wives of traditional potters, whose houses I had visited in historic pottery villages such as Bizen, Tatchikui in Tamba, Karatsu, and Mashiko, Nishijin wives sat side by side with their husbands at the *kotatsu* [low table with a foot-warming heater underneath] during the interview and participated actively in the discussions, except when they disappeared briefly to prepare and serve tea. They often spoke in tandem with their husbands, completing their husbands' sentences, and sometimes corrected their husbands' accounts or contradicted their interpretations.

Even women in the villages in the Tango Peninsula had assumed a different posture after becoming weavers and were treated somewhat differently by their husbands. Mrs. Uebayashi, whose husband is a fisherman, combines eight hours of weaving with housework, and gets up at 4:00 A.M. to prepare the *bentō* [lunch box] for her husband, and to see him off when he goes to his boat. When I came for the interview, though, it was her husband who arranged the *kotatsu* and the *zabuton* [cushions] on the *tatami* mat; then he ushered his wife in and joined us for the interview. His wife, however, did most of the talking. Older men in these villages are concerned with the new style of behavior of women weavers. As Mr. Okamoto (seventy-two years old at the time of the interview), in a Tango village, put it:

I think that women gained some rights to express their own opinions after they started weaving. They order their husbands in their work, too. Their way of speaking has become imperious. It was influenced both by weaving and by general trends in the world.

Nishijin women weavers acted with greater flexibility than their husbands in moving back and forth between weaving in their own households and weaving in the factory, especially during periods of economic depression. Women were more willing than men to change assignments or take on part-time work. Following the spread of powerloom weaving during the 1930s, women weavers often shuttled back and forth between the cottage industry and the factory. They learned to weave in their own homes, as apprentices in another weaver's household, or in a manufacturer's house. They then worked in small factories or in another weaver's cottage until their marriage. After marriage they wove at home, side by side with their husbands, but in times of economic crisis they returned to the factory. Most Nishijin women weavers had done both household weaving and factory work.

In contrast to men, women weavers who had experienced factory work preferred it to weaving at home. Most women whom I interviewed in the small Nishijin factories expressed a clear preference for working there, rather than in household production. These women, who were in their thirties and forties, viewed the factory as an opportunity to be treated as an individual worker, rather than as inseparable from the family as a work unit. They were paid individually for their work, and the cloth they wove was evaluated and judged as their own product, rather than as part of the household's collective production. The factory enabled women to work a fixed number of hours without recurring interruptions for child care, housework, and assistance to their husbands. Most important, women weavers also valued the sociability of the workplace — the opportunity to enjoy the other weavers' company and to chat during tea breaks. A woman powerloom weaver (forty years old at the time of the interview) responded to my question as to which she preferred, weaving in the factory or at home:

I prefer to work here in the factory. When I come in here [to the factory] my time is my own. When I worked at home, we all worked together — my mother-in-law, my husband, and me. But my husband kept interrupting me and asking me to help him, and I had to help him, and I had to do things around the house. It is not fun to watch television at home. There is no one to talk to at home, except my husband and my mother-in-law. When I come here, I talk with all the people during our tea breaks.

Contrary to the prevailing perceptions of factory work as a form of exploitation, and contrary to the stereotype that women are better off working at home, this woman weaver and many others preferred the factory, because women were recognized and paid as individual workers, and because of the sociability that the workplace offered.

Ambivalence and Conflict

Despite their deep commitment to their craft and their high sense of perfection, Nishijin weavers are conscious of the internal contradictions in their roles. These ambiguities emanate partly from their being at the interstices between traditional craftsmanship and industrial work, and partly from the conflicts and insecurities inherent in Nishijin's ongoing economic crisis. Because Nishijin weaving is defined not as an art but as a traditional industry *[dentō sangyō]*, these weavers are considered craftspeople *[shokunin]* rather than artists. Even their status as craftspeople is ambiguous because of the organization of production. They are not independent or self-employed artisans; they weave *obi* in accordance with the manufacturers' designs, as specified in the orders and in the patterns punched into the jacquard system. They cannot choose the designs or colors they use. Their main challenge is to translate the design into a flawless web. Even the finest Nishijin weavers could never aspire to become Living National Treasures unless they started making and weaving original designs.[1] In the past, Nishijin has had two Living National Treasures, one manufacturer and one designer. The manufacturer, Tatsumura Hyogi, became famous for reconstructing the traditional design and weaving technique of a seventh-century brocade from fragments found in the Shōsō-in Museum in Nara. The designer, Kitagawa Heirou, excelled in recovering traditional designs and in adapting them to current Nishijin weaving, including the fabric used for the crown prince's adulthood ceremony. Mr. Kitagawa compared his creative work to "orchestrating an opera."

As employees of capitalist manufacturers, Nishijin weavers have little control over the type of *obi* they produce or over their terms of employment. They also have little control over their working conditions and pay rates. Even when they weave in their own households, they are neither independent artisans nor small entrepreneurs. The manufacturer provides the raw materials, design, and punch cards for the jacquard *[mongami]*, and then pays them for the finished product. The weavers prefer to be assigned as many *obi* of the same design and color as possible, even though it is more challenging to weave different designs. Since the weavers are paid by the piece, they lose time by having to change the threads attached to the jacquard for changing colors and designs. In order to curtail production, manufacturers assign fewer *obi* of each design and color to the weaver, and the need for frequent changes causes the weaver further loss in time. As Mrs. Konishi put it:

1. A Living National Treasure is an outstanding craftsperson or artist who has been given this special title by the national government. The program recognizes exceptionally high skills and the creation of outstanding traditional products. One of the main criteria for the selection of Living National Treasures is having recently been acknowledged for recovering lost skills and designs of a traditional product.

Earlier we used to weave about ten *obi* with the same design, but now we have to change the patterns of the design after every five *obi*. If you are now doing a design of roses and you have to change next to a design of ships, and so forth, it is hard to weave very efficiently, like before.

Cottage weavers have always been concerned about maintaining control over their work schedules. Flexibility in working hours has been an important distinguishing mark of Nishijin weavers' identity as craftspeople, as it was for European and American craftspeople in the nineteenth century. As Mr. Nishitani put it, "I've never thought about working in a factory. I have always worked in my home. I can't stand to be tied down by time schedules [laugh], especially in the morning." Like pre-industrial craftsmen in Europe, Nishijin artisans working in their own homes treasured the opportunity to exercise flexibility in their time schedules. Some preferred to "play" in the daytime and work in the evenings. They wanted to have this freedom, as long as they completed their assignments. After World War II, the passage of the Fair Labor Standards Act established the eight-hour work day and weavers lost some of this flexibility. They felt increasingly pressured to stop work in the evenings. When some weavers continued to work late, neighbors requested that they stop. The clicking of the looms during late hours was gradually silenced under community pressure. This was partly a result of the fact that Nishijin neighborhoods had become increasingly interspersed by residents who were not engaged in the production of textiles.

In Matsumoto's 1962 survey administered to weaving households in Nishijin, weavers were asked whether they thought it was better to weave at home or in a factory. Among those who claimed it was better to weave at home, the majority of the reasons given (63 percent) cited freedom, flexibility, and a more relaxed atmosphere as advantages to weaving at home. For some informants, flexibility meant no fixed hours. Others explained that working at home was more relaxed because they did not have to worry about relations with co-workers and did not have to dress up in order to go out to work. Another group felt that work at home was more efficient, and therefore provided a better income. A few respondents, most likely women, claimed that working at home enabled them to take care of the family and the household as well, and made it possible for them to be with their children. Some claimed that at home they could benefit from the help of other family members. Several replied that at home they were able to continue working, even when they were weak or old. One comment was particularly revealing of the Nishijin mentality: "There are many workers who cannot 'switch their mind' [compartmentalize] from work as work and family as family, so they need to work at home."

On the other hand, people who thought it was better to weave in the factory claimed that factory work was more efficient because schedules were fixed. That meant working fewer hours and not having to work on Sundays. This raises a question about income. Since they were being paid by the piece, does this mean that weavers were prepared to sacrifice income by working more limited hours and taking Sundays off? Another group found it an advantage in factory work not to need to ask for family help, and appreciated the opportunity of learning from co-workers or competing with them. As one weaver put it, "Competitive spirit leads to better work." Some emphasized the advantages of having fewer interruptions and separating work from the family home—a concept that was not characteristic of Nishijin.

The ambiguous status of Nishijin cottage weavers as employees or as semi-independent artisans is expressed in their ambivalence toward the labor union. Only a fraction of weavers belong to the Greater Nishijin Textile Labor Union. As Mr. Sakane Shigeru, the former labor union chief, explained bitterly, "There are approximately fourteen thousand weavers in Nishijin. . . . Our union has three hundred members, and among these, approximately one hundred people or less are *debata*; one hundred or less!" Mr. Matsushita, a highly skilled handloom weaver in a famous Nishijin company, sees the source of the problem in the fragmentation of the labor force, resulting from the isolation of weavers in their households, and in their separatist mentality, which is not conducive to unionization:

One thing we can say is that the cottage weaver's sense of solidarity is very low. This is because the unit of work each weaver does is defined individually. You weave each *obi* by yourself[2] and are paid by the piece-rate system *[deki-daka]*. So each individual is isolated and, instead of getting unionized, each works for himself and receives the wage for that. So the weavers' thoughts aren't directed at making our situation better, at making Nishijin better, at making it easier to work, or at making a good atmosphere.

Nishijin weavers feel betrayed and exploited by the manufacturers, especially during the industry's decline over the past decade and a half. As Mr. Fujiwara stressed:

2. The emphasis on weaving "by yourself" does not contradict the family system. It means that the *obi* is the product of that individual and his household, rather than a communal factory effort.

Nishijin is really feudal. . . . The factory where I work does not give us holidays with guaranteed pay [yūkyū-kyūka] and retirement pension [taishoku-kin]. The pay for our labor [kōchin] is low and not stable at all. We get no bonus, either. When there is a big gap between our needs for a livelihood and what the employer pays, it becomes difficult to make a living.

The weavers feel that the manufacturers exploit their sense of pride in their skills and their loyalty. As Mr. Matsushita put it, "The manufacturer is taking advantage of our pride." He is acutely aware of the contrast between the magnificent product he and his fellow workers are producing and the difficult working conditions:

Nishijin textiles are recognized for their beauty and their tradition. But no one is paying attention to what is behind this beautiful obi—the difficulty we have in creating it, our hard working conditions, and the great difficulty we have in making a living. We who are working here have to make a better Nishijin situation, so that we can live more like humans, rather than just work under these bad conditions.

The Nishijin weavers' sense of betrayal is intensified by the breakdown of the paternalistic relationship between manufacturer and weaver. The weavers feel that the manufacturers take advantage of their loyalty, especially when they use tricks to curtail production. The manufacturers slow down the weavers, without fully laying them off, just long enough to avoid paying unemployment compensation. Mr. Konishi described the sly way of curtailing production by putting cottage weavers on hold. Like Mr. Fujiwara, Mr. and Mrs. Konishi were bitter about the manufacturers' shrewd techniques of stalling production. As Mr. Konishi said in anger:

To keep a weaver waiting, they use the excuse that the work is not ready. Sometimes they keep weavers waiting for days. Companies play games. Weavers do not have any idea of the color they should use. They come to the company to get the silk thread and the design, but the orimoto [manufacturers] delay telling them the color arrangements. The manufacturers plan these underhanded maneuvers on purpose. They don't want to just send a weaver home without any orders. It would become a legal problem [having to pay unemployment compensation]. So they keep them waiting.

Mrs. Konishi added:

They do it very cleverly. . . . If they told us in advance and asked us to wait for a whole day, then we would know it and we could expect that we would get zero pay for that day. When they say they will bring an order soon, and they want us to wait for just "two or three hours," or when they ask suddenly if we could change the colors, we have to stop for a while. We don't really complain about that sort of "little" thing, you know. Well, suppose we've woven a big piece today, and the next day when we have to do the next order, they tell us that they want to change the colors this time. So they ask us if we could wait until they finish preparing the new threads; so we agree to wait. If it is now about 4:00 P.M., they say they will have the threads ready first thing in the morning. It only takes two or three hours to have them ready. We plan to start working at 7:00 or 8:00 A.M. But for them, "the first thing in the morning" means 10:00 A.M. or noon, you see. Then after we receive the threads, we have to wind them, and so on, so we can finally start weaving only after lunch. These delays mean almost a whole day for us, but for them "the first thing next morning" was delayed just a little [laugh]. That's the point—they don't make us wait long enough to qualify for unemployment compensation. We have to be unemployed one whole day in order to get compensated.

Many weavers perceive the fundamental problem in Nishijin as emanating from the dead hand of the past—the survival of the exploitative and paternalistic relationship between the manufacturer and the weaver, without the benefits and protection that were inherent in this system in earlier times. As Mr. Konishi explained:

There is a hierarchical line between the manufacturer *[oyakata]* and the weaver *[kokata]* in Nishijin. So if the *oyakata* taps on my shoulder and says, "Would you please wait for a while?" I have to accept this. The tapping means that I cannot make money now, because I am not paid by the hour.

Mrs. Konishi added: "If we were unemployed for one day, we would get about six thousand *yen* [through compensation], instead of the normal ten thousand *yen*, but when they say 'just wait a little while,' we don't receive anything." The weavers feel that the manufacturer is taking advantage of the paternalistic relationship. "That's the peculiarity of Nishijin," emphasized Mr. Konishi, "*Oyakata* and *kokata* always see each other," so the *kokata* has to comply. Mr. and Mrs. Konishi and other weavers felt that the manufacturers were exploiting the "family" metaphor of an earlier paternalistic relationship. As Mr. Konishi put it, "The worker is manipulated under that concept of 'family.'" Mrs. Konishi added, "I definitely think that the employer used the concept of *kazoku* [family] for his own convenience. Maybe the worker was treated as someone without brains and was cared for like a child [laughs]. . . . But the modern weavers can't be like them. They would protest."

The weavers' frustration is intensified by their inability to exercise the one form of escape they used in the past, namely changing employers. They feel trapped in non-negotiable working conditions, because it is impossible to change manufacturers during periods of declining production. As Mr. Yamada, a seventy-year-old weaver, observed bitterly, "If we quit this job, there would be no place for us to go. What they are doing to us is just like beating babies." Mr. Konishi also recalled better times, when weavers were able to exercise some choices:

When we were young, it used to be that if we didn't like the wages or conditions of one manufacturer, we could move to another one. We would walk around Nishijin with a pair of scissors in our hands. We used to look for signs on the houses saying "weaver wanted," and we'd find another manufacturer. We used to make twice as much money as ordinary salary men. Now we have nowhere to go, nowhere!

As noted in chapter 1, Nishijin weavers see the worst injury in the manufacturers' tendency to subcontract *obi* weaving to rural workers in the Tango Peninsula, and in China and Korea. As a result, traditional weavers have been losing their jobs to rural weavers who are willing to work for lower wages. As Mr. Fujiwara explained:

There exist many ugly things behind such beautiful *obi*. If you visit the manufacturer, they would speak beautifully about their business, but it is false. . . . Manufacturers do not make any effort to sustain successors in Nishijin. They just keep giving orders to weavers outside of Nishijin for lower wages. . . . The manufacturers are shortsighted.

Witnessing the precipitous decline of their craft and the erosion of their livelihood, Nishijin weavers feel betrayed by the industry that they and their ancestors have served loyally over several generations. Former labor union chief Sakane Shigeru lamented about employers' failure to replace weavers who quit or retire with young ones, and worried about the extinction of Nishijin:

So because they don't hire new workers, although there are jobs . . . production here will become less and less. Then the name of Nishijin will end as a well-known name for weaving *obi*. As a result, young people do not want to succeed to our work, because this industry has no future.

Mr. Fujiwara said sarcastically, "I belong to the 'young' generation. I am forty-eight years old. Some weavers are older than seventy. Really good handloom weaving will disappear from Nishijin when my generation gets old."

Despair over Nishijin's shrinking industry has led weavers to revise their family strategies concerning succession. Since the 1960s, weavers in their fifties or older have discouraged their sons from continuing their craft in an industry without a future. As Mr. Koyama explained:

I did not ask my son to be a weaver. Now he also thinks that it would be better not to be a weaver, I imagine. At the present time, we cannot make a living unless we do something extra, in addition to the ordinary. In comparison with what I did, nowadays they must work twice as much. After all, fabrics have become more difficult to weave.

Mrs. Konishi also explained her preferences for her children's future:

The most important thing is to get our kids out of the Nishijin village. . . . I found that weaving is quite hard, so we decided to let our children go to the university. Also, I wouldn't want my daughter to marry a weaver. I think a man, like a salary man, leading an easygoing life, would be better.

Mr. and Mrs. Konishi sent their son to a technical school and their daughter to a junior college. After graduation, the daughter worked temporarily in a law firm. Within the year, she married a salary man and moved to a middle-class suburb to co-reside with her husband's parents. She had a child a year later.

One of the contradictions inherent in Nishijin is the sense of semi-isolation of Nishijin weavers and their families in their households, by contrast to the strong community pressure for conformity. Unlike factory work, the household production experience isolates individual weavers from each other, a phenomenon also expressed in the weakness and low membership of the union. While Nishijin weavers share a common identity in terms of their craft, production, and identification with the process and the product, their primary identification is with their family. This type of behavior does not necessarily imply individualism. In Japanese culture, individuals are defined in terms of their contribution to a group. In the lives of Nishijin weavers, that group is the family, rather than the larger community of manufacturers. This lack of communal identity among Nishijin household weavers is the result of the manufacturers' competitiveness with each other and the divisiveness among weavers, induced by the manufacturers' basing the pay rate on individual negotiations with each weaver.

In their efforts to interpret Nishijin and explain their lives to me, Nishijin craftspeople expressed their inability to understand their own world in all its complexities. Most of all, they felt helpless in coming to terms with what they felt was betrayal by their employers. After being interviewed for many hours, Mr. Konishi asked me, "Have you come to understand Nishijin?" Before I had a chance to respond, Mrs. Konishi followed, "It is also hard for us weavers to understand each other's feelings," and Mr. Konishi added: "Maybe that's one of the unique things about Nishijin." Their bewilderment emanated partly from the manufacturers' wage system, he explained:

There is no stable wage system, except that people talk with each other and draw the minimum line to base the pay rate on. I think this is why Nishijin is so complex and hard to understand. . . . [T]his is the major cause of complexity. I was born in Nishijin and my wife has been involved in Nishijin for over twenty years, and it is still hard for us to understand it.

PART TWO

The Nishijin People's Own Stories

Mr. Yamaguchi

Manufacturer and Creator
of The Tale of Genji *on Handwoven Scrolls*

Mr. Yamaguchi Itaro, one of the most distinguished and creative manufac-
turers in Nishijin, was eighty years old at the time of the first interview. He
has spent many years designing and supervising the weaving of four surviving
scrolls illustrating scenes from The Tale of Genji. *As Mr. Yamaguchi ex-*
plains, he was engaged in a creative process that involved not merely the re-
production of paintings on textiles, but an artistic translation of the ancient
paintings into Nishijin weavings. The Genji scrolls are being woven in Nishijin
by three master weavers on wooden handlooms in a traditional small workshop.
In 1994, Mr. Yamaguchi donated the first two scrolls to the Guimet Museum
in Paris.

Mr. Yamaguchi lives with his youngest son, Nonaka Akira; his daughter-
in-law; and his grandchildren. Their home, a grand, traditionally designed
Japanese house, was built in the 1970s on the outskirts of Kyoto. Mr. Nonaka,
Mr. Yamaguchi's son and also a Nishijin manufacturer, is more inventive
and innovative than the traditional Nishijin manufacturers. Mr. Yamagu-
chi's two older sons from his first marriage head their own Nishijin weaving
companies. In 2002, Mr. Yamaguchi celebrated his hundredth birthday.

These are the paintings of *The Tale of Genji*. I made a copy of the paintings by looking at the originals. This picture was painted by Tawaraya
Sotatsu [a famous Japanese painter] in the early Edo Period in the beginning of the seventeenth century. I took on such a big project because
I wanted to recreate these paintings in textiles. The original paintings

FIGURE 12. Mr. Yamaguchi in his manufacturing office. Photograph courtesy of Nonaka Akira.

used to be much more colorful, but the bright colors faded away. I think that the original painter's intention was to express *The Tale of Genji* in colorful images. Since the colors are gone, we cannot tell what aesthetic sense of color people used to have at that time. I wanted to recover the original vibrant colors in the weaving. All the techniques of Nishijin textiles come together in this weaving of *The Tale of Genji*.

The art of Nishijin weaving was transferred to Japan from some places on the Silk Road. We also learned a lot about weaving from China. However, we invented more sophisticated techniques in Nishijin than those imported from other places. The costumes of Noh plays are nothing more than the direct imitation of imported weavings in which we can observe the cultural progress created here in Japan. In China, they used to weave this kind of textile with motifs of paintings, but from my point of view the Chinese weavings look too simple. The Chinese seemed to have intended simply to reproduce the original paintings in

FIGURE 13. A woven scroll depicting a scene from *The Tale of Genji*, designed by Mr. Yamaguchi. Photograph courtesy of Nonaka Akira.

textiles. However successful the Chinese might have been, the outcome was too simple. Paintings have their own particular beauty; so do textiles. I wanted to express in the weaving the beauty, which cannot be described in paintings alone. There is nothing like that in the Chinese weavings. But Chinese-like weavings that used paintings have existed in Nishijin. However, I am the first to do this type of weaving in Japan.

So when we try to translate the paintings from *The Tale of Genji* into weavings, we have to do it with our contemporary sense of beauty. As much as we research the original colors, we cannot use them because they may not fit contemporary aesthetics. Consequently, we can use all the modern techniques of weaving for this project. We do not have to depend on the traditional methods. This is my philosophy. We use only these new techniques for weaving, but the colors are produced with my own sensibility.

Look at this sample! I even changed the size of the paintings in order to make it easier for people to see them in the weaving. I wanted to introduce to people today the gorgeous lifestyle of the court culture from that time. This is my interpretation of that style expressed in the colors and in the weaving method. This is not a copy of the paintings, but a new creation. If you look at this weaving technically, you may find how hard I worked on this piece. Even specialists in textile museums say that they have not seen textiles similar to this one. I concluded that most of the weaving techniques in the world converge in the weaving techniques of Nishijin. I wanted to use these techniques, as much as possible, to their utmost perfection.

People are saying that Nishijin is declining. This is because the machine technology has improved a great deal. The production capacity of powerlooms has increased much more than handloom weaving. In Nishijin, they produce now more than necessary, but there is a limit to the demand. Supply and demand are unbalanced. It is natural that the market does not go well when they overproduce. We see the same phenomenon in various modernized productions in capitalist society. Even in food, when we get an excessive crop of rice, the price goes down. But I do not know what the solution is. What is the best way to reduce production in Nishijin? Since there are tremendous numbers of manufacturers here who are not organized into big companies, it is difficult to follow a unified policy. All of us have been advised to develop some cooperative action. So far, we have tried to do something but could never achieve the cooperation we needed. Part of the problem is the division of labor in Nishijin. People who make *obi* make *obi*; people who make *kimono* make *kimono*; people who make fabrics for interior decorating make only that; and necktie makers produce neckties. They are all divided into groups. So since the manufacturers compete with each other, it is impossible to achieve organized action.

Nowadays people cannot wear *kimono* daily. On the surface, it looks as though fewer and fewer people wear *kimono* but, in fact, the demand for the high-class products of Nishijin is high. *Obi* has become very elaborate, because of the rise in the living standard of ordinary people. They buy *obi* now as well, and we expect them to buy in the future. Many girls today wear *kimono* for the celebration of the adulthood ceremony *[Seijin Shiki]*, but this was not possible a few years ago. They wear long-sleeved *kimono* with *obi* during that celebration on January 15, but earlier nobody could afford this.

I founded my company and started production sixty-four years ago. I formed a corporation after World War II. My father was a cottage weaver working for someone else. I was going to elementary school when I was living with my father, till the age of twelve. There were four looms at our house, and he was employing weavers there. I helped my father, and then went to my uncle for apprenticeship *[hōkō]*. My uncle was a manufacturer *[orimoto]*. The name of his company was Sano. He was my mother's younger brother. I stayed in his house for training *[minarai]* to weave *obi* until age eighteen. Then I became independent and started as a manufacturer.

My father was a craftsman-weaver *[shokunin]*. I am the oldest son. Traditionally, the oldest son used to get the highest support in the Japanese family. But my father did not help when I decided to become independent. I had many brothers and sisters, so my father was poor and did not have extra money. Because my father was not an independent small manufacturer *[jimae]*, he wanted me to be educated in order to become a manufacturer. So he entrusted me to his wife's younger brother. My brothers stayed with my father. We were four brothers and four sisters. Even though I was still eighteen years old, I supported my younger brothers to some extent. I was not given anything by my father. My sisters and one of my brothers were already weaving then. Since they were working, my father did not have to work so hard at that time. I was young and easygoing.

My father's family was very poor. My father started as an apprentice at age five. Age five is the same age as when kids go to kindergarten today! His older brother was already doing an apprenticeship in Nishijin, and then my father was sent to the same place to apprentice. At that time, parents used to "get rid of extra mouths to feed" *[kuchiberashi]* by sending children away. Parents with too many children used to make some of them leave home and live and work in someone else's house, in order to reduce their financial burden. My father came from a family of "drinking-water peasants" *[mizu-nomi by-akushō]*, meaning they were extremely poor. So they wanted to reduce the number of children in the house as much as possible. My father was just being fed in exchange for doing trifling errands like boiling water for baths or wiping floors with rags. He did not have a chance for an education; he was illiterate. He became a weaver later. Though he was a good weaver, he could not start his own business because of his illiteracy. His mother did not weave, but she helped by winding the thread. Such was the situation in Kyoto at the early part of the Meiji Period [late nineteenth century].

As I was finishing my apprenticeship, my uncle quit being an independent manufacturer. His company was absorbed by another company; he became an executive of the newly merged company. After the new company was started, the war in Europe [World War I] ended. The war stopped the high demand for goods in Japan. They were unable to import dyes from Germany, and the prices were raised as much as a thousand times. Because of the war, the price of every item, such as thread and dye, for the weavings was extremely high. They made lots of money due to this abnormal economic boom. But the market crashed suddenly, as soon as the war ended. All the prices came down to one-third of the pre-war period. I was one of the employees in my uncle's new company, but they had to reduce the scale of business in February. Though many employees were fired, I was not. I was, however, disappointed with the weak structure of the company that my uncle had joined. Finally, I quit my uncle's company on June 30, 1920. Then, on July 15, 1920, I started independently as a manufacturer. I was eighteen. My uncle suggested that I start a new company, because he knew how efficient I was. He did not have any expectations from his company for the future. I guess that he could not use me in his company, so he encouraged me to start something new.

Yes! It was very unusual to start a company at such a young age. But when I was working with other workers in that company, I found that I was just as capable as people ten or twenty years older than myself. Nothing inferior! When I started this company I was living separately from my parents. I was still living in my uncle's house in Nishijin, until I got married. The house was large enough to enable me to stay there. I started living there as an apprentice, but later we changed the arrangement to my renting a room. All of us — my parents and my uncle — were living in Nishijin. It was a wooden house, something like the "sleeping place of the eel" [unagi-no-ne-doko]. I built my own house when I got married.

When I started this company, I did not need much capital. Hand-looms did not cost very much. Nishijin was a convenient place where we could prepare things without paying cash, by buying supplies on credit. We could start an enterprise with just a little money. My first product was wide obi [maru-obi], which was sold on August 10. I did not have advance cash for it. We usually do payments at the end of each month [getsumatsu-barai], so I could pay the weavers first, in the beginning of August. I paid cash to the weavers as soon as the obi was completed [oridema]. All other expenses I paid by the end of August. We were able to make two maru-obi on the tenth and the fifteenth of August. The next one came out on the twentieth of August. After all, I could produce five obi in the same month, and I could earn some money when I sold them. It was right after the depression, the economic panic, in Taishō 9 [1920]. Companies in general were not daring with their businesses. They were quite hesitant. I was crazy from just working in order to survive.

A little while later, department stores like Mitsukoshi and Shirokiya were strong. They were willing to buy my products. Once I produced original designs, the department stores bought my entire stock. They bought five or six rolls *[tan]* of newly designed *obi*. They preferred something new and unique. Since they bought the *obi*, the wholesalers *[ton'ya]* bought our products, too. They did not have a hard time at all selling my *obi*. They just went to the stores to sell my products. Since I produced excellent quality *obi*, I did not have to worry about money. They were glad to buy my products. Despite the general depression in Nishijin, I was young enough to work like crazy.

It was 1920 when World War I ended. I was designing for myself. The company grew bigger and bigger. It was growing till World War II. It was a good time. We had ups and downs even then. Nothing went that smoothly. For example, in 1923 we had the Great Tokyo Earthquake *[Kantō Daishinsai]*. Because I was mostly doing my business with people in Tokyo, it was really shocking when Tokyo broke down. It was indescribable damage for us. The government issued a moratorium which allowed people to postpone payments, because the earthquakes caused serious damage to the economy. However, there was a strange phenomenon after that, which was called "recovery market" or "boom" *[fukkō keiki]*.

When Tokyo started to recover, money was invested in construction and so forth. Then it stimulated other businesses. The licensed prostitution quarters *[yūkaku]* in Tokyo were prosperous. At that time, the fashion trends and boom for *obi* were set by the prostitutes, rather than by the townspeople. I use the term *yūkaku* in a general sense. In fact, there were two kinds of women in *yūkaku*: one of them was commercial prostitutes *[shōgi]* and the other type was women entertainers *[geisha]*. Women in *yūkaku* wore luxury items, unlike in the present *yūkaku*. Those prostitutes and *geisha* bought their own *obi*, because they made lots of money. We used to call them "Fujiyama *geisha* girls." They wore really conspicuous clothes and were different from the contemporary *geisha*. The Mitsukoshi department store used to issue a magazine called *Time*; the magazine covers had pictures of famous *geisha* in the Shinbashi district in Tokyo who were wearing luxurious kimono.

In Tokyo, top politicians had meetings at Akasaka, Shinbashi, and so forth, where *geisha* entertained them and made enormous amounts of money. When people invited guests for special occasions, they entertained them by hiring *geisha*. Politicians and top businessmen made use of *yūkaku* in feasts. Top-class *geisha* appeared at the important political meetings, which were influential enough to govern Japan. Rich people tried to use *geisha* to gather information from them. They bribed the *geisha* in order to be informed about who got together at feasts and when. The *geisha* had such special relationships with the rich patrons that they visited those wealthy people for New Year's greetings.[1] If the *geisha* were wearing excellent *kimono*, they received "big" celebration money as gifts *[shūgi]*. They could gather enough celebration money to buy such luxurious *kimono* just by visiting these people for greetings. Of course, there were rich people's wives and ladies of the nobility who wore much better *kimono* than the *geisha*. But women of the nobility did not show up in public. By contrast, the *geisha*'s business was to display good *kimono* and they were willing to appear on posters. Naturally, *kimono* had to be advertised only through the *geisha*. When Tokyo was destroyed by the earthquake, wealthy people from all around the country visited Kyoto and played around in the Gion [*geisha* and entertainment district]. They spent lots of money here. They also bought *kimono*, particularly during the recovery period after the earthquake. I don't have any connections with *geisha*. The kimono store *[gofuku-ya]* is in contact with them.

I quit my textile business once during the war [World War II]. There was a government regulation at that time prohibiting the making of luxury products. Only those who could not survive without textiles kept making textiles. And those who had excellent skills were allowed to keep weaving in order to preserve their skills. I could have gotten a permit to continue production for the sake of the preservation of skills, but I decided not to accept it. I thought that to keep weaving in the midst of the war was unfair. Powerlooms were destroyed in order to recycle the metal for weapons. But I was just using wooden looms, so that was not a problem. During the war, we were not allowed to waste anything. Luxury was regarded as the enemy. At the beginning of the war, I decided to quit weaving and started to work in a wooden-airplane factory, because I thought I could manage to support myself. I had to survive the war somehow by making a living. These airplanes were designed for the "death-for-honor" strategy *[gyokusai]*. This was a small subcontract factory where about one hundred people were making parts for air-

1. In Japan, the heads of companies, government agencies, small businesses, and families hold open houses during the three days of the New Year's holiday and receive customers, clients, friends, and relatives. It is still customary for *geisha* to visit the open houses of their customers and to offer New Year's greetings.

planes. I founded that company with some other people. The government bought the parts. During the war, we were not allowed to waste anything. Luxury was regarded as the enemy. But after the war, I returned to weaving. I started it for my own sake and wanted to make something satisfactory for myself.

During the later part of the war, I was sick in bed with tuberculosis. I was away from work. I got sick in Shōwa 18 [1943]. Because of lack of nutrition, I spent the rest of the wartime in bed without recovering. There was no way to be fed proteins . . . I survived on starches. Antibiotics did not exist then. I was taking zolo-amin medicine, which weakened my body extremely. But we did not have any financial problems. Since I was a representative in the municipal government, I was receiving an annual salary.

After the war, when we started production again, there was no supply of silk thread, so we obtained raw, unprocessed silk thread [kiito] in the black market and dyed it secretly [yami]. We produced and sold textiles in the black market. After the War, the entire economy in this country was functioning in the black market. Everybody was "put in a fork" [experienced a squeeze], whether he or she survived or not. We were eating wheat chaff imported from America, which was fed to pigs there. It was at least supplied legally. Everybody was suffering from malnutrition. We used to have swollen faces because of malnutrition. We are reminded of those days when we see the starving people in Africa nowadays. Those who appeared strong were doing something illegal through the black market. We used to grow vegetables on the roadsides. We burned the trees from our garden for fuel. In such a situation, we had to do something critical for survival. No choice! We had to use the black market to get threads.

I was not physically strong. I could not do physical labor. Theoretically, people like us had priority to be covered by some welfare policy, but that did not happen. Instead, those who kept weaving through the war were rude to us, because they were able to get a supply of thread legally, even after the war [since they were not weaving luxury products]. Yes, most of the craftsmen [shokunin] were killed. Lots of young craftsmen died. Those who remained alive were either old or in ill health. Even the physically lowest-ranking soldiers like my younger brother were sent to the battlefields.

In the summer when the war ended, Shōwa 20 [1945], I started weaving mufflers for the coming winter. I wanted to make proper weavings, but there was no way to get appropriate silk floss [mawata]. What I got was cotton thread, or junk silk thread *[kuzu kiito]* that was left over from parachutes and re-spun into another thread. I bought these threads in the black market. I made mufflers from them, since people did not have enough warm wear in the cold winter. I was crazy to make them with the expectation of selling. Right after the war in 1945, I could not find any weavers. So I looked for old women living in the countryside who had some experience in weaving family stuff at home, and I asked them to make mufflers. The mufflers sold very well in the winter. Even top-class department stores bought them. These would be considered worse than rags today. But at that time I could sell those mufflers at good prices, and finally I found weavers. I did not have any idea where I could have contacted them right after the war.

I was able to start producing *obi* again from March, Shōwa 21 [1946]. Then I hired one weaver. In 1946, I increased the number of weavers. My business became more and more successful after the law controlling the sales of thread was revoked, in Shōwa 25 [1950]. I then employed about twenty weavers. Two were working in my shop, and all of the others were cottage weavers.

These problems during the war were not specific to World War II. They were historically consistent in Nishijin, because during war situations fancy textiles are never needed. Before World War II, Japan used to have some kind of war every ten years. Whenever a war occurred, Nishijin had to confront the same situation. I was not too shocked, therefore, with the situation.

Ups and downs are sort of the characteristic way of life here. In Nishijin, we can have a business only with the anticipation of those kinds of things. We had these problems many times before the war [World War II]; for example, bankruptcy of the wholesalers. Before the war, however, we used to use handlooms. The production was not as rapid, so that adjustment to crisis was easier. In the worst depression, some kind of *kimono* could be sold somehow. In my father's generation, there was the Sino-Japanese War *[Nisshin-sensō]* in Meiji 28 or 29 [1895]. People were really upset to fight with such a huge country, and it caused a serious depression in which weavers lost their jobs. People used to serve rice gruel to starving weavers in the temple or shrine areas. I heard that in Nishijin they called this depression "rice gruel panic" *[o-kayu sawagi]*. Even in such terrible situations, they could have the market open in the fall in order to sell *kimono* for the New Year. It was my mother who told me this, when I was experiencing an economic depression during the difficult period after the war. My mother advised me that whatever depression we experience, we should just wait for a while till recovery comes.

After my company developed, my younger brother became independent. My uncle didn't help him at all. I helped my brother in every respect. It was the same kind of business but in a separate company, and we compete with each other now. In fact, I don't think we had such terrible times together. So far, we somehow managed to survive. We really participate in our work, unlike other business owners [not in textiles], who only subcontract factory work. We, as manufacturers, do everything by ourselves. Other company owners just let their employees work in the office. We have our own values and our ways of doing business. My third brother is also a manufacturer. The fourth one died in the war [World War II]. Two younger brothers are still working. Three of us are running weaving companies.[2] I helped my brothers a lot when they wanted to be independent. They did not get any help from our parents, but they got help from me. My sister also married a manufacturer *[oriya]*.[3] I also helped them. Whenever any of them have important changes in their lives, I always help them.

Nishijin is a convenient place where we can find all kinds of specialists in textiles. If we need original design paper *[genshi]* and thick-and-thin thread *[ito]*, we can order them. There are some special supply stores in Nishijin. We ask the dyeing shop to dye them in various colors. We ask the weavers to weave them. We are following this procedure even now. It is really surprising that we, who are doing all kinds of specialized work, are surviving here, even though we do not have any guarantee about when we can get our next orders.

For example, in the case of the dyeing workshop *[some-ya]*, they may have the capacity to dye threads for a hundred *obi*, but they do not always have enough orders to use their full capacity. Yet they constantly keep getting some orders and they manage to survive. Sometimes they are working with a hundred *obi*. Another time, they are working with only

---

2. The brothers have developed separate identities. For instance, one kind of *obi* is recognized as Mr. Yamaguchi's and another kind of *obi* is the other brother's.

3. During the interview with his father, Mr. Nonaka said: "In Nishijin, the manufacturer does not usually have a wholesale department. He is just a maker. Seiko Company is different. So we are competing with each other, but every product goes to the wholesale store. It is half competition and half cooperation. But the other family of Yamaguchi . . . his brother has five sons and five daughters, and all of them are working for their father in one company. They are cooperating, not competing. Seiko is different. Each son has a company."

fifty *obi*, even though they have the capacity for one hundred *obi*. They require payment to cover the gap, and we pay it. The price per piece [*tanka*] is high, so we can lower the price when we give them more pieces. If we were to do the dyeing in our own place, we would be able to cut the cost a lot. But it is troublesome, for we need special dye and other equipment to dye the threads. So it is better to ask dyers to do the job, even though it may cost three times or five times more than if we did it ourselves. In Nishijin, there are interdependent relationships between weavers and dyers. The relationships between the manufacturer and the different specialists, such as dyers, are very important. We are allowed to change our subcontracts [*shita-uke*] with these specialists as we like, but we are related to each other in sincerity. If they do something insincere, we may switch to another dyer.[4] We could start a business without capital only if we had trust from other craftspeople to whom we subcontract the preparatory work. We could ask them to do some work without cash payments, if they had trust in us.

We moved to this house seventeen years ago. Before this house was built, there were forests and meadows here. It was somewhat like a suburb. I did not really feel lonely when I left Nishijin, because I had my work here.[5] But Nishijin has a division of labor [*bungyō*], so I had to go to Nishijin to cover some part of the [preparatory] work, which could not be done here. We have to go all the way through the preparatory processes in Nishijin before weaving.[6] Nishijin is a strange place where everything is fully organized for weaving. In Nishijin, one subcontractor can take orders from several manufacturers; this is impossible with a subcontractor in the Toyota automobile factory, for instance. We can assign each process of the auxiliary work to a different subcontractor, and the whole job can be accomplished. In this respect, it was inconvenient to have a business outside Nishijin.[7]

The relationships among manufacturers and weavers did not change very much as long as they used to produce within Nishijin. But in the

---

4. Mr. Nonaka said: "Actually, the biggest change in the community relations is happening in the relationships between manufacturer and weaver."

5. Mr. Nonaka said: "It was inconvenient to move here, because all other companies were located in Nishijin."

6. Mr. Yamaguchi is referring to the organization of production in Nishijin, where the manufacturer subcontracts each prepatory operation prior to weaving to a different craftsman—for example, dyeing the thread, preparing the warp, making the punch cards for the jacquard, and making the design and the patterns.

7. The actual production of Mr. Yamaguchi's weaving takes place in Nishijin.

Tango [Peninsula on the Japan Sea], they introduced new looms in order to produce more *obi*. We have a law called *chōsei-hō* [regulation of production for adjustment] that regulates the scale of equipment and machines. We cannot exceed certain quotas in the number of looms we are authorized to use. The law was made in Shōwa 30 [1955] in order to avoid the dumping of textile exports in the trade market. The law also became effective for the products made for the domestic market. Under the law, we cannot easily increase the number of looms. In the Tango Peninsula, however, they were equipped with special equipment for looms *[hata-zao]*, even though this circumvented the law. Because the *chirimen* cloth [textured white silk used for *kimono*] woven in Tango had become unpopular in the market and the fishing industry declined there, the Tango people got permission to be equipped with looms that produce Nishijin *obi*. It was apparently illegal, but they insisted on their right for survival. In fact, the number of these looms increased as if the law did not exist at all. This alone had a great influence, since the labor cost is lower in Tango. Nishijin weavers have been getting less and less work, while the weavers in Tango have been getting more and more orders.

People in Tango advertised themselves as ready to weave any time when they got orders. The relationship between Tango and Nishijin was rather cool because of the distance. Sometimes Nishijin manufacturers offered work to the weavers in Tango, and another time they stopped ordering it quite abruptly. This was due to the contracting system *[ukeoi-seido]*. In this way, the manufacturers used Tango weavers when they needed them, and other times they dropped them. Since subcontracting to Tango became the main production policy of *obi* in Nishijin, we are not handling the adjustment system well. The idea is that we should adjust to the declining market by stopping production for a while. We should be doing this through negotiations among the manufacturers.[8]

Though Nishijin is sometimes depressed, it usually recovers from a depression sooner or later. In Nishijin, there are not only manufacturers of *obi*, but also manufacturers of neckties, costumes for Shinto priests

---

8. Mr. Nonaka said: "Tango has fifteen thousand looms. In Nishijin, even at its peak, we had only thirty thousand looms. At present, I guess the real number of looms should be around twenty thousand. In fact, there are just ten thousand working looms in Nishijin. Tango has a much larger number of looms after all. We should say now Tango *ori* [textile] rather than Nishijin *ori* [sarcastic comment]. I have cottage weavers in Tango. The manufacturers' relationships with weavers in Tango is very different from their relationships in Kyoto."

[shinkan], robes for Buddhist priests, and so forth. Since garments for religious use are made to order, they are free from depressions and booms. When temples have big anniversaries, the sales of robes get really preposterous. So even when the market of *obi* is depressed, it does not necessarily mean that the markets for neckties or robes are depressed, too. So when people get fussy about an occasional depression in Nishijin, some other parts in Nishijin in fact are not so depressed.

You may see several weaving houses in the same block of Nishijin, but a few of them may have a hard time and the rest may have a good time. It is hard to tell the real situation of Nishijin from the outside. We have a saying in Kyoto that Honganji [the head temple of Pureland Buddhism], the Gion entertainment district, and Nishijin cannot be penetrated by outsiders. The function of business in Nishijin is not simple. The market of robes for priests is also complicated, so they say that things in Gion and Honganji are incomprehensible.

Mrs. Shibagaki

Artistic Handloom Weaver

Mrs. Shibagaki Kimie, forty-seven years old when I first interviewed her in 1982, is one of the most highly skilled weavers in Nishijin. She worked as a demonstration weaver on the traditional wooden handloom in the Nishijin Textile Center. She uses the technique of fingernail weaving, meaning that the fingernails are filed like a saw and used for pulling the weft through. The tsuzure *weaving in which she specializes requires exceptional skill, bordering on artwork. She translates the design with the bare eye and follows it through a mirror, which is placed under the warp. Since our first meeting, Mrs. Shibagaki had become progressively more famous in Kyoto and in western Japan. She was commissioned in 1984 to reproduce a five-hundred-year-old Chinese tapestry that is hung each year on one of the traditional floats in the parade of the Gion Festival in Kyoto. This tapestry is now viewed and admired by thousands of people each year. In 1986, she was commissioned to produce a special hanging depicting an ancient Japanese motif (angels with musical instruments) from the wall-paintings in Nara. Her tapestry was hung at the entrance to the* Silk Road Exhibition *in Nara. In 1990, she was commissioned to weave a table cover as a present for the Emperor and the Empress. Her husband, Mr. Shibagaki Mitsuo, is also a highly skilled weaver. He worked on a wooden jacquard loom at a well-known company in Nishijin. He was given early retirement (at age fifty-eight), because of curtailments in production. Mrs. Shibagaki and her husband were labor union organizers. They live in a modest modern house in a concrete building in the northwestern part of Kyoto near Ryoanji Temple, which they consider a step up from the traditional wooden house. Mrs. Shibagaki's husband's parents, both of whom were retired weavers working part time, lived in a tiny wooden house in the oldest district*

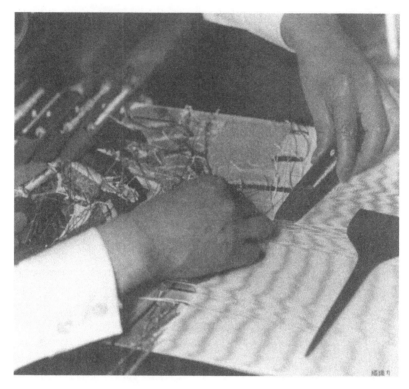

FIGURE 14. Mrs. Shibagaki Kimie's hands *tsuzure* weaving (fingernail weaving). Photograph by Matsuo Hiroko. Courtesy of Nishijin Textile Industrial Association.

in Nishijin behind the Kitano Shrine. Mr. Shibagaki's mother and father were both seventy-five years old at the time of the interview. (See their interview below.) Mrs. Shibagaki has since retired and weaves at home for outside orders. Her husband was employed by another company in 2002.

My parents' jobs had nothing to do with weaving. My father was a tailor, and my mother was a housewife. I wanted to have a job. For women there were not many jobs. I thought that *tsuzure* [figured, handwoven brocade] weaving was the work that a woman could do from the beginning to the end. I knew that many women were working as weavers.[1] I was familiar with a *tsuzure* workshop that was near my home, and

---

1. This type of *tsuzure* is also called "fingernail weaving" because the weaver's index fingernails are filed like saws, in order to pull the weft through in this delicate work. For

then became interested in it. I thought weaving would be the most appropriate job for me.

I considered learning to knit, but it was difficult to study with a perfectionist teacher. Also, since people who teach knitting or sewing and people working in beauty salons are so elegant and fashionable, I did not think that these jobs would be appropriate for me. I was fifteen years old when I started weaving as an apprentice [hōkō]. I learned in a small weaving factory in Omuro [western part of Kyoto near Ninnanji Temple], which is famous for tsuzure. There are many brocade factories in that area, so the product is often called "Omuro tsuzure." While we were apprenticing, instead of receiving a wage, we were taught such things as sewing, flower arranging, and the tea ceremony. As a result, we had a very small wage. We could only have free time on the first and fifteenth of the month. But since the Fair Labor Standards Act was enforced [after World War II], we now have an eight-hour work day, as well as vacation with salary. So a good employment situation was established. The law was fully enforced by the time I was twenty-two or twenty-three.

I had an agreement to work for three years as an apprentice and thereafter to get wages according to the amount I produced. So I could earn enough to buy the things necessary for getting married. It was generally expected that young people would work for five years as an apprentice, and work another five years to "show gratitude" to the employer [o-rei bōkō]. For the first five years one was not paid, but the second five years were with pay.[2] Anyway, I worked there for fifteen years in all. In the second five years, my wages were the same as those of a regular weaver. Some people quit before putting in the extra five years, though it was expected that they should stay. If you work hard and finish the ten years, people around you will think that you have successfully accomplished the task. Since Nishijin is a small area, it was important what other people said about you. The factory where I was working paid less even in the second five years. When I became an apprentice, the agreement was made just verbally, not in writing. But this agreement could not be honored because of the new labor standards law. After the law was passed, it turned out that we did not have to

---

purposes of consistency, I will keep the term tsuzure in Japanese, because it designates a specific product woven by a unique technique, and there is no exact English equivalent.

2. The standard system in Nishijin was three years to learn the craft, three years to perfect it, and three years to show gratitude.

work on Sundays and we could get a bonus just like other workers. When I left my apprenticeship, I was treated as an ordinary worker.

Nishijin has a complicated wage system. Basically a weaver is paid by the piece. On a loom that uses punch cards [for the jacquard mechanism], you can count how much you should earn by counting the number of openings through which the shuttle passes. It is impossible, however, to count when you weave *tsuzure*, because this is done completely by hand. It is also difficult to set a fixed hourly wage, because of the differences in weavers' individual skills. The wages are set through negotiation between a weaver and a manufacturer. Because of the special tasks and skills required, it is hard to evaluate *tsuzure* weaving and to compare it with other products.

Even if the design is the same, it takes more time for an unskilled weaver to finish it. The finished cloth is different from the one made by a skilled weaver. As I went on learning, I could insist on the quality of my own products against the person who was judging my work, if they disagreed with me. After ten years, we had become able to judge the quality of our own work.

As I went on weaving, it was getting more interesting. I stayed on afterward because I liked the place. By that time, a labor union was established and I was one of the oldest members. I stayed there to help the union as an important member. I had also made many good friends there. I left that factory, where I had started as an apprentice when I was thirty years old. I am now forty-seven years old.

The weaving I am demonstrating is called *tsuzure*. To weave this pattern, I do not use a jacquard loom with a programmed design. Instead, I put the picture with the design under the warp and weave in accordance with the basic image. My weaving is more specialized, because it does not require programmed punch cards, such as the loom using the jacquard. It takes more time to learn this method. It took me ten years to learn everything.

There are three kinds of weaving: *tsuzure*, which is completely handmade on the wooden loom; handloom weaving, which is partly hand made on the wooden loom, but where the design is programmed by punch cards in the jacquard system; and the powerloom, which is run by machine. Many handloom weavers rent their looms, while many powerloom weavers own their looms. In large companies, they use powerlooms. Some families own one or two powerlooms.

Today we have factories making *obi* by machine to look exactly as if it had been done by hand. Although the powerloom enables us to produce more quickly and make cheaper products, handweaving is still superior. Today, truly good handwoven products are needed and appreciated. So, machine-made *obi* will not push out handmade *obi*. Handloom weaving has to be even and smooth—no ups and downs. And we cannot hurry in our weaving.

Weaving is still difficult for me now, but after ten years I came to enjoy the work. I like the idea of creating. I can hardly be satisfied; I always want to create better products. Whenever I look at things in nature, I want to recreate them in a weaving. At home, I design my own patterns. For my own enjoyment, I have made my own *obi* and wall-hangings. And when I look at the product I successfully made, I feel really happy. Here at the Nishijin Textile Center, the employer tells us what designs to weave. I have to work here for eight hours, but after retiring I will be able to have more free time to make my own things.[3]

There may be some difficult aspects to working here, but you can get more money here. We demonstration weavers are not paid by the piece, but by a fixed salary. Generally there is no bonus in Nishijin, but here at the Nishijin Textile Center there is. We also get retirement money. Here the pay is in accordance with the wage system the city government has for its employees. If you want to get a pension, you have to do it yourself by using the pension plan for small-factory workers.

So there is a minimum wage, which the textile industry and the Greater Nishijin Textile Labor Union agreed upon. But it does not work well. If a person works normally, his wage naturally goes above the minimum. The minimum wage requirement is just a law without meaning. It is not observed. The government insists that the minimum wage be observed, but it means nothing for the weavers. It does not work in other areas, either. The minimum wage is too low for ordinary workers. The union is trying to make sure that the minimum wage is observed. In Nishijin, there are thirty thousand weavers, but less than three hundred people have joined the union. The workers in Nishijin, though uneducated, can weave if they have the skill. Because the weavers are usually ignorant and uneducated people, they do not understand the importance of the union to protect the rights of workers. If you do not join the labor union, you can work until you die. There is no required retirement age in Nishijin.

The employers do not want their workers to join the union. They rather want the workers to remain ignorant. They give easier jobs to the workers who do not join the union. For example, if there are two kinds of cloth to weave that are paid by the same rate, but one of them requires

---

3. Mrs. Shibagaki has retired since and is weaving art products at home.

more skills, the employer usually gives the more difficult design to a union member. Another reason why workers do not join the union is that weavers can increase their wages if they are highly skilled; they can move to other factories and get more money. Each large factory has its own company union, which is affiliated with the Greater Nishijin Textile Labor Union. Individuals are allowed to join the union. But despite this, they try to hide their membership.

Nishijin weavers do not want their children to be weavers any more. So many of the weavers now are from the countryside. There used to be a tendency among people in Kyoto to look down on the people in Nishijin, though not any more now. As for *tsuzure* weaving, the situation is different, but weavers on powerlooms are looked down upon. I myself have pride in my occupation, but up until ten years ago there were some weavers who tried to hide their identity. Also, some workers in Nishijin themselves felt inferior because of their job. Recently, however, there has been a general social tendency not to look down on any jobs.

Weavers in Nishijin have become fewer and fewer. The average age of the weavers is getting higher and higher. Japanese people do not wear *kimono* as often as they used to. We have to cut the amount of production. Since wages in urban areas are high, some Nishijin weaving jobs are done in rural areas. We call it "cottage industry" *[kanai kōgyō]*. So, instead of giving work to Nishijin craftspeople, the manufacturers send it out to the countryside.

Young people come to cities from the countryside to learn how to weave. They learn in factories. Some live in a company dormitory while learning. These young people come from various parts of Japan—Tango, Kyushu, Shimane, Fukui. . . . They do not come from big cities, but from places outside of Kyoto, mostly from the countryside. They remain in Kyoto after learning the trade. In addition to bringing young people here, factories are also sending work to villages to be done there. There are not many young people coming to Kyoto. We send jobs to the countryside.

The industry is getting smaller, because the *kimono* is not used as often any more. But I am certain that *kimono* is a traditional Japanese art and it will never disappear. People wear *kimono* when they get married and on New Year's Day, too. I myself wear a *kimono* more often than other people, but I do not wear it in the summer at all. I do not wear it as casual wear, except in January for the New Year's festivities.

I got married when I was thirty-one years old. This was considered

late in Japan. One reason that I married late may have been that I had
a job; a more important reason was that I did not come across the right
man. I have one child, my husband's child with his former wife. This
daughter is twenty years old. She is married now, and lives separately.

I stopped working for five years after getting married. I worked at
home. I bought a loom. So I worked by myself and sold my products
to friends or to companies. To make *tsuzure*, you can do everything by
yourself. You do not have to get *mongami* [punch cards for the jacquard]
and you can draw a picture by yourself, though it takes time to master
tsuzure. So it is different from weaving on a loom with a jacquard. When
I was weaving at home, I got my raw materials from a weaving factory,
and I made weavings for the factory. But if I wanted to make something
for myself or for my friends, I had to prepare my warp and designs
myself. When my daughter was in junior high school, I returned to the
job here at the Nishijin Textile Center.

More people still work at home on handweaving than in factories. If
a weaver works with a *tsuzure* loom for five years in a factory, she knows
enough how to do it at home and looks forward to doing it at home.
As a housewife, she can be with her children. If women are teachers or
workers with special skills, or if they really are dedicated to their jobs,
they take employment after marriage. But generally speaking, women
remain at home after they get married, and when their children get old
enough they may take part-time jobs. Half of the saleswomen on the
second floor in the Nishijin Textile Center are part-time workers. We
three [demonstration] weavers are full-time employees and also housewives.

Some men who do not like to work in a factory, because of difficult
human relations, prefer to work at home. My seventy-five-year-old
father-in-law is working at home. He has worked in factories twice or
three times in his life, because he thought it was warmer there in the
winter. But he found that he liked to work at home better, because he
could work whenever he wanted to and could have a freer time schedule.
He prefers working at home now. He is still working.

My husband is a weaver. He weaves on a handloom *[tebata]* for eight
hours a day. My work, *tsuzure* weaving, needs higher hand skills, but
not high mechanical skills. As for the mechanical aspects, the handloom
is more specialized, and the powerloom is even more specialized. So
there is a balance between my skill and my husband's.

I often insist that my husband should share the housework, but he
will not move. Since he was brought up that way, he cannot change

now. I am angry because I do not have time for myself. I wanted to weave at home. I like working here, but I also have to do all the shopping and the housework. Japanese men, including my husband, cannot do housework. I will make my grandson into a person who can do everything. He is just two months old. It may be the fault of women that men behave this way. I do shopping after work, and on the days when I do not work. The Nishijin Textile Center closes at 5:00 P.M. It takes me fifteen minutes to go home on my bike. It is usually 6:00 when I get home, after shopping on my way. We usually have dinner at 7:30 or 8:00. I think that the new generation will have men with different outlooks.

My daughter is more family-oriented than I am. I do not like the idea that a wife is supported by her husband. I want to live my own way. My daughter is more like a traditional woman. She does not have a job and stays home. I do not want to make my daughter into a weaver; I let her do whatever she wants to do. Once I wanted her to become a weaver, but she chose another direction. She got married then. She is a housewife.

In Nishijin, women work as hard as men and earn as much money as men, because they were already working at home before they got married. In Nishijin, women are more likely to have jobs outside their homes after marriage than in other places. In my generation, more women are working, since our parents told us to learn weaving. Young people growing up in Nishijin now do not want to work here, because they have seen their parents weaving at home and they know how hard it is. So there are fewer and fewer people from Nishijin working here. Almost no graduates from a junior high school in Nishijin take jobs in Nishijin.

Mrs. Fuwa

Artistic Handloom Weaver

Mrs. Fuwa Emiko, thirty-nine years old at the time of the interview, works as a demonstration weaver in the Nishijin Weaving Center. Mrs. Fuwa had apprenticed with Mrs. Shibagaki. Her technique is fingernail weaving or tsuzure. She specializes in weaving portraits and landscapes on the traditional wooden handloom. Most of her products are considered works of art and are commissioned by Kyoto City public institutions and by the Imperial Palace. In 1979, she was sent by the Nishijin Textile Industrial Association as a demonstration weaver to the Fogg Museum at Harvard University. She married late in life and had one child at the time of the interview. She had a second child in 1985 and quit her position as demonstration weaver. She continued, however, to weave at home on commission. She made highly specialized textiles, including flags. Mrs. Fuwa is now back working part-time at the Nishijin Textile Center.

Some people are better at weaving in factories, and others are better at demonstrating the craft for tourists. When I visited Harvard University and demonstrated the weaving there, people didn't ask me too many questions. They just said: "*Nishijin-ori* [textile] is wonderful and beautiful." That's all. And they said something like, "Although it's expensive, I want to have one to decorate my home." I spent more time showing my fingernails than weaving. We cut our nails in the shape of saws. It's easier to pull through the threads of the weft. But those who weave genuine *tsuzure* [figured, handwoven brocade] don't have fingernails like this.

FIGURE 15. Mrs. Fuwa displaying a weaving based on a *ukiyo-e* painting. Photograph by Tamara Hareven.

I weave for the City of Kyoto government and for Kyoto Prefecture. They commission from me art objects as gifts. This is completely different from what the other demonstration weavers make. Mrs. Shibagaki weaves *obi* and some kinds of traditional *tsuzure,* while I weave *bijutsu-hin* [works of art] and other products, such as a big *kake-jiku* [a long vertically hanging scroll picture] for various events, such as the founding of KBS Hall in Kyoto.[1] I also get private commissions for weaving gifts. I weave things like school flags and company flags, but nothing really for individuals, because I weave large objects. All the orders come through the Nishijin Textile Center.

Here at the Nishijin Textile Center, I get my salary whether there are any orders or not. But if I were a cottage weaver, the work would be easier and I would also get paid more. It would be mentally easier, too. Well, here you have to deal with many different customers. So you need to pay attention to them in many ways. Sometimes drunk tourists confront me. And some people get angry if I don't respond to their ques-

1. KBS is a television company.

tions. I get letters of complaint sometimes [laugh]. Still, I prefer to work here.

I prefer working here; if you are a cottage weaver, you only weave. Here you can meet and talk to a lot of different people, so you learn. On the other hand, if you are a cottage weaver, your tension is only with your work. But as an employee here, you have tensions with your co-workers—your colleagues. However, being with other people also promotes friendship. So if you compare the money you get, it's not so different to work here from being a cottage weaver. Also, here we get paid a bonus as city employees. For example, the amount of our first salary for the newly employed is the same as that for city employees working in the Sightseeing Department. So we get a five-months'-salary equivalent of bonus per year.

When I first learned to weave, Mrs. Shibagaki was my teacher [see pages 121–28]. The *bokashi*[2] technique is the most difficult aspect of *tsuzure* weaving. I often think, when I look at the glory of the evening, that it is difficult to reproduce shades of color that blend delicately into each other. It should be difficult to reproduce them in a painting, and it's even harder to reproduce them in my weaving. In the case of *tsuzure*, two threads join together and we can only mix a dark color with a light color half-and-half. The results depend on the experience and skills of the weaver. Even if I get the same design and colors as Mrs. Shibagaki, the weaving technique I use is different from hers; the images are different.

My parents were not weavers. My father was a salary man. He worked for a movie company—To-ei. He was like a carpenter and made sets for the company. My mother was a housewife. I had just graduated from junior high school, and I thought it was better to start working earlier instead of waiting till I graduated from high school. I was fifteen at that time. At first, when I thought about my occupation, I wanted to do something others didn't do. I finally found that there were only four masters who could make the hair for *ohina-san* [sets of dolls that are displayed during the Girls' Festival on March 3]. I decided to become the fifth master and entered apprenticeship. However, it was so feudal! And they didn't allow me to commute. Instead, I had to live in the master's house and work till very late at night. Otherwise, they wouldn't teach me the skills. The four masters didn't want to let their own secret

2. *Bokashi* is a technique that produces a range of nuances on the cloth, like in an impressionist painting, rather than abrupt transitions from one color to the next.

skills be known to each other, and they wouldn't show me the most important points. It was also hard to mix with the master's family.

During meals, we were provided only with half the portion that a regular family member was given. We couldn't have hot rice, either. Also, we servants and apprentices were the last to take the bath.[3] So the water in the bathtub was always cool at the bottom. Whenever I went home to visit, I had to bring some cold medicine back with me. We went to bed at 11:00 P.M. If the master's family was missing some money, they would regard me with suspicion.

The master's house was about a twenty-minute bus ride from my home. But I wasn't allowed to go home. They told me that I could go home whenever I wanted to, but actually I could do so only less than twice a month. My parents felt sorry for me, because I was so young. Well, on the rare occasions that I was allowed to go home, I used to write my parents in advance what I wanted to eat. They would prepare for me something like *zenzai* [thick, sweet, bean-meal soup with rice cake]. Since I wanted to be the fifth master, I really worked hard. The master's family had a son, but he didn't learn the trade because he didn't want to. So they were teaching it only to strangers. Since their son didn't like to learn the craft, the master wanted to have someone else.

I had been asked to come to apprentice three years earlier. I don't know why I was chosen, but I got the opportunity. I was the only non-family member. They wanted me to learn the skill and start helping with their work. They got very angry when I finally left [laugh]. I just told them I couldn't endure it and wanted to quit. My father came to take me home. Well, in the neighborhood it was known that no housemaid could stay more than three months in that house. I stayed six months. I think my father understood [laugh]. I suspect he thought I would be back home in three months at the longest [laugh].

I knew that it would be hard to master any kind of skill, but making dolls' hair was especially feudal, because it is one of the very traditional Japanese arts. It required more rigid discipline. The master never taught me the secrets, but I learned by observing—*nusumi-dori* [to steal or

---

3. The traditional bath in a Japanese home is shared by all members of the household sequentially. Everyone uses the same water in the tub. People first wash with soap and water outside the tub. After they are clean, they enter the tub to soak. First goes the head of the household, or the retired father living in the household; next the grandmother (if she lives in the household); next the sons; then the daughters and the wife. If there are servants or apprentices, they come last. Younger children bathe together with the grandmother or mother.

acquire]. They never instructed me directly. For instance, on a sunny summer day I would make the shape of dolls' heads. Or on a cloudy day when humidity was high, I would stretch dolls' hair using an iron. I learned when to do these kinds of things by observing my master.

I was like a maid and an apprentice combined. I had to do the wash for the master's family, too. They even demanded that I bring rice as tuition. I didn't bring either money or rice. The master often told me that he had brought some money and a bale of rice to his master when he had taken instruction and that I should feel lucky that I didn't have to. I didn't bring any because it was not customary at my time to bring money or rice to do *hōkō* [apprenticeship]. Since I didn't get enough food, when I went out to do some shopping in the evening, I often bought some snack with the money that I'd brought from home and hid that in my drawer. And I used to eat that before going to bed [laugh].

The master's son was one year older than I. Well [embarrassed], he was not mean, but at night he would sneak into my room. I couldn't stand it. This was one reason why I quit [still embarrassed]. Well, I couldn't allow him to peep, nor could I scream. I just hid in the *futon* at the corner of the room. Of course, he never attacked me, or I couldn't have endured for six months. He peeped into my room, because he was interested in knowing what a girl of his age was doing, I suppose. He opened the door and looked at me. I couldn't stand that. A servant and her master's son were in totally different positions. He knew that.

I quit the apprenticeship and didn't have anything particular to do. Then I found that a woman next door to my home was weaving *tsuzure*. I got interested in it and asked her to show me. The design was beautiful. It was quiet there, and the loom didn't take much space. I thought I'd be able to continue it even after I got married. So I decided to become a weaver. I went to a weaving factory near my house and met Mrs. Shibagaki there [laugh]. She was already my senior by eight years when I began my apprenticeship. She was also my teacher. Later, when I expressed my interest in a bigger job to her, she introduced me here at the Nishijin Textile Center.

When I apprenticed in the weaving factory, I wove the same design as my seniors did, but I did a better job. It caused trouble. In my generation, it was not uncommon to have such problems. Most of us were ready to endure difficulties as apprentices, to some extent. You have to experience such difficulties if you want to master some skill. Well, I believe you start by coping with such troubles to get the skill, really.

I got married two years ago, soon after I returned home from Boston. I came home in September. On October 30, I left for Hawaii and got married there on the thirty-first. I married late in life. When I was younger, most of my friends who were employed were working just enough to register the time cards. They got their salary, left the office, and went bowling, hiking, or skating. They played a lot. But I didn't. I was young—but I felt that I had wasted the half a year that I spent at the doll master's house, so I devoted myself even harder to mastering *tsuzure* techniques. Well, when I was younger, it was much more common for women to get married and to quit their jobs. Now I think it is more common for women to want to work as late in life as possible. Some of my friends once quit their jobs when they got married. Their children have grown now, and they want to resume working again. I may have been exceptional. Well, we liked our jobs. I originally learned how to weave *tsuzure* because I thought that I'd be able to continue this kind of work after marriage. But as business got more demanding, I couldn't get married. The more I devoted myself to my work, the more I liked it and I didn't really want to get married. I often used to say to everybody I met that I had married *tsuzure*. I said I decided to remain single.

But I got married two years ago, and later realized that I was already married to weaving [laugh]. I now regret getting married. I want to do more work [laugh]. Well, what I mean is that I want to spend two-thirds of my salary for living expenses and the rest for my own weaving activities in the evenings. Well, in the evenings I spend time with my husband and child, and on weekends and holidays there are other things to do. My baby is not even one year old yet. My mother takes care of the child. We live with my husband's mother, but my mother takes care of our baby. Usually the mother-in-law takes care of the children, but my mother-in-law doesn't like to do it. She wants to enjoy herself. I am now thirty-nine. This was a big change in my life—to get married at thirty-seven and become a mother.

My husband does not object to my work, because I like the work and he promised before marriage that I could continue working. That was my condition to marriage. And he has not changed his mind yet. No, not yet [laugh]. He works in construction. He is a builder. My husband does not take care of the child. He says, "It's a woman's job to do child care" [laugh]. Yes, I sort of knew this in advance. But he takes care of her more than I had expected. Because normally he is the kind of person who doesn't even stretch his hand out to pick up an ashtray or a newspaper.

So I think that the powerloom has its own merits. It makes more beautiful lines, but *tsuzure* [which is completely handwoven] has its own traditional beauty in its colors and appearance. For example, if you look from a distance at women wearing *obi*, you can identify a real non-*tsuzure obi* from among them instantly. You can tell at first glance that the good one is made by a handloom. *Tsuzure* has a future despite the powerloom. While the powerloom can produce a lot of products with the same design, *tsuzure* is not made that way. Unless we receive a specific order, we don't make one. So *tsuzure* will probably be more valuable.

There are few people who want to specialize in *tsuzure*, partly because of the low wages and partly because your eyesight gets worse. And, well, we still have feudal traditions in Nishijin; I don't think young people can tolerate them. Once it was believed that if your eyesight got weaker it meant your skills were higher. These days, since the effects are known, people try to rest their eyes between jobs. Factories are better lit now than when I was younger. I started wearing glasses since I began to receive *tsuzure* jobs fifteen years ago. I wore glasses only in the afternoons [laughing shyly] because I felt embarrassed to wear glasses. But as my eyesight got worse, I had to wear them all day. I think it was about ten years ago. It's troublesome to wear glasses. Dust sticks on the surface, and they get dirty. If you don't have glasses, you don't have to feel that way. Also, there is an eye disease, *haku-naishō* [cataract], the kind of eye trouble that old people often get for using their eyes very hard. Some weavers suffer from cataracts, and others get even more shortsighted. But, I think if you are careful enough, you do not suffer from it, although the problem of shortsightedness is hard to cope with.

Mrs. Fujiwara, Mr. Fujiwara, and Mr. Nishitani

Handloom Weavers

Mr. Fujiwara Tuneo and Mrs. Fujiwara Hiroko are both highly skilled hand-loom weavers. Mrs. Fujiwara, fifty years old at the time of the first interview, works as a demonstration weaver in the Nishijin Textile Center [Nishijin Ori Kaikan]. She was one of the first people I interviewed in Nishijin. Mr. Fuji-wara, forty-eight years old at the time of the first interview, works for a major manufacturer producing handwoven obi. They live in one of the very tradi-tional wooden houses in a neighborhood into which Nishijin expanded in the 1920s. Mrs. Fujiwara's father, Mr. Nishitani Hidetaro, was seventy-five years old and already retired at the time of the first interview. He continued to weave at home on a handloom for a manufacturer. Mr. Nishitani died in 1997. Noriko, Mr. and Mrs. Fujiwara's daughter, still lived at home during the early interviews and participated in some of them. She studied English in order to become an interpreter. Noriko married in 1988 and moved to Tokyo. Mr. Fujiwara has retired since. She now lives with her husband and their two children in Germany.

Mrs. F. =Mrs. Fujiwara

Mr. N. =Mr. Nishitani (Mrs. F.'s father)

Mr. F. =Mr. Fujiwara

MRS. FUJIWARA

MRS. F.: No, I do not want my children to be weavers. For their hap-piness, I don't want them to be weavers. There were three generations before me weaving in Nishijin. As far as we know, we are the fourth

FIGURE 16. Mrs. Fujiwara weaving on the handloom at the Nishijin Textile Center. Photograph by Tamara Hareven.

FIGURE 17. Mr. and Mrs. Fujiwara during an interview in their home. Photograph by Tamara Hareven.

FIGURE 18. Mr. Nishitani displaying an *obi* he wove. Photograph by Tamara Hareven.

FIGURE 19. Mr. Nishitani tying the warp to the loom *[tate-tsugi]*. Photograph by Tamara Hareven.

generation. We guess so, but we don't have any family tree. This is all according to my father's memory.

My family was a weaving family and I was urged to weave against my will. I grew up with the weaving sounds. I was seventeen years old when I started weaving. Even before that, while I was still in school, I helped my parents twist and spool the thread. I did many errands for them. My mother died early and I had to help my father. My father is still weaving *tsuzure* at age seventy-five. I was ten years old when my mother passed away. I had one older sister and three younger brothers. My grandmother took care of us. She was living with us. She was like a mother to us. She brought us up—five children. We also took care of her. She lived to age ninety-six. She was also a weaver, but she said that she did not like it very much, and finally gave it up. I resisted weaving, but my grandmother persuaded me to acquire weaving skills in order to survive. Eventually, I came to like weaving, though. I am proud of my job now. I love it and I can see many people while working here.

I have been working for five years for the Nishijin Textile Center. I have a twenty-year-long career of weaving. Before I came here, I used to work for a company where I was allowed to work any time I wanted. I was paid by the piece. I was not allowed to make any errors, though. I felt too much pressure to work with complicated stuff, so I came to work here. I have to work here on holidays when people come to visit. I like this job, because I have good friends. I am impressed to see many interested foreigners. I study a little English with my daughter. I enjoy that and I get excited to see foreigners. I am old, but my spirit is young. I am forty-six years old. I try to forget my age. I never imagined I would study English at this age. I did not go to college. Ups and downs are usual for me. I take it for granted. There is no way to tell if people are happy or not.

My husband works at a weaving company owned by one of the richest families in this country. My husband does the same type of weaving I do. He also weaves on a handloom. The loom he uses is good for detailed work. Some wives do the preparatory work for their husbands. I prefer using my own skills. This way I can make more money. Also, I wanted to accomplish something for myself but I also love housework. I never use instant food and I knit and sew for my family with my own hands. I never depend on anybody else. I even educated my children in that way. It is all right for women to work outside the home, but they should also take care of their families. My husband does not help me, not at all. I do not want him to do housework. He has his own job outside. I do not care that he doesn't help me at home. He works longer hours than I do. But my daughter tells me that I should educate him to help me.

When I was raising my children, I worked only part-time in the factory. I did not work in the factory till our first son went to elementary school. Then I started working part-time jobs. I did not want to excuse myself from taking care of my children because of my work. In the factory, they did not rush me at all, but I had to do a good job. I took care of my children when I came back home. We lived near my husband's parents for fourteen years. At that time, there was a big demand for weavers in Nishijin. I started working for the Kawamura Company half-time when my daughter [Noriko] went to nursery school at age two. I participated in PTA activities for my children. It was the only occasion when I could socialize.

Most of the women in the factory work full-time. I guess these women trust mothers to take care of their children, or they may take them to daycare centers. I also heard that there are many children left alone at home. We call them "latchkey kids" [kagikko]. Women who have skills cannot be satisfied with the housework only. Some women do not have to depend on men. They have skills to survive for themselves, so they marry later. I did not want to lose money despite my skill, either. My husband does not care about whatever I am doing. We have never fought in our twenty-six years of marriage.[1] Even our children admire that. Compared to salaried men who work under strong pressures from senior workers, Nishijin weavers have less stress. So they do not have to take it out on their families at home very much, I guess.

I got married at age nineteen. Ours was a love marriage. We did not have any wedding celebration. Our parents opposed our marriage very much. It was great love! My father thought I was too young. My older sister was not yet married. The custom is changing now, but at that time, our parents were quite rigid about the rule that the older daughter should marry first. My father could not stop me from marrying. He opposed the marriage, though. That was very exceptional. My father finally accepted us after we had children. After we got married, we rented a small apartment in a neighborhood in central Kyoto, in Demachi. We stayed there for two years. Later, my father built a house for us behind his house. We have been living in this house ever since.

---

1. Mr. and Mrs. Fujiwara maintained a peaceful relationship by using humor and bantering.

MR. F.: I did not know why my father-in-law opposed our marriage. I was twenty-five years old.

MRS. F.: Maybe he did not like the poverty of your family. My husband also had a complicated situation with his family. His father died when he was six years old. His mother remarried. In a sense we had greater freedom, because my husband's parents died when we were young. But we did not have anybody to depend on. We could not help but be more independent.

We came back to this house after two years, because our lease was over. Also the neighborhood in Demachi was very bad. It was a place for gambling. My husband got involved with gambling. Our first baby died. We were going to be separated, but my husband's mother called us back to live with her and my husband's stepfather. I got along with my mother-in-law, but my husband did not get along with his stepfather, so I was involved in conflict. My mother-in-law thought that I pushed my husband to say controversial things.

I would not object at all if my daughter found her husband on her own, as long as they love each other. I have a son who is now in love with a girl and they got engaged recently. They will marry in two years. I am very happy. He is a student now. My older son has a food management job at McDonald's. He married a flight attendant for Japan Air Lines. She said that she would quit her job three years after her marriage.[2]

MR. F.: I am content with my life.

MRS. F.: My husband's life is a shame for our children.[3] Since our children are growing up to become independent, my husband is the only person whom I can rely on. Noriko says that her father is a person of integrity, though. That is why I could be with him for so many years, she says. He did many things that we disagreed with, but he is not ill-natured. He does not insult anybody except his company's boss. He does not deceive or trap anybody. Next year is our thirtieth anniversary. I wonder which of us has been more patient. My husband took me to Hokkaido last year to celebrate our anniversary. Thanks to our daughter-in-law, we do not have to pay for Japan Air Lines.

2. Two years later, Noriko, Mrs. Fujiwara's daughter, married in a love marriage. The older son and the flight attendant later divorced, and the son remarried and now has three children.

3. She is referring to his frequent change of employers and his gambling.

Our son is making much more money than his father. He makes 3.5 million *yen* a year, in his second year of employment. His wife also gets high pay at Japan Air Lines, so they are quite well-to-do people. They bought a new car and paid in cash. We also wanted to provide an opportunity for a good education for Noriko. We want her to do whatever she wants later. She seems very interested in English. Still, she is not sure what job she wants to get.

MR. F.: We are doing an out-of-date job. Our work has no future, so we hope that our son is successful in his own field. Our job is out-of-date in many ways. First, the conditions of labor, and second, there is little opportunity for our future personally, and for the whole of Nishijin. We will be the last generation to work in traditional weaving.

MRS. F.: We did not say anything particular to our son about his career. He had his own idea to go to college and to work for a company, since his childhood. We knew what he was thinking by reading the compositions he wrote in elementary school. We had discussions about the Nishijin situation in our family, many times. Noriko seems to be somewhat proud of Nishijin as a traditional industry. She is grateful to her father, and she knows that she was fed by her parents' jobs. But Noriko probably does not want to be a weaver. If I were well educated, I would not have done this job. But I had many brothers and sisters, so I could not have a higher education. Had I been born in a rich family, my life would have been different. But I had to give up my hope. I want to let Noriko do whatever she wants to do.

My mother died early, when I was ten. My father remarried to a *geisha*. My mother died in January, and my father married the *geisha* in April. He used to be a ladies' man. He had another woman even while my mother was still alive. He was always fooling around with women. While I was still in elementary school, I remember one of the quarrels between my mother and my father. Mother was crying when she discovered that father's *kimono* had been repaired by someone else. I did not understand why she was crying, because I was too young. My father was forty and the *geisha* was twenty-nine when they got married. He divorced her several years later. When my father had money, she was happy. But once his money was spent, she ran away. After the divorce, it was impossible for the second wife to go back to being a *geisha*. I heard that she remarried later. My father used to play the Japanese string instrument *[shamisen]*, and I also used to play it. The second wife did not oppose it, but she did not like us to play the *shamisen* in the detached house. When they divorced, the wife took her first son and daughter with her, but left her second son with my father. Now the second son still lives with my father. One of their children died. My father's ex-wife is still alive. We do not have any contact with her or the daughter she took with her, because she left us when the daughter was three.

MR. N.: The daughter came back to my house when she was fifteen for half a year. Later, her mother wanted to remarry me, but I refused. She married twice after our divorce, and then she sent her daughter to arrange for her to come back to me. The daughter married later. My ex-wife called me sometimes and said she would like to come back to see me some day, but she did not show up at all. The second husband of my ex-wife was older than seventy, and her daughter married his youngest son. My ex-wife should be stable in her family life now. At that time, it was easy to divorce with only one witness. It is really complicated to divorce now. They have to pay alimony, which did not exist at that time.

MRS. F.: My father's mother tried to hide that my father was fooling around.

MR. F.: My wife's father was an independent small manufacturer *[jimae]* at that time. Many manufacturers *[oriya*[4]*]* have traditionally been playboys. They have money. Weavers do not have money or time to play. Both my stepfather and my wife's father remarried three months after the deaths of their first wives.

MRS. F.: My husband's mother also complained to me about many things concerning his stepfather. My husband's father died when my husband was four. His mother remarried when he was in the fourth grade. Then she had another son later. My husband was mistreated after that. The other son is still alive. My husband's younger brother became the successor. My husband has conflicted feelings toward his stepbrother, even now. After my husband's mother passed away, his stepfather took another woman without getting married. She does not live there, but she has been commuting to his house for sixteen years. She is a widow with four children.

4. *Oriya* is another word for "manufacturer" *[orimoto]*. Both words come from *ori*, meaning "weaving." *Oriya* is a more old-fashioned term.

MR. F.: My stepbrother, who lives in that house, did not accept that woman at all. His wife never visits our father, even though she is living nearby. I did not like my stepfather at all. He worked hard for six months, then he spent all the money on gambling. He and my mother fought all the time. I have many memories about their quarrels. I was quite antagonistic toward my stepfather and often spoke frankly to him. My mother stopped us when we quarreled. I don't think that my son does the same thing with me. My stepfather gambled with cards [hana-fuda] at home, so I learned gambling from him. He charged people for the use of his house for gambling. If I had been a little more clever, I would not have learned to gamble.

MRS. F.: Once he [husband] starts gambling, he loses control of himself.

MR. F.: I have been here for thirty years. I learned to weave at my home, where my stepfather was weaving. I was trained under him. It was sort of practice for me. I began to work in the factory after working at home for two years. I could choose better wages and learned many skills outside. I went to the factory because I could get much information from other weavers about the working conditions of various manufacturers [orimoto]. If a craftsman [shokunin] stays in one place, he is supposed to make the same kind of textiles repeatedly. By changing workplaces, actually, we can improve our skills. Each manufacturer does different kinds of weavings. I believe that I have mastered all kinds of weaving skills. I have worked in maybe twenty places. I am not used to working on rigid time schedules. I need freedom. I cannot stand the kind of place to work where you have to show up regularly every day, because I have been working so freely. Yes, I do play pachinko during the day. However, I haven't gone recently. Originally, there was a rule that we should work steady hours. But nobody is there to supervise our work. We can do anything we like.

Yes, my stepfather is a weaver. My parents [real father] were also weavers. They were cottage weavers [debata]. I learned to weave at home. When I was young, I did not like to weave, so I did many things. I worked for a bakery, then in photography. . . . I even tried to be a Buddhist priest, which I did not like. I had a chance to be employed at the state house. I think I should have taken that job. Right after the war [World War II], salaried men had poor conditions. Craftsmen earned much more then. So I drifted a lot. Now I regret it. I was twenty-one years old when I started weaving.

MRS. F.: We met when his family moved into this house, which my father owned. It was a destiny for both of us to meet here.

MR. F.: My family was poor.

MRS. F.: Since my mother died, my father had had to rent out this house in order to make money, so that he could be with a *geisha*. Just like in our son's case, my father failed the university entrance exam. He went to a not-so-great university a year later. Then he met his wife there, at some party. I feel that they were also destined from their former lives to marry. Destiny is a mystery. I feel so happy with my life now. The only thing I am concerned about is Noriko's future. My husband brought many troubles to our home. Recently, he has been all right. If only he had kept working constantly, we would have had no troubles, despite the ups and downs of the Nishijin business.

MR. F.: I stopped working when I was paid too little. I was devoted to gambling then.

MRS. F.: He could escape from life that way, but I always had to face life. Noriko says that I should write my autobiography. Whatever troubles I had with our marriage, I never complained. Since we got married against our parents' will, I could not complain to them. I never complain to my son's wife. I treat my daughter and my son's wife equally. Our son's wife is our daughter, now.

MR. FUJIWARA

MR. F.: [To Hareven] I came back from the *pachinko* parlor because you made an effort to come here. I want to tell you everything about Nishijin. You can ask anything about Nishijin. This may be the last chance for us to talk [before Hareven's return to the United States]. This is the first time for me to have an opportunity to speak to a professor from an American university. I feel familiar with you because you are the same age as my wife. I admire that a woman is a professor with a Ph.D. My wife and daughter scold me all the time. I am quiet like a cat at home, though I am outspoken outside. I want to be frank with you. Most people in Nishijin are too timid to speak out. They do not even try to join the Greater Nishijin Labor Union [*Nishijin Ori Rōdō-kumiai*]. They are afraid of their bosses. The Nishijin industry is really pre-modern.

There exist many ugly things behind such beautiful *obi*. If you visit the manufacturer, they would speak beautifully about their business, but it is false. I work for a weaving company, and I know that many weavers have a hard time there. You are asking how many times I changed employers?

MRS. F.: Well, so many that I can't count.

MR. F.: I probably changed employers more than twenty times [laughs].

MRS. F.: How many times do you think that you will continue to change jobs? Remember! This is not America![5]

MR. F.: [to Hareven] You know me by now. Can you imagine me not speaking my mind? Nishijin is really feudal. First of all, the wage system is old. Their way of thinking is so old that the manufacturer *[oyakata[6]]* doesn't like it if we say what we think. So we do not exactly have discrimination, but it is something similar to being discriminated against. The factory where I work does not give us holidays with guaranteed pay *[yūkyū-kyūka]* and retirement pension *[taishoku-kin]*. The pay for our labor *[kōchin]* is low and not stable at all. We get no bonus, either. When there is a big gap between our needs for a livelihood and what the employer pays, it becomes difficult to make a living. Well, the first problem is the low pay. The employer does not like what I say, and I feel that I am discriminated against by him. The way of thinking in Nishijin is old. The manufacturers speak about fairness, but we have our own pride as *shokunin* [craftsmen]. When they pay so little and take our jobs away, we feel that they do not appreciate our skill. If they put the wages so low, we feel like our skill is looked down upon as cheap.

MRS. F.: In some cases, people with long careers have not received the reward certificate of "master of the traditional arts" *[Dentō Kōgei]*. Instead, others with shorter careers got it. It is ambiguous how they decide who should be rewarded. I cannot tell what criteria they use. Some companies do not tell the weavers that they are qualified to receive the certificate. Other companies want to get the certificate in order to

5. The comparison to America was provoked by my earlier statement that in the United States it was common for workers to change jobs and employers.

6. *Oyakata* means "father." It is an old-fashioned, paternalistic term for "manufacturer."

dignify their products. I think that anyone who qualifies should get such a certificate. Even I would be able to get it. [to husband] Nobody would recommend you for traditional arts *[Dentō Kōgei]*, because you have changed jobs too many times. Many of the craftsmen with this title have been working at one place.

MR. F.: I have a lot of skills, and have had a long career. I know how to weave many kinds of things. The company would be pleased if I were rewarded.

NORIKO: But you would not be able to get the certificate for *Dentō Kōgei* because you have changed jobs too many times.

MR. F.: I believe that weavers who move around many places have greater experience in making different things. If we stayed in only one place, we would only know how to make limited items for one company.

MRS. F.: I think so, too, but that kind of theory does not work in Nishijin. Nishijin is still feudalistic. Even now Nishijin is quite old-fashioned. You lost something by changing your employers so many times, I think. In particular, you took financial losses. It is different here than in America. We do not get advantages by changing jobs. In Japan, it is not considered good to change jobs many times.

MR. F.: I don't like weaving. But just after the war, if I had become a salary man, the salary would have been very low, right? [to his wife] It is good now, though. So, at that time, the income of a weaver was good and it was better to become a craftsman *[shokunin]*. And if you could weave, you could make money right away. I couldn't eat if I didn't do this job, right? I don't have any other skills. I only know how to weave. So I can't say I dislike it, and I can't say I like it.

Well, there is a difference between the generations. Of course, *oyaji* [Mr. Nishitani] really knows very well about the production of textiles and so on. We don't know this so well. For example, we don't know the quality of the fiber in such detail. My father-in-law knows it very well and I'm still learning it now. I learned from my stepfather, and then I went out to weave. So, after all, I couldn't learn all the techniques if I only wove at home. I went here and there. If you change manufacturers, you learn different skills. I acquired my skills on my own. I have not been through a formal apprenticeship. Well, I couldn't do an apprenticeship, considering my character [laugh]. So, if you are a salary man, you have to care about your superiors or your president. If you are a craftsman, you only weave. The only things the manufacturer *[oyakata]* cares about is if the job is done well. Isn't it right? Yeah, it's a hard living. Well, my wife may have had a hard time, I guess, because I changed employers so many times. For us, it's more comfortable to weave outside the home. Well, considering my character, I can talk about stupid things and make jokes with other people when I go to work.

MRS. F.: In the factory, he says whatever he likes. Since we don't need to take care of the children so much, we have much free time. Our children go to work. Often in the evening the two of us are alone. So he goes to play *pachinko* to kill time, because he has nothing to do. When the children were young, he took them somewhere. He babysat quite often. I think therefore, this must be a lonely period for him.

MR. F.: The place I work at is a rather big company in Nishijin. It has about three hundred workers — it is large.[7] In the generation of the president's father, it was a small company. The current president made it large, and he earns a lot. They don't have a retirement allowance, paid holidays, or a minimum wage. Also the bonus isn't stable. The company gets a good price for products of the handloom. But although they sell their products for a good price, the weavers cannot get as much of a benefit from it. This is the reality. We say this from our side, but the manufacturer *[oyakata]* doesn't think so [laugh]. Well, he is not the only one. Generally, most of manufacturers *[oyakata]* in Nishijin are like this. If there is a difference between the wages that I expect and what they pay me, I am not really happy as a worker. Also, it is tough for me to make a living.

In our system, we are paid for each piece *[deki-daka-barai]*. We are not paid by the day. So you get more if you can weave more. Of course, we have individual differences in pay. This is also the reason why we cannot have a union, because the pay system is by the piece. The person who weaves well can make a pretty good income. In our company, we don't have such a thing as a minimum wage or a guaranteed wage, even though it exists nationally. If you don't weave, you don't make any money. The wage for the piece is generally the standard price.

7. In the small sub-factory building where Mr. Fujiwara worked, there were only eight weavers.

The procedure of deciding payment for the weaving of *obi* is too complicated. There are three categories of wages even if you produce the same quality of work. Even for each piece, there is no uniform wage. There are many ranks. Each individual weaver negotiates separately with the *oyakata*. Quiet people do not say anything, but I am fussy about that. When I insist on good pay, the bosses sometimes mention that I should work for somebody else. If you complain too often, you'll be treated like an eyesore. If you complain too much even about small things, they fire you. And among us craftspeople *[shokunin]*, only those who are very close can trust each other to talk to each other about our wages. The system is inconsistent. If the manufacturer *[oyakata]* pays me at a certain rate, he should pay the same to everyone, but he doesn't.

Even if we threaten the employer that he will lose his best weavers, it won't matter to him. Today, the business is dull. The employer's attitude is that it doesn't matter what I say. And among craftspeople, also, the way of thinking is wrong. We can't do anything when we are in a dull business period and the company wants to cut down on the number of workers. If we could have gotten together and had organized the labor union while the business was in good condition, we could have talked, couldn't we? I think so, I do. Where I work, the union amounts to almost nothing. Everything is the way the *oyakata* says. They do not have any union and people have to obey the employer. Craftspeople are also egocentric. The company where I work exploits this tendency.

The employers do not want to see unions at all. They are afraid of a movement to increase wages through the unions. They prevent us from having a union. They give some extra pay to the person who complains. This is how things are. If you don't complain, you get less. After all, it's also the weavers' fault that we don't have a union. Most of them think it is okay as long as they can be satisfied. They are used to such a situation.

If we organize a union, the manufacturer would be in trouble. He arranges things to prevent us from having a union. And after all, if we organize the union he will have to raise the wages every year. The workers protest in the bonus season [springtime, when the wages are negotiated]. The manufacturer does not like this kind of thing. The Greater Nishijin Textile Labor Union exists only in name, although I don't want to say it—they have no power. Even the craftsmen *[shokunin]* have the wrong idea, I guess. They are all old now, and when you get to be old, you have to be careful. For example, if I am fired I can still work. But if one is over sixty-five years and receives a pension *[kōsei-nenkin]*, they are not allowed to work. People receiving old-age pensions weave secretly *[yami]*, even if they are paid low wages. Still, their incomes are better than ours.

Earlier, they used to pay an extra one thousand to two thousand *yen* whenever we demanded it. However, this is not true any more. The business is not going well, so we are paid less. I was paid more than other weavers two years ago. People who have to support their families have the most trouble. Under conditions like this, the youth don't want to inherit their parents' jobs any more. Also, the parents don't want to pass their jobs on to their children. That is the reality. And recently in Nishijin, the companies have been sending work out to the countryside, like in Tango [peninsula on the Japan Sea in Kyoto Prefecture] or to Kyushu. Although they have to teach the skills to new weavers, the wages are cheaper in such remote areas. Of course, the quality of the product made in the countryside is bad. There are lots of flaws.

Twenty years from now, the real good products of the handloom *[tebata]* won't exist any more. We can work just a little longer. But it will end when we get old. At that time, there won't be craftspeople *[shokunin]* who can weave on a handloom in Nishijin. It's going to be powerlooms. I'm sure this is going to happen, because the young people won't inherit their parents' jobs. The products woven by handloom *[tebata]* are very expensive. I think if they were less expensive, we could sell them to general consumers and we could sell more products. After all, I guess the exploitation by the wholesalers is too heavy [meaning that they price the products out of the market]. Today I finished making two *obi*. If a customer were to buy these in a retail shop, each piece would cost three hundred thousand *yen*. The cost of labor is thirty-one thousand *yen*. Yes, yes! The middleman [wholesaler] is the one who makes a lot of the profit.

It takes me about four days to weave an *obi* with gold thread. This piece can be made by handloom only, because we have to pull the gold thread through twice; it requires two kinds of thread. You cannot weave this on a powerloom.[8] For more ordinary designs, weaving by powerloom is really fast. It is at least twice as fast as handloom weaving. Physically, it is easier to work on powerlooms. On the handloom, we have to move our hands and feet. The powerlooms can weave for you. The

---

8. Subsequently, a technique was developed for pulling the gold thread through automatically on the powerloom. A robot-like arm was attached to the powerloom; that arm pulls the gold threads through automatically.

only thing you have to do is operate them. In the case of plain weaving, a powerloom weaver can make about five pieces a day, while I make two pieces. I don't like to use powerlooms, because they are so noisy. Also we need funds to buy them. If you weave without owning your own powerloom, the wage is really low. I think the handloom is good. If I weave with a powerloom, the product has no meaning. The powerloom product looks good at a glance, but just superficially. With a machine you are not weaving, just playing. We run through a row and "pon!," pull it tight and weave, but that is just playing for me. There is no feeling like when we truly weave by hand. I love the handloom.

MRS. F.: It is just beautiful. The durability and characteristic texture of handwoven cloth are totally different. Even like in a knit product, the handknit fabric and the machine-made fabric are completely different, right?

MR. F.: Nishijin is rather strong even in periods of low business. Every time the manufacturers talk about losing their business, they still manage to continue. But in ten or so years from now, there will be nobody left to weave. The youth don't want to inherit this work. I hope that they could improve the conditions in Nishijin so that it would be attractive to young people to stay on weaving on the handloom and have a hope for the future, but in fact there is no hope that this might happen.

Well, in earlier times, when we lost our job, we could get another one, except if they blacklisted us. Manufacturers [oriya] sent messages to each other saying, "Don't take that man." But if they didn't send a message, it was okay. One could get another job. If I run into trouble in one place and the manufacturers communicate with each other and notify others not to employ me, I would not be able to find work easily, but I could be employed by other manufacturers who were not informed about me. Manufacturers usually have a group consisting of about ten firms, where they can communicate immediately that "Fujiwara should not be employed." Yes, I was blacklisted. Now I am getting older and am losing the energy that I had when I was young. The older we get, the more we learn to live easily by having to obey those stronger than us.

Four or five years ago, the sales of the company where I work were extraordinary. No matter how much they increased the number of products, all sold out. But since last year, the sales got stuck all of a sudden. They started giving us less work and they tried to delay the supply of raw materials to us. They are doing many illegal things in their violation of the Fair Labor Standards Act. For instance, they are obligated by law to cover 60 percent of the repair costs of cottage weavers' *[debata]* looms, but they never pay that. We can't help but quit our jobs. We do not have any written document for a contract. They do not fire us directly, because they are obligated to pay retirement money by law. Instead, they treat us badly until we leave by ourselves.

The company where I work does not give us a chance to negotiate. We have to catch the senior officer *[bantō]* to negotiate the pay, but if he is not there, nothing doing. I think that this is a general pattern in Nishijin. In a small company with few workers, the boss would talk with us directly. But in the company where I work, the boss does not maintain contact with us. The manufacturer is extremely pragmatic. Some other employers are, however, more humane. The young companies that are trying to develop their business give us better working conditions. Once they grow big, they become cold to their employees. As far as I know, good companies that treat their weavers well tend to go bankrupt.

In many companies, when we wanted to negotiate, the manufacturer *[orimoto]* used to fire us easily. I had a terrible time with a company where I worked earlier when I negotiated for labor pay and tried to organize the union. Suddenly they fired me. I was really angry then. It was about twenty-five years ago, right after we got married. The labor union is concerned with the fact that manufacturers *[orimoto]* do not make any effort to sustain successors in Nishijin. They just keep giving orders to weavers outside of Nishijin for lower wages. The union exists, but it is too weak. It is controlled by the employers. The manufacturers are shortsighted. As I said before, most of the union members are old men *[o-jii-san]*. They'll die out in twenty years. They don't have power.

MRS. F.: I belong to the union. They say that our monthly membership fees are wasted, because it doesn't amount to anything.

MR. F.: The union doesn't amount to anything. I just belong. Well, if I am laid off, I can say that I have my rights under the law if I belong to the union. This is the only reason I belong. I also used to work at yet another weaving company. I resigned though [laugh]. When I go there and they see my face, they turn their heads the other way because I'm trouble [laugh]. After I resigned, they established a company union. At that time, I didn't think much about organizing a union. I left that company because of the pay. It seems that I fought with the president [*oyaji-san*, literally, it means "father"]. Actually, the president's wife runs the company. She is strong in sales. Since my resignation, more young workers have come. They are young over there, compared to other factories. Therefore, their union is strong—yes! Yes, Matsushita-san, for example, is from Kyushu, too. He is strong and young. If people like Matsushita-san put their best in Nishijin, then the Greater Nishijin Textile Labor Union will become stronger.

At least I still have a job! There are many things that make me angry, but I keep working patiently. Although I have changed jobs many times before, if I quit I will have no other job. The company fires workers under a certain plan. They now fire people older than sixty. I am under that age. Those who are eligible for a retirement pension *[nenkin]* must be fired first. This is the same thing with all companies. The working conditions are not good at all. The pay per piece of work has not changed for the past three years, but the price of every item is climbing rapidly. The labor for cottage weavers or factory workers is worth eight thousand *yen* and up per *shaku*. I make about two *shaku* or three *jaku* [*shaku* and *jaku* are measurements of length, each equal to about thirty centimeters]. In principle, I do not work extra hours. I try to make more cloth within the fixed hours. I can make more in the same number of hours, but I cannot do it every day. So my average is one meter and twenty centimeters a day. When the manufacturers make weavers work more, they have to pay high labor charges *[kōchin]*. They usually prefer to place orders with weavers in the countryside instead of us. In order to do this, they have to teach the country weavers how to weave.

They pay less to weavers in Tango. They should attract young people by paying much more. I told the manufacturer to change the name from "Nishijin *ori*" [textile] to "Tango *ori*" [sarcastic comment]. We are getting less and less work in Nishijin. There are fewer and fewer workers here. They keep the cottage weavers waiting for their next assignment. To keep a weaver waiting, they use the excuse that the warp is not ready. They often change the color arrangement within the same design and claim that it is not ready. We heard that they sometimes harass the weavers by keeping them waiting for many days. Weavers come to the company and get the silk thread and the design, but the manufacturer delays them by not telling them the color arrangement.

NORIKO: During good business conditions, they used to tell the weavers the color arrangements in advance.

MR. F.: Companies play games. Even if the manufacturer saves one hour from each person, they do the same thing to ten workers. They plan these underhanded maneuvers. They can't just tell a weaver to go home without supplying the thread; it would become a legal problem. If they did it publicly, the labor union would do something about it.

There are many people, however, who are modest and just quit without protesting anything. The unions don't have the power to do anything about it. Even among union members, those who are receiving pensions [nenkin] avoid getting involved. They are afraid of being noticed by the company if they do anything public. They know that they will retire in a couple of years, so they try not to complain, even about low pay. They are afraid of being fired. There is no change at all. The weavers are so old. They do not want to do anything different. In twenty years when I become unable to work, I will not find anyone here weaving on a handloom [tebata].

I seldom have difficulty getting enough work. When I complain a lot, the company does not punish me by giving me too much work or difficult work. Now the times are hard. It is dangerous to complain under these circumstances. I cannot go too far. I try to keep my complaints under control. I have not yet fought with the president himself. I usually fight with the managers.

I mentioned the Japanese mentality before. A smile can sometimes be a negative expression. It means that you are being ignored. But I am not doing anything with the union; I just refer to issues relating to me personally. So I don't think the manufacturer is afraid of me. I am concerned not only about my problems, but about the other workers' problems. I can receive what I demand. Later, other workers go back to demand the same thing and they get nothing. Such is the situation. The company is afraid that if they don't listen to me, I might do something with the others against the company.

MRS. F.: They want to keep the noisy ones silent.

MR. F.: If I were fired, I would get help from the union. Probably the company fears that most.[9] About the other workers' feelings, I tell my friends that I get some concessions for myself, and I encourage them to ask for the same thing. I do not say anything to the workers whom I

---

9. There is an obvious contradiction between Mr. Fujiwara's recurring statements that the union doesn't mean anything and his statement that the company fears the union's reaction if a worker gets fired. The fear of the union that Mr. Fujiwara refers to here is in cases of firing that are related to legal issues, where the union could cause trouble.

do not like very much. I do not know what they feel when only I get something. On the surface, they never say anything against me. If I were too frank with fellow workers, some people would make use of it. I mean, somebody may complain that the company gives me special treatment. Then I would have to take the consequences and get less. I tell things only to my close friends. Some people are sneaky.

I am not active any more in opposing my employers. If I am outspoken, I just lose their favor. But when everybody keeps silent, I have to say something. The other weavers do not confront me. They confront each other. Some of the eight weavers working at the company where I work now never talk to each other, because they fought once. They have never talked since.

MRS. F.: They don't behave like adults. They are childish! If women had a fight, they soon would start to talk. Well, in the case of women, we do worry what they said, but in the case of men, they don't really worry about small matters, right? Don't you think it's childish?

MR. F.: Well, if weavers fight often, the manufacturer is very happy. He doesn't like most of all that weavers become friendly with each other and get together. After all, the capitalist is stronger than us. And in the end, we have to do whatever the capitalist says. There is no fighting spirit among workers in Nishijin. The bosses must be happy when weavers do not get along with each other. If we are united strongly, they must be worried. It is possible for the manufacturers [orimoto] to plot conflicts among workers. In Nishijin, there is no solidarity among workers.

MR. NISHITANI

MR. N.: Only old persons like me can tell the deep personal history of the Nishijin industry since the Meiji Period. My life was full of ups and downs. The present is quite calm. My children are very affectionate to me. My mother lived to age ninety-six. I wish I could live that long. Now I can receive a pension [kōsei-nenkin], so I don't need to work. Of course, I want to do something so I will not be a burden on my children, right [laugh]? I can't do anything else except weaving. So I weave and contribute extra money if I can. Yes, I still enjoy weaving. If I don't weave, I have to babysit my grandchild, right? Then if I weave, I just concentrate on weaving. Since I've been weaving for sixty years, my lower back is bent out of shape. It is an occupational deformity. I have had x-rays taken. Although I feel pain sitting upright, I am okay when I start to weave. Even this lower back pain goes away, because I have been doing this for sixty years. So, my spine has got to be bent [laugh]. I work very hard when I weave. But when I think of something else besides weaving, such as spending time with friends or playing mahjongg, something will go wrong with my weaving. I have to concentrate very intensively when I weave. Only old weavers can concentrate that way. When they are young, they tend to think of many other things while weaving, so their product cannot be free of errors. I cannot weave easily. I have been doing this for sixty years, but still it is impossible to be perfect. I still enjoy weaving. Although I have been weaving for sixty years, I really don't know everything. Weaving this cloth requires deep knowledge. I still study weaving, and I haven't done anything so perfect that I can say, "This has been done without any mistake." There is always some part I don't really like. So that is the spiritual exercise: I want to make a perfect weaving without any mistake. This is what keeps me going.

MR. F.: And this spiritual condition is not easy. We can't measure our product in meters. I'm hardly able to say I really like all of it from the beginning to the end. I can't be completely satisfied, even if there is no flaw. I don't make any flaws, but still the design cannot come out perfectly. This always happens [laugh]. I set my own standards. Even if I don't make an actual mistake, I still wish this part could be done more perfectly. So it is difficult. Honestly, I say now that I cannot easily achieve a perfect score.

MR. N.: I cannot do it easily. I have been doing this for sixty years, but it still is impossible. Well, well. I try to weave perfectly from the beginning to the end. I can't achieve easily what I want, but that might be the high standard of handloom weaving. There once was a proposal to designate Nishijin weavers as Living National Treasures. If I was a Living National Treasure, I could get a pension. That would be good. But if I receive only a citation, I would decline it [laugh].

MR. F.: It may be better than nothing.

MR. N.: Well, like Mr. Shibagaki was praised, right? He received the title of *Dentō Kōgei* [certificate of "master of the traditional arts"].

Since he received this honor, he has been assigned only difficult designs to weave. His income has become lower, because it takes him longer to weave these pieces. So he was angry.

I started weaving at age twelve. The weather, the climate, and the tradition make Nishijin a special place for weaving. When I was in sixth grade, I stopped going to school in the second term . . . well, actually I was stopped from going to school. I was working from age twelve. My parents were also weavers. They were living here. We moved here when I was six years old. We moved to the Taiho district around 1920. My parents were very poor, and we lived in crowded quarters in Nishijin. When the *orimoto* [manufacturer] offered them the opportunity to move, they decided, "Let's go ahead and have a new start." We were so poor at that time we could not even afford to pay the movers. We sold our chest of drawers *[tansu]* and sideboard so that my father could buy a cart. We then loaded all our possessions on the cart and we started our walk, pulling the cart. It took several years before we had electricity there, and my parents were weaving by the light of the kerosene lamp. We were far from Nishijin, so I had to keep running back and forth to deliver the *obi* and pick up the threads. I was happy most of the time. Sometimes they would give me a bowl of rice or a sweet in the *orimoto*'s house. During my long run from Daitokuji [temple] to Nishijin, I kept wondering what they would give me this time. So I have lived here for seventy years.

MR. F.: In my childhood, there was a bamboo thicket behind this house. There were only two houses. Now there are houses and garages all along the way.

MR. N.: There was no electricity. I was weaving by the light of a kerosene lamp. There weren't any streetlights. In those days, we had one lamp between two looms. My stepfather *[oyaji]* and I were working together.

MRS. F.: My grandmother used to tell me that the lamp chimney became really black with soot if you didn't clean it. The lamp chimney had to be cleaned. It had to be wiped each time and it broke easily. I used to be told when I was a child that my father broke the lamp and he was scolded.

MR. N.: I broke so many lamps.

MRS. F.: We used this kind of lamp quite often during the war. And even after the war, I remember that we still used this type of lamp when we had a blackout. It's a dear memory [laugh].

MR. F.: [to Mr. Nishitani] You were weaving with such a thing in the old days? Did you see well?

MR. N.: Yes, I could see. I could see somehow. I still don't wear glasses. We got electricity when our neighborhood was incorporated into Kyoto City. Electricity first came around when I was in the sixth grade, so that was Taishō . . . Taishō 8. But there already was electricity in town. It was late around here. There was a lottery. The electric company came to encourage us. They gave us something. Since we became part of the city, the municipal government adjusted the land tax here and there, consolidated the roads, and set up the streetlights. Since then, things became better. This happened about Taishō 8, when I was twelve years old. Now this neighborhood is on the edge of Nishijin. In this area, the farmers' families used to live along with the *obi* weavers of Nishijin. There were not so many salary men. Most of the people who lived here were small manufacturers *[jimae]* or cottage weavers *[chinbata]* from Nishijin, and more than half were farmers' families. There were also the people who became land profiteers, who sold their land and became owners of apartment buildings. More than half of the people sold their land, but they lost because of speculation. Really, only one-third of them have survived. In the beginning, when we first moved here and the streetlights appeared, I could still hear the sound of looms all over the neighborhood.

When I was young, I did not do indentured apprenticeship *[nenki-bōkō]*. My mother did it till she got married. She was an apprentice till age eighteen, but after that she had to do gratitude service *[o-rei bōkō]* till she got married. During the Taishō Period and until the beginning of Shōwa Period, parents would lend their children out under a contract. For example, parents received fifty yen with the contract to make their son work as an apprentice *[bōkō]* for three years. After that, they could renew the contract to get more money. When the children reached age eighteen and were considered to have the necessary skills, they began to earn some money, which they frequently sent to their parents. But they had to continue to do gratitude service[10] and make money for the master, before they left the place of apprenticeship.

The hardest times I remember in Nishijin were in my childhood when I was about fourteen or fifteen years old, in my junior high school age, about sixty years ago. Around that time, we couldn't have days off. We had off only twice a month, on the fifteenth and the first, but if we rested on these days, we couldn't eat. Rice was our main food [shushoku]. We only got about one shō of rice for our work.[11] On the way back home, after delivering the product to the manufacturer, I could only buy one or two shō of rice. It was really a hand-to-mouth existence [sonohi-gurashi]. Yes, yes, sixty years ago, all of us, my father [oyaji] and I also, all of us worked together. I worked at home. The first time the artisans [shokunin] in Nishijin became content was after the war [World War II].

The market for weaving was terrible about sixty years ago. The Nishijin Textile Industrial Association told us to stop work for two weeks or so. During that time, when I was a child, the sales of obi started to decline. When I was fourteen, there were crises [kiki] for the weavers when obi did not sell well. We had to stop the looms; it means you are not allowed to weave and you are told by the union of manufacturers to stop the machines [kyubata].[12] They stopped work because obi didn't sell well. It was a terrible depression and everyone stopped the machines and left their weaving jobs. I was weaving then. But in the Taishō Period, we were often told to stop weaving for a couple of weeks. So I pretended I was seventeen years old in order to be employed by a cigarette company. I have been smoking since the age of fourteen, because I worked at a cigarette company.

MRS. F.: My family lived here. I was born here. If you work on Nishijin weaving for forty or fifty years, you can't do anything else besides Nishijin, right? That is one reason why we all continue to live in the same place.

MR. N.: Originally, my grandfather was a carpenter for the Imperial Palace and for shrines and temples [miya-daiku]. After the capital moved

10. An apprentice was expected to train to perfect the skill for three years, without pay, and then work for another three years with minimal pay, as a way of saying "thank you" [o-rei bōkō] to the master.

11. A shō of rice is approximately 1.4 kilograms.

12. Kyubata means "resting the looms."

from Miyako [Kyoto] to Edo [Tokyo], my grandfather lost his job and he started to weave. At that time, they were not weaving on mechanical looms. It was all plain cloth. Well, my father was weaving plain satin during his youth. When I stopped going to school at the second term of sixth grade, my father first wove *obi*. So my father was the first one in my family to weave *obi*, seventy years ago.

I remember when we were still using the "human jacquard" *[sorabiki-bata]*.[13] Nowadays, the machine does it. I went up to the top of the loom and I pulled the threads of the warp in batches. We switched to the jacquard loom about sixty-five years ago. My parents were small independent manufacturers *[jimae]* all their lives. When I was a child, we were three brothers and sisters and my parents, all weaving together. There were five looms that we used in my family. I learned weaving from my parents. Our whole family lived a hand-to-mouth existence *[sonohi-gurashi]*. When I was about seventeen years old, we had the Great Kantō [Tokyo] Earthquake. I went around to sell our family's products. I went by myself. I went to the wholesalers, and depending on each wholesaler, the price was different. I used to wait and visit five or six wholesalers and sell to the one who had the best offer. Yes, I went to Muromachi, too [the wholesalers' district in Kyoto]. It was the Muromachi of the old days.

MR. F.: That's a hand-to-mouth existence *[sonohi-gurashi]*, after all. First you have to bring the product to the manufacturer, and then you get money; then you can buy rice for the day.

MRS. F.: After all, in the past the wages were very low, according to what father said. He couldn't make much money from eight hours of work, like now.

MR. N.: I have supported my family since I was sixteen. My father did not work hard; he played around. He was playing Chinese chess *[go]* in temples. Yes, it was common for men to play around. We would have been made fun of if we had let our fathers keep weaving after they were fifty years old. In most poor families, they had to work after age fifty.

13. The "human jacquard" was the old system of the two-tier loom, where a woman or a child sat on the second tier of the loom and batched the warp in relation to the design, while the weaver put the weft through. The jacquard system, which was introduced to Japan from Lyon, France, in the late nineteenth century, replaced the "human jacquard."

But our fathers were playing *go* or fishing . . . doing anything besides their occupations. We could not eat unless we worked. So I had to quit elementary school in the second semester of the sixth grade in order to support my family, because my father was loafing. I was twelve years old. My father did not drink, though. Many young kids used to work part-time early, but I started weaving only when I had to work full-time. I could not reach the loom to weave the wide *obi*, because I was too short. I asked to work on the half-width *obi*. My legs did not reach the pedal, so I had to use a platform to step on it.

I went back to elementary school just to get my graduation certificate, and then I went part-time to commercial school while working. I went to school at night for four years. Finally I graduated. Yes, it was hard. My younger brother and sister were too young to help me. I enabled them to go to junior high school. I completely supported them. Later they became weavers. My sister used to weave till she got married, and my brother used to weave till World War II began. After the war, he became an x-ray technician at the Red Cross hospital in Otsu.

I was drafted into the army during the war. While I was in the army, my wife kept the weaving business going. I kept in contact with her on the phone. She used to make *obi*, but weaving *obi* was prohibited at the peak of the war. My wife changed the production to cotton slacks and military-looking jackets. She exchanged half of the products for food. She was not working for a manufacturer, but for herself. My daughter [Mrs. Fujiwara] was young and working at home. I spent seven years in the army. Then I fought in China for two years. I served as military police in Korea. After I completed the compulsory period in the army, I passed the police exam. Later my parents called me back to Japan. My wife died right after I came back from the war. We felt lots of pain around that time. During the war, we did not have to suffer from a lack of food and clothes, because Korean weavers exchanged food with us. I was supplied with clothes by the army.

After I came back from the army, I was going to keep the same business as a small manufacturer *[jimae]*. However, the supply of thread was under government control. We had to pay a tax for each loom. We could only get the thread supply according to the number of registered looms we operated. Then I moved to Otsu, on Lake Biwa, and organized an association of weavers in order to get more supplies. My mother supervised four Korean weavers in Otsu. They made *obi*. The average price for thread for *obi* was one hundred *yen*, but I paid double in order to get more thread. I got thread through the black market

[yami]. Only brave people could run that kind of business. The market for textiles was much better than now. I think that we worked there for eight years. Since I earned so much money, I became addicted to gambling and spent all the money I earned in three months. I did professional gambling with Japanese cards [hana-fuda]. I could not even pay the tax. All the furniture except the *futon* in my house was seized by the tax office.

I could not work as a cottage weaver, because the government seized my looms, so I went to work in a factory. I worked there from noon till late at night. I was not covered by insurance, but they paid me by the piece. I was weaving on the handloom. I took my daughter [Mrs. Fujiwara] to work with me. She started working with powerlooms [shokki] at age fifteen or sixteen. I took both her and her sister to weave together. After one year, I started again as a small manufacturer [jimae] by myself at home. Since I did not have any capital, I went to borrow money from the wholesaler to whom I promised to sell my products.

I used to pay the workers in the factory as much as I paid the cottage weavers [chinbata]. I used to work with my wife. I had this business till recently. Even after the Korean weavers left, I kept running the business. I managed it with my family members. I paid them the same pay as I used to pay to the regular cottage weavers. We did weaving without using the jacquard. We placed the paper with the design under the cloth we were weaving, and the weaver followed the design just like *tsuzure*. At the time, I was a member of the Nishijin Textile Industrial Association. That was the union of manufacturers, not weavers. I used to belong to it until twenty years ago. During elections for president of the association, the candidates used to pick us up in a cart pulled by a human [jinrikisha] and paid us when they wanted us to vote for them. The association controlled the payments to the cottage weaver, and made many policies in favor of the manufacturer, not for the weaver. A labor union did not exist at that time.

My son is now working as a taxi driver. After he graduated from junior high school, he used to drive for the manufacturers. He drove the manufacturers' agents around to collect their products and deliver the yarn. A young man does not like weaving. The older we get, the worse our skills get. But salary men can be paid better when they get older. So I wanted my son to work for himself. My daughter, who is also a taxi driver, used to prepare weaving equipment. She is ready to retire from driving any time.

I stopped being a small manufacturer two years ago. I managed to handle every kind of job [for production] by myself. When I worked as a small manufacturer, it was as an individual. Large manufacturers preferred to form a corporation because of taxation, though. I visited several wholesalers in order to choose the best one. I do not think I would become an independent manufacturer now. We cannot run the business without cash. We have to wait for several months to cash the promissory notes [tegata] that the wholesalers pay us, but we have to pay for silk thread in cash immediately. If one of the related wholesalers goes bankrupt, we go down with him. As a cottage weaver, you are paid for as much as you produce. I close my eyes and try to be patient when I work as a cottage weaver.

Weaving is not all we have to do as craftsmen. If the loom is in trouble, we have to fix the loom, too. If the punch cards for the jacquard [mongami] have trouble, we have to know a little how to handle it. The loom has many rods and we have to keep them in order. We have to do everything. Once we know how to do everything, we can become independent craftspeople. I will prepare the tying of the threads for the warp [tate-tsugi] tonight. It is heavy work. I have to do it once a month. In a factory, they use machines for that. In some cases, the manufacturer comes with a machine to the weaver's house. But the machine cannot work on my thick thread, so I have to do it myself. For tsuzure we use thick thread, which must be handled by hand. The number of these threads is also smaller—around four hundred. From a roll of thread, we can produce fifteen or sixteen obi. Look at these designs in relief on the cloth. They are unique. They can be done only by the tsuzure technique—one needle for one thread. These days, even the design for the relief can be done by computer. Look at this design. We used to punch holes in the punch cards for the jacquard. This is not necessary any more, because of the computers. We can change the number of colors with computers. With this jacquard system, we do not have to think very much.

The jacquard was first introduced to Nishijin during the Meiji Period. After all, it's been 110 years. It became commonly used about 65 years ago. In the beginning only manufacturers could use it. Big companies, like the Kawashima Weaving Company, introduced the jacquard much earlier, but for ordinary cottage weavers, it was impossible to buy a jacquard. Weavers like us, working with two or three looms, couldn't buy a jacquard because it was too expensive. My parents used to weave only plain cloth [muji] and black cloth [shishu]. Initially, they did not use a jacquard. When my father reached age fifty, he started using a

jacquard. Later my parents bought the jacquard by monthly installments. They learned from another weaver how to use it. I learned how
to use it from my parents. The manufacturer bought the machine for
ordinary cottage weavers and taught them how to use it.

The jacquard system became popular among ordinary weavers in the
Taishō Period. By then, almost all weavers in Nishijin were using it. It
does not require original design by hand, and it produces very quickly.
It also can produce complicated designs. When we started using the
jacquard, we got a day off every Sunday. We did not have holidays
[yasumi] every week—twice a month only. Our income became stable
and we could buy more food. After the technique of the jacquard was
improved, weavers got greater income than before. The jacquard requires less skill. It can produce a design automatically, without the
weaver manipulating the threads. The powerloom [riki-shokki] is also
very efficient, so the labor pay is low. For example, they paid one hundred yen for handloom weavings, but sixty yen for powerloom weavings.
We can produce more with powerlooms. We can buy punch cards for
the designs more cheaply now. But the manual work of tsuzure demands
the highest skill. The designs became complicated by the use of the
jacquard. Before the jacquard and the powerloom came into existence,
tsuzure was the only way of weaving complex designs.

Even handlooms function with motors these days. Big factories at-
tach motors to the handlooms, so there is less labor for weavers. There
is no visible difference in the product. I cannot afford a motor, which
costs two hundred thousand yen. The manufacturer will not buy it for
me. Powerlooms can be controlled by power through the entire process.
At first, the powerlooms could weave only two or three colors, but now
they can weave more colors. It has become elaborate. But, after all,
the high-quality products in Nishijin cannot be done by powerlooms.
They still must be done by the handloom. We have to weave each obi
one-by-one.

Many things are different in Nishijin since the time when I was
young: the design, colors, and so on. The way of weaving itself is
different. However, these changes are not fundamentally different from
the past. Design and colors are modernized each year. We now use
synthetic dye. In the past we used ashes from grass and wood for dyeing.
They had a more subdued color. Synthetic dye has a larger number of
colors, which can compete with the ancient dyes. But the color from
the natural ash [usaki-zome] was more beautiful. People are now trying
to make closer imitations of the ancient colors. They visit the Shōsō-in

Museum at Hōryūji Temple in Nara to see the old textiles. Hōryūji has many kinds of ancient textiles. Nowadays, some specialists are again using natural dyes from the ashes of grass and trees. The major companies, such as Kawashima and Tatsumura, for example, have special orders using natural dyes. But certain products from the past cannot be reproduced any more. The natural dyes produce dark and light shades in the cloth, but the recent synthetic dyes are uniform all over the cloth. They are very flat and too even. Natural dye is incredibly expensive now. I don't think we can reproduce the five-hundred-year-old designs, such as the ones in the Shōsō-in Museum in Hōryūji Temple, with power-looms. These textiles are the basis for contemporary weaving. Weavers learn the ancient designs at Hōryūji Temple. There are lots of old weavings that were made several hundreds years ago. We cannot weave similar ones today. It is difficult to make this by machine. Of course, in the past it was all done by hand; everything was done by hand.

MR. F.: We can make similar weavings, but it is difficult to make exactly the same ones, and, of course, it will go wrong. All of the designs seem to be adaptations of original old designs. The designers use original old designs, but they change them to a modern taste. They compete to sell designs at as high a price as possible in exhibitions. The manufacturers buy the designs. Designers also collect very expensive art books to pick up unique designs. They also compete to survive. There are independent designers, who occasionally get together to have exhibitions and auctions to sell their works. When they really want to buy a particular design at an auction, they present blank paper without mentioning any price. Manufacturers buy a single design even for six hundred thousand *yen*. This means that they are ready to bid the highest price. The big traditional weaving companies employ their own designers, though.

MR. N.: Of course, there were many changes in Nishijin after the war [World War II]. There are so many things I can tell about. Nishijin became stable after the war. So many changes have happened, I tell you. Every time we had a war, the business became brisk all of a sudden and then it became dull again. Such things happened so many times in my life that I can't count them all. After the war [World War II], the business gradually stabilized and is balanced now.

Recently all the residents here have become salary men. Now all the weavers' sons don't inherit this occupation any more. More than half of them have become salary men. Only the elderly still weave little by little at home. Elderly people like us, who can't become salary men, weave. The youths are all salary men. I never considered becoming a salary man. Never! I don't like to be tied down by a time schedule.

MR. F.: Well, I complain here and there, but I've never thought of becoming a salary man [laugh]. Yes, my wife is now a "salary man" [as an employee of the Nishijin Textile Center].

MRS. F.: Cottage weaving is really different. I don't have to produce the same amounts as factory workers. I enjoy it. I don't want to work together with my husband in the same factory. No, thank you! It is not good for husband and wife to work in the same place.

MR. F.: In her demonstration job, she doesn't need to improve her efficiency. She has to explain as much as possible to the visitors. That's her job.

MR. N.: Well, nowadays, nobody knows how things were done in Nishijin; like, the young people now do not know how things were done. In my youth, we couldn't even receive compulsory education. Unless we stopped going to school in the second term of sixth grade and we didn't work at home, the parents and the children couldn't eat, you see.

MRS. F.: The standard of living was so low then. It was a feudal era.

MR. F.: Right. It was much better if you could graduate from sixth grade. Even before the children entered sixth grade, we had to practice to wind the weft or other things that had to be done. Nowadays, nobody works later than 9:00 P.M. or 10:00 P.M., like in the old days.

MR. N.: In earlier times, I experienced worse depressions than this one. We stopped working, even for thirty or forty days. We used to have more controlled labor action than now. I don't remember any major strikes in Nishijin. Young weavers sometimes went on strike. It is impossible for all cottage weavers in Nishijin to be united in one group and to do something against the manufacturer. We have no single example like that in the history of Nishijin. It is not very effective for weavers to strike inside their own company. They usually compromise easily in negotiations before they start a strike. After the negotiations, the leader of the strike is always fired. I think that Mr. Fujiwara [son-in-law] quit many jobs after he represented the opinion of weavers. We now have the Government Office of Labor Inspection. We can complain there when we feel troubled. This did not exist when I was young. We had to negotiate with employers by ourselves. The union in Nishijin is nothing, but we can trust the Office of Labor Inspection about such things as retirement. After the war, the labor law [*rōdō-kijun-hō*, Fair Labor Standards Act] — the eight-hour labor law — improved our conditions. The Americans came to be stationed. They introduced democracy. For the first time we, the craftspeople, too, could rest every Sunday. I think this is thanks to America. Yes, I honestly think so. . . . After the war, really!

MRS. F.: Well, it is true. Before the war, we had a rest day only twice a month. We were working like this during my time as a young woman.

MR. F.: It is the reality. We worked at night until 9:00 P.M. or 10:00 P.M. We worked until late, even after the war. It was like that just after the war. Today conditions have improved.

MRS. F.: Around the time when we were getting married . . . well, thirty years ago . . . we still worked at night [*yonabe-suru*].

MR. F.: Yes. We call it *yonabe*. We were weaving at home until late in the night.

MRS. F.: Yes, yes, so even thirty years ago, in factories that had fixed schedules, the work was finished at 6:30 P.M., but in some private places work went on really late, right? It was not uniform. So the way it is now that people work eight hours wasn't really . . . really the case several decades ago.

MR. N.: The system now is payment by the piece [*deki-daka-barai*]. So if I thought I was short in pay this month for eight hours labor, I would have to work for ten hours [laugh]. Because we do work in our home, not like in a factory, we can work as much as we need in order to cover our expenses.

MRS. F.: Well, Daddy [*oto-chan*], don't you weave until 10 P.M.?

MR. N.: Right. I start late in the morning, because I weave late in the evening, until 10:00. Well, when I wake up, I don't eat breakfast. I have two meals a day. I have breakfast and lunch together. I weave about ten hours; maybe not so long as ten hours. I start to weave around noon. If I don't want to, I stop. In other words, well, it isn't ten hours at the end. I do it in a relaxed way. I guess it's eight hours of actual work [*jitsudō*].

MRS. F.: If he finishes early, it's only four hours because he is late in the morning [laugh].

MR. F.: Grandpa [*o-jii-san*], in this case Mr. Nishitani, still has the same strange schedule as before. The old weavers are losing their jobs. But he is always busy. The wages haven't changed at all. But if the elderly had their work taken away, they'd become old. Grandpa's work keeps him young. If he continues his work, he must be alert. It must be good for him.

MR. N.: I have never been away from Kyoto because of work, except during the war. The rest of the time I worked in my father's house. Yes, I've never thought about working in a factory. I have always worked in my home. I can't stand to be tied down by time schedules [laugh], especially in the morning.

MR. F.: Even if I tell him all the time to stop, he still stays up until 10:00 P.M. or 11:00 P.M. His feet get cold from early morning to early evening. He is free to do what he wants.

MR. N.: I am free to do what I want.

MRS. F.: He goes to the public bathhouse [*sento*] at 11:00 P.M. He watches midnight movies on television until 2:00 or 2:30 A.M., usually. He is a "corrupt" grandpa [*gokudō o-jii-chan*] [laugh].[14]

MR. N.: Well, let me see, before television, we had the old, old radio with a trumpet. I sat up with the crystal radio. I liked such things. I went to Osaka, gathered and bought the parts, and constructed it at home.

14. *Gokudō* usually applies to gangsters.

MRS. F.: And now he devotes himself to *karaoke*. Yes, *karaoke*! Before this, there was a time I had been weaving at home, and I wove in my parents' home when this child [Noriko] was small. At that time, my father set up the radio. I could hear Miyako Harumi's songs when he pushed the button. Even though I felt it was too loud and I didn't want to listen, he played the songs of his favorite singers, like Misora Hibari. He set up a kind of device that you could hear the songs when you pushed the button. He connected the lines from the house next door to this one by himself. [They lived in two separate, adjacent houses.] He sings *enka* or *natsumero* [laugh].[15]

MR. N.: When I work, I get freedom from all thoughts *[munen-musō]*. I don't think of anything. If someone says, let's say, "the wind will blow tomorrow," I don't listen. I avoid worrying even if I don't have rice for today. I try to forget about today within this day, yes. You can say weaving on a handloom is very exhausting. That's true! I don't worry even if I get sick. I've been told I have diabetes, but I eat sweets and I don't put myself on a diet. Even when the doctor gives me medicine, I don't take it. I used to play baseball until I was about fifty-three years old. I still ride a bike.

For me, the best time is right now. Finally I could retire as I liked. Since we lost the war and were occupied by the United States Army, our society has become stable. All of my five children have a happy life. I am very happy about that. I do get a pension *[kōsei-nenkin]*, but it is social security from the government. The manufacturer and the weaver pay for this pension—fifty percent each. I did not have any support from the manufacturers for any of the various contributory pensions *[kōsei-nenkin, kokumin-nenkin, kenkō-hoken]*. Even if we do not contribute at all to social security, when we get old we can receive twenty thousand *yen* per month from the government. I receive that money, and the medical charge is free for anybody over seventy. Yes, I can work.

If my son had a good business, I would not be eligible for social security. My mother could not receive a pension when I was making 1.3 million *yen* every year. She passed away when she was ninety-six years old, more than ten years ago. I supported her. She used to live with me. My father died at the age of seventy-six, after the war. Times in Nishijin

---

15. *Enka* are popular ballads sung by street singers in Japan during the period from 1900 to 1930 and *natsumero* are once-popular sentimental songs that evoke nostalgia for one's youth or for particular periods.

are better now. In the old days, we had only two holidays a month. If we rested a full two days, we couldn't eat. Usually, we worked until noon and took a rest in the afternoon. We usually had a half-day's rest and we worked until noon on a holiday. We had to work on Sundays.

MR. F.: The same was true for us. At night, we had to work after supper until 10:00 or 11:00 P.M. You are paid by the unit. So if it takes you one day or two days to weave that piece of cloth, you are still paid the same for the piece. If you couldn't finish, you had to weave until even 10:00 or 11:00 P.M., extending your hours into the night. Otherwise you couldn't make a living and your accounts would become unbalanced.

MRS. F.: It was this way. After all, the wage was low compared with today's wage. This means that today the income is better. Nowadays, it is not rare that you can earn more money besides just for eating.

MR. F.: Now nobody works until 9:00 or 10:00 P.M., like in the old days. If you do so, you can make a lot of money. People today do not wear much *kimono*. It is too expensive now. *Kimono* should be sold at a lower price. People do not buy cheap things. They need precious *kimono* for special occasions.

MR. N.: I do not think that companies are thinking of the future deeply enough. They are just shortsighted in their effort to sell goods right now. Nishijin should keep its own unique skill that nobody else can imitate. Everything is produced by machines now. What we used to produce when I was a boy had the fine taste of Nishijin. Nowadays the products are getting worse and worse.

After the war [World War II], the big manufacturers started a group employment system. After everyone completed their schooling in accordance with the new post-war compulsory education system, they were hired and trained in Nishijin. Those young people were from the countryside. They came to Nishijin after they graduated from middle school.

MR. F.: It was once like that. But today, even though we try to recruit people from high schools, they won't come to Nishijin. So now the manufacturer *[oriya]* goes to the countryside again, and he trains housewives for part-time weaving *[naishoku]*, locally.

MRS. F.: There are lots of workers who came to Nishijin from the countryside in Kyushu and also from Shiga Prefecture. The weavers' situation has changed since you left Japan last time. They have four more holidays a month. They are not allowed to work from the thirteenth through the sixteenth of August during Obon time [the Buddhist All Souls' Day, held in July or August]. Production has been cut down due to the decline. When sales used to go well, we had days off only on the fifteenth and sixteenth of August. Since last year, the holiday time has been radically extended. Many other places have cut down on production. In his [husband's] company, since there are only a few weavers, they do not have to worry about a shortage of work. Rather, they are asked to work more.

MR. N.: In our company, there are only six or seven weavers. I am not sure if small companies can survive in Nishijin. This company proves that they are doing well. It must be difficult, but they are managing. I do not think that this company overproduces. They have a low stock. We make extra for inventory. The amount of work assignments has not changed. The number of looms is small.

MR. F.: Gradually the number of weavers is going to decrease. We have fewer and fewer workers every day. In the company where I work, nobody wants to be employed there because their conditions are bad for workers. Because of this depression, I think they still want to decrease the number of looms. There are many other places with better employment conditions. But all manufacturers are having fewer workers and more empty looms. If we could find work somewhere else with better conditions, we would change our jobs. But the situation is not going well, so I am patient. Now cottage weavers are buying new powerlooms for five million *yen* each, so they can produce more in less time. I think that they are preparing for when the handlooms disappear completely. They need machines that can compete with the high ability of the handloom to produce complex designs. A powerloom would have to be quite sophisticated in order to make a product similar to handloom weaving.

The work schedule at the company where I work is free and flexible. The people who work regularly weave in an orderly fashion. But it is unusual for weavers to have so much independence. It is not the same in other factories. Our workshop is far from the office and no one cares what we are doing. But because of the system in which we are paid by the piece *[deki-daka-barai]*, we cannot loaf very much. We cannot start work too early, because we bother the neighborhood with the sounds of looms. We have an approximate schedule, but generally our starting time is fixed. The schedule is clearly posted on our board, but nobody cares. If the company requires us to work longer, we work as long as possible. So it is selfish on the company's part to force us to have two days a week as holidays because they can't sell their products well.

In our job, the weaving is often difficult and there is a deadline. If the company puts pressure on us with a time limit, we can't improve the efficiency. Then our income will become lower. We can manage to put up with any difficult work. After all, we weave any kind of design, even if it is a very difficult one. They don't pay more for the difficult work. But it takes many days, and then if the wages become lower, we will have no work to do. And if you can't earn enough to make a living, you have to quit. There is no way!

More and more weavers leave the company where I work. Mr. Sakurai [a fellow weaver of Mr. Fujiwara],[16] for example, now has a difficult assignment and he seems quite disillusioned with his work. To work with silk is not easy. He has to work very carefully and slowly, and he earns less. If he leaves the company, he can find work as a guard or something similar. He is now sixty years old. He is eligible to get social security [kōsei-nenkin]. So even if his pay is low, it's okay for him. The company pays a retirement lump-sum grant [taishoku-kin]. Mr. Sakurai is sick of working here. He doesn't want to stay after all. Weaving requires a lot of patience, because it is very delicate work. But Mrs. Sakurai will continue to work here.[17]

There are some manufacturers who prefer to use old people, because usually the old ones don't care so much about their wages; however, we are concerned with it very much. They can employ Mr. Nishitani because he is healthy. He is working as a "secret" weaver [yami]. In fact, he should get 20-percent less of his social security. There are many kinds of "secret" weavers in Nishijin, especially in small businesses. The old weavers are not concerned with their illegal status. Employers do not have to cover them with health insurance and some other benefits, so they can use these people more cheaply. Some of the old weavers who are receiving social security are well off. They don't complain about low pay. It is not easy, therefore, for us to complain to the company. Older weavers usually have a hard time working on a sophisticated job because of their weak eyesight.

16. See interview of Mr. and Mrs. Sakurai.
17. Mrs. Sakurai retired subsequently (see interview).

We do not tell Professor Hareven good things. We are too frank and we expose everything.

MRS. F.: We are happy to have her in our house. We are real craftsmen *[shokunin],* so we have nothing. We are embarrassed, though. I don't know why we are getting along with you so well [to Hareven]. I am thinking of divorcing him [her husband] the next time he plays *pachinko* too much [jokingly]. Now that our son got married, I can leave my husband.

MR. F.: When I win in *pachinko,* I can make money. But I don't win very much . . . not very much.

MRS. F.: So, it must be thrilling and he really likes it. He is a little bit strange.

NORIKO.: In fact, he likes mah-jongg most, but it is easy for him to go to play *pachinko.* Japanese people have difficult human relations in the businesses and service division. Everyone has pressures in personal relations and their work is not interesting at all. So, they want to forget annoying relationships by playing *pachinko.*

MRS. F.: [to Noriko] People in other businesses may not have any time to relax, but your father does not have any stress. Your father is on a blacklist in Nishijin, but still he plays *pachinko* during working hours. It's not to his advantage, but still he does it.

MR. N.: There were many, many bad times in Nishijin. We had interruptions of production *[kyuki]* all at once in the old days, when they couldn't sell well. We tried to keep up.

MR. F.: Now they can standardize.

MRS. F.: I think *kimono* was also expensive in the old days.

MR. F: I really think it's too expensive and they should sell it more cheaply.

MRS. F.: After all, we make good *obi* for the adulthood ceremony *[Seijin Shiki],* and many people buy at least one *kimono.* The very cheap *kimono* doesn't sell, no!

MR. N.: I have never seen the *obi* we made worn by someone.

MRS. F.: There are many *[obi]* just stored in a wholesaler's store, right? The manufacturer *[oriya]* sells the *obi* to the wholesaler and sometimes the products circulate among the wholesalers, I heard.

MR. N.: The people keep the *kimono* in a drawer.

MRS. F.: There are some *obi* which are not sold. If the retailer can't sell it, he sells it at the listed price, below cost.

MR. N.: Well, I don't know what we should do. I think the manufacturers don't think about the future. They only think how to sell the products anywhere they can sell. They only see the immediate profit and don't worry about the future. Well, I wonder what they should do? We in Nishijin weave fine products—complicated works—like in the old days. The country weavers cannot imitate this kind of work.

MRS. F.: But now, with the powerlooms, we can weave anything mechanically.

MR. N.: Well, gradually. . . . The products we wove when I was about fourteen or fifteen years old were much more complicated and required higher skill. They were more like "Nishijin." But gradually the products have become worse.

MRS. F.: They used to weave with forty or fifty colors of thread. Now such products have become very expensive.

MR. F.: But now no young people want to succeed to our work, because this industry has no future. I belong to the "young" generation. I am forty-eight years old. Some weavers are older than seventy. Really good handloom weaving will disappear from Nishijin when my generation gets old. Maybe twenty years from now, there will be only powerlooms. I agree with you: it is very sad. [But there is] no way to avoid this. The market is not too bad, but the price is too high. They should set a price which ordinary consumers could afford. Then they would be able to sell many more *obi* than they do now. Exploitation by the middleman *[ton'ya]* is serious in our marketing. Nishijin is feudalistic. Nishijin is strong even in the depression. They said it would go bankrupt a thousand times, but it has not yet. What I am concerned about is the lack of young labor power. They should prepare something for the future, but they do nothing.

MR. N.: Now the skilled weavers *[jukuren-kō]* who can weave anything are over fifty. This is really a problem. And let's say weavers with artistic weaving techniques *[gijutsusha]* and skills will disappear in twenty years or so, I think. But if the young people will become considerably more skilled in twenty years, the tradition of Nishijin will continue forever. If there are no skilled weavers, one's students will become skilled after all. Yes! And I think Nishijin will continue forever, yes! The skills I learned have been passed down from my father's [*oyaji's*] skilled weavers.

MR. F.: Nishijin will not go out of existence; only the number of people who can weave will decrease in Nishijin. Nishijin will become very small, but it will never die.

Mr. and Mrs. Konishi

Handloom Weavers

Mr. Konishi Hiroshi and Mrs. Konishi Nobuko work as cottage weavers in Nishijin. Mr. Konishi was fifty-one years old at the time of the interview and his wife was forty-six. They live in a traditional narrow wooden house, which had belonged to Mr. Konishi's parents. The weave shed was attached to one end of the house. Both husband and wife worked in the same shed, their looms facing each other. The looms were sunk in a ditch in the packed-earth floor—both because the ceiling was too low for the looms and because the silk requires a certain level of humidity. Mr. Konishi was weaving obi on a handloom—the jacquard, where the pattern is controlled by punch cards—while Mrs. Konishi wove tsuzure brocade on a wooden handloom and translated the design with the bare eye. Mr. Konishi died in the year 2000 after serious surgery.

Mr. K. = Mr. Konishi

Mrs. K. = Mrs. Konishi

MR. K.: The silk threads usually look really pretty. Indeed, they have different colors and so on So the threads are not what you would get dirty from. But you have to work on it in various forms. Just explaining does not make people understand that you do, in fact, get dirty working.

MRS. K.: We are proud of our work. However. . . . [hesitation]

176

FIGURE 20. Mr. Konishi weaving on his handloom. Photograph by Tamara Hareven.

FIGURE 21. Mr. and Mrs. Konishi in their home during their interview. Photograph by Tamara Hareven.

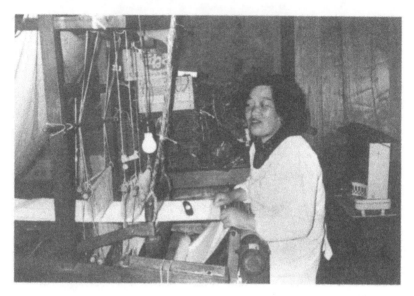

FIGURE 22. Mrs. Konishi weaving on her handloom. Photograph by Tamara Hareven.

MR. K.: However, the demand for this kind of work has been declining. I am sure that some weavers will survive, though. I can't imagine that *kimono* will cease to exist. It will continue in some form. But thinking about our son, if this business shrinks so much, what could he do?

MRS. K.: The most important thing is to get our kids out of the Nishijin "village" *[mura]*. We want our kids to leave. It is true. If you look just at the starting salaries, the outlook is really good in Nishijin. But we know from experience that once you have a family and you grow old, your income drops suddenly. Therefore I really want my children to get out. My son did not show any interest in being a weaver.

MR. K.: This is not the kind of work for college graduates. I haven't seen weavers with a college education. Better jobs must exist for them. I am worried about a decline in demand for *obi* in the future of our industry. I know some weavers' pay was cut in the depression. The stores around here do not sell as many things as they used to, because the weavers' income decreases and they do not buy very much. Nishijin seems to be experiencing pretty bad times. There used to be crowds shopping on Senbon Street [the commercial shopping artery on the edge of Nishijin] at the end of the month. This is not true now. I heard that the sales in the stores have gone down considerably. Their income has decreased.

MRS. K.: When our children were small, we used to spend a great deal of money on them. Now, although our daughter is working, our financial situation is much harder.

MR. K.: I hope that the situation in Nishijin will improve, but actually I am pessimistic. I see women wearing *kimono* a little more than before, though.

MRS. K.: We are quite concerned with how many people on the street wear *kimono*. I have not seen anybody with *kimono* made by my husband, yet. I wonder who is wearing his work. Only once, we saw somebody on television wearing *kimono* made by us. My brother-in-law made the *obi* for Princess Michiko [the current empress].

MR. K.: He was a weaver in a factory, but he worked for the Tatsumi Weaving Company, and they got an order from the Imperial Family. He made *fukuro-obi* [a special style of *obi*] for her.

MRS. K.: When the company we work for is unable to sell its products very well, they tell us to cut down on the production of *obi*. For example, if normally we were to make twenty *obi*, they tell us to make just fifteen. That means we earn less by the amount earned for five *obi*.

MR. K.: We are never told explicitly by the companies how much we should weave. The companies limit the amount of thread they give us in order to control the number of *obi* we weave. That is the so-called production adjustment *[seisan chōsei]*. This did not happen often before. It started in 1980. Since 1983, the decline in *kimono* production has become apparent. The company has not been able to sell, so the inventory has increased. They tell us to cut back on production so that the inventory will not rise.

Our company tells us to stop working on Saturday. When the company is closed, we are able to work only if they supply the materials. But usually they are clever and stop the supply of raw materials. Relative to other companies, we have better conditions. We do not take advantage of these, though. We want to work to make money. Our income has not increased for ten years. In most cases, incomes have fallen here.

MRS. K.: The change has been coming little by little. There is a possibility that the industry will continue to decline. Earlier we used to weave about ten *obi* with the same design, but now we have to change the patterns of the design after every five *obi*. If you are now doing a design of roses and you have to change next to a design of ships, and so forth, it is hard to weave very efficiently, like before. The way the manufacturers deal with the decline is not really to tell us that they are reducing production. But they are reducing our work time by changing the orders, or asking us to wait for just a short while because they "are now having the threads dyed." They do this to us from time to time, but they don't ask us to stop weaving completely or anything like that.

MR. K.: To keep a weaver waiting, they use the excuse that the work is not ready. Sometimes they keep weavers waiting for days. Companies play games. Weavers do not have any idea of the color they should use. They come to the company to get the silk thread and the design, but the *orimoto* [manufacturers] delay telling them the color arrangements. The manufacturers plan these underhanded maneuvers on purpose. They don't want to just send a weaver home without any orders. It would become a legal problem [having to pay unemployment compensation]. So they keep them waiting. This is the characteristic of Nishijin.

MRS. K.: They do it very cleverly [laugh].

MR. K.: This sort of thing is unthinkable in other businesses. There lies the peculiarity of Nishijin [laugh].

MRS. K.: If they told us in advance and asked us to wait for a whole day, then we would know it and we could expect that we would get zero pay for that day. When they say they will bring an order soon, and they want us to wait for just "two or three hours," or when they ask suddenly if we could change the colors, we have to stop for a while. We don't really complain about that sort of "little" thing, you know. Well, suppose we've woven a big piece today, and the next day when we have to do the next order, they tell us that they want to change the colors this time. So they ask us if we could wait until they finish preparing the new threads; so we agree to wait. If it is now about 4:00 P.M., they say they will have the threads ready first thing in the morning. It only takes two or three hours to have them ready. We plan to start working at 7:00 or 8:00 A.M. But for them, "the first thing in the morning" means 10:00 A.M. or noon, you see. Then after we receive the threads, we have to wind them, and so on, so we can finally start weaving only after lunch. These delays mean almost a whole day for us, but for them "the first thing next morning" was delayed just a little [laugh]. . . . That's the point—they don't make us wait long enough to qualify for unemployment compensation. We have to be unemployed one whole day in order to get compensated.

MR. K.: There is a hierarchical line between the manufacturer *[oyakata]* and the weaver *[kokata]* in Nishijin. So if the *oyakata* taps on my shoulder and says, "Would you please wait for a while?" I have to accept this.[1] The tapping means that I cannot make money now, because I am not paid by the hour. They determine, therefore, how much to pay after the waiting is over. That means the longer we wait, the less we get paid.

MRS. K.: They say "wait just for a little while." This is their style. If we were unemployed for one day, we would get about six thousand *yen* [through compensation], instead of the normal ten thousand *yen*, but when they say "just wait a little while," we don't receive anything [laugh]. We have to be unemployed one whole day in order to get compensated. At least, this pattern was reduced greatly since the [Fair] Labor Standards Act was adopted. Our employer formed a corporation.

MR. K.: In this respect, we are treated better. In Nishijin in general, you are brushed aside with, "please wait, I'm really sorry." Therefore, it is very rare that weavers receive compensation [for unemployment]. Only a few of the places in Nishijin, I think, give employees compensation. In our company, if we wait one day, they will pay approximately sixty percent of our wages, at least.

MRS. K.: But we are usually not sure about that sort of complicated thing. They don't ask us explicitly to wait each time. We mark the day spent waiting as a paid holiday. We are allowed twenty paid holidays

---

1. *Oyakata* is the old-fashioned term for manufacturer in Nishijin. It means "father" aänd *kokata* means "child." The paternalistic relationship between manufacturer and weaver was described as that of father and child.

per year. We rarely take a day off. After one year, the twenty vacation days are canceled and you are allowed a new set of twenty days for the next year, from September to September. When we tell our president that we would use the waiting day as a paid holiday, they just let us do so. When they tell us to take the next day off or they want us to wait the next day, I tell them I would make that a paid holiday. I'll have other things to do anyway. It is a disadvantage to take a day off, even if it is a paid holiday. Actually, I take a day off as an unpaid holiday quite often—when I want to go out with my children, for example; but my husband hardly does that. My husband takes a day off only about five times a year, when the company offers him a paid holiday. [Mr. K. laughs.] Those times are usually the days off that the company gives— for example, the New Year's holiday and the company's large-scale cleaning break in December.[2] If you take time off, you cannot sustain your living. Our pay is determined by how much one *koshi* [movement of weaving] is worth. If it were people from Tokyo or other places, they might demand compensation explicitly after having waited for a day. People from Kyoto or Nishijin do not speak so frankly. I think there is hesitation . . . and I think that's where the Kyoto people are different.

MR. K.: That's the peculiarity of Nishijin, so to speak—*oyakata* and *kokata*[3] [traditional name for manufacturer and weaver, with paternalistic meaning of "father and child"] always see each other. For instance, we see our president all the time. In most companies outside of Nishijin, you don't usually see the president because you are at the bottom. At best, you would see the manager if you were in a firm. But we see our president whenever we go over to the headquarters. On New Year's day, we all assemble at the president's house. We listen to our president's New Year's speech. Also we have some drinks to toast, and after that we say good-bye. The contents of his speech change every year. For example, this year he said, "The economic outlook is severe, the production of last year was bad," [laughs] or he would say, "So many goods still remain in the inventory." His topics are like this. Our president doesn't simply end it with just saying "Happy New Year!" He also encourages us [laughingly]. In the past two to three years, these

2. It is customary in Japan to clean the whole house at the end of December, in order to start the New Year fresh.

3. Whenever *oyakata* and *kokata* are used, rather than *orimoto*, I repeat the Japanese terms, because they designate an earlier mindset of the manufacturers and the weavers mention them with bitterness.

parties weren't fun [laugh]. He keeps us lined up in front of him, and speaks to us [laugh]. Our president talks about what's left in the inventory very concretely, such as how much thread remains. Nobody wants to hear such a thing right at the beginning of a New Year. Who would want to hear it [laugh]! For the New Year's party that the employer gives, probably everybody working on powerlooms shows up. Let me think . . . including about fifty people.

MRS. K.: There are some factory weavers who don't show up. They are women who have to prepare dinner at home. The company takes attendance for the New Year's party about ten days ahead of time [laugh]. They send you a sheet for attendance. We can't really reply "no" to the company. We feel obligated to go.

MR. K.: When the business was going well, they used to hold a party at some hotel or restaurant. Now the business has fallen drastically [laugh], and all we get is our president's speech at his house!

MRS. K.: This year was nothing but his speech. He uses two or three rooms together in his house. The old houses in Kyoto have sliding doors that can be removed. One can transform the adjoining rooms into one big room. Our president has a gorgeous house. He was adopted by his wife's family when they married.[4] Even when the old president was alive, the current president was already working here at the company.

MRS. K.: Mr. President *[shachō-san]* is always there. We always talk to him—at least we say hello all the time.

MR. K.: The way they pay us in Nishijin is strange. We are paid by the unit of weaving *[koshi]*.[5] If the market is not going well, they pay us less. If it goes well, they pay us more. The price of each single item *[tanka]* is the same as last year. At least we get work steadily. Last year, there were times when we did not have work. For example, for ten thousand *koshi* we get seven thousand *yen*. If you want to make seven thousand *yen*, you have to move the shuttle through ten thousand times. The price

4. The former president had no son to inherit the business, so the current president married the former president's oldest daughter, was adopted as a son and took the president's family name, and later inherited the family's business.

5. A *koshi* is one movement of the shuttle—meaning one unit of weaving.

of *koshi* varies according to each company. But in Nishijin seven thousand *yen* for ten thousand *koshi* would be the average. That is because the number of *koshi* varies with different designs. Also, in order for us to support our family, we must weave fifteen thousand *koshi* a day for sure.

MRS. K.: That amounts to approximately ten thousand *yen* a day. This is just for my husband, who is one of the more serious weavers. He is serious! The pay varies according to the design. If the design is complicated, the *obi* is more expensive.[6] *Obi* with simple designs are cheaper. I earn only one-third of the income my husband gets. When my son entered junior high school, I was earning very little. I was still learning at that time. Recently my husband's earnings started to decline. He used to make more money. Once I started weaving, my hips started to hurt, so I did not like it very much. I was often asked if I was enjoying my work. A long time ago—that is, already eight years ago [laugh], when I started work—I earned twenty thousand *yen* per month. Now I earn sixty to seventy to eighty thousand—that depends. When I have something in mind that I want to buy next month, I work extra hard for about an extra twenty thousand *yen*. One *obi* earns me about twenty thousand *yen*. If I want to make sixty thousand *yen*, I have to work rather hard. It is a bit strenuous, but when I have promised my daughter that I would buy her something next month, I work hard [laugh]. My pay per unit is good. It is about double his [husband's], but it takes more time to make the kind of *obi* I am weaving.

MR. K.: It works this way: there's no set time limit. I work back and forth on different kinds of *obi*, but my wife always weaves *tsuzure*. For *tsuzure*, the unit price is high, but it takes many days to make one *obi*. So it is not suited for a man's work—it is not very profitable. So this type of weaving is mostly done by women.

MRS. K.: I think that people weaving *tsuzure* are not weaving in order to make a fortune. It's like a hobby, so to speak. It is really enjoyable. I might get scolded if I say this, but I have a lot of fun doing it, actually. It's fun. You can watch the cloth getting longer and longer. Also you can choose the colors that you like. So it is mainly for fun, but men

---

6. As Mrs. Shibagaki explained (see interview), weavers do not get paid extra for more complicated designs. It takes longer, however, and therefore they lose money on complicated designs.

would not be able to do it for making money. I can't weave with a jacquard system like my husband. If someone could teach me, then I would be able to, especially because the thread guide is the same. But if I did that, I could not weave as leisurely as I do now. I think it would be a mistake to take my husband as a model. In Nishijin there are many weavers, regardless of whether they are men or women, who are earning money. But the women cannot take care of the household if they are weaving as rigorously as their husbands. There aren't many who weave at home, you see—not even one out of ten women who weave make additional income for the family as I do. Women who weave are usually weaving along with their husbands. Some women are even better than their husbands. Sometimes the husband goes to the supermarket to buy food [amazed]! My husband never goes into a supermarket. He waits outside around the corner all the time until I finish shopping. There are many households like this in Nishijin. When we go to the market, my husband helps me carry the bags to the bus. But when we get off the bus and turn into our lane, only I carry the bags. Yes, yes!

My husband is the major breadwinner in the family! [Mr. K. laughs.] Oh, it couldn't be me. Well, my daughter is already a senior in the university, so she is pretty much independent, and my son is going to start the university next year and he is going to a private one, so it will cost us a lot of money—about a million *yen*. I did not work at all while my children were young. Once my son entered junior high school, he did not give me much trouble any more, and also I didn't have to go to school for parents' day, like in elementary school. I started working a little before my son entered junior high school. By then my daughter was already in high school; then I had the time to stay at home and do nothing. I do not want to leave anything undone. I am too old for a part-time job outside, so I can't do it. And when my husband is weaving at home, I hesitate to go out [to work], although there are wives working outside.

MR. K.: I started to get weaker. I am paid by the piece, so as I got older I could not weave additional pieces in order to increase my earnings. When we were young, our pay in Nishijin was much better than what we would have gotten working in other places. Even now, a junior high school graduate who becomes a weaver in a factory right after graduation can become qualified enough to start at a new place after two or three months of training. He can make about two hundred thousand *yen*, you see, if he weaves over fifteen thousand *koshi* per day. So if you think about working in a corporation, the pay in Nishijin is much better—and that is why we decided to enter Nishijin right away, too. But actually, this is not relevant to young people today; it is apparent that the pay in Nishijin will decrease substantially once we start getting old, because in Nishijin there is no such thing as seniority, like in usual corporations. The peak for men in Nishijin is in their forties. Nowadays there is no fixed period of apprenticeship for weavers. But even during the learning period, the relative wage can be said to be better, compared to that of young people of the same age range in other businesses. Although the pay wouldn't be that good during the period of apprenticeship, once you weave for three months, you'll get to that level.

MRS. K.: You would then be considered qualified *[ichinin-mae]*.

MR. K.: The pay in Nishijin is good while you are young.

MRS. K.: But when you get older, after forty, the income starts to decline gradually. By contrast, in a company your pay increases steadily. So we take this into consideration when we think about our children's careers.

MR. K.: That is, when you are young you can get ahead of others very easily; but when you reach our age, the speed of production declines. The legs get weaker and the whole body is not as vigorous as before. Probably . . . in their forties weavers start to feel weaker and tired.

MRS. K.: My husband is young; he is fifty-one. I am forty-six.

MR. K.: I feel more and more tired these days.

MRS. K.: For instance, he cannot go out in the evening for enjoyment. Gradually people begin to feel greater stiffness in the lower body, don't they?

MR. K.: Certainly. It's the weakening of the whole body. Weaving is said to be handwork, but it is actually the same as physical labor, and one must do it with the entire body . . . we use our legs and arms.

MRS. K.: In my case, the eyesight has worsened. I have to watch very closely. My body is too healthy [laugh]. I have grown plump, because I am sitting all the time [laugh]. I'm young in spirit. I'm always playing like my daughter; I mean, chatting and having fun.

MR. K.: Well, I would think that there is a force of habit, to some extent. Even if we are to live until around seventy, I suspect that we will also be weaving at that time. We ought to be able to do it, supposedly. Eyes, legs, and hands would be the most important, after all.

MRS. K.: Sundays, I don't work. In the near future, I will take Saturdays off, too [laugh]. If our president were here, I would be scolded, because I'm not supposed to say something like that. I have never considered the possibility that my husband would work less and I would work regularly [laugh]. Never, never! I couldn't think of such a thing!

MR. AND MRS. K.: It's the men who are supposed to work.

MRS. K.: I get tired of working, too. I don't know if it's because I'm old, but I can't go on and on weaving. When my children get home, I start chatting with my daughter. I soon start playing [laugh]. I can do only about one-third of what my husband does. Also, I usually go to the manufacturer to deliver the finished *obi* and pick up the new orders, because it is more profitable this way. When we go on errands, we don't earn much. It is better for my husband to continue weaving while I run the errands, because I don't earn as much as my husband, due to house-work. It is very common for women to go over to the manufacturer and deliver all their husbands' finished products, because men work more efficiently.

MR. K.: For me, there would be a loss of money if I went to deliver my products. In the Nishijin industry, handloom weaving is different from machine weaving. A powerloom will continue to work once you switch it on, but handweaving doesn't work that way [laugh]. Once you leave the work for a little while, it takes time to get back into pace when you come back. So if you spend one hour at the manufacturer's office, that means you've already lost two hours.

MRS. K.: I go over to the company around 4:00 P.M. because I work until then. Right after I return home, I have to start preparing supper. Once I get away from my work, I cannot go back to it.

MR. K.: Among the handloom weavers, it is very unusual for a man to run errands to the manufacturer's office. In the old days, for example, in my father's day—when I was a child—they sent children over to the manufacturer to pick up supplies and deliver finished products.

MRS. K.: Children don't go nowadays.

MR. K.: Of course, Nishijin weavers don't make children work any more. Parents don't make children do such things. Children don't do that willingly, either. Children hardly even come to the side of the loom to watch [laugh].

MRS. K.: About eight years ago, I was told not to weave. I could not do the household chores because of the help I gave my husband with his weaving [preparatory work]. But I promised to do all the house-work. I asked to be allowed to weave, too.

MR. AND MRS. K.: All the women in Nishijin are working.

MRS. K.: They used to leave the children alone.

MR. K.: In the old days in Nishijin, people always had to leave their children alone.

MRS. K.: It would not be proper if I just sat around; meanwhile, the expenses for our children have also increased. They now want a lot of things.

MR. K.: We have become pressed financially. I suppose there is that much work to be done by women in Nishijin. For example, if only men do the real weaving, then the wives do the preparation for it.

MRS. K.: One must wind the thread and do the preparation for the next day before one goes to sleep. The wife can do that for the husband during the day. This way, the husband can have supper, take a bath, and go to sleep, after he finishes the weaving for the day.

MR. K.: [joking] So women cannot go out to enjoy themselves because they have to do that preparation for their husbands.

MRS. K.: Nowadays, I don't do any preparation for my husband. Each of us does his own work. My husband has to work hard and check each one of his products every day. But I have to wind the thread just once a week. I do not have any other tasks for preparation. For instance, when he is winding, I'm sometimes watching television [laugh]. It's hard to know how others want to have things done. My husband knows what to do for his own work. Because he knows what is best, it gets harder for him to ask others to do things for him.

MR. K.: However, we have additional work beyond the actual weaving. We have to do preparation for the next day. This takes about one hour or, when it is bad, two hours. Our schedule is: get up in the morning, have breakfast, work, clean up the tools, prepare for the next day, take a bath, and then sleep. So the only free time available to us is when we go to sleep. This means that we need to do so much work all the time. Yes, that's how it is.

MRS. K.: When I work at home, I can't stop working exactly at noon. For my own reasons, I may prolong work time for an extra fifteen minutes or so. I may go shopping for a little while. Again, I may not resume work exactly at 1:00 P.M., maybe fifteen or twenty minutes later. Then I take a break and have a cup of tea at 3:00 P.M. During my break I watch television and take a rest till about 3:30 P.M. I know you can't do this in an office. They take only ten-minute breaks. Then I work till 6:00 P.M. When I speak with the president, I can't tell him that I take a break for a cup of tea [laugh]! When he comes over here and asks me when I finished working, I say "about 6:00 P.M." But I should have said "5:00 P.M.," because that's the rule. My husband works till 7:00 P.M. I begin cooking supper and taking care of my children a little bit around 4:00 or 5:00 P.M. So I can't really get absorbed in the weaving. The children come home and tell me one after another that they are hungry.

MR. K.: Ever since the [Fair] Labor Standards Act was put into effect, the manufacturers in Nishijin began enforcing working hours strictly. Prior to that, weavers used to play around in the daytime and work in the evening.

MRS. K.: Weavers used to play ball with children around the street corner, have dinner, and work slowly till 8:00 P.M. They took time off during the day, thinking that they would make up for that later at night. When a person works at home, it doesn't matter how long he works. Our schedule is left to our independent judgment. Only factory workers observe the eight-hour day. But those of us who have families can't keep those hours when working at home. At any rate, our wages are so low that we won't be able to make a living otherwise. I don't think we have inspectors.

MR. K.: Yes, we do sometimes. They come from the Labor Standards Bureau.

MRS. K.: Once a year, someone comes around and asks questions, such as, "How many hours do you work?" and "What time do you stop working?" I don't know where he comes from. I just make four rolls of *obi* a month. I am not making much money; I have children.

MR. K.: Though her income [his wife's] is not big, it is an indispensable part of the monthly income for us. Wages have not increased. Our company has its own union. Of course, I have to join them. There is also the Greater Nishijin Labor Union. It has only approximately 350 members. Some of the *debata* [cottage weavers] are members of this union. Yes, I have joined it. Our company union is not part of the larger union [Greater Nishijin Labor Union]. There are two separate unions that we belong to. The company union serves only to raise wages. It exists only as a friends' association.

MRS. K.: We joined the Greater Nishijin Labor Union as individuals. We are the only ones from our company who belong to this union.

MR. K.: I am a member, but my wife is not a member.[7] The Greater Nishijin Labor Union is supposed to protect us and negotiate on our behalf, if somehow the entire Nishijin business goes broke [hesitation]. Some companies have unions now. Workers in these companies with unions may also join the larger Nishijin union. Only those people who agree with the Greater Nishijin Labor Union join. It doesn't mean much. Whether one belongs to the union or not is one's personal choice. When an organization invites one to join, he can join individually. Sometimes, the whole company union may join the larger Nishijin union. The workers in our company do not belong to the Greater Nishijin Labor Union. I think that is because of financial reasons; also because of the fear that this union may be too vigorous in negotiating with the company. In short, the workers there are elderly. In their minds still

7. There is an internal contradiction here. Mr. Konishi claims that his wife is not a union member, while she claims that she is.

remains the *oyakata–kokata* relationship [the "father-child," paternalistic, relationship with the employer]. They say they don't want unnecessary friction . . .

MRS. K.: Our manufacturer does not know that we belong to the Nishijin union. Nobody knows that. It doesn't really matter. My husband rarely speaks out at the company union, although he talks a lot here. He doesn't have much social contact with other workers in the company, either. When he goes out to a union meeting, he never opens his mouth [laugh].

MR. K.: In spite of the problems in the market, the wages have been going up, thanks to the labor union. I recognize that kind of good aspect. Of course, there are fewer youngsters.

MRS. K.: Yes, that's right. My husband is considered young. He is the youngest member in the Nishijin union. Even among the elderly workers, we don't see someone who provides leadership and speaks out. They will get into trouble if they speak out too much. They'll get fired by the company. The old folks were elected to be leaders of the union because they are senior people. We are among the youngest members of the union. Many of the union members are about seventy years old. They think that they are too old to argue and demand. Some of the old folks don't even join the union because they say they are too old. They don't want to rebel against their president. They say they would feel sorry for their president if they pushed him and made demands on him. They say they would rather quit the union if they have to do that kind of demanding [laugh].

MR. K.: In other words, if the *oyakata* collapses, they are afraid that they will share the same fate. That's on their minds. For example, whenever we go to the company office and are told repeatedly that the company 's products are not selling and that they are piled up, this penetrates into our minds. It becomes difficult for us to insist that we are unable to maintain our livelihood unless the wages are raised. We would feel disappointed if our president tells us that he is in no condition to raise our wages.

MRS. K.: In the old days, the manufacturer used to respond better when young people complained about their wages and threatened to leave.

He would raise wages and even ask them to stay in his company. I no longer see this now.

MR. K.: The advantages of the union are that we can benefit from health insurance through our work. Also, we are insured for the minimum wage to some degree. The union can negotiate with the manufacturer and draw up a certain wage scale. Our health plan is administered by the union. It is applied only to people in Nishijin. It is not administered directly by the government. The workers are irritated and discontented inside themselves, despite the peaceful atmosphere on the surface.

MRS. K.: I think that all the weavers are feeling this way. People said to him [husband] in a meeting, "You should become a union leader next time." When they actually wrote down the names, however, everybody voted for the oldest person. Five or six people had told my husband that they would vote for him, but no one voted for him. Everybody, in fact, voted for the oldest one. They were just saying this to him.

MR. K.: Things like that remain unchanged.

MRS. K.: My husband is too naive, so he believed them. He told me that they would elect him at the next meeting, if he showed up. He wanted to avoid it and told me that only I should go. Also they were going to serve a dinner, naturally paid by our dues. But when I went in, everyone agreed to elect the oldest person. They clapped their hands for him and had the dinner. After that was over, I came home and said, "Oto-chan [daddy—the way a wife usually addresses her husband], you should have come. You only missed dinner!" [Laugh] When I came home, we laughed about that. He did not expect that to happen. My husband was wondering what the hell he was going to do if he were elected [laugh]! The union leader will negotiate for bonuses and increases in wages . . . [laughing voice] but most of the time, the president won't listen and will raise wages only a little bit. I think that someone old working for a long time may have sympathy for the president during the negotiations. That's what I think. Don't you agree?

MR. K.: That happens most of the time.

MRS. K.: I think if my husband becomes a union leader, he would surely quit his job. He would feel that it is his responsibility to see the wages raised. If he goes out to the president to negotiate, and he feels he fails in his negotiations, he would quit the company. He would do that because he has that kind of attitude. In Japan, we have heard of strikes. For example, people asked for a raise in wages and went on a strike for one week. This did not happen recently. Well, there used to be more young people who did this in the past.

MR. K.: I also think they don't go on strike any more because there are problems in making a living now. Strikes were almost unheard of in Nishijin. We've heard about a strike among cotton-mill workers in Japan. Around 1922, there must have been strikes in two cotton mills during the Taishō democracy. I am almost sure that there were no strikes in Nishijin. Due to the unique characteristics of the Nishijin family enterprise, the weavers probably were not able to go on strike.

The manufacturer's family business in Nishijin is now called "company," but it used to be a small shop. The relationship between the manufacturer and the employee was like that of a family. I don't understand it in detail. As far as I know, an employee was absolutely subjected to the manufacturer. When an employee was ordered to "turn right," he had to turn right—that kind of thing. Yes, it was just the same for the cottage weaver. The manufacturer could halt the weaver's work by not sending threads.

Yes, one could change manufacturers. One had that possibility. But it was more true for a cottage weaver; an employee in a factory did not have that much autonomy to be able to change employers. If we are ill-treated, we may have to prepare ourselves for changing manufacturers in order to protect our livelihood. Yes, this is how it is now, in modern times. In earlier times, the factory weavers used to be terribly exploited. They had to obey their superiors' orders as one must obey the Emperor. This system must have continued since feudal times. It was the so-called Japanese *kazoku* [family] system. The father had the absolute power. The head of the household had absolute authority. Well, young people can't believe this [laugh].

MRS. K.: I think that whoever was superior to a weaver described the relationship of a weaver to a manufacturer as *kazoku* [family member] for his own benefit. Then he took advantage of the weaver under that concept. I also think that the weaver thought his superior was taking care of him like his own child. But in fact the president *[oyakata]* wouldn't really be caring for him [laugh]. Don't you agree [to husband]?

MR. K.: The worker is manipulated under that concept of "family."

MRS. K.: I definitely think that the employer used the concept of *kazoku* [family] for his own convenience. Maybe the worker was treated as someone without brains and was cared for like a child [laugh]. . . . In the olden times the ones who couldn't read and write could be "good" weavers. But the modern weavers can't be like them. They would protest. We live in different times now.

MR. K.: So when you take someone old, say, who was born in the Meiji Period, who is a cottage weaver or factory weaver, he would be absolutely obedient to his company even now.

MRS. K.: I heard that at the times of bad economic conditions in the past, a weaver would work for no wages, even for our manufacturer.

MR. K.: That was before the labor law [Fair Labor Standards Act]. The law did make a difference. Also, as the economy in general moved upward, free labor without any wages ceased to exist. The manufacturers who did not pay wages had to shut down. Some manufacturers did not pay their weavers until they received their pay from the wholesaler. The length of the period for a promissory note *[tegata]* paid by the wholesaler *[ton'ya]* to the manufacturer might be a problem. Depending on various companies, the waiting period varies.[8] The weavers often had to wait to be paid until the promissory note could be cashed. The term *oyakata* [paternalistic term for employer] has been used since the Meiji Period and is still used by people in their seventies. I think that we may see a similar problem arising again in the future.

MRS. K.: No, we don't use the term *oyakata* any longer. If the president of a company hears that word, he will correct it to "president." He wouldn't like the word *oyakata* either [laugh].

MR. K.: The weaver was also called "child" *[oriko]*. Though I don't know the origin of the word, female weavers were called *oriko*. We no longer use it now. The word is sort of derogatory, I think.

---

8. The wholesaler sells the manufacturer's *obi* on consignment. He gives the manufacturer a promissory note *[tegata]*, which often is not cashed until nine or ten months later.

MR. K.: Yes, yes. In the old days, the kids had an education only up to the fourth grade. After that, they were forced to leave for *nenki-bōkō* [indentured apprenticeship] for three or five years. I'm not sure for how long. After that, they would be recognized as independent weavers, return home and work as a *debata* [cottage weaver] in their parents' house or in a rented house, once they had their own family. For the first time, they would receive wages. During the *nenki-bōkō*, they did not receive any pay and they could not leave their master by any means because the parents borrowed money in advance from the master [in exchange for their child's service] equivalent to the pay a child would earn in three years. The child would have to work without pay for the next three years. There was some monetary transaction, like a loan between the owner and the parent who sent him for *bōkō* [apprenticeship]. So the length of the apprenticeship period was to cover the amount of the loan borrowed by the parents. It's like selling a human being. You know how young people won't listen to parents now? Nowadays, if they were sent for *nenki-bōkō*, the kids would say it's illegal. In those days, they must have been so impoverished! In whatever way you got treated, you couldn't say anything about it. That was a long time ago.

MRS. K.: You know how young people wouldn't listen to parents now.

MR. K.: The system disappeared long before World War II. I think that it must have ended about the beginning of the Shōwa period [1925 on].

MRS. K.: Even now people talk about the old times and remember when they were apprentices. Someone like the executive director in our company refers to his apprenticeship *[detchi]* days when he started out. The *detchi* is someone young who became an apprentice after graduating from junior high school. He would be kind of lost, not knowing what to do.

MR. K.: You don't hear the same terms now. There still remain unspoken ranks like that. Yes, you can find a similar ranking among the factory workers as well, even when they appear to be engaged in the same kind of work. In short, someone who is senior in the company can possibly receive narrower material to weave, while a recent worker may only get the wider one and be slowed down in his work.

MRS. K.: In the case of fabric with designs, only the most senior weaver would be given the kind of work that is easy to earn money from. On the other hand, the newest weaver will end up with the most difficult work. It will be hard for him to earn money. The traditional apprenticeship system does not exist any more.

MR. K.: Two years ago, our company's president said that they were bringing young girls from the countryside. But these girls quit their jobs; they are back in the countryside working as *debata* [cottage weavers].

MRS. K.: Those girls were employed here as a group, directly after graduation from junior high school *[shūdan shūshoku]*. The president of our company graduated from Kyoto University. One of his classmates is teaching at a high school in Shikoku, which sent girls here in group employment every year. Our president used to ask his friend to send these girls and took the responsibility of taking care of them. The young girls had very little experience and were the sort of people who used to be called *detchi* [apprentices]. They used to live in the dormitory of our company's president. These girls usually stay for a few years. But the girls from Shikoku quit their jobs in one year and went somewhere like Osaka to work in companies. When they did not like weaving, they wanted to leave and join friends somewhere else. Even so, four or five girls from Shikoku were sent to Kyoto every year in order to get used to life in the city. But they were like frogs in a well [trapped]. When they woke up, they started the day with the sounds of weaving. When they finished working, they just ate supper and went to bed. They just repeated the same thing day by day; no chance at all to see the outside world! They could hardly leave the dorm. The curfew *[mongen]* was strictly at 9:00 P.M. Since their life was like that, I guess, it was easy for the girls to dislike their jobs. But the managers of this company are somewhat rigid and are not open or generous toward the freedom of young people. For instance, they want to keep them strictly in the dorm at night. Since they were entrusted with the care of these youths, the managers were afraid something bad might happen to them. There was a notice on the door of their factory dorm saying "off-limits." This prevented the young workers from receiving friends from other places. If they were living by themselves, they could have enjoyed themselves in many ways. It was not true in their case. When they eventually came to feel too little space for personal freedom, they quit. This type of dormitory arrangement does not suit the feelings of young people today. The industry of Nishijin weaving is not progressive. It is a very conservative business forced to follow old routines. The young people have to be educated to place their hands neatly on the *tatami* [mat] when they bow.[9] The president's wife tries to educate them to polite behavior, but youth today do not like that kind of thing.

There is no chance for the girls to go out. On Saturday, they learn flower arrangement from teachers who come over there. The president's wife is trying hard to make them into "good girls," but it turns out to be oppressive for the girls. This kind of educational attitude of employers, trying to get the young girls to behave like ladies, is not popular among girls nowadays. Employers want to make them into good girls, since they have the responsibility for supervision. This is the old tradition. At least our president's wife is doing this. She is friends with somebody in Urasenke [the headquarters of the biggest tea ceremony school in Japan, which is located in Nishijin]. The president's wife herself is a teacher of flower arrangement. So the girls take classes with her. If our president offered our daughter such a deal where she could learn how to do the tea ceremony and flower arrangement, we might agree with pleasure. But if the employer lets girls do whatever they like, even at night, we would worry. We would be able to trust our daughter with an employer like our president. When the girls leave their jobs in our company, their parents must be very worried about where they go. There are plenty of girls who come from Shikoku to work in this area. So they gather information from each other and compare their work situations. Some of them become dissatisfied with their jobs. I wonder where they go.

MR. K.: It does not seem that they go back home. They have nothing to do there, even if they go back. In fact, our president is just teaching them skills and they go to a different place with those skills. There is no way to keep them from leaving once they say they want to quit. Since the young girls quit their jobs so soon, it is necessary to bring new girls from Shikoku. They bring them even though there are not so many jobs

9. Refers here to the custom of formal polite greetings, which involves getting down on one's knees on the *tatami* or on the elevated threshold at the entrance to a traditional Japanese house, and bowing deeply with the head almost reaching the floor while the hands, with the fingers elegantly together, touch the *tatami* in front of the knees.

in Nishijin. These girls can be employed with low wages, for they come from the countryside.

MRS. K.: Moreover, the costs of their room and board are deducted from their pay, so they receive very little. I think the girls are paying for the boarding house. The president provides a woman to cook their meals. He asks her to manage in a way that she spends only three hundred *yen* per person. She must be receiving money from the president as part of company expenditures. What the girls pay for the dorm fee should be cheaper compared to apartment rent, though. In the old times, when they first did apprenticeships *[hōkō]*, young people spent three years learning the skills and another three years working for lower pay, in gratitude to their employers. There are no such girls today. In the old times, they used to work very hard without getting a penny.

MR. K.: That's not true. They received a little, and their parents occasionally borrowed the pay from the employer in advance.

MRS. K.: They were not allowed to go back home even during the Obon holiday [the Buddhist All Souls' Day, held in July or August]. Instead, they used to do so on July 15 and 16 *[yabu-iri]*.

MR. K.: You can see that it is really hard for youngsters to stay with a job in Nishijin, even if they come from the countryside. Nowadays, more women tend to work on powerlooms and more men on handlooms with the jacquard system because of the men's skills and physical strength.

MRS. K.: Recently the powerloom has been making good products, and so the handloom has to produce even better ones.

MR. K.: The design is made by someone else. Our skill is tested in how quickly we can weave the new design into a product. The products are becoming more and more refined. For instance, you can easily find many textiles made by powerlooms that cost three hundred thousand *yen* in retail price. The handloom weaver will lose money if he makes the same sorts of things and gets paid the same amount of money. He would have to make things that are too difficult to make on the powerloom or to combine colors. Then he would be able to receive five hundred thousand or six hundred thousand *yen*. Once women got used to weaving more complicated designs, they would be able to handle them. But it may get too much for a woman to keep pushing the jacquard pedal with her feet. The pedals are heavy. The threads have to be pulled tightly. The final outcome of the weaving varies depending on how tightly the threads of the warp are pulled. Each thread has a lead attached on one end underneath. The more refined the weaving is, the more weighted down the threads are. That's why one's feet get tired. In order to stretch the threads, there are stones attached underneath the warp. Depending on the weight of the stones, the threads either get too loose or they overlap. The adjustment is difficult. [to Hareven] Haven't you seen a heavy stone under the warp or small pebbles attached to the threads in most of the places? Did you feel the tension in the thread?

The quality of the products has been improving in recent years. They are definitely getting better and more refined. Powerlooms can handle multiple colors now. Suppose you want to weave the design of a circle. The powerloom has a device that can determine the dimension of the circle. A weaver can adjust the machine to the number of times he has to move the shuttle to make the circle. If you make the circle by hand, you can't help the slight difference in the way you hit the pedal each time. The powerloom will make a perfect circle. Even though you could make the same kind of circle by powerloom or by handloom, the difference would be in how the product feels when one touches it.

MRS. K.: We are predicting that sooner or later powerloom weaving will come to an end, because of lack of capital. For example, a powerloom would cost ten thousand to fifteen thousand dollars if one wants to make good stuff. A wooden handloom will certainly not cost more than two thousand dollars. The payments for the powerloom will take one year or so, whereas one can pay back for a handloom sooner than that. So the question is how much capital the manufacturer can invest in the powerloom. That's why in the case of the powerloom the manufacturer depends on the cottage weaver, because the weaver has to buy the loom.

MR. K.: A refined powerloom of good quality would cost 250,000 to 300,000 *yen*. The cottage weaver will buy his own looms, get threads from the company, and make the products. But it will be hard for him to pay back the money for the loom. The question is whether the manufacturer can buy all the looms or not. Quite a few weavers work on powerlooms at home, especially in the countryside. They are called "hidden weavers" *[yami]*. It's something about tax. The manufacturer has to report to the Internal Revenue Service how many looms he is operating. In order to hide his income, he does not report certain weavers. The manufacturer must get an advantage in tax. It affects maybe only the manufacturer. There are particular areas where people do only that kind of "hidden" work. You know, it is done in small places but where the pay is a little better. In addition to that, there is a possibility that "hidden weavers" cannot have formal contracts with a manufacturer. Powerloom weaving is in a terrible economic condition. Handloom weaving is better off. There are too many powerlooms and they produce three times more than handlooms.

MRS. K.: The handloom produces better work, too. Powerlooms tend to overproduce.

MR. K.: Earlier, people preferred *kimono* woven by powerlooms, but now they have started appreciating handwoven cloth again. The powerloom makes the surface of the cloth too flat and smooth. The handloom produces some variety in texture, which people did not like before. Rich people must like the products of handlooms better. Ordinary consumers do not prefer handwoven products. Only special people, who like high-class things, prefer handwoven cloth for special occasions. When daughters get married, their parents want to buy *obi* for them. But I cannot tell which of the handwoven or powerloom *obi* they buy. It is a matter of price. Handloom products are not for ordinary people. Some people are satisfied with fake diamonds. The same is true for *obi*.

Very good powerlooms have come into existence. One can make quite sophisticated *obi* with them. So I cannot talk too simply. Handloom weaving is superior in quality, but people's criteria are changing a lot. Handloom weavers are getting older. If powerlooms are improved just a little more, they will eventually drive out the handloom. When machines reach the same level of technique as that of old weavers, they win. Nowadays, no young people succeed to the techniques of handloom weaving. But with the newest powerlooms, one can weave things similar to the handlooms. The powerloom stops each time when it changes the thread to a different color. In the past, powerlooms could not stop each time when the thread was changed; consequently, they could make only simple designs. This is not true any more. Now powerlooms can deal with each thread as well as the handloom does. They do it automatically, while we handloom weavers have to stop the loom each time. At least weavers do not tire themselves out with the powerloom, though. We will never buy new powerlooms. It costs five million *yen*. We cannot afford it. I think the manufacturers worry if cottage weavers do not have new looms. But even if we have new looms, it does not mean that the manufacturers will give the weavers appropriate work for these looms. I guess that weavers could not help buying new looms if they want to survive in Nishijin.

MRS. K.: The weaver is worried that his present loom may not qualify to make something new. He buys the new loom to be competitive. Let's say, for example, that his old machine could handle work with only eight colors, but the new one can work with twelve colors of threads. This difference of four colors is very important. It can make a much better product. These days we cannot survive on tradition alone. Companies need new methods for business. They have to be prepared to move along with the preferences in the market as fast as possible. Weavers who buy new powerlooms are in their thirties. After age fifty, nobody wants to buy such a thing by borrowing money from the bank. They cannot make much money. Weavers with new looms expect to get more work and better pay. I doubt it. Right! We do not have to bother ourselves by using complicated machines. Who in their sixties and seventies would bother to master new skills with the machine?

MR. K.: Some people who could work only with four-hundred-needle looms were asked to work with six-hundred-needle looms, which can make much more sophisticated weavings. When they said that they could not work on them, they had to leave. It means that the company did not have to "fire" them and pay them special money [for compensation]. I do not know what the weavers' fate is in the future. There will have to be some demand, but business will not go well. The manufacturers have too much stock in the warehouse. If I were younger, I would be floating along the stream, but I have to consider my age. When we were young, it used to be that if we didn't like the wages or conditions of one manufacturer, we could move to another one. We would walk around Nishijin with a pair of scissors in our hands. We used to look for signs on the houses saying "weaver wanted," and we'd find another manufacturer [see fig. 23]. We used to make twice as much money as ordinary salary men. Now we have nowhere to go, nowhere!

MRS. K.: If one large company goes bankrupt, many other companies linked with it go down with it.

FIGURE 23. Announcement on a Nishijin manufacturer's house seeking a weaver for mechanical gold-thread weaving [*hikibaku*]. Photograph by Tamara Hareven.

MR. K.: Every day, the whole of Nishijin is producing enormous amounts of textiles. How could they sell all of them in this country? Those who survive the depression will be much stronger. They can import Chinese products and put the Nishijin label on the product and sell it for a good price. I am not very optimistic, even about that. Some people used to do the same things with Korean weavers, but finally they overproduced. Things made in Korea are different from domestic products. Handwoven fabrics made in China and Korea have a different touch. It is paradoxical to have to buy new machines when the market is not going well. The *kimono* market is a matter of demand. I doubt if women wear *kimono* in the summer. If they did, the number of women who wear them would be very limited. It is absolutely impossible for my wife to purchase a *kimono*. It must be hard to make profits on those things.

MRS. K.: I agree with you. Even if someone insisted that I buy a *kimono*, I would just have to refuse.

MR. K.: The manufacturers are just producing *kimono* to store in their closets. If the manufacturers want to make money with that kind of thing, they have to produce something good enough to attract high-class people.

MRS. K.: We wonder what kind of people can afford the special kind of *obi* that my husband is making now. We have never seen people wearing such things. Even if we go to Shin-Kyogoku Street [covered pedestrian shopping street in the center of Kyoto, especially attractive to tourists from other parts of Japan], we do not see people wearing them. So we came to the conclusion that people buy them to collect them in their closets. They want to show them to other people in order to boast that they possess such wonderful things. Rich people maybe just enjoy shopping. People who are wearing *kimono* every day do not buy it so often. They buy reasonable stuff, but not expensive ones. I bet people just boast about their possession of expensive stuff to other people.

MR. K.: In various times, there were many people like that. They bought *obi* to boast about it—for example, medical doctors' wives or stockbrokers' wives. In the case of Nishijin, when stocks go up, our business is not good. When stocks go down, they buy *kimono* or *obi* with their floating money. Nishijin manufacturers are going to survive only by producing technically superior things. Most companies pretend to ignore the skills of the weavers. Otherwise craftspeople *[shokunin]* would have been given many more advantages. Even though they know the value of the craftsperson's skill, the manufacturers are greedy to make profits for their companies.

MRS. K.: There are few young men weaving on handlooms *[tebata]* today. Most people working in this field are sent out on a national pension for senior citizens *[kōsei-nenkin]*. Even powerloom weavers are mostly in their forties. When people lose their jobs now, there is no way for them to find new jobs. I wish I could have taken a much longer leave after I was hospitalized for my gall bladder operation. I was afraid if I stayed out too long I would be fired, so I decided to come back to work. The employer said that I should take a longer leave, but I could not take their words honestly. They could have shut my loom down. Once that happens, there is no more job. Though I could not make much money, I kept working. I was afraid to lose my job, even though the employer said that I should take a rest as long as I liked. In fact, when I went to see the president after my absence, he immediately asked me if I was leaving. I was really surprised. I realized then that I had made the right choice to go back to work earlier. In earlier times, when we complained about cheap wages and threatened to quit our jobs, the manufacturer made every effort to keep us. Nowadays, if somebody does the same thing they must leave right away. We cannot even make a joke. In the past, when we mentioned that we would quit our jobs, it was the only strategy in our wage negotiation. The manufacturer would try to keep us. They raised our pay whenever we mentioned quitting. So we could keep working at the same place for many years. But we could never use this in negotiations these days. This strategy does not work any more. One weaver threatened to quit during the negotiations. Despite his twenty-five-year–long career, the employer said right away that it was all right for him to leave. He had to leave then and there.

MR. K.: There are laws for the protection of workers and even for wage regulation. But none of the Nishijin manufacturers applies these laws to their employees. If there was a strong union, companies would be careful with the laws. In our company, the union gets along with the employer very well. So they do not start arguing. I do not think that they fire weavers. Firing weavers costs the manufacturer money. So they set up a situation so that weavers will leave by themselves. They accuse weavers of having defects in their work, even if they do not have any. Or they may complain that such work cannot be sold. They can find as many excuses as possible to insult weavers so that they leave on their own.

MRS. K.: They often accuse weavers that the cloth is too soft. It is the worst insult for weavers. It means that weavers have to worry a lot while weaving. Handloom weaving requires emotional stability, so it is very hard for us to keep working after they complain.

MR. K.: Anyway, first they complain about our work and then they complain that the product cannot be sold. We know it is a sign that we have to leave. It is not reasonable.

MRS. K.: We cannot afford to get angry even in that situation. We usually ask them for the next assignment the day before. They tell us to leave a note to remind them. They do not prepare it on the next day at all. So I usually ask them three days in advance for an estimate of their delay.

MR. K.: Since we keep in touch with the company all the time, we feel through our bodies how well our works are sold. When we go to the office, the clerks whisper to each other to let us hear that the handloom products sell well, but not the powerloom products.

MRS. K.: Yes. We have to be patient. Our manufacturer is regarded in Nishijin as being rather modern. I think that he has a sense of the modern times. Though when you look at his company, it's old and traditional. Of course, it's hard to say with certainty in these severe economic times whether Nishijin manufacturing will survive. We are not that worried about ourselves in our generation. We are still used to the thought that we could move around with only a pair of scissors in our hands and find another manufacturer. Our employer is not the only one around. We know we can get a job somewhere else when his business becomes sour. Like in the old times, a pair of scissors means to us what a sushi knife is to a chef. You know, a chef could get a job if he has his knife. It's the same way. We use our own scissors anyway.[10]

MR. K.: I think that this kind of attitude has been the negative characteristic of the old-time workers. The workers frequently used to change jobs in the old days. Now you don't see that very often. They pretty much stay with the same jobs. Yes, the workers used to move around where they got better pay. One decade ago, they began stabilizing. I think that it's because the wage system became stable and the same happened everywhere. Yes! Earlier there was a lot of discrepancy in wages. I think that part of the reason was that people moved around to a certain extent. In other words, the workers pursued better-paying jobs and moved out from the low-wage jobs. When this happened, the owners with low wages could no longer keep their businesses going. In addition, although minuscule, the labor union exists in some companies in Nishijin and helps stabilize the wages. The Fair Labor Standards Act sets maximum hours from 8:00 A.M. to 5:00 P.M.

The Koreans are threatening Nishijin with competition. I think they started entering the Nishijin business after World War II, when they began weaving velvet. They have good skills. You know our technique originally came from Korea. The real threat to us occurred when the manufacturers in Nishijin began sending orders for weaving to Korea

10. One year later, Mr. and Mrs. Konishi actually changed manufacturers. By then, this was a rare occurrence in Nishijin.

directly. This started in the early 1980s. It was just like the case of Oshima *tsumugi* [a textile woven in a southern island of Japan, Amami Oshima], known as a luxury fabric, some time ago. Weaving Nishijin products in Korea has forced the price to come down drastically. This imposed a serious threat. But recently we haven't seen much of this. Not only the products from Nishijin but also other products, such as *yūzen kimono* [hand painting on *kimono*], were made in Korea. These things matter to the manufacturers and have little to do with us, except if you are hand-loom weavers. The products made in Korea are certainly cheaper, because the wages there are lower. The manufacturers still make profits, even after sending raw materials there and bringing the products back here.

MRS. K.: The labor is cheaper in Korea. I think manufacturers prefer cheap labor and they send out more work to Korea. That's why there are fewer weavers in Nishijin. But I don't know whether or not the expensive, good stuff is also being made out there.

MR. K.: I think that by sending products to be made in the countryside or in Korea, the manufacturers in this Nishijin business are choking their own necks like suicide.

MRS. K.: For example, the type of work sent to Kanzaki, Maizuru [places in the countryside on the Tango Peninsula on the Japan Sea], and so on, is woven by the people there and the products are called "Nishijin." The raw materials and the designs come from Nishijin. Regardless of where they are woven, it is called a Nishijin *obi*. Are these still Nishijin products if they are woven outside Nishijin [hesitation]?

I think there is a middleman system in the countryside. I am certain of the fact that the manufacturer and the cottage weaver transact through the middleman *[daikō-ten]*. I suppose that it is cheaper this way than using one's employees in Nishijin. Probably the manufacturer gives a certain allowance to the middleman for each cottage weaver, I think. The middleman goes out and recruits the cottage weavers. If the manufacturer himself were to go outside Nishijin and recruit in the countryside, people would criticize him by saying, "What kind of a man is this who ignores his own home ground in Nishijin?" That's why he has someone else, a middleman, do it, as if the middleman is operating independently. So the manufacturer can pretend he has nothing to do with it.

MR. K.: Sending work to the countryside means that the number of weavers in Nishijin has been decreasing. I think that is why the work is being sent out to the countryside, where housewives can work as weavers. Compared to us, who are skilled, independent workers, those farm housewives provide cheaper labor; their pay is about one-third of our wages. In other words, although the demand has been declining, the whole Nishijin business world has not reduced the number of looms. . . . How can I explain this? I guess that they can't help operating the same number of looms for profit. In this area of Nishijin, the number of looms in operation is restricted. The manufacturers compete to obtain looms for themselves within Nishijin. When they send work out to other places, they can gain more looms. But he is only increasing the sheer number of looms while being unable to sell *obi*. Needless to say, the work done in Nishijin is superior. The quality of the product is declining when it is produced in the countryside. Certainly, it is true. In Nishijin, we have our own circle of friends with whom we get together about twice a year and exchange our techniques and discuss various matters. This group is formed privately. We discuss, for example, what we will be given to weave next and what is the best way to weave it.

MRS. K.: I myself was not from a weaving family. I had no intention of marrying a weaver. I've already forgotten such a thing [how they met]. It was not an arranged marriage [feeling of embarrassment].

MR. K.: We were married twenty-five years ago. Our first child is already twenty-one and will turn twenty-two soon. Well, where was it that we met? It was a romance [shyness]. Shall we tell [laugh]?

MRS. K.: When we were young, ballroom dancing was extremely popular. For example, in dance halls such as Senbon, Mimatsu, Soshu, and Belami. I don't think I've been to Belami since. Mimatsu was very popular. At that time, we went dancing.

MR. K.: In our time, about half of the Nishijin people had arranged marriages and half met each other. It was the post-war period, when recovery had started, I think. Many weavers had romances with other weavers. Weaving girls knew that women in the weaving industry must keep themselves busy. They would have to start working soon after they got married because they knew the weaving techniques. Men in the weaving industry very often wished to marry weaving girls who would be able to help them [laugh]. But girls, knowing how hard a Nishijin wife's life was, did not want to marry a weaver.

MRS. K.: In my case, because I'm not from a weaving family, I could not help him much. My husband has suffered a loss.

MR. K.: No, no [laugh].

MRS. K.: Had I been a weaver, he would have put me to work right away [laugh]. Well, I was spending my time on nothing for seventeen or eighteen years. I didn't have any outside part-time job, either. My father was a salary man. I was not raised in Nishijin. In my parents' generation, in salary men's families, women did not work. My mother, for example, did not work, either. We were not rich, but [laugh]—well, we didn't know at the beginning that my husband was a weaver. He didn't reveal this to us. I myself didn't know exactly what weavers do. My parents didn't, either.

MR. K.: Some people, you see, have looked only at the bad aspects of Nishijin. Women in Nishijin have to work from morning to night; this is the tradition, so to speak. We felt that if it was revealed that I was from Nishijin. . . .

MRS. K.: He thought that I wouldn't go out with him any more, so he didn't mention that he was a weaver in Nishijin. When we went out, he would be properly dressed.

MR. K.: [to his wife] You would not have possibly thought of going out with me if I wore a sweater like I wear now, right?

MRS. K.: He wouldn't wear a sweater like this; he looked neat when we would go out, so my parents and I couldn't tell where he was from. He was very relaxed about such matters as time, too. He would ask me in midday, for example, if I wanted to go to the movies or something in the early evening. So I was impressed that he was so free, and also that he seemed to have a lot of money. In fact, he had a lot of money. He used to buy me all sorts of things, like shoes. If I said I wanted a dress, he would buy me one right away; so I really liked that [laugh]. He had a lot of money before our marriage.

I knew always that he had money, but I didn't really know what "weavers" were. I would have felt that weaving was indeed hard work, if people had let me do the work. But everybody said that I didn't have to do anything, so I haven't done much [tone of excessive modesty].

MR. K.: [to his wife] But you started to understand when you began to work. I mean, when you started thinking about helping me do the preparation.

MRS. K.: I found that weaving is quite hard, so we decided to let our children go to the university. Also, I wouldn't want my daughter to marry a weaver. I think a man, like a salary man, leading an easygoing life, would be better.

MR. K.: Most of the people in Nishijin think that way, too.

QUESTION: Do you feel that your wife should be helping you more?

MR. K.: Oh [laugh]. It would be nice, wouldn't it?

MRS. K.: Oh, my. Do you think so [laugh]? You are just joking [laugh]. I get all the money, though [laugh]. I get all the money.

MR. K.: You get all of it.

MRS. K.: Yes, all of the money, I get. Well, I tell my husband: you've earned this much, at least. If not . . . [laugh], if not, he wouldn't know how much we've earned, right? [laugh.] That's a foolish thing [laugh]. I just show him the account to show "you've made this much money." I get the money, nevertheless, just saying "thank you" [laugh].

MR. K.: When we have to decide on the use of money—large expenditures—we talk it over, don't we?

MRS. K.: Oh, we talk over any kind of spending decision. Well, when our children say they're going to special winter sessions and they need twenty-five thousand *yen*. We decide together to give it to them. For heaven's sake. . . . I don't spend all the money by my own decision [laugh]. Yes, consultation is the first thing. On trivial things, such as beef, I don't tell him every time. I don't tell him what today's menu is going to be, or anything like that. My husband does not say anything about expenses on food or about trivial matters concerning money. Well, I don't know how it is in other households. There are a lot of couples in the neighborhood . . . In fact, in some families, the husband keeps the money; but in our family, that's not the case. My husband does not care about little things and that's fine with me [laugh]. Well, well, I give my husband allowances. [Mr. K. laughs.] But whenever he gets his allowances, he gives them to the kids pretty soon. He says, "Do you need some money? I'll give you two thousand *yen*." He asks the kids these things and gives his money away [laugh].

MR. K.: Traditionally, we take a holiday on July 15 and 16 as *yabu-iri* [summer holiday].

MRS. K.: Workers from the countryside go back home to see their families. This is what we call *yabuiri*.

MR. K.: We are not going to celebrate Obon. We do not have a home town to go back to, because we were born and brought up here.

MRS. K.: We don't go anywhere.

MR. K.: We just lie down and take a nap.

MRS. K.: We were just relaxing here. If we were receiving a monthly salary, we would agree to take a holiday right away. Salary men get lots of money, even during the holidays. In our case, we are paid by the piece-rate system. We lose money if we take a holiday.

MR. K.: In fact, a holiday is not relaxation for us. We were just hanging around the house because we had neither a particular place to go to nor a visitor. For us craftspeople *[shokunin],* holidays are not holidays. Emotionally, the next weaving assignment keeps coming up in our minds. So even during the holidays we cannot be relaxed from our hearts.

MRS. K.: Sure! We are working in our mind even then.

MR. K.: Yes, we are so in our mind. I think everybody needs to relax sometimes and forget about work. In this respect, ordinary Sundays can be our relaxation. But if we take a long vacation, we cannot stop worrying about our job.

MRS. K.: It is true that life is short and we should take advantage of the holidays; but even so, we cannot do that. Travel is very exhausting for us. It would be good to travel when you are young, but we just get tired whenever we leave home.

MR. K.: Yes, travel is something for the young. During this time of year, wherever we go it is just crowded. We prefer staying in Kyoto. Even after people leave for vacation, we cannot take off for even one day. If we took a day, we would be fired. However, by comparison with last year, the work load has been so-so. We had little work to do in this period last year. There is an old saying that during February and August we have less work. In February, production is reduced because they do not start the sales of summer cloth [natsu-mono] until after February. Until then, they deal with winter cloth [fuyu-mono]. February is too early for summer cloth. It is a blank season in-between, a preparatory period. But it means that the stock of goods keeps increasing, then. In the case of Nishijin, production for stock is based on estimates of future demands [mikomi seisan].[11] Therefore, even if we prepare, for instance, one hundred rolls of cloth, nobody warrants that they would be sold out in March and April. This August is a little better than last one. It means that the preparatory period was set up a little earlier than before. So, earlier, August meant the preparatory period for winter stock. People used to have less work before the sales of the winter stock started. But now each company wants to start earlier than the other one. The routine of nippachi [February and August] that people used to follow is deteriorating.

Another factory extended the Obon holiday from two to three days, in order to reduce production. They used to be too successful with their business. We say, "A standing nail has to be hammered down." They were once warned to slow down their production. Our employer is making new things. They seem to be working very hard with those new products [sarcastic expression]. We cannot work during the holiday, because the manufacturer plans the total amount of our work for every

11. As in the fashion industry in Europe, Nishijin manufacturers produced in advance for the next season and for stock. Production of excessive stock rendered Nishijin manufacturers vulnerable.

month. For instance, if we make ten *obi* regularly, we cannot make more than eight or nine *obi* in July, for that month has more holidays. We are paid less for those days. It depends on the design. In general, we make twelve or thirteen rolls of *obi* in a month.

MRS. K.: Last year, we were told strictly not to work during *Obon*. We did not prepare a reserve of threads. But this year, we prepared extra so that we would have some work. It means the supervision was slack. They pretended not to see anyone working, even if they were working. Last year, we did not get any thread, because the company wanted us all to have holidays together. So we could not work, because of the lack of thread supplied by the company. But this year, they were tolerant enough to give us thread for a few *obi*. I guess that they meant that it was all right for us to work. Even so, we could not work in this hot weather, in spite of our desire to work. We were encouraged to take a trip for five days or a week during *Obon*. We would have liked to do so, but we did not have any guarantee payments [*hoshō*]. If we could have gotten that payment, we would have taken a vacation comfortably.

MR. K.: So we want to get as many raw materials as possible. There is a limit to how much silk thread they can give us. Because of piecework, it is possible to work for an extra two or three hours and then take a day off on the next day. In theory, if we wanted to, we could take a vacation when people are not traveling. In fact, we cannot do that because we feel guilty taking a holiday. But on the other hand, we cannot make noise with the machines when others have a holiday. They may insult us, saying that we are overworking. So when there is nobody working on Sundays, there is no sound at night. Then we cannot work. A few years ago, it was possible. People used to work even at 10:00 at night. It should be each person's choice. But nowadays, such a thing does not exist any more. It is very quiet in the evenings. As a matter of fact, there is the problem of noise. Nobody dares to make noise. In Tango [region by the Japan Sea], it is possible to do that kind of thing. It is a rural place with few people. If they are asked to make an *obi* in a hurry, they can work through the night.

MRS. K.: In this area of Nishijin, we cannot do that. But in other more remote parts of Kyoto like Kinugasa [northwest of Nishijin], people sometimes work until late at night. People work till very late and start working from 6:00 A.M. I heard so.[12] They can do it there because weavers' houses are concentrated in those areas. So if they hear neighbors working late, they just join them. In our place, we have few weaving neighbors. Here, of course, there are some neighbors doing something related to our work. For instance, people in the house next to us are making linings for *obi [shitae]*. There is only one weaving house besides us. Another neighbor next to us goes out to work for a weaving company. Other neighbors are doing something different — nothing related to our business. It is quiet here. In Nishijin, there is a tendency for the concentrated area to expand more and more toward the north.

MR. K.: At one time, there were many weavers around here, too. But then their children started working outside Nishijin for other companies. We, too, will end this job in our generation. Our children won't succeed us. Our daughter is a salary woman. It is probably the same with all the children in the neighborhood. None of the weavers expect their children to succeed them. If they were running their own company of powerloom weaving *[kioriya-san]*, they might do that. But in our neighborhood, everybody is doing cottage weaving, just like we do. So I guess that none of them will let their children succeed to their job. I guess the people in major companies *[ōte]* may be thinking that the small manufacturers *[jimae]* may do that.

MRS. K.: In the case of *shokunin* [craftspeople] like us, children do not want to do the same thing as their parents. My son says that if he were a weaver, he would not be able to find a wife. He has said this since his childhood. He wants to go to a company where he will wear a necktie to work. He is at school now. I bet that my daughter will not marry anybody in a weaving family. She would say, "No," if it was a weaver, because women in weaving families are pretty busy. Young men can be well paid as weavers in some companies. If they go to work in weaving, they work with powerlooms. They are able to make money — nearly two hundred thousand *yen* a month.

MR. K.: Some of the weavers' children listen to their parents' words and start doing that kind of job.

12. Kinugasa is to the northwest of Nishijin, along Nishioji Street, near the Temple of the Golden Pavilion.

MRS. K.: I admire them.

MR. K.: I do not think that it depends on their education. I think they make more money as weavers than ordinary salary men.

MRS. K.: If their educational background is only high school, they would be able to get one hundred thousand *yen* at most in ordinary companies. In the case of weaving, if young men work very hard, they can produce lots of *obi*. Our son, he is not that bright [modestly], but we, as parents, tried hard to get him into a university. He has seen some government institutions on the local level and does not like that, either. So once he gets out of the university, I hope he can find some easygoing job. My daughter likes social studies. She did not make it into a national university. We thought that Kyoto Sangyō [Industrial] University would be good, because they have a good law faculty. We figured Kyoto Sangyō University would be better for finding a job later. She tried only Kyoto Sangyō University and some other schools for backup. She thought that if she was not successful, she could try a national university the following year. She applied to Kyoto Sangyō University and was accepted. So we decided not to wait another year to try a national university, especially because she is a girl. She enrolled in Kyoto Sangyō University. That's all. There is no deeper meaning or anything. She has been working very hard. Our son will also go to the university.

MR. K.: I wonder what he is going to do in the future.

MRS. K.: We want him to go to college. But even if parents say they want to send their children to school, the school does not just say, "Then please come." There are entrance exams, as you know [laugh]. He's been working hard and is hoping to get into a university. Yes. He goes to Horikawa High School. There, only six students are planning to get employment after high school. All the others will go on with their studies. All are enrolled in the general curriculum.

Well, you see, in our family it is very usual to go out together. We always go out together, for example, to department stores. It is not often the case for other families. I hear that only the husband goes out for fun. But in our family, we were always going out—all four of us— together. Nowadays, our children are grown up and don't want to come with us. Also our daughter has a car. She sometimes drives us to where we want to go. She has spare time, you know. But that's about all there is. My husband does not drive. The two of us are having dinner out. Our children rarely go out for amusement, so they are waiting for us at home. My daughter, too, goes out very rarely. If she gets a boyfriend or something, she probably wouldn't come back until late at night. But now, she gets back by late afternoon whenever she goes out. Our son, too, is already home. He gets back from school around 3:30 or 4:00 P.M. He is now upstairs and is probably watching television. With the car we go, for example, to Arashiyama [scenic area west of Kyoto] or the areas nearby. Sometimes our daughter takes us around her university.[13] Our daughter is working. She worked as a private tutor. She bought the car with that money, so it was not a burden on us. Our family is a happy family [laugh].

MR. K.: Yes, in Nishijin it is more common that only men go out. But we often go together to the Shijō Street area [fancy shopping street in Kyoto], where there are lots of department stores.

MRS. K.: I have never seen my husband's younger brother going out for fun. Only this one [pointing to husband] went out for fun when he was younger; nobody else did. When he was out, I thought I had to be up, waiting for him. So I used to fall asleep right at the kitchen table and so did his younger brother. I remember he would come home late without being noticed by us. Then I would wake up in the total darkness among his family members, who had fallen asleep. Yes, that's right. They used to be awake till 11:00 P.M. They worked until about 10:00 P.M. Even if they wanted to go to the public bath earlier at night, it was impossible. They could go only at about 11:00 P.M. If they showed up at the bath early in the evening, they would get a sarcastic comment from the owner of the bath, like, "You finished work so early."

MR. K.: The elderly were kind of exempt, though. If you were young and in your prime, you were expected to go to the public bath at the very end. The last bath is called "finishing bath," at about midnight or 1:00 A.M. The latest bath was the worst—at 2:00 A.M. I hear that in my father's days, the dream was to have *geisha* girls around. That means that the men were making the wives work until late at night, while they were hanging around in *yukata* or *ki-nagashi* [informal summer kimono]

13. Later their daughter married a salary man. The couple and their son live with her husband's parents in a suburb.

in the Senbon Street area [red-light district]. This was a bad habit that manufacturers in Nishijin used to have. It was not only my father. It was a common problem. The weavers' goal was to behave in the same manner as the manufacturers. There were only a few weavers who could afford it. Those were the ones who were called "top masters" [*ōdanna*], I suppose. The average weavers could only wish for it.

MRS. K.: But then, some go to play *pachinko* at present, very often in the evening. My husband does not play *pachinko*. Some people go to *pachinko* parlors after weaving all day. I don't understand what attracts people to *pachinko*. Lots of weavers do it often. Nowadays, the nature of *pachinko* is more gambling than pleasure. What can we enjoy at our age, even when we go out?

MR. K.: Yes, this is the most popular entertainment for weavers today. In the old days, they sat by the glass doors on the porch extending to the garden [*endai*] and played *shōgi* [Japanese chess] or *go* and spent time talking. But nowadays there are no occasions for weavers like us to meet and talk together. Earlier, I used to sit on the porch in the late afternoon, especially in the summer, sometimes with a mosquito guard. We gathered there with friends to enjoy the time. Sundays, when I was young, we went fishing. I go fishing on the Kamo River [Kyoto's main river].

MRS. K.: I like shopping [laugh] with my children. We rarely go out, so our children don't go out, either.

MR. K.: I think certainly that people in Nishijin have stopped going out. Senbon Street, where Nishijin people used to walk, has become lonesome and sad. The shops and markets on Senbon Street reflect the economy of Nishijin. When the economy improves, they become prosperous. Nowadays, you don't see anyone walking on the street after 8:00 P.M. Now only the *pachinko* parlors are open. Since the number of cars began increasing, shoppers from Nishijin started going beyond Senbon Street. When the trolley was running, the stores on the street were already quiet. It must have been about ten years ago.

MRS. K.: In Kyoto, the area around Shijo Street is very lively until 1:00 or 2:00 A.M. People play with toy pistols and shoot at dolls lined up in front of them. Bang! It is said that the place near Kawaramachi Street is unsafe. My children say that the Shijo area is dangerous at night and they have to come home early. What I mean by unsafe is not a threat by pistols. What I mean is that we see youngsters hanging out. As you know, a bunch of twenty seventeen- to eighteen-year-olds will crowd together. I am not scared of them, though. We don't go out near them late at night, at any rate. We don't have to worry about that kind of thing in Kyoto. You'll find violent motorcyclists on Friday or Saturday night. They speed even on the sidewalk. I can hear them running violently on Horikawa Street near our home on Saturdays, for example. Young people are more clever now. Some people work part-time and use the rest of their time for pleasure. They have their parents buy clothes for them. We have nowhere to go.

MR. K.: Don't you think that nowadays there are too many goods? You know that children in the old days used to wear hand-me-down clothes, even when parents could afford new ones. The kids now would never put up with hand-me-downs.

MRS. K.: Young people today can earn six thousand *yen* through a part-time job. My daughter used to earn more when she tutored privately. When she became a senior in college, she quit tutoring. She worked a bit in a supermarket.

MR. K.: Parents must earn a lot. Also, there are too many goods around us. Young people want attractive goods. Parents don't discipline their children. They may say at best the children should take care of themselves, but that's it.

MRS. K.: The parents are mild. . . . A friend of mine told me that she urged her son to study. When I asked how she talked to him, she said, "Are you studying hard?" The son simply answered, "Yeah," and that was the end.

MR. K.: We didn't stay outside late at night because our parents worked at home till late. I guess there is no other way for us but sticking together as long as we are in Nishijin.

MRS. K.: I guess that we get along well with each other. Our children also behave well.

MR. K.: [to Hareven] Have you come to understand Nishijin?

MRS. K.: It is also hard for us weavers to understand each other's feelings.

MR. K.: Maybe that's one of the unique things about Nishijin.

MRS. K.: It's like everybody is hiding what's going on.

MR. K.: I must say that the main reason for that is the weavers' wage system.

MRS. K.: Depending on a person . . . someone would say that he earns a lot [of money] and others say they earn very little.

MR. K.: Of course, for salary men, too, one's salary varies from company to company, or from office to office. The Nishijin business world fluctuates all the time. It has no stability. There is no stable wage system, except that people talk with each other and draw the minimum line to base the pay rate on. I think this is why Nishijin is so complex and hard to understand. Everybody in this business wants to survive, no matter what happens. Even if some people go bankrupt, others want to survive at their expense. No matter how hard the economic depression might be, on the surface people pretend with smiles that everyone is getting along well with each other, and yet they are very competitive at the bottoms of their hearts. I think that this is the major cause of complexity. I was born in Nishijin and my wife has been involved in Nishijin for over twenty years, and it is still hard for us to understand it.

Mr. and Mrs. Shibagaki

Two Generations of Handloom Weavers

Mr. Shibagaki Yūrokurō and Mrs. Shibagaki Yoshie, his wife, were the parents of Mr. Shibagaki Mitsuo. I interviewed the three of them together, with their son's wife, Mrs. Shibagaki Kimie, present (see headnote for her interview on page 121). The senior Mr. Shibagaki died in 1987 and his wife died in 2000.

Mr. S. = Mr. Shibagaki

Mrs. S. = Mrs. Shibagaki

Y. Mr. S. = Young Mr. Shibagaki

Y. Mrs. S. = Young Mrs. Shibagaki

MR. S.: Thank you very much! I really appreciate your effort in coming to such a messy small place and to such an old man *[o-jii]* who doesn't really speak well. I stopped working full-time about five or six years ago, when the manufacturer *[oriya-san[1]]* where I worked went bankrupt because of economic recessions and the company dissolved. Our company was making *obi* and more complicated weavings. Maybe they went broke because they had overproduced. We made more *obi* than the orders we received. When I became seventy years old, I began to receive pensions as well as some unemployment insurance. Also my children gave me some money *[ko-zukai]* occasionally [laugh].[2] After I quit working for

---

1. *Oriya* and *orimoto* both mean "manufacturer."

2. It has been customary in Japan when parents get old that their children give them some petty cash as a small, casual present *(ko-zukai)* when they visit them.

FIGURE 24. Mr. Shibagaki senior weaving on his handloom. Photograph by Tamara Hareven.

FIGURE 25. Mrs. Shibagaki senior during the interview. Photograph by Tamara Hareven.

the manufacturer, some of my old friends asked me to help with their work, providing me with some weaving machines. I first declined the offer because my legs were getting weak.

My mother was already weaving when she had me in her womb. Yes! I was born a weaver. I was listening to the weaving sound when I was born [laugh]. We have been doing only handloom weaving [tebata] since my father's time. My parents first started dealing with *obi* and other products as merchants. Well, my grandfather was a peasant. He was from the Midorogaike area in Kyoto Prefecture where there are a lot of Shibagakis. My grandfather came to Nishijin after he left Midorogaike. I heard some rumors about his leaving home, but I don't know for sure what's happened to the original family place. Well, my grandfather was the oldest son. But he did so much gambling and playing around that he was driven out of the family. After he left the farm, he peddled draperies in Nishijin. He married a woman he met when doing business, and my father was born to them. I don't know for sure where my father learned to weave, but I assume he did it when he was living with one of the manufacturers *[oriya-san]*.

When I was a small child, the weaving business became prosperous and my father became independent. He opened his own new weaving establishment. In those days, things went well. But later, as the war [World War II] broke out, everything deteriorated and the prosperity of Nishijin was gone for a period of time. During the war, the *obi* industry was completely halted, because it was considered a peace industry. The whole of Nishijin stopped producing *obi*. My father worked sometimes as a cottage weaver *[chinbata]* and other times as a small independent manufacturer *[jimae]*. It is a complicated story [laugh]. He spent a lot of money playing around when the business went well, and sometimes he was not industrious enough.

MRS. S.: Once he earned a lot, he spent a lot; then he could not continue his business and he had to work as a factory weaver.

MR. S.: He was doing the business at home. He had five or six looms, and when he was busy, he rented out two looms to cottage weavers in the neighborhood. Our family worked as well. My father once took me with him to Fukui Prefecture to factories in places like Kurotomo and Shirotomo. We looked for cheaper labor there. When I was around twenty years old, in Shōwa 2 or 3 [1927 or 1928], we went to Fukui to find a factory. We were asked to do that by capital holders in Nishijin.

My father used powerlooms *[riki-shokki]* when he opened his factory in the countryside. Powerlooms were more widespread in the country-side than in Nishijin, where the handloom has dominated. In the Tango Peninsula, they mainly use powerlooms now. I don't think that any products made outside are better than those in Nishijin. My father gave his factory to someone and came back to Nishijin. He then worked as a cottage weaver, and I myself worked in a factory as a weaver. My parents worked together. My mother wove at home and I went out to work.

MRS. S.: His father didn't work a lot [laugh]. He usually told others to work, and he didn't concentrate on work himself.

MR. S.: We children sometimes had to worry about our family and brought our salary home. I had four siblings, but two of them died.

MRS. S.: He had brothers and sisters from his father's "second" wife, too.

MR. S.: [laugh] The "second" mother was my father's lover, a *ni-gō*, so-called. I haven't mentioned this yet, but when we went to Fukui, the second mother and her children also came. The story is getting compli-cated [laugh]. Well, it is an old story. I must have been embarrassed to talk about it at the time, but it's all right now. I just began to talk about my history because I referred to the second mother's children.

MRS. S.: Well, this is about the old days in Nishijin. In those days, manufacturers *[oriya-san]* took pride in having more than one woman around. So I knew some of them were spending a lot of money, more than we could imagine, but they were also making a lot of money. The manufacturers, especially men, often played a lot and were called very bad guys *[gokudō]*. They played with *geisha-san* or had two wives. They had no hesitation in doing things like that. It is not the case today, though. We have more usual families around here. Yes, in those days it was common. They were proud of behaving like that.

MR. S.: My second mother was a young girl who originally came from the countryside to work in my father's factory as a weaver. My father trained her as a weaver, and he seduced her. When my real mother learned that the girl was pregnant, she left home, leaving me behind, still a small boy. So my real mother left my father and divorced him. After she left, my mother worked mainly in a university hospital as an aid to patients, and she took care of my younger brother. Then the second mother came to live with us. In those days, two of my big brothers were with me, but as they grew up, they missed their mother more. She often came to see them. They got angry with our father's way of doing things and eventually left home. As for me, I couldn't leave.

I had to take care of those younger stepbrothers. Therefore, my stepbrothers call me "brother" even today. So I might have picked a wrong straw [a bad lot] [laugh]. I am seventy-five years old now, and I remember carrying my brother, who was four years younger than me, on my back. He is dead now. I just remember I felt some responsibility for taking care of my poor younger brothers after my big brothers left. Because my father didn't work diligently, I couldn't leave home. In those days, my father was doing some work, I suppose, because I vaguely recall seeing him leaving home with his lunch. But since my father played a lot, our family faced difficult circumstances. I think I was the unluckiest of all.

When I was twenty-one, I was drafted during the war with China [Dai-Tōa Senso] in Shōwa 14 and 15 [1939 and 1940]. I served in the military for maybe two years and came back when I was twenty-three. I thought I was old enough to get married, and I also wanted to buy a kimono for myself [laugh]. I was exempted from going to the war because I was two inches too short. When I learned that I was not to be sent to the war, I made a promise to my father. I told him that once I came back from the military, I would not leave his house until two years after my return. When I came back from the army, I went to visit my big brother's house. I think I could have lived on my own, but my brother insisted that I come, and also I missed my real brother. He often advised me to leave my father's house, saying that the longer I stayed there, the longer I wouldn't make anything of myself. I responded by telling him about my promise to my father. Had I tried to leave earlier, that might have caused problems. I was determined to keep my promise. As I had promised my father, I left home after two years. My younger brothers and sisters still continued to work at home. At that time I often went to see my mother, but I kept away from my father's house. [The second mother had become the main wife of the household.]

My wife and I got married in the eighth year of Shōwa [1933], and we will have been married for fifty years next year. I met my wife in a weaving factory [embarrassed laugh]. When we got married, I had earned some money, so we rented a house and bought all the new things. We had five children. We had to live in a small house. There were a lot of difficulties in managing family life, but they were worth coping with because it was our own family.

MRS. S.: It really was difficult.

MR. S.: It was a common thing, especially in Nishijin, to meet your future husband or wife in the factory, because both men and women worked there. There were a lot of marriages among people working in the factory. We were all in the same boat. That is, we didn't have to teach the weaving techniques to our wives. It is to the advantage of a Nishijin weaver to marry a wife who is a weaver, because she can help at home in weaving when we need help. My wife is helping right now. Women continued to work in the factory after marriage, usually until they got pregnant and their babies were born. After they had babies, they couldn't go out to work.

MRS. S.: After our first baby was born, I continued to weave at home. Well, I was weaving on powerlooms for a long time. I started on a handloom and then I used a powerloom. I had worked as an apprentice [hōkō] for a big manufacturer, and I learned the techniques of handloom weaving. When I turned twenty, I left there and I commuted from home to a factory to master powerloom weaving. Then, after our marriage, I used the powerloom.

MR. S.: Depending on the circumstances, I sometimes worked outside and I also worked at home. Well, when I worked outside, I used the loom of the manufacturer [oyakata-san] at home. I went to weave with my wife at that time. My wife used the powerloom and I wove on the handloom. So, we had two looms. If you want to earn more, the hand-loom [tebata] pays well. The powerloom doesn't yield as much profit as the handloom. When our children got bigger, my wife got a job as a yarn-spinner at the Yamazaki-ya factory in this neighborhood.

MRS. S.: I worked for ten years. . . . After that, I stayed home. I stopped weaving a long time ago. I am seventy-five now.

MR. S.: She was busy taking care of the children. Women have to do many miscellaneous things in housework, when compared to men. And that kind of work is more worthwhile than weaving. For instance, the wife has to clean around the house, go shopping; everything depends on her. That's why we can concentrate on our jobs.

MRS. S.: Well, unless I worked, we couldn't have eaten [laugh].

MR. S.: Our livelihood depended on that, so to speak.

Y. MRS. S.: I weave for both joy and money. Both! I like my work, but I don't know if I always enjoy it [working as a demonstration weaver].

MRS. S.: I just follow what is necessary—nothing special [laugh].

MR. S.: My wife has acquired sophisticated skills, and when she looks at her product, I think she likes it the more for her commitment to weaving.

Y. MRS. S.: I enjoy my work more than anything else. At this age, working gives me the most meaning in life. Well, I like having to think of the weaving strategy every time I do it. My earnings are reduced if I make any mistake, so I must be more careful. And when I look at the product that I successfully made, I feel really happy.

MR. S.: Nishijin people have said repeatedly that our work requires practice all the way until we die. We deal with different designs all the time, and we make samples whenever we get them. We examine our products and seek reactions to our samples. At this age, I can take orders for any type of weaving. When a weaver feels confident about his product, he cannot say that he is unable to make something. Production in Nishijin changes and designs change. Even at this age, we still face some difficulties that laymen wouldn't recognize, but we accept almost any order. I think you may say that the quality of Nishijin products has declined in certain respects that laymen wouldn't recognize. In the past, people could criticize us just by spreading the cloth and feeling its surface. They could tell which part was hard or soft. But now you will rarely see such a response. Even if you think you have woven a very fine cloth, you feel somewhat sad when others treat it without much care. In the past, people cared for the quality of products more than for efficiency in production. Nowadays, the treatment of quality products is the same as of non-quality products. Now the manufacturer seeks profit by asking weavers to produce more and faster, and we elderly weavers cannot compete with younger people in terms of efficiency. So younger weavers, who may lack in advanced techniques and quality but who weave faster, are more welcome. This is the tendency of today. In this respect, you may well talk about the decline in quality.

Whenever there is a war, Nishijin collapses. During the war [World War II] they issued *shichi kinrei* in Nishijin. That was an order prohibiting the use of gold or silver thread in Nishijin weaving. Suddenly we had no sales [laugh]. The Greater Asian War *[Dai-Tōa Sensō]* started in 1941. At that time, more than before, Nishijin silk production came under heavy restrictions because it was a peace industry. You had to do this and couldn't do that, or you couldn't use gold or silver thread. The government's restrictions were very severe. Because the restriction became gradually tighter, we couldn't make enough products for a living. The government recruited us to work as civilian war-industry employees *[gunzoku]* in the factories it established. I felt that Nishijin's future was gloomy. I received offers from the army to work for them. I went into the army during Shōwa 15 [1940], and the war broke out the following year. They offered us higher wages than what we were earning in Nishijin, because of our declining industry. They used more and more of the people for the war purposes. For example, you couldn't make even five hundred *yen* from your own work as a weaver, but if you accepted the government's offer, you could make six hundred or seven hundred *yen* for a day. So if you could make money in industries for war supplies *[gunju-sangyō]*, when you could hardly make any money on your own job, you wondered if you might be better off in the war-supply industry than as a lower-class worker.

The government policy was such that it restricted peacetime industries for the purpose of expanding military power. Thus the government recruited *gunzoku* for military purposes through the Employment Security Office. If you refused, they threatened to recruit you forcibly for military service. Then, if you were drafted, you would be paid by the government the lowest wage, just like pocket money. So it was much better to go for *gunzoku* than to be conscripted or drafted. And, of course, for your own family's safety, your life was much more secure and much more stable if you went as *gunzoku*, and you could send the money to your family. It was just like going on a trip at the government's expense, rather than feeling that you were a victim. What shall I say? It was an illusion or a hasty conclusion. This is how we were thinking before the war, and I went to *gunzoku*.

I went to the war in November 1940 and I came back in the autumn of 1942. I was sent to Hainan Island near Vietnam. During this period, I was paid four *yen* and twenty *sen*, including meals. I had thought that if I went over there and ate over there *kuchio azukeru* [literally meaning "keep your mouth over there"], I could better support my family. I went over there by myself, and I received all the wages, and I sent them to my family, and my family had one mouth less to feed. This was much better and we could make our income more stable. My family stayed in Kyoto. We had two children, and *obā-chan* [grandmother, meaning his wife] went to weave.

MRS. S.: Because we had to feed these children, we had to stand in line at the small lunch place *[meshiya]*. For lunch and for supper we used to take this one [young Mr. S.] and the other child to the noodle shop *[udon-ya]* and we stood in a line there [laugh]. We couldn't make food at home. It was a rationing system with food tickets. We had a little bit, but it wasn't enough. The quantity of food was limited. The government decided how much food we could have in a day. So it was very little; it was not enough for us to support our children. We went to these restaurants so we could eat something. These shops were run privately, as businesses. Restaurant owners received food that was specially distributed in this rationing system. They had rice to sell to customers. The beans were always cooked with rice. I had to stand in line to buy everything, I remember. Anything we saw that one could eat, we had to stand in line for. Even clothing we went to buy with tickets. Children used to stand in line, taking turns with each other.

MR. S.: If you lived only on the rations, you would become malnourished. The rice was served in a bowl without seconds *[mori-kiri]*. We got one big bowl with rice gruel and one bowl of miso soup and some pickles. Sometimes they gave us hot peppers or pumpkin *[nanban* or *nanka]*, and sometimes soybeans cooked together with the rice. This was in order to stretch the quantity of rice. I do remember. After the war broke out, around the eighteenth year of Shōwa (1943), my younger brother [real] who was a carpenter in Yonago City, in Tottori Prefecture, invited us to move there. So we lived in Yonago during the war. You [addressing his wife] were pregnant with Yasuko. And after the war, when Nishijin was recovering, we came back.

Because of my brother, the village people were nice to us. At that time, evacuees from other places in Japan were still rare in Yonago. The village people were curious about us newcomers from another place. They were kind. Everyone was kind at that time. And since they knew that we were not farmers, after they came to feel closer to us they brought us rice, vegetables, and fish whenever they caught them. Our children grew up easily and we did not have a hard time like Kyoto people did. The people over there didn't get used to us and the local dialect was . . . quaint, what shall I say? But once we got closer to them, we began to understand each other and communicate more naturally.

MR. S.: We lived in Yonago for about five years. We came back here when he [young Mr. S.] was in the first grade in junior high school. After the war was over, we returned to Kyoto to work for a manufacturer in Ogawa [a neighborhood within Nishijin]. They asked us if we could weave, and they offered us a house. Before we left Yonago, we played [gambled] pretty hard, so money was tight. We had to borrow money from other people in order to be able to return to Kyoto. We had some trouble with money at that time. I met the manufacturer who hired me in Ogawa during the war. During that time, I often came to Kyoto to sell rice from Yonago while I was killing time anyway. Yes, yes, it was black-market rice. They produced a lot of rice over there in Yonago. But then black-market rice did not sell well here in Kyoto, and I was sort of "between the two boards." So the manufacturer in Ogawa, to whom I sold rice, asked me if I wanted to weave velvet for him, because he knew I was a weaver. He said that the weaver whom he had hired originally had left. He asked me if we wanted to come and work for him, because he had already rented a house for us. We very much wanted to come back home, but we had no funds to build a house. It was difficult enough even just to come back here with many children. So we decided to settle down in Ogawa temporarily and thought we would decide what to do later. The manufacturer said he would pay me by the piece for as much as I wove. Also he would let me borrow money when we moved in.

I began to work and I pushed myself hard when I started to weave here. But the manufacturer gave me nothing to do for over a month after we moved in, and we had no work. We were able to eat, because we brought back enough rice. The manufacturer told me he would have a loom ready for me on such and such a day, but he didn't. Because he did not get it ready, I went to weave one or two days at our neighbors'. Then the manufacturer heard about it from my wife and came immediately to the place where I was weaving and scolded me, forgetting that he did not get the loom ready. So I told him that we had to eat and needed pocket money, too. I was forced to work elsewhere and earn less money than he had promised me, because he did not get the loom ready. When he saw me working for someone else, he finally said he would get the loom ready. He showed ill-nature. So I asked him to get it ready quickly. He felt at ease keeping us waiting, because we lived in his house. We had trouble dealing with him from the beginning. He thought we were going to cause him trouble and that we would never leave the house he gave us, because we moved in with many children.

We stayed with the manufacturer in Ogawa a little bit over a year. Of course, since the job came with a house, they made unreasonable demands on us. Sometimes we couldn't bear it, and if I responded sharply to his harassment, he would say, "Just leave, if you don't like it." So I said, "Okay, we will leave." One day, he said, "Get out of here." Since I wasn't really happy with that job, I said, "Okay, we'll get out." Then he said, "I didn't really mean it." Actually, we were getting ready to move out before he even said it. I couldn't take it any more, so I said, "I resign." And when I told him we would leave, he said I should return to him the bonus he gave me for the New Year. So I did not say anything, and I borrowed the money from other people and went to return the bonus. I asked my younger brother for money (he was a taxi driver), and I took the bonus money back to the manufacturer and gave him as much as he had demanded. When I came to him with the bonus money, he asked me to stay on and tried to prevent me from leaving. He invited me for a *gochi-sō* [feast] one night; he asked me to stay on and take the bonus money back home with me. But later, when I insisted on leaving, he said to me that I owed him more. He reminded me that he had invited me for dinner. He said, "Don't forget fifty *yen* for that meal." Actually, he didn't want us to go. He then offered me a higher wage, but I thought that I would be controlled by him and I knew by then that we could move here into this house [current residence]. I rejected his offer and moved out. I still owed him some money. So I managed to pay it back.

MRS. S.: He [husband] had worked for another Korean and he had a lot of suspicion about such promises. I didn't have a good impression of the manufacturer in Ogawa. Anyhow, I had a bad feeling about him. He was a Korean.

MR. S.: Maybe I can say it. . . . The manufacturer himself was Korean and at that time anything he did was not honest. He never did what he said. We were fed up anyway. Although I worked from early morning till late in the evening, he told us stories about other weavers who worked harder and said I should work more and should improve my efficiency. We felt we could not stay any longer, and when he told us to get out of his house, we took him at his word with the speed of a ferryboat. So we felt we had to search with all our energy and asked my wife's brother for this house [where they were still living during the interview]. First he gave us a pretty strong refusal. But I had taken good care of his father when we were in the country, so I reminded him of that and finally I got the brother to say okay.

MRS. S.: So I asked my brother to let us pay just as much as the manufacturer requested from us. So we moved here into my brother's house.

MR. S.: This house was built one hundred years ago. The landowner of this neighborhood wouldn't sell the land. All the families living around here don't own their houses.

Y. MR. S.: They had two children in Yonago and had one more when they came back to Kyoto. The last child was born here in this house.

MR. S.: I used to weave at home and my wife helped me with the jobs related to weaving. We call these "under jobs" [shita-shigoto]—for example, rolling the thread for the weft or helping with anything in preparation for weaving. After the war, hantō-jin [peninsular men, or Koreans] started the velvet industry. Velvet was used for the thongs for sandals [hana-o and geta]. At that time, since Japan was a defeated nation, Japanese people didn't do business, although they tried to deal with velvet. At that time, velvets were the main product in Nishijin. I worked in many factories. I used to work there pretty long, too.

Y. MR. S.: The loom I first wove on was brought to this house by the manufacturer I worked for. [to his parents] And what did I weave?

MR. S.: You wove tsuzure.

Y. MR. S.: Oh, right, tsuzure. I wove for that manufacturer for two years. When I quit afterward, the manufacturer said I could keep this loom.

MR. S.: The manufacturer let him keep the loom, because if he broke it down or gave it to someone, it would be trouble for him, and if we built the loom in our house and broke it down later, it would be trouble for us. So he said if we didn't mind, we could keep this loom and do with it whatever we wanted. Since that time, we took advantage of this loom. It was not so common to be given such a gift, but if you work many years, then, like in the Sanyo Company, too, weavers keep the loom when they quit their jobs.

What shall I say? [speaking to his son] Even though you hadn't done good work, the manufacturer had a good will, I guess. For us, it was such a big difference from the job I quit in Ogawa. We were very happy that this manufacturer told us very clearly that he did not need the loom and some other tools, because we might be able to use them. Anyway, it was the [customary] relationship between two Japanese from the beginning.

After that, I worked for different companies. At the company [where his son worked at the time of the interview] the people were all good and also there was a union [kumiai]. We were able to negotiate each time through the union for raising our wages or for retirement. If the company said okay, the union took care of it. That's why we felt quite comfortable. Although I say this company is good, if there were no union it wouldn't be so good. Their textiles were not the usual type. The prices of the products, which were woven by powerlooms [riki-shokki], were generally decided by the market in Nishijin. But because we were starting to produce unusual goods, we could request extra work and the manufacturers' profit was better than the others, and it was good for everyone. Yes, yes, we needed the skill, too. All the people who left there left because they had short tempers. But they discovered later that they couldn't make such good money working for other companies like they had for Sanyo. All the people say this very clearly. Well, of course the union making too many demands also influenced the situation. The company became depressed and they came to a deadlock with the weavers. They stopped their business for a while in order to adjust their stock.

After the war [World War II], the pay structure was leveled. This has lasted to this day. You get paid one thousand *yen*, for example, whether you are a factory weaver or a cottage weaver. And when the union was organized in Nishijin, the so-called small cottage weavers' *[debata]* bonuses were introduced. There are quite a few problems, but our biggest concern is the method of payment. At the time when we got married, many years ago, there were differences in pay between cottage weavers who work at home and weavers who weave in a factory *[orite]*. We used to get paid double if we wove at home, compared to the weaver who went with his lunch box *[bentō]* to the factory.

Y. MR. S.: The union helped us make a distinction between the two.

Y. MRS. S.: Basically, the payment is determined by the number of pieces woven. Some weavers rent the loom and pay for it.

Y. MR. S.: Nowadays, payment is not so different for those who own their looms and those who don't.

Y. MRS. S.: In the past, those who owned their looms got better pay, but now the system has changed and the wage difference has almost completely disappeared.

MR. S.: The rules have been modified for the benefit of the manufacturer.

Y. MRS. S.: And also there are different approaches among the manufacturers. Some give a good bonus and some don't; others give nothing. It varies from one manufacturer to another. But the basic part is the wage paid by the piece.

MRS. S.: Working hours have been reduced, right? Under the Fair Labor Standards Act, eight hours is the maximum.

Y. MRS. S.: People in Nishijin were working hard from morning till night, but since the Fair Labor Standards Act was passed, working hours have decreased. If people work late, others complain about the noise from the looms at night. In the past, people got shamed for not working, but now they get shamed for working late. Sometimes a neighbor complained that we were violating the labor law. In this way, people started to work fewer hours.

MRS. S.: People started working at 7:00 [A.M.] and worked till 10:00 or 11:00 at night. Until about 11:00, right? When we had a lot of children. . . .

MR. S.: We worked fifteen to sixteen hours a day. Anyhow, I had to feed six or seven children then [laugh]. I couldn't complain about my fatigue, working from early morning or till late at night. That was common in those days. Because the wage is paid by the piece, you get more money by working longer. But once the labor union was organized in Nishijin, emphasis was on how you get the maximum by working for shorter hours. The labor union movement pushed the demand in that direction. But recently, fewer people join the union and the business in Nishijin is not good. . . .

MRS. S.: For example, my husband had to work long hours because we had many children. Nowadays, even when they have three or four children, they can manage if the wife goes to work part-time. They can send their children to high school if the husband works only eight hours a day. I think this is progress.

MR. S.: Some families maintain their livelihood by having only the husband working, but in other families that have more than three children, both husband and wife work. The value of money has changed much. The wage I got twenty years ago for weaving plain white cloth was two thousand *yen*. It has increased about seven-fold? Six- or seven-fold, I suppose. Mostly I worked alone and supported the family. Also the living standard was lower. In those days there was nothing like a pension, but today we can get some kind of pension from the government when we get older. On the other hand, young people, even if they don't really commit themselves to hard work, can earn a decent living. So life has become easier to cope with in that regard.

Y. MRS. S.: Well, when we worked in factories, we paid premiums for the pension. Mother [meaning mother-in-law] did so, too, when she was working in a factory. And now the elderly get pensions even if they paid premiums for only a short time. We younger people cannot get a pension unless we pay the premium continually. We are now in a kind of transition period regarding the pension system, and the elderly can get it even by paying the premium for a short time.

MR. S.: When the company went out of business, I went to get compensation. I did not have to prove anything there. For young people now it is much harder. They ask you why you are not working or if you really cannot find a job. They think that it is not hard for young people to find a job. Young people would be embarrassed to go to receive compensation.

Y. MR. S.: In Japan, you can only receive compensation for one year at the most; under special circumstances, you get a sixty-day extension.

MR. S.: In times of recession, some companies do that. If they have unions, they usually tell the company to pay more because they could not work as much as they wanted to.

Y. MR. S.: In times of recession, they slow down the supply of orders and materials on purpose. I don't think they are slowing down the handlooms these days, but it might happen for powerlooms. That's true. When someone from the Kawashima Weaving Company gave a speech in the study meeting, he said that in the future Nishijin will become a "think tank," while the actual weaving will be done in rural regions and in developing countries, such as Korea and Taiwan. I think that will probably happen. I think it will gradually happen.

MR. S.: The handloom can make things that are not easily done by powerlooms. So I think the handloom can survive.

Y. MR. S.: I think that we are laborers. Anyhow, the Bureau of Labor Standards [Rōdō-Kijun Kyoku] has not come up with a clear definition. First of all, it is easier to manage weavers in the factory rather than having cottage weavers outside. Also the quality of the products, such as the design and colors of obi, can be more easily managed in a factory. We can start at 8:15 A.M. and work till 5:15 P.M.

MR. S.: When I was young, there was no such thing as labor unions. Our position was like that of day laborers. If you were told that you were no good, even if you had been working for the company, you were fired. Now, there is a labor union.

Y. MRS. S.: There is also a Fair Labor Standards Act.

MR. S.: In every respect, there are more favorable conditions to laborers today. As long as the company has a union, cottage weavers [debata] can join it like other factory workers, and they receive the same treatment. For example, when I worked for the company as a cottage weaver, I received the same retirement allowance from our reserve fund. What differs from the past is that the work is the same for factory workers and cottage weavers. However, cottage weavers used to receive a special allowance because they did the work on their own at home. It was a certain percentage of their income. That's about it. For example, the company used to pay one thousand *yen* for factory workers, for the same work, while they paid two thousand *yen* to cottage weavers. Now cottage weavers are treated the same as factory workers.

Y. MR. S.: The labor union was only limited to the factories where they have unions. When they don't have a union, they really cannot do anything. What has clearly changed since pre-war times is that now we have health insurance and a welfare pension. Before the war, we didn't have any sort of insurance at all.

MR. S.: It has nothing to do with insurance, but when I was young, before the war, everyone had to go to a taxation office to get an assessment. They told you how much you had to pay. There were many kinds of textiles. They taxed separately, according to each item. Unless you had stamps to prove that you paid taxes, it was illegal to carry products around. Now this system doesn't exist any more. We could make as much as we wanted before. One of the reasons why they abolished the system was that there were too many unauthorized products floating around. Before the war, the rolls of cloth *[date-maki]* that we made in one day could not be sold without the stamps. If one tried to sell them without stamps, he could get caught immediately. Without paying taxes, we could not sell the products in the market. This didn't restrict our production at all, but if we wanted to sell any products in the market the first thing we had to do was to get those stamps at a taxation office. But after the war we could sell anything before paying taxes. That's the big difference. Though the government tried to restore the old system, it did not happen due to the opposition of the representatives to the Diet from Kyoto. After I quit the company. . . .

MRS. S.: You played, and you were killing time while receiving unemployment insurance. . . .

MR. S.: I was over seventy years old — I just went over the peak of seventy — so I relaxed with unemployment insurance for a year. Also I had an annuity *[kōsei-nenkin]*. Although this annuity was just a small amount, I also had some help from my children. So rather than calling what I do now a job, I would call it physical exercise for the elderly. Yes, after that I have worked properly less and less . . . and also my children told me, "Don't push yourself." Although I don't mean to avail myself of their advice. . . . Well, I try not to work so hard. . . . Generally, we call this kind of work *naishoku*. It means that you go out to work part-time. We also call it *arubaito* [means part-time work, derived from German "Arbeit"]. The manufacturer brings the materials and comes to pick up the product, and we don't need to go out. So when I don't like to do it, I refuse it. For example, I say, "No, because I don't feel well." And I don't do it if I don't like to. Today when I wake up, my granny [*obā-san*—his wife] and I look at the travel guide. If we think it's fun to go somewhere, we just fly away together [laugh]. It's really easygoing . . . just doing whatever I like. . . . Rather than calling it a job, it is my physical exercise.

It has been fifty years since we married. Thanks to the Gods, although various things happened in fifty years, it is going to be our fiftieth anniversary in August next year [all laugh]. We have too many memories, although we had more hardships than good times. Well, but our hardships were also a part of joy. Although various things happened, well . . . thanks to [the Gods], the two of us have been healthy until now like this, and we have five children. All of them have been making an effort; none of them are so bad. Only these children make my life worth living. Well, when we had the youngest one here. . . .

MRS. S.: That time was the worst in our lives.

MR. S.: That time was the worst time in our economic conditions, yes. She [wife] didn't go to the hospital; she delivered the baby here. We couldn't pay for the midwife. After all . . . the midwife "closed her eyes" [ignored the lack of pay]. On the day of the birth, I went to borrow one *shō* of rice from her [wife's] brother and also went to gather the firewood because we didn't have any. Well, that was the hardest memory. I went to work, and when I came back home that evening, our neighbor told me that my wife had swept and cleaned here, and that day she delivered the baby. Our neighbor was so surprised, and asked her, "Are you okay doing such things?" and she advised her not to do it.

MRS. S.: I was doing housework; since the baby was born, I couldn't rest well.

MR. S.: Well, when I review our life after being together for fifty years, I really think today is comfortable, yes! Our children have been making an effort, each of them, and also they worry about their parents; they ask how we are. It is the best time now with my health [laugh].

MRS. S.: Well, me, too, the same way. This is the best time for feeling easygoing [laugh].

MR. S.: The two of us go wherever we want to.

MRS. S.: It's really easygoing . . . [laugh].

MR. S.: Conditions have become better for old people. We elderly not only get health insurance and benefits from pensions, but we can also use city transportation without charge. And we don't spend money on things other than what we use. Medical care is free and we receive a welfare pension. We are more privileged in every respect. We receive money even if we forget about it. When we are tired or sick, we receive free medical care. So it is a lot better for old people.

Y. MRS. S.: Although the government takes care of older people, I still think that children have to support their parents. Mentally, I don't think that has changed. Life in Nishijin has gotten better through the creation of unions and the Fair Labor Standards Act. Even when we did not have unions, some people actively negotiated with the company to pay us bonuses. Under pressure, the company paid a little. So I don't think it has gotten worse. Even though there is not a union, the companies cannot ignore these demands. Such companies will not be able to attract good weavers. So they pay a little, as well.

Y. MR. S.: The standard of living in Nishijin never gets better than the average. But as it gets better in other places, the standard here follows the trend. When I was twenty years old, not many households had washing machines, and no one had a television set. Over the past twenty years, the standard of living has gotten much better. Since twenty-five years ago, working hours have been cut down. The standard has risen in every respect.

Y. MRS. S.: It has been changing. When I was small, there was no water tap in the house and there was no gas.

Y. MR. S.: Since the standard of living has risen, it has become impossible to live without the new amenities. Over the past twenty-five years, bicycles were replaced by motorcycles, and motorcycles were replaced by cars. In Nishijin the standard of labor is still below the average. As far as factory workers go, I don't think there is much difference.

Mr. and Mrs. Sakurai

Handloom Weavers

Mr. Sakurai Takesumi and Mrs. Sakurai Akiko, his wife, were both employed as highly skilled handloom weavers in a weaving company at the time when I first met them. Mr. Fujiwara, who worked in the same place, introduced us. By the time I had the opportunity to interview them in their home, Mr. Sakurai had quit his job at the weaving company and worked as a night guard near his home. His wife continued to work side by side with another weaver in the adjacent workroom, where Mr. Fujiwara was working. I first talked with Mrs. Sakurai briefly during the lunch break at the factory. I subsequently interviewed them in their suburban home, halfway between Kyoto and Osaka. The factory where they worked, and where Mrs. Sakurai continued to work, was in a large shed in the historic part of Nishijin. Only six weavers were working there at the time of my first visit. The number declined to four the following year, after Mr. Sakurai retired and another weaver took leave because he was injured in a car accident. Mrs. Sakurai retired two years later. The interview took place in the home of Mr. and Mrs. Sakurai.

Mr. S. = Mr. Sakurai

Mrs. S. = Mrs. Sakurai

MR. S.: This tapestry came from my family. I took it to the Kyoto National Museum. They told me that it is something precious. My ancestors used to work for Nakayama Dainagon [a noble family connected to the Imperial Palace], so I think that they were able somehow to get this. My ancestors lived somewhere near Arashiyama [west of Kyoto] for a long time. In the Meiji Period, after the occupational classification of families was abolished, my ancestor lost his job at the imperial court [kyūtei]. He did not know how to do anything, because he had been a court attendant, and he was really troubled. Then my grandfather learned how to weave for a living. He became a cottage weaver [debata]; so did my father, and he worked at home. They worked for a manufacturer in Nishijin. My father died when I was two years old, and my mother left for her parents' home. I was brought up by my grandparents, and after I grew up I went to the army. When I came back from the war [World War II], I did not have a place to live. I lived with my relatives. I learned how to weave with a relative who had a branch company [bunke], as a cottage weaver. My family is the main house [honke].[1] My father was the oldest son. After his death, I represented the status of honke. I was doing cottage weaving at my grandmother's house. Then the Greater East Asian War [Dai-Tōa Sensō] broke out and we all had to stop weaving. I worked in Maizuru [a town in the Tango Peninsula] for the war industries. Then I was drafted, and later came back from the war to live with my relatives. I could not do cottage weaving at my relatives' house, so I went out to weave in a factory. I changed manufacturers many times. I did handloom weaving, necktie weaving, and other kinds of weaving. My entire weaving career was thirty years long. It is the only thing I could do. I used to work for some other manufacturers before I started weaving for the weaving company I currently work for, where I have worked sixteen years. At the company I work for I used to weave the highest-quality product. I retired from that weaving company on August 10 last year. I retired right after I saw you last time.

MRS. S.: Another weaver came to take my husband's place on the newest loom, but the product did not sell well at all. So the manufacturer changed back to a simple loom and the weaver has been working on the same type of things as I do. He helps me when the loom has to be fixed. For one week after my husband left, I felt lonely when I had to work all by myself. After that, Okamoto-san joined me, so I am okay.

---

1. In the Japanese succession system, the oldest son usually succeeds the father and heads the main house and family business (honke). Another brother or relative may establish a branch (bunke).

MR. S.: Since the market has declined, the profits of the company I work for are less than 50 percent. The market for products of the sophisticated loom is even worse. I suffered from an occupational disease — arthritis — so I decided to retire and receive *nenkin* [retirement pension], which is much easier for me. I suffered from pain in the shoulders and the waist. If I wanted to work, I could have worked. But the profit was too low, so I decided to stop working. Of course, I am not satisfied with the way they treated me. The company I work for is very changeable according to business conditions. I don't really like my current job as a guard. I have to work for twenty-four hours every other day, even during the New Year. The job itself is easy, but I cannot take days off when I want to. I can have meals at the office, and I can take a nap from 11 P.M. to 6 A.M. I bet that my wife is comfortable when I am not home, because I take up space in the house [meaning he keeps her busy] [laugh].

MRS. S.: We have other members of the family living here, so I do not feel lonely even when he is not home. I leave home at 7 A.M. for work; I go by bicycle to the station. It takes me an hour by train to my work-place. I stop working a little before 6 P.M., and I take the bus and train to get back home. I am back home by 7 P.M. I work even on Saturdays. My son's wife cooks for us. I can have dinner right after I get home. When my husband used to work with me at the company where I cur-rently work, I used to come back an hour earlier than he did. We used to work together for a different manufacturer when our two children were small. Since my son got married and came to live with us, I can devote myself just to my work, because my son's wife does the house-hold work.

MR. S.: I used to cook and wash when our children were small. But after they grew up, I became lazy. Even though I did not do household work, I prepared things for the next day's job, such as winding the thread for the weft [*nukimaki*], which took an hour. I took this work back home with me, so that we would be ready to start weaving right away at the factory next morning. This way, we could save time to make more *obi,* and we were paid more according to the piece rate [*deki-daka*].

MRS. S.: I do the preparatory work now at the factory.

MR. S.: We have one hour for lunch time at the factory; that is when we smoke. We are supposed to work from 8 A.M. to 5 P.M. But if one wants, he can go to play *pachinko* just like Fujiwara-san. In principle, we are not supposed to do that, but the factory where I work is separate from the office, so we have no supervision by them. I do not think that the company where I work is so alert to our pace of work. Their business is not going well right now. So they do not expect us to work so hard. Fujiwara-san may be able to make more money by playing *pachinko* [laughing facetiously].[2]

MRS. S.: The kind of weaving that I do is doing well in the market. They change the color each time, but I do not have to wait to get my next order. The design is the same, and I get used to it. But I have to change the color arrangements, so I cannot work faster. Physically, it is not easy for me to weave on a handloom, but I can make as much money as men do; there is no gap between males and females in terms of pay.

MR. S.: In other fields, women are paid less. In Nishijin, the skill is valued in itself.

MRS. S.: I make more money than Fujiwara-san does [laugh]. He often sneaks out for *pachinko*. He takes lots of breaks. I work strictly for eight hours, and I work intensively; I get tired just as much.

MR. S.: In a sense, he [Fujiwara] is a happy person, because he does what he wants to do. I heard that he sometimes makes money from *pachinko* and takes it back home, though.

MRS. S.: I was born in Kyoto, but my grandparents came from Tsuruga [a town on the Japan Sea]. My father came to Kyoto when he was young. My mother was born in Fukui, and they got married by arrangement and then came to Kyoto. I am the only one in my family who kept weaving. My siblings got different jobs, but one of the younger ones married a wholesaler for *kimono [naka-gai]*. She is sewing *obi,* not weaving. My four brothers are running a company for collecting wine bottles. Another sister married a businessman in Yokohama. He sells shutters for garages and stores.

I had the responsibility for taking care of the younger children. I only graduated from elementary school. After that, I lived in the countryside

---

2. This statement comes from the first interview, when Mr. Sakurai was still working in the factory.

in Fukui Prefecture during the war, in order to avoid the bombings. I had to help my family. My father had to work for the army and my mother used to farm. After our father came back from the army, he came first to Kyoto and worked alone for a few years. I came to Kyoto next and lived with him. After we found a place, we called all the other members of our family. I was working as a live-in housekeeper with bad pay. So I decided to start weaving. I started weaving at age eighteen before we had a baby. I learned how to weave from one of my father's acquaintances in Nishijin. They pay differently for weaving in different companies, so I moved later to another place to weave for better pay. I was weaving on the handloom. There I met my husband. Yes, it was a love marriage.

MR. S.: In fact, I could have married much earlier if the war had not occurred. I had a girlfriend when I was working in Maizuru. We used to live in the same factory dormitories, but at that time close relationships between boys and girls were strictly prohibited. I used to correspond with her even after I joined the army. But since soldiers had to move from one place to another, our correspondence did not last long. After I came back from the war, I wrote her. She replied to me right away and said that she was ready to come to Kyoto to live with me. I was so frightened by her reply, for I had no place and no money to receive her. I wrote back and asked her to stay with her parents in Maizuru for a while, but I did not hear anything from her any more. If the times had been peaceful, I could have married much younger.

I came back from the army in Shōwa 21 [1946]. I was twenty-seven and my wife was nineteen when we got married. I think it was normal for a man to be married at twenty-seven. Nowadays, some students get married early, though. It was right after the war, so age twenty-seven was normal. I came back from the army at the age of twenty-three. Then I had a hard time finding food every day and I could not think of marriage at all. I "forced" her to marry me [joking]. For us, no such thing as entertainment existed. My parents were already dead and her parents were having a hard time. We had to buy everything to set up a household, to acquire things such as chopsticks and rice bowls for our new home.

MRS. S.: We got married without any preparation, and we had to buy every single thing while both of us were working. We started living in a company house [shataku] and then moved to a rented house. Finally, after our children grew up, we could buy our own house. This house is the second one, for we used to have our house in Takagamine [a rural area outside Kyoto]. We bought this house six years ago.

Even when I was pregnant, I kept weaving. I took leave just in the month when the child was due. I just took a one-month leave after the delivery. I had to stop weaving when I nursed my babies. I have two children. I took my babies to my workplace, because we used to live in a house in the factory complex. I kept a box beside the loom in which I laid my baby down. I think it was common for women in Nishijin to do that. Most weaving women kept working while taking care of their children in their workplace, I think. Nowadays, they can entrust their babies to nurseries. There was no nursery at that time. My mother raised seven babies in that way [keeping them near the loom]. She was a cottage weaver at home. It was easier to raise children and weave at home than to do it in the factory. I wished I could have worked at home, but it was not easy to find a house suitably built for weaving. We need a large space with a high ceiling to place a loom in the weaving house [oriya dachi].

I raised my children at my workplace till they reached elementary school age. The company had a large yard, so my children used to play there with the children of other workers. My husband was also working at the same place. We were four couples working together, and the other couples also kept their children at the workplace. Our children were about the same age, so they played together. When my children became junior high school students, we left the company house and rented our own house.

MR. S.: The manufacturers preferred to keep married couples in their dormitories, where both husband and wife worked for the company. There was a divorced woman with a child living in the dormitory, though. There were apartments only for women weavers in front of the Imamiya Shrine in the Nishijin district. The manufacturers had to hire young people from the countryside, because they could not expect enough youths from Kyoto to work in Nishijin. First we were weaving gold brocade [kinran] for the Hosoi Company. Kinran was mainly for Buddhist priests' robes and ritual clothes.

MRS. S.: We also wove neckties, and then came to the town of Sakurai [near Osaka] to make obi. When we worked for the Hosoi Company in Nishijin, we used to live in the company housing. It used to be in Takagamine, but it does not exist any more. Some people commuted to work. Since the pay was low, the employers tried to provide company housing [shataku] in order to attract more weavers. It was very difficult to get housing at that time. They paid us very little, so that we did not have to pay for electricity and gas. They did not charge us rent for living there. There was no difference in the pay between us and the workers who commuted. We had only a four-and-a-half *tatami* room, though. [The size of apartments is measured by the number of *tatami* mats per room.] There were four houses in the factory. Each family had a four-and-a-half *tatami* room, and we had to share just one communal kitchen outside our rooms. We had another room within the factory building, though. Our house was narrow and long, just like a "sleeping place of the eel" [unagi-no-ne-doko]. Once you opened the door, our room was in the innermost place of the house. We shared a toilet with the other families. We used the public bath. The two of us and the two children crowded the small room. We had to cook quickly because all the families were cooking at the same time.

MR. S.: We used wood fuel to cook rice, and charcoal in a portable clay pot [shichirin] to cook other foods outside the house. Even when it rained, we had to cook outdoors. We used an empty kerosene can in which we put the wood in order to cook the rice. Every family used such a pot for cooking at that time.

MRS. S.: Of course, we also did washing, and the washing machine did not exist then. So I washed clothes by hand in a wooden tub. I did shopping, too. My husband helped me in some ways.

MR. S.: [to Hareven] I hope that you don't expect Japanese men to behave in the same way as American men. I believe that there is a big cultural gap between Japan and America.

MRS. S.: My father did not help my mother at all, though she was working. She did everything by herself.

MR. S.: These days, many couples both work, and they help each other. As far as I know through television movies, American husbands do much domestic work and they tell their wives every day, "I love you." That is impossible for us, even if we love our wives in our hearts. I used to help her [wife] by doing laundry when we had small babies, but people often laughed at me, saying, "Look! A man is washing clothes!" I did not care what they said to me. I had to help her when our children were small. I did my best as a Japanese husband. At that time, we did not have the notion of getting together with other people for recreation.

MRS. S.: We only had one day off on the first and fifteenth day of each month. We worked even on Sunday at that time. We started weaving at 8:00 A.M. and finished at 6:00 P.M. We sometimes visited my parents and relatives.

MR. S.: In those days, I did nothing in particular for recreation. We sometimes took a walk with our children. We had no money to spend for fun. Once a year, we took a small trip with all the members of the company on chartered tourist buses. We only made a day trip to Nara and Hirakata. In this company, we made one overnight trip to a hot spring once a year—to Tottori—and to Shirahama in Wakayama.[3]

MRS. S.: We enjoyed these places. Only the people working in the company could participate in the trips, because the company paid some money. If a spouse was not working at the company and wanted to join us, they had to pay the full charge of the trip. Our employer started doing this about fifteen years ago, after many other modern business companies started treating employees better. At present, our employer has stopped doing that due to the depression. Very few companies in Nishijin organize trips for their workers nowadays.

MR. S.: They stopped it about three or four years ago. Employees used to pay installments every month for trips, and the manufacturer paid one million *yen* to cover the difference. There is a big difference in the scale of business between Japanese and American companies. The way of thinking here is also very different from America.

MRS. S.: The company where I work used to have these trips so that workers would feel closer to each other. It was quite recent that we started this sort of recreation. No such thing existed at all for cottage weavers in the old times. My mother had no chance to enjoy trips like we did. Old weavers in Nishijin were miserable. Since the former prime minister, Mr. Tanaka, encouraged the rapid growth of the economy, we

3. These are popular tourist and resort sites in Japan.

started these modern ways. Before that, we did not have anything like that. My mother was also paid by the piece, but she did not have any regulation of working hours. So she used to weave very late at night. After she put her children to sleep, she kept working until midnight. She did not get any bonus pay, though, or overtime. She had a holiday only two days a month. She had no health insurance and no pension from the government. Later my mother became eligible for a pension. Only workers who had worked a long time were eligible to get support from the company to cover insurance and pensions.

MR. S.: After the war, Nishijin introduced its own insurance and pension system. Then the weavers were supported by the manufacturer for the charges for those programs, but people who joined the company about ten years ago were not supported by them. No cottage weaver today gets any support from their company.

MRS. S.: Since three years ago, we have not been receiving any support or any bonus. They pay bonuses to the office workers, but not to the weavers. I think the workers in big companies are paid a bonus, too.

MR. S.: My employer hates the labor union. If weavers belong to it, they are treated badly by the employer. The manufacturer accepts what the weavers demand through the union, but then, if the weavers make small defects in their work, the employer cuts their pay. My employer avoids firing employees because they have to pay them extra retirement money. But they plot something so that the weaver will leave on his own. Now none of the weavers in the company where I work belongs to the union. Workers in big companies do belong to the union.

I heard that the union in one company does strike sometimes. Anyway, in Nishijin office workers are treated much better than weavers. Originally, all big companies started from very small-scale businesses. The boss arranged the colors, wove, and went out to sell the work by himself. As the business grew gradually, he had to employ people to help him. And finally the business really became big. The relationships between the employer and the weavers were interdependent and humane. When weavers had troubles, the employers tried to do the best to help them. The Japanese character for "person" consists of two strokes. One of them is the employer and the other is the weaver. Either of the strokes can be left out. We have another character that means "between." It is applied to the first character to construct the whole term of "human being" *[ningen]*. So the two strokes in the first character are *orimoto* [manufacturer] and *orite* [weaver], and the second character in between is "office worker," who should be ranked lower than us. But in Nishijin things are upside down now [meaning that the traditional paternalistic relations are not maintained any more].

Something basic is wrong with the working system in Nishijin. The company officials tell us the color arrangements, according to the way they are told by the president of the company. The scale of business has changed in Nishijin. When the employer has a few looms, he can keep close contact with the weavers. But when the number of looms gets really large, the situation also changes. The system of Nishijin industry originated from the direct relationship between the employers and the weavers. But now many salary men [administrators] in the company stand between us and the employer. They are treated much better than the weavers. This change probably took place after the war [World War II]. They will not be able to get any good weavers in the future.

MRS. S.: Office workers are paid from the profits of the work done by weavers. They [the company] are forgetting that.

MR. S.: In the old days, office workers were treated just like *detchi* [the lowest-ranked employees or apprentices].

MRS. S.: Nowadays, a *detchi* is treated better than a weaver *[orite]*

MR. S.: As I said, my parents died quite early, so I don't know much about their working conditions, but I guess that my grandmother had a good time working as a weaver. When she was sick, the employer visited and consoled her. This is impossible, nowadays. The human relations have changed a lot since then.

MRS. S.: My mother did not tell me very much about that, but I think that they had much closer relations with the manufacturer. When they needed money, or when their relatives got sick, the employers used to support them—so I heard. Even now, a small-scale manufacturer with about ten weavers has good relations with the weavers, I guess. Big companies like the one where I work have changed greatly, and they only run after profits.

MR. S.: The working conditions were the same as today, since weavers were paid by the piece. But at that time they were paid better than ordinary salary men. We are paid less than salary men now. In the present, conditions are easier for weavers but the wages are low. A carpenter is paid fifteen thousand *yen* per day. We used to be paid better than carpenters. Still, by comparison with the past, our life has improved.

The industrial system is based on capitalism, and in capitalism the human relationships have disappeared. The company managers can make lots of money when the market is going well. When I was young, I do not think that bonus pay existed. But the salary men are now given a bonus. When the market gets worse, we become victims because we do not have a labor union or any other organization to fight through. What we are doing in Nishijin is still feudalistic. Nishijin is functioning on domestic demands for goods *[naiju]*; it does not have foreign markets. We cannot export *kimono* to foreign countries. Modernization has improved many other fields in Japan, but not in Nishijin. Even compared to other craftsmen, such as carpenters, we are having a harder time. When the domestic demand is not going well, craftsmen have to face hard times first. Nishijin in particular has to confront these difficulties.

MRS. S.: Some companies build their factories in the countryside and employ people from the surrounding villages. Then housewives and young daughters would not have to come to Kyoto. They are paid less than the workers in the city.

Mrs. Yasuda and Mr. Yasuda

*Manufacturer's Widow and Manufacturer's
Mother; Manufacturer, Manufacturer's Son,
and Manufacturer's Father*

---

*Mrs. Yasuda Toshie, age seventy-five at the time of the interview, still worked
eight hours a day in the Yasuda Tsuzure Company, of which her husband
had been president. Her son, Mr. Yasuda Genichiro, was president at the time
of the interview, and her twenty-seven-year-old grandson (who was present at
the interview) was being groomed for the presidency. The Yasuda Company is
typical of a traditional family business in Nishijin. It was turned into a corporation after World War II, but continues to be owned and run by the
family. Mrs. Yasuda's daughter-in-law, wife of the current president, has
worked alongside the senior Mrs. Yasuda. The grandson's wife was slated to
start her training as soon as her children started going to nursery school. Two
years after interviewing Mrs. Yasuda, I interviewed her son, Mr. Yasuda,
then president of the Yasuda Company and vice president of the Nishijin
Textile Industrial Association. By that time, the senior Mrs. Yasuda had
retired but continued to come into the company from time to time in an
advisory capacity. The Yasuda Company is known in Nishijin for its original,
high-class tsuzure weavings, all of which are done on the traditional handloom
without the jacquard. I was first introduced to the Yasuda Company by the
director of the Nishijin Textile Industrial Association. Mrs. Yasuda's Japanese
style of discourse reflects extreme modesty, using third person rather than first
when she refers to herself. Mrs. Yasuda died in 1999.*

MRS. YASUDA

In Nishijin, the head of the company takes care primarily of the man-ufacturers' union and sales, and his wife, in the background, engages in management of the factory and in blending colors. Most of the time, this is the way in a Nishijin family.

Nishijin is such a place where family members work together. All textile families are busy. Everyone in the family helps each other. The men mainly work in public areas, such as sales and management, whereas other family members look after the weavers. This is what you find in most of the Nishijin family companies wherever you go. How-ever, we do separate our family life from our work. We [individual family members] receive wages for our work here. The working hours are between 9:00 A.M. and 6:00 P.M. Everyone keeps his schedule. Now I live with the president and his wife [son and daughter-in-law]. And this child [grandson] got married last year and has a child.[1]

My husband frequently went to handle the association's business, and his own business tended to be neglected. But our business had to be taken care of for our livelihood, so we hired craftsmen and all of us took part in the work. The current president of the company [her son] has also mastered the skills well. Otherwise he could not use employees, because he needs to explain everything to them. He has also become a member of the board of directors of the Nishijin Textile Industrial As-sociation since my husband's death. Now my grandson manages the business along with my son, especially when the president is still so busy with the affairs of the association.

The president tends to be out often—for example, he goes to other partners' stores and on sales and business trips. So the rest of us talk with each other and decide how to divide the work. We say, "This person is good at this, that person is not good at that." People have individual characteristics in this business, and we are very careful about this.

I teach the young weavers how to weave and I assign them work. They live in our dormitory. Once the weavers get married and have families, they move out of the dormitory. They work at home [as cottage weavers] and return here with their products in the evening. When I give them their next work assignment, I instruct them as to the colors

1. The grandson says, "So my wife will go to work and learn the business. Then grandmother will help take care of the child."

and how the work should be done. They take the materials back home to work. Then they bring back the products. The ones who live far away mail their products to us. I make a package of the raw materials with written instructions. I send the package back to them. They make the next product according to my instructions. We also discuss on the phone if they have any questions.

In other kinds of business in Nishijin, once they select a design, they repeatedly weave the same design, but with different colors, and so on and so on, for 100 to 150 lengths required for *kimono*. In the case of *tsuzure,* we look at the weavers' work and decide who is good at it and who isn't. Then we give each design to the weaver who is best suited for it. We look at the weavers' personalities, not only their skills. I determine the assignment of work. Since I have done it for so long, I haven't forgotten how to choose who fits which work, who is uniquely qualified for a unique product, and who likes what kind of work. For example, some weavers prefer to weave landscape designs and others prefer human figures. There are different kinds of patterns and designs. That's the uniqueness in this business. The machine-woven cloth is done in accordance with patterns from the punch cards for the jacquard *[mon-gami].* If two weavers weave exactly the same design pattern on the jacquard, the product is the same and looks the same. On the other hand, in the case of *tsuzure,* even if they weave the same design, the end product is never the same. The individual expression in the weaving differs from weaver to weaver.

We recruit our young employees through the high schools. My grandson selects healthy, young people. All of us decide together. [Grandson says he decides 80 percent of the time whom to employ.] In the old times, I also supervised the dormitory for the weavers. Even now, we have a dormitory. Each room is independent. Those whom we hired recently are at least high school graduates and junior college graduates. Some come from a technical design school. They are mostly over twenty years old, and they live by themselves.

Yes, yes, before World War II, we did require much more supervision over the young weavers. We have had this building since pre-war times, with these floors, too, where the workers live in their own rooms. As for their food, we hired someone to cook for them. But nowadays they say they find it stifling to live here. Now there is a Western-style building next door that has five floors. The fifth floor is for single employees and the others are for married couples. The couples stay there temporarily until they can purchase their own houses. In the meantime, both husband and wife work and save up for the down payment for their housing loan. Then they move out to where they have their own family life—where they like. There are some couples where both husband and wife work for us after their children grow up. Also some work at home while their children are still young.

A long time ago, I did prepare the food for the employees. I used to do it even after World War II. But it got beyond what I could take care of. Then we had someone who could cook come over and prepare the food for us, as well as for them. We followed this pattern for a while. Ever since the building next door was built, each worker has had her own room in a women's dormitory. We have another house for a men's dormitory near the Imperial Palace.

I have acted as a go-between for marriages for my weavers many times. We always serve as a go-between for our weavers, especially for the ones who meet each other in our company [laugh]. I also listen to their various problems. Everyone . . . well [hesitation], it may be a bit too much to say, but many of them have come to see me with their problems, as if I were their parent . . . even about their personal problems. And the president took care of their housing, and guaranteed their loans to buy a house, and other things.

Nowadays, there are advertisements for financing and other loans for housing, aren't there? The weavers think about how to borrow money. Then we advise them what to do, and if they are short of money, we borrow money from a bank on their behalf. The current president takes care of this sort of financing for those weavers who have worked diligently and who want to spend a lifetime in this business.

Well, until twenty-five years ago, most of the *tsuzure* business was managed in individual manufacturers' houses, where the head of the company slept in the main room and the employees in the next room. Even now, you can find this kind of household. But this becomes stifling for each other. When we had this house built twenty-five years ago, we decided to make the third floor a dormitory. We decided not to put two people in the same room. This is likely to cause trouble between them. So we made one room for each employee. We even had to check who was in and out at night. After this, we expanded the dormitory next door and had these employees transferred into it. The dormitory has separate rooms for each person. It is apartment-style. They can lock the door whenever they go out, even on a holiday. In the old days, whenever someone went in or out, he had to check in and out. Now they can come with their key whenever they return. In modern days, people wouldn't work for you otherwise.[2]

I did not grow up in a Nishijin family. I grew up in Nara Prefecture. My father was a Buddhist priest for the Shingon sect. What brought me to Kyoto [laughing in embarrassment]? What shall I say . . . the person who my older sister knew was the owner of the Shungetsu restaurant in Nara. My husband had lots of customers and used to take business trips to Nara to show his products to them. They often took him to the restaurant, and the owner arranged the marriage for us as a go-between.[3] I was eighteen when I married. I had been to Kyoto before. But this was the first time I went to live there.

Once I got married and my husband was running the family business, my husband's mother told me that I, too, had to learn the family business. Then she taught me how. After that, my husband branched out from the main family. He was the second son. The first son — my husband's older brother — inherited the family business. But he didn't like it. Then he passed away and his son got some sort of a job at a court-house in Osaka. Then my husband and our family — a branch family — succeeded to the business. At that time, when I married, my husband's company was only a family business. He was the so-called president. My husband started the business in 1934 when he branched out and moved to the Nishijin area. I was about twenty-six years old at that time.

About twenty-some years ago, the company became incorporated and we made my son president. My husband's father was the chairman of the board. When my husband inherited the company, I was about twenty-six. I had two little children at the time. The current president was in first grade then. His younger sister wasn't born yet. When she was born, we hired a woman called *myoto-san* [helper], and she took care of her until she entered elementary school.

In those days, we were only three of us — my husband, my son, and

2. The grandson says, "The dormitory was established twenty-five years ago, at the same time that this company was incorporated. The company didn't exist at this site twenty-five years ago. It used to be at Karasuma-Oike streets [closer to downtown Kyoto]. There we lived and worked in an ordinary house. When I was a child, my grandfather, grandmother, parents, and I lived there. The workshop was across from our house. We had no space to build such a dormitory then."

3. A go-between is the "broker" who arranges marriages at the request of the young man's or woman's family. When Mrs. Yasuda describes her own role as a go-between for her current or former employees, it is a more informal, ceremonial role, where even couples who meet on their own and decide to get married use a go-between as an intermediary between their parents.

myself—and we had a small business. In addition, several male weavers commuted to our house. Then the war broke out [World War II]. All those boys were drafted and left for the army. Then we closed our business for a while. After that, when General MacArthur came around, we decided that we should no longer be inactive and slowly resumed the business.[4] At that point, we had business allies and all of us were saying that we would amount to nothing if we did nothing. We also thought that we should get a ration of silk and decided to establish an association of manufacturers. Thirty-some people gathered and started an association. After that, we talked about needing an executive director. They nominated my husband and made him the executive director. The Nishijin Textile Industrial Association was created after World War II. At that time, the silk had to be allotted and rationed. My husband used to be the chairman of the association, and he determined the allotment of silk and what kinds of products to make. Then the supply of silk became unrestricted and the association was dissolved. However, the association of manufacturers was rebuilt after the war by all the manufacturers and continues today.

My older sister told me that my marriage in Nishijin would be hard and troublesome, and so she suggested that I marry a Muromachi man [a wholesaler who lives and trades in *kimono* in the wholesalers' district on Muromachi Street]. I had no idea what Nishijin was about and what a wholesaler's family in Muromachi was like then. Had I married a Muromachi wholesaler, my life would have been different. It would have been utterly different. The tasks of a wholesaler are to stock the finished cloth and sell to retail shops, and in Nishijin it is to manufacture and sell the products to Muromachi. You can't get a real picture of what a Nishijin manufacturer's life and what a Muromachi wholesaler's life are about until you become part of their family. I grew up in a priest's family, and so I didn't know the differences. I think now it would have been just the same . . . just the same. The old Japanese saying is that one goes into a bog for a lifetime. The life would have been similar. The Muromachi district has its own difficulties. All my married life, I was always absorbed in this work and so I can't say particularly when was the hardest time.

Nishijin has undergone a great change. What shall I say . . . Nishijin

---

4. The grandson says, "During the war, extravagance was forbidden. We were not allowed to make any luxurious products. Only so-called daily necessities were permitted. All of us closed down our businesses, because what we were making was high-class and extravagant. Five to six of our employees returned home and the men left for the army. We halted our business for a while, until the prohibition was lifted."

used to be all family businesses. Now the businesses have become in-corporated. The contents of the business have changed, too. Neverthe-less, the backbone still remains in the family businesses. Several family businesses are sometimes under the same corporation. The family busi-ness makes the best products. There has not been much change in the Nishijin community itself. I think that most of the people in Nishijin are good. They are nice. It is an easy place to live in. You can still find the old relationship, like a parent and a child, between *oyakata* [manu-facturer] and *orite* [weaver]. The major strength of Nishijin is in the family business.

The economy doesn't really affect Nishijin too much. Large busi-nesses may go bankrupt in a depression. By contrast, Nishijin stands strong in such a time. It is said that in Nishijin we will never go bank-rupt, because everybody has a small business. For instance, in our neigh-borhood, if you visit during the daytime, many would be out to work. Everybody—wives and their husbands—is out to work. We also have several neighbors who are housewives and they come to work for us part-time. The husbands may go to different jobs, whereas the wives work for textile companies. Even grandmothers and grandfathers can find work in Nishijin. You can find families where the young generation doesn't want to work in weaving. Some young people may switch their jobs after their elders pass away. But you also find people who would like to inherit only this kind of work. All of our employees really enjoy this work. We continue to have contact with families of weavers who have worked for us for several generations.

MR. YASUDA

I turned our family weaving establishment into a corporation. Our busi-ness was started after the Meiji Restoration as a private family enterprise. During the Meiji, Taishō, and early Shōwa Periods, it was a private business all the time. It is now managed as a corporation. The founder in the Meiji Period was my grandfather. I am the third generation.[5] As a corporation, we have to be concerned with labor conditions under the law of a joint-stock company *[kabushiki-gaisha]*. In the company, work-

5. Even though Mr. Yasuda defines himself as the third generation president of his family business, as the story unfolds it appears that he and his father did not follow traditional patterns of succession. Mr. Yasuda founded his own company, and then invited his father to join his company. Similarly, Mr. Yasuda's father had broken away from his father's company and founded his own company.

ing hours have to be fixed regularly. The evaluation of employees' work efficiency has to be recorded in precise numbers. We also have to disclose gains and losses publicly.

The traditional relationship between master and apprentice in Nishijin has changed into one between employer and employee. My family members are all company employees. I am also one of them. If the company makes bigger profits, I can be paid more, and vice versa. Even my family members are paid according to their effort. The company does not belong to any particular person; it belongs to all of the workers. Management, staff, and employees should have this attitude. We are different from the Kawashima Weaving Company, for example.[6] They have a much longer history and operate on a much larger scale. Their management is not all family-based. In our case, if the owner's son were stupid and became president, the company would go bankrupt. So we would have to select the president among the most excellent employees. My son is the vice president of this company.

When the war [World War II] was over, I was a junior high school student. I learned how to weave in my father's company before the war. I am the only son. I have a younger sister who is married and lives in Osaka. This company has a thirty-year-long history since I established it. I founded my own company in Shōwa 30 [1955]. I brought my father, who was working for his company, to work for my company in Shōwa 31 [1956]. For us, the hardest times were when the company was established. I was still young. I did not have any money, so my father gave me all the capital. One year later, I invited my father with all his employees to work for my company. But the capital was too small to support all of them. At that time, Nishijin did not experience any particular hard times. It was something peculiar to my own company. Though I got some advice from my father, I do not think that this company experienced any big change in business policy after my father joined. I have kept it consistent. My father passed away six years ago. He worked with me until his death. I did not know what he had done earlier in his company, because I was too young. He gave me some advice based on his experience.

The reason I did not inherit my father's company is due to the heavy taxes after the war. Officials used to make extremely subjective estimates of businesses for taxation. To prevent this, I decided to begin a new joint-stock company. My father stopped his business so he could be free

6. The Kawashima Textile Company is the largest corporation in Nishijin.

from heavy taxes. Otherwise they would have charged him enormous taxes each year. I started my company from zero in Nakagyō-ku [center of Kyoto], while my father had his company in Kamigyō-ku [the Nishijin district]. This is the reason why I founded my company and became the president. I employed my father so we could pay less tax. We shared the market for sales.

My father's parents had many children. My father's older brother did not work at all, but as the oldest son he was legally qualified to inherit all his father's property. My father was not happy about that, and left home. He started his own business in Kamigyō-ku. His company began growing from Shōwa 25 [1950], but it suffered from heavy taxes. The tax office did not expect me, such a young guy, to make very much money, and charged me less tax. This is the reason why my father did not become president.

Very small-scale family businesses in weaving have a hard time finding employees. Young employees prefer a company system with an eight-hour day to a feudalistic apprenticeship. We can find about five employees every year. When the family industry really needs somebody to work, we tempt our workers with very high pay. Since the large companies do not have to invest money to train the experienced weavers, they do not lose any money by paying higher wages than we do.

Before Shōwa 20 [1945], workers were mainly concerned about money. Contemporary workers want to work because they are interested; they do not care about wages. They want to enjoy their work by doing what they want to do. Before the war, they had to make money anyway to support their poor families. The current problem of the stability of the labor force is similar to the pre-war period, but the in-between period had its ups and downs. In Shōwa 20 [1945], there was a surplus in labor and nothing could sell well in the market. In the Shōwa 30s [1955–64], all kinds of companies were created and Nishijin suffered from a labor shortage. *Obi* was selling well, but the labor supply was short in the 1950s and 1960s. They even wanted retired workers to fill the labor shortage. Younger workers preferred more modern types of work. Our company was too small to attract young workers. At that time, I had to employ retired people, but they did not work very well. I fired them later.

Times have changed, and people started applying for work even in my company. Japanese society has become more individualistic, and parents could not help but trust their children's own choices of jobs. So girls changed their minds and want to find jobs, which they can continue even after they get married. If they work for banks or something like that, they cannot continue their careers. A little while ago, most parents used to be poor and they expected their children to get jobs with better pay. But since their living standard has improved, they encourage their daughters to work at what they really want. Some women complain that they have less chance of finding men to marry if they work in a place like ours.

In the Shōwa 50s [1975–1984], employers began selecting good, qualified weavers. We invited candidates for interviews at our company before we decided to employ them. They also got a chance to feel the atmosphere of our place. They came here with school transcripts, by which we could tell how well they studied in school. We interviewed them and we said "no" right away when we did not want to employ a certain person. The rest of the candidates were given time to think over their decision at home by consulting with their parents.

The girls we employ come from various places, such as rural areas, as well as from Kyoto City. The ratio is fifty-fifty. They come from everywhere except Kyushu and Hokkaido. We recruit them through a local employment office in Kyoto [shokugyō-antei-shō], which is in touch with employment offices outside Kyoto. After the agency contacts them, the girls start making contact with us directly. I do not see any difference between girls from rural areas and ones from Kyoto. I do not think that rural girls have particular difficulty living in the city. The modern girls are much more adventurous than girls in the old days. They can speak the same language as the other girls. Transportation has been greatly improved and has shortened the distance from their homes. Also communication, such as phones, got really convenient. They can talk with their parents on the phone any time.

In contemporary Japan, it is very rare for relatives to recruit each other for jobs. None of the girls working here are related to each other. There is a big diversity in the job market. Each person has a different idea. Even if a girl weaves in Kyoto, her sister may want to work for a bank in Tokyo. Her own preference and income take the first priority. They are now more individualistic. I do not think that weavers try to recruit their sisters and friends. Till the Shōwa 30s [1955–64], they might have done that way. In the Shōwa 60s [1985–88], it would have been impossible.[7]

7. The Shōwa 60s correspond to 1985–88. On January 7, 1989, with the change in emperors, the numbering of years shifted to Heisei 1.

All the girls come without any weaving experience. They learn from zero. Well . . . it takes three years till they begin weaving simple things, and five years to make more sophisticated ones. They all come here when they are single. Some of them may get married while working here. It is their own choice whether they keep working here after their marriage. If a girl marries somebody who has a store, she has to quit the weaving job. The ratio of women who remain to work here after marriage is about fifty-fifty.

We built a five-story building next to the factory. Working girls have private rooms on the fifth floor. They used to stay on the third floor of the same building two years ago. All of us have our lunch delivered from a restaurant, but the girls take turns cooking dinner for themselves. Some of them may eat outside. Yes, my mother used to cook for us, but only before the war. We had a maid who cooked for all the employees. When I started this company, I employed a cook who was a licensed dietician; she cooked for all of us. But the employees complained about the monotonous menu, and then I let them do as they liked. They can go out to eat, or order whatever they like to be delivered. Some cook by themselves. When they used to eat at the company, the meals were deducted from their wages. As a result, it is the same for them. As for the dormitories, the employees pay rent, because not all employees are living in the dormitory. They are required to pay 60 percent of the average rent of an apartment. They also pay for electricity and other utilities. We give them what we should give, and they pay what they should pay.

The dormitory arrangements have been adapted to the modern system. Each person has a different hobby and personality. The workers do not want their lives to be regulated in a communal setting. I would like them to develop their own personalities. It is their own choice whether they live in the dormitory or in an ordinary apartment. If the company were pretty big and had a large space, and if it were located in a rural area, employees would have to live together in the company area. Our company is not so big and is located in the city, so we do not have any reason to have communal living for workers. Before Shōwa 20 [1945], all the workers lived in the same place, ate the same food, and wore the same uniform. Nowadays, people want to be more individualistic. They like to have their own lifestyles.

On the average, our women employees work from three to six years. Then they usually get married. Yes, they get married after they learn the skills. About half of them keep weaving at home. Some employees leave us to work for another manufacturer and earn higher wages after they have learned their skills here. We do not put any restrictions upon them. We cannot interfere at all with their choice of job. It is possible for a girl to move from our company to another company. I am not concerned about leaking the secrets of our techniques, because it takes ten or twenty years for the weavers to master our own designs and colors. *Tsuzure* weaving demands a high level of technique. In two or three years, they cannot gain any substantial knowledge about our production methods.

We have lots of cottage weavers. Some girls who come to work for us from other places marry here in Kyoto; they take looms back to their home communities to work there [as cottage weavers]. We have a few cottage weavers in Tango,[8] but most of our company's cottage weavers are in Ise, a city in Mie Prefecture, and in Sakata, a city in Akita Prefecture, because some girls from those areas who worked for us got married and took looms back to their home towns in order to keep weaving. We do not use a middleman [*daikō-ten*] at all. Truck transportation is quick [system similar to UPS]. We send two units of raw materials to our weavers at one time, and when they finish one of them they send it back. Then we send again new materials for two *obi*.

Many among the twenty-five hundred manufacturers of *obi* in Kyoto have stopped their business or changed their kind of business. Even though we are having hard times now, we may reach a good balance of supply and demand after certain manufacturers survive the depression. No, we do not reduce production. Since we have capital, we can keep producing the same amount and keep it in stock till the market improves.

We did not exhibit any of our *obi* in the manufacturers' exhibition at the Nishijin Textile Center last May.[9] Manufacturers want to steal designs from good companies, and they do many tricks to bother other companies. Though we used to exhibit in the past, we stopped participating a little while ago. We have our own exhibition for the wholesalers. We just stopped exhibiting in the Nishijin Textile Center in order to avoid having our original designs stolen.

Our designs and colors fit the current taste of consumers, but the

8. The Tango Peninsula on the Japan Sea is a major center for cottage weaving farmed out from Nishijin to the countryside.

9. In this annual exhibition, Nishijin manufacturers exhibit their *obi* for the wholesalers to view and select. Some major manufacturers refuse to participate, because they fear their designs might be stolen.

prices are generally higher than those of other manufacturers. We also have a direct advertisement system, which challenges any other company to compete with us. I do not determine the designs by myself, because I might be too committed to one pattern. All the executives in the company participate in the decisions. Each person has a different taste. Frankly speaking, we earn a lot. So we consider almost all opinions expressed, though using some designs may cause some loss of profits. Because we encourage our managers to be creative, we expect potential errors any time.

I can do every kind of job, but most company owners do not know how to weave. The modern division of labor has made company presidents unable to weave and to do accounting. Long ago, owners of small companies were able to do that, too. My son is studying both sales and management in order to be the future president. My wife is in charge of supervising the weaving once a week. She takes the place of *obā-san* [his mother], who is too old. My wife also fixes the warp every other day. She does warping *[seikei]* at home, also.

There should be a separation between family and company. At 6:00 P.M., we close the company building. We do not live in the same house as our employees. But in earlier times, the employees used to live with the employer's family. Even my son is not living with us. My mother *[obā-san]* is living with us. My son's wife comes to learn how to do office work every other day. My son and his wife have two children. From my point of view, one business can feed three generations, so we must be careful not to lose the business. If we are conscious of that, we do not have to fight.

Family problems come from the kitchen. We have separate kitchens and bathrooms in the same building. We do not have to argue over the priority of the use of the kitchen. My wife cooks for my mother, but if my mother does not like it, she cooks something else by herself. I was too stupid to do something other than textiles. If a son is smart enough, he would start his own career. Inheritance of the family business, though, is the easiest way for survival.

The weaving of *tsuzure* is a traditional industry *[dentō sangyō]*, but I do not stick to the idea that only Japanese can make it. We could ask Chinese or even American weavers to make it, and we could import it. The products of Japanese traditional industries should not be monopolized by the Japanese alone. This is the way I believe. I do not think the location of Nishijin matters very much. People in Sakata or Tango are already making products for Nishijin. We should not have narrow ideas. We should share every kind of work with all people over the world. Even Buddha statues could be carved by a French sculptor. In the old days, the transportation was pretty poor. Now anybody can go anywhere in the world. Any kind of product can be produced by anybody on this earth.

Mrs. Maizuru Michiko

Manufacturer's Daughter, Manufacturer's Widow,
Manufacturer's Mother

Mrs. Maizuru Michiko, fifty years old at the time of the interview, is the daughter of Mr. Maizuru Masajiro, the retired president of the Nishijin Maizuru Company — one of the most distinguished companies in Nishijin for their artistic obi. Mr. Maizuru was still president when I first interviewed him and his daughter. He retired formally in 1986, but he continued to work in his former office and guided his grandson, who succeeded him as president. Mr. Maizuru had no sons, and therefore no heir of his own. Mrs. Maizuru's husband was adopted as Mr. Maizuru's son and successor and he was groomed to be president. In such marriages, the son-in-law is adopted into the wife's family and bears their name. He died, however, in his thirties, and Mrs. Maizuru's son, Mr. Maizuru Kazuo, was designated and trained as successor. The elder Mr. Maizuru continued to supervise the company's management after his grandson became president. Following his official appointment, in 1986, the young president introduced various innovations into the company. These were not always favorably accepted by his grandfather and the older production managers. This caused tension; Mrs. Maizuru was caught in the generation gap. She was also concerned over her son's love marriage to a woman from outside Nishijin.

Mrs. Maizuru's own career was unusual in that she worked in the company office, alongside her father, as the office manager. She perceived this work as a professional career, as well as a contribution to the family's effort. After her husband's death, Mrs. Maizuru lived in her father's house in Omuro — a wealthy suburb in the northwest of Kyoto near Ninnaji temple. The family's magnificent new wooden house was built in traditional Japanese style and has an outstanding garden. Mrs. Maizuru's father and his second wife inhabited

FIGURE 26. Mr. Maizuru displaying an *obi* woven in his
company. Photograph courtesy of Mrs. Maizuru Michiko.

*the main part of the house. After Mr. Maizuru's death in 1995, the second
wife has continued to live there. Mrs. Maizuru keeps a separate apartment in
the house, with her own kitchen. When she entertains, however, she uses the
main formal spaces of the house. Before her eyesight got worse, Mrs. Maizuru
used to drive her father to the office every morning and bring him back in the
evening. Her father usually sat in the back seat.*

*Several years before her father's death, Mrs. Maizuru became more inde-
pendent of her father and her son. She has many hobbies characteristic of
women of her class, such as flower arrangement, tea ceremony, and Japanese
dance. In addition, however, she goes hiking in the Kitayama (the mountain
range north of Kyoto) and travels once a year to Europe. She has lost, however,
some of her independence because she is not able to drive anymore due to a*

FIGURE 27. Mrs. Maizuru Michiko in her garden. Photograph courtesy of Mrs. Maizuru Michiko.

degenerative eye disease. She still goes to the company office once a week. Her son, the company's president, has built a house next door to hers and lives there with his family.

I was introduced to Mr. Maizuru and his daughter by Mr. Kimura, a wholesaler of kimono, who is the blood brother of Mr. Maizuru but was adopted in his childhood by the Kimura family.

My son married for love *[ren'ai-kekkon];* he and his wife went to the same college. I was surprised to find them sitting together during the graduation ceremony at Doshisha University. She is not related to a textile family at all. I know that my father wanted someone related to textiles to some extent, and he was concerned with her family's class. Also he wanted my son to marry someone much younger than himself. I encouraged them to marry, even against my father's will. My son's wife is the only daughter in her family. Her father runs a transportation

FIGURE 28. Mrs. Maizuru Michiko performing traditional Japanese dance. Photograph courtesy of Maizuru Michiko.

company. She worried in the beginning that she would have a hard time in the Nishijin community. I think they worried about the traditional way of life in Nishijin. I know that my son criticized the integration of business and family in our company that my father had, but actually my father was more modern than that.

In Nishijin, the business and the family are often mixed together on ceremonial occasions, such as weddings, funerals, and so forth. People usually have the factory and their home in the same place, but my father did not like that and separated them. In old Nishijin, manufacturers could not have any private time because of the intimate relationship between business and family. My father was a new type of person in old Nishijin. We respected our father. I think my parents were quite a democratic couple; they went everywhere together. At that time, even a married couple could not walk together on the street. But my father took my mother dancing, too.

Many wives of the business owners in Nishijin were in charge of business at home, too. The owners could go out to have their private life with the "second wives" [concubines]. Such things were still possible even during my father's time. I know many business owners, my contemporaries, who play around with *geisha* in the Gion, but I do not think that they are having them as concubines; rather, it is just a relationship of customer and hostess. In the old times, if someone wanted to have a particular *geisha* as his own concubine, she had to give up her career first. A *geisha* belongs to the teahouse *[ochaya]*, which sends her out to many places to entertain. I think that wives endured it and, to some extent, took it for granted from men. Some wives became devoted to their hobbies. At that time, marriage was arranged for the sake of the family lineage.

In the old times, I think the concubines were humble enough not to show up in public with someone's husband. So the first wives could sustain their pride and authority in their families. Some wives had greater power than their husbands; they were acknowledged by society, too. We cannot simply say that these women experienced oppression. I am sure that the wives had hard times emotionally, but eventually they gave up their jealousy as something they took for granted. It would have taken time for them to adjust their minds, though.

In old Japan, it was considered a big shame for women to divorce. Women were not given any inheritance rights before the war [World War II]. If they divorced, they had to go back home without taking back anything they had brought with them when they got married. All the property and the business belonged to their husbands. When the husbands died, their sons had a right to become successors, regardless of how young they were. The senior managers in the company *[bantō]* took care of the business till the children grew up. In cases where the manufacturers had only a daughter, their wives were probably made successors to the properties. This was before the war.

I share my husband's inheritance with my son. My father still keeps his own property, except for some stocks. If my husband were alive, he would be eligible to inherit my father's property, because my husband was also adopted as my father's son. In that case, my husband would have had a right to take it all.[1] The oldest son used to be given all the rights of inheritance. None of the other brothers inherited anything. I think they arranged something special for women, case by case, because

---

1. It was customary for heads of business families who had only daughters to have their daughter marry an appropriate man, who trained in the family business and was then adopted, took the daughter's family name, and became the inheritor.

fathers were very devoted to their daughters. If the oldest son did not want to inherit the business, they would have brought in the younger brother or their daughter's husband as a successor. The first son would have been given just a part of the properties, not all. Parents usually negotiated with the first son to arrange something particular for him. Some people kept their first son as an heir in name only, and entrusted all the business to the senior manager. Those sons just hung around, for they did not have any capacity to run the business.

In one major manufacturer's company in Nishijin, the four brothers are suing each other over the inheritance. Anyway, they are managing to run the business, so far. I do not know anything in detail about them. Their fuss was reported in the newspaper, so everybody knows it. In contrast, the Kawashima Weaving Company is growing rapidly with the production of interior decorations and is becoming less of a family company. Since the company is linked to the upper class in the stock market, it would not be so simple for a family member to inherit the president's position.

In Nishijin, there are so many occasions for manufacturers to get together and to exchange information. The secrets about the business are kept strictly. There is an expression — "Nishijin *mura*" [village] — because the business owners get together so often, even for playing together.[2] There is a close group among the younger generation as well. They also meet together with wholesalers, but not with outsiders to the business. The wives of the older generation do not show up very much at these meetings, but young couples have started socializing together. Even in my father's time, three or four couples got together and made trips somewhere for recreation. On that occasion, the wives accompanied their husbands. This occurred frequently, in particular, after the war [World War II]. My father was a little unusual. He and my mother traveled together with other couples. Of course, there were also meetings for men only. My mother shared hobbies with other manufacturers' wives. Usually, for her, contacts with the people in the neighborhood were important. We had contacts mainly with the people connected with Nishijin, but not always with the manufacturers. Nowadays, manufacturers join the Lions Club or Rotary Club to communicate with other professional people. Prior to my generation, Nishijin was a closed society.

People under age forty are more open, because they have had a mod-

2. "Playing together" means going to tea houses, being entertained by *geisha*, and gambling.

ern education. People my age did not have a college education. I am now fifty years old. I was born and raised in the midst of Nishijin, but my personality is not something peculiar to Kyoto. I cannot behave like an *oba-san* [an aunt, meaning a matron]. I feel rather like a student. I am the type who is impressed with many things. My father was also a kind of modern person, and he influenced me.

In my childhood, fathers were feudalistic. They pretended to have absolute authority. But my father talked to me as an equal. When he traveled with my mother, he told us children to take care of the home. Then, when I wanted to make a trip with my girlfriends, he generously allowed me to do that. He was understanding, indeed. Most fathers fuss over their children's behavior. My father took the whole family swimming every summer. We often went to have dinner at a restaurant. He gave us lots of time to talk with him.

It is a difficult question as to why he was so unusual. My grandfather was a son of gentility *[shizoku]*. He did not fool around and he took very good care of the family. I heard that when he was young, my father hung around with *geisha* in Kamihichiken ["Seven Houses" is the *geisha* district in Nishijin]. He took care, however, of his family. He babysat for us when my mother was busy. I heard that he took us, babies even, to the teahouses where the *geisha* were. It should have been very rare for men to do this at that time. I have a slight memory of that before I was three. He babysat while visiting a *geisha*. He was a playboy-type, and liked a joyful atmosphere. Even now, he is happy when his relatives visit him. All the relatives get together at his house on his birthday. He likes visitors.

We have dinner parties when someone from our family and other relatives goes somewhere or graduates from school. We all like getting together in our house. We have many Buddhist services for our ancestors, in which many cousins get together. After we visit a temple, we—forty or fifty members of our family group—go to a restaurant to have dinner together. I have eight brothers and sisters, and twenty-one cousins. Other relatives and the company staff also join us. We usually invite the executives only, but occasionally other staff members from our company also come.

Yes, Mr. Hiraoka and Mr. U., the two production managers of our company, join us. They belong to the executives. These two men started working for the company from their elementary school age. They were drafted during the war, but then kept working here afterward. They want to share their destinies with this company, and they do not have any desire to establish a company of their own. Rather, they are eager to help my son in succeeding my father as president. I believe that they put the company as their first priority. They show their devotion and loyalty to the company just like the *samurai* used to in the old times, rather than as modernized businessmen. They get bigger bonuses when the business is going well.

When my husband was young, he used to work for his father's cotton company in Osaka, but the cotton industry was declining and big companies absorbed small ones. Before marrying me, he did not have any particular relations with Nishijin. I still keep in touch with his family in Osaka. I have to take care of things related to my deceased husband and his mother. My son is treated just like a son by the uncles and aunts in my husband's family. He gets advice on business and personal things from his uncle, in particular. I also consult with this uncle and his wife. My sister and her husband are also good consultants for me.

Mr. U. gives me good advice in the company. I have another advisor concerning my physical and mental health. I sometimes talk about education with my son's former tutor. My uncle, Mr. Kimura, used to be a good advisor for my father's brothers and the company.[3] He occasionally attended conferences in the company. One of my former school-teachers is also a good adviser to me. I talk to these people case by case. I am very grateful to all of them. Whenever I confront crises, somebody appears to help me and lead me.

I leave for the company at 8:15 A.M.; I can do many things before that. I gave up driving, because I was involved in a small accident due to my poor eyesight. One of my eyes has very poor sight. I miss driving a lot, because I had been driving for twenty-two years. My job demands sharp eyesight, so I have to take care of my eyes. My son [president of the company] gives me a ride when I go to work. On the way back, I use either a bus or a taxi.

When I first started working here, it was only in the mornings. I had a hard time due to my lack of knowledge, but now I enjoy working. I, myself, started using the computer and programmed the software. Under good business conditions, we could just make and sell the products and get profits. Nowadays, the supply is bigger than the demand. So we restrict the use of materials and production in order to keep the prices stable.

When I started working, I had no problems with the executives who

---

3. Mr. Kimura was a well-known wholesaler of *kimono* in Nishijin. He was the blood brother of Mr. Maizuru (Mrs. Maizuru's father), but was adopted by the Kimura family in his childhood.

have had long careers in the company, because my husband used to tell me everything about the company. The accumulation of this knowledge was so helpful! He and I used to walk around department stores and other shops in Osaka to see many kinds of *obi*. I knew well the human relations in the company, for I worked on a part-time basis in this company for one month before we got married. Originally we could survive because we produced high-quality products. We could roughly guess the management of financial affairs in Nishijin.

When I got married, I was shocked to see the antiquated financial notebooks that our company used. I went to management school for one year to help my husband as his secretary and bookkeeper. Eventually I changed the record keeping to something more rational. We had a woman clerk who was in charge of recording all the financial and production information. I used to check the results and look at the statistics. When the clerk reached retirement age, we got the computer. The computer and I share the tasks she used to do. I take a walk every morning and I enjoy the beauty of nature; the morning is indeed wonderful. The Higashiyama [Eastern Mountains] around Kyoto are so beautiful in the winter when the sunrise is late. I meet many other people taking walks; we all exchange greetings.

I have a fixed appointment every month for wearing the *kimono* that is made for the next season. I have to keep wearing *kimono* regularly so I will continue to be accustomed to *kimono*. I wear a silk *kimono* woven in stripes *[tsumugi]*, which is easy to get around in. I dance traditional Japanese dance, in which I wear *kimono* or the summer cotton *kimono* *[yukata]*. I started traditional Japanese dance again thirteen years ago. I had danced for seven years before I got married. I am a poor singer, so I decided to dance. I used to dance to my father's singing.

I listen once a month to a sermon by a leader of lay Buddhism. I wrote the biography of my husband after he passed away. This became a spiritual backbone for me. When I finished delivering copies of my book about my husband to all his relatives and friends, I happened to meet this leader. Through him, I could encounter very good people and books. It was miraculous that I encountered the right person at the right time. I have had many valuable encounters in my life. I am very, very grateful about that. I never imagined that I could have survived so far just with my own ability. People supported me, and my children grew up all right.

Mr. Hiraoka

Production Manager at
the Nishijin Maizuru Textile Company

Mr. Hiraoka Masao was in his sixties at the time of the interview. He was
the production manager at the Nishijin Maizuru Company when I first in-
terviewed him. He has since retired. I was introduced to him by Mrs. Maizuru
Michiko, daughter of the president of the Nishijin Maizuru Company (see her
interview).

My job includes various tasks, such as planning for the design of the
cloth, studying the organization of production, development new products, and so on. I also supervise the cottage weavers *[debata]*. So half of
my job is to supervise the weavers and the other half is to design and
manage the products. I can't leave my work until 2:00 or 3:00 A.M.,
because the cottage weavers visit every day. I do not design myself, but
I supervise the designers. I give orders to the designers and to the various
subcontractors.

Well, since Nishijin is situated within the city, it is getting more
difficult to recruit weavers here. Most of the sons and daughters of cottage weavers do not succeed to the family business. They find other jobs.
One reason why we chose to employ weavers in Tango [by the Japan
Sea] is that the production of the plain white cloth *[shiro-kiji]* in that
region is declining and their dependency on Nishijin has increased year
after year. Now the amount of production is almost the same for white
cloth and for *obi* from Nishijin. Another reason is that there are factories
in the Kameoka region, the Sonobe region [West of Kyoto], and in
other places in the countryside around Kyoto where we tend to look for
a labor force. So we compete with the factories for labor recruitment.

Children in pre-war Nishijin usually didn't attend school above *kōtō-shōgakkō* [higher elementary school of the seventh and eighth grades in the pre-war school system]. But after the war, girls began to go to high school and to junior colleges, while boys went to high school and colleges or colleges or universities. Thus they preferred other occupations. Consequently, we had to recruit the labor force in the countryside. Also, Nishijin has an advanced technology and is beginning to have cottage weavers in Fukui, Kanazawa, and in other places, such as the Bizen region.

Earlier, we had an apprenticeship system under which we recruited young women, had them live with us in dormitories, and trained them. Sometimes we saw them off for their marriage. Now we have difficulty recruiting people in that way, and we tend to maintain our production in the form of a household industry. The number of weavers is decreasing, and we have to recruit in Tango. We have observed this transition. We depend on cottage weavers who work with their families at home. Most of our workers in Tango are cottage weavers. We have middlemen [*daikō-ten*] there, each of whom takes care of several weavers. We have a couple of hundred of these middlemen. We communicate with the middlemen; they inform us of their available workforce. The middlemen carefully keep their eyes on quality and we convey our evaluations to the weavers through them.

I think the middleman is a recent phenomenon that developed primarily during the 1970s, though it happened later in our company. As we came to want more weavers, our recruitment coverage expanded. Now we recruit from all over Japan.

Cottage weaving in the Tango Peninsula is an old system, but the use of middlemen in Tango is new. We have about 150 *debata* [cottage weavers] scattered, say, from Kinosaki to Maizuru [in Tango]. We are not so familiar with the region, and it works better and is less costly to have local people deal with the weavers rather than to keep our staff there. We give the middlemen the payment for the work of the cottage weaver, and they deduct their 10 percent commission. For example, suppose there is only one manufacturer [*oyakata*] like us and he has, say, thirty cottage weavers. He can't oversee all of them. By using this system of middlemen, the manufacturer can send jobs and receive products. In the meantime, he can sell the products and solicit orders. It is more reasonable.

Once there were some manufacturers who had labor unions in the company, but they went bankrupt. The manufacturers reduced the workforce and some workers were re-employed by other manufacturers or by newly created companies. Now I don't know of any existing company unions in Nishijin. Well, some skilled workers get fifty thousand *yen* a month, while other low-skilled ones get one hundred thousand *yen*. If you try to equalize the salary, those skilled workers suffer. Usually lower-skilled workers call for unionization and the skilled workers don't like it. When you lose those skilled workers in the process of unionization, you cannot expect the same high quality of work from the low-skilled ones.

Cottage weavers usually work between eight and twelve hours a day, but we don't really know exactly how this is done. Weavers get paid by the amount of the product they make. We estimate that an efficient production per day is worth ten thousand *yen [seken-no-sōba]*.[1] It is common in Nishijin. And it has been getting better recently. According to the labor law [Fair Labor Standards Act], working hours are regulated. But our relationship to weavers is one of subcontracting. It is not the normal employer–employee relationship [meaning employees in a factory]. That is one important thing to keep in mind. The regulations in the labor law are not clearly stated and different interpretations are possible. The labor situation in Nishijin is very difficult to understand. For example, the labor law requires eight hours of labor as the maximum length for one day. But we wonder who keeps records of the working hours of the cottage weavers here in Nishijin. There is no time limit on cottage weavers. Does a housewife stop her work after eight hours, if her tasks are not finished [laugh]?

Since we make much of technical skills, our complete compliance with the law seems to somewhat dehumanize our relationships. Human relationships do count a lot in this industry. If it was necessary, both the weavers and I used to work when it was New Year's Day or at midnight. Human relationships are more important than the labor law. The law is one thing, and flexible human relationships coexist with it. It seems to me that some weavers in Nishijin voluntarily worked late without being asked to. When you use machines, you can easily adapt to regulation by labor laws. But handweaving *[teori]* is different. Weavers may sometimes sleep during the day and work at night, but no weaver works day and night. It is more the case with handlooms than with powerlooms, because sometimes you hit upon a new idea at night and

1. *Seken-no-sōba* is a reasonable price, wage, or income, neither much above nor much under the level of price or wage informally set by people concerned.

if you wait till the following day, you feel different about it. You can't tell what the application of that new idea might result in unless you try it in practice on the spot. If you come across a new idea at, say, 10:00 at night, you have to try it right then. I recently heard from one *hata-ya* [weaver] that he was thinking about a new design at midnight. This happens because people are concerned about the human relations. If it is only a matter of money, they only concern themselves with the time. But the situation is such that each person tries to work harder than the others. We don't really tell them to do so. This is the complexity within this business. During the day, you are sometimes too busy to concentrate on new ideas, but you might think of something new at night. It is a difficult topic to describe well [laugh].

I have worked with this company for about forty years. One big change has been the switch from handlooms to powerlooms. I'd say the major change came especially after the war. But there still is a future for handwoven cloth. Handwoven *tsuzure* is finer and softer than the machine-woven one. It feels smoother. This kind of difference will still be maintained, I think.

The industry itself has been declining. Before the war, women usually wore *kimono* and *obi* sold well; we had a lot to produce. But after the war, they started to wear clothing other than *kimono*. Today, only upperclass women who love *kimono* wear it.

Mr. Koyama

Weavers' Assistant in a Factory

Mr. Koyama Takashi[1] was eighty years old at the time of the interview. He worked as a weavers' assistant in a small factory that specialized in high-quality obi woven on powerlooms. I first met Mr. Koyama during the tea break, along with other workers, most of whom were women weavers. I subsequently interviewed him in an office in the factory that the manufacturer made available to me.

Young people today don't know about life in Nishijin. We couldn't even receive compulsory education. If we didn't stop going to school in sixth grade and didn't have work, parents and children couldn't eat. Even before we entered sixth grade, we had to wind the weft.

I have been weaving for more than fifty years. My parents had no relation to weaving. My father was a peasant. He lived in Nagoya. After all, it was a custom that in the old days, before the present family system emerged, the oldest son inherited the family estate. Second and third sons were kicked out [from their parents' farm] to be apprenticed. One day my father said, "What about my son?" He decided without asking me, because at that time we obeyed our parents. Without thinking anything, when my father told me to leave home, I went to Kyoto. I learned to weave with a relative. He was a cottage weaver. Based on a contract, they promised me some money after ten years. So I stayed at his house for ten years. After the term was up, the master said I could somehow

---

1. This is a pseudonym.

earn a living by working independently. I went out to rent a house; I found a small house where I worked on a loom that my former master gave me. That was when I was twenty-four. When I was twenty-five, I got married.

I did weave in the past. But now, because of my age, I make preparations for weaving, such as winding the weft, preparing the threads, and winding here. I have been weaving since the age of eighteen. Now I am eighty. I came to work here in January. Nobody wants to use an eighty-year-old. Here I had some acquaintances for a long time. They asked me to come because one employee quit. So I came in that way. I have been weaving almost everything that was made in Nishijin, long before the introduction of the powerloom. We used handlooms. Then I practiced weaving on powerlooms. I have used powerlooms for the past fifteen years. I think that powerlooms are the best method now. The new advanced powerloom is the most difficult and valuable machine. It is the weaving of the future. The new powerloom has twelve boxes. In the beginning, there was only one box. Later it became three, four, six, eight, ten, and now twelve. This is the maximum. If this is used, it is sure to be successful. Nishijin weaving has become high-grade in general. There are few places in Nishijin that make cheap cloth, as in the past.

In our work we must use our hands. We learn by doing. But it has not been as interesting to work on the powerloom as on the handloom. If we make a mistake, after all, the product will be damaged. We must be pretty careful with this type of loom. As you see, twelve shuttles are moving here and there. If one does not work well, it becomes complicated. We are fairly nervous. Surely the handloom was easier. I can work with handlooms as I like. With powerlooms, I can't. With a handloom, I can work faster if I want and I can work slower if I want. I work in this way, or that way, if I want. But the powerloom is rigid, moving here and there. Naturally I like the handloom. With the powerloom, I can take some rest, though. But with some products, taking a rest is not good. Once we begin to weave, we should weave continuously. I take a rest when defects come out. Only a skilled person can produce continuously. I first learned to weave by watching. In the case of the handloom, you can teach with your hands. In the case of powerlooms with the electricity running, it is difficult to learn while watching.

My wife was a weaver and she had some contacts with manufacturers. At that time, they would say, "Do not get married." It was a time when people said that a man should not get married unless he was able to support his wife. Society in general followed this custom. A man could not let his wife stay at home, unless he was able to support her. Two people had to make a living from the husband's work. By now everything has changed. Husband and wife are both working soon after they get married. Nowadays this is necessary. In the old days, when only a man worked, he could earn a living for two while having children and letting them graduate from school. A man did feed his family, and he endured hardships.

My wife started work after the children entered school; she then had some free time. There were no washing machines. Washing clothes in the morning, cleaning the rooms, and cooking took the whole day. Even if the wife had some free time, she did not work outside. A man could support his family by himself. After World War II, things were changing. Both my wife and I were forced to work. A man alone cannot make a living for his family. My wife, for example, basically did housework. After I went out, she took care of the weaving. Or after I stopped working early in the evening, she wove. By doing these various things, she became a weaver.

We had two children, a boy and a girl. Actually we had four, but two died. Although my son said that he would not do the same work as I do, he was forced to succeed in my business, because of the general situation. He is now a weaver. He is forty-five years old, or so. He has been weaving since he graduated from junior high school, since he was fifteen years old. He has been weaving at home. Yes, I did want my son to be a weaver. But after all it is up to the wishes of the sons. It is better these days. It is not a time any more when fathers make sons do this and that. So fewer and fewer sons become weavers.

When I was young, we could make a living by weaving. Now it is impossible. If you are a low-skilled weaver, you cannot earn a living after all. It is impossible now to let boys become weavers. Earlier, the cloth we produced was sold at once. Now it is fluctuating. Sometimes it sells well; other times badly. It is difficult to say, but just after World War II was the best time. I did not ask my son to be a weaver. Now he also thinks that it would be better not to be a weaver, I imagine. At the present time, we cannot make a living unless we do something extra, in addition to the ordinary. In comparison with what I did, nowadays they must work twice as much. After all, textiles have become difficult to weave.

In the case of the handloom, almost all the weavers were men. When the powerloom was introduced, women replaced men, as if they had been waiting for this. After all, the handloom requires hands and feet. It requires physical strength. The powerloom does not; just watching. They have to use their hands only. Weaving is not men's work any more; to tell the truth, it is work for women. I cannot imagine weaving as men's work. Though men make some special things like big curtains for the theater [donchō], which require four to five people to weave together. Ordinary things such as obi are not men's work here. After all, women are patient with their work. Men soon get tired. Women do more detailed work. I think so.

I worked in a factory for five years. After all, working outside is easier. When one works in one's own home, everything should be done at home. When weaving outside, wages are a bit lower, but we do not have to worry about electricity costs and so on. At home, we carry electricity costs and, after all, we tend to be lax at home. When weaving outside, we work hard because there are fixed time schedules. But at home, things are done more sloppily. Weaving at home is bad for our health. I think weaving in factories is better because health conditions are maintained.

It is better working here than at home. Well, at home, there is nothing special, no obligations. If I stay at home [idle], my health rather declines. If I do some work, it is good for me. But when doing nothing, I become senile. If I work here, I do not become decrepit. I am alert here, but at home I am lethargic. Even when I get tired, I totally forget it, until after I finish my work at 5:30 in the evening. This is not a kind of work that gets me tired. In the factory, my body becomes sober.

In the old days, people stopped working at age seventy-five and took care of their grandchildren. At the present time, this practice is not working well. It would be better for an old person to work outside for himself and his family. At home, I cannot make precise work. I did badly at home. When I first came to work outside, I felt that I should have come out earlier. Considering wages and so on, it would be the same at home or in the factory. In the factory, I am forced to work according to a time schedule, but when I worked at home, I tended to think that I could work longer at night instead of finishing now, so I interrupted my work. Whether we weave at home or in the factory, the savings are not enough if something big happens.

Mr. Aioi

Warper

Mr. Aioi Eiichi works in his family's warping shop in one of the narrow streets in Nishijin. Warping is one of the main auxiliary industries in Nishijin. The manufacturer sends the silk thread and the design to the warper and commissions from him the tied warp. The warping and spinning operations took place on the second floor of his workshop on a narrow street of Nishijin, where I first met Mr. Aioi. The big drum was turning the colorful silk threads and batching them into separate groups according to the design. Mr. Aioi's brother's wife was tying the threads, while he was operating the wheel. Mr. Aioi's brother and his family live downstairs, where they also have their office. Mr. Aioi was forty-three at the time of the interview. I was first introduced to him by Mr. Nishiguchi Mitsuhiro, Kyoto City's director of the Division of Traditional Industries, during our walk through Nishijin. The Aioi family business provides an important example of a dual arrangement. On the one hand, they own a warping workshop, which places them in the position of small businessmen to whom the manufacturers subcontract orders; on the other hand, they also work as cottage weavers, who would be considered employees of the manufacturers.

The process of warping itself is very simple. We just make the warp *[tate-ito]*. The manufacturer *[orimoto]* delivers to us bundles of dyed silk thread. Then the winders *[kuriya]* wind them into the rolls. This is it. We arrange the threads for the warp, depending on the number of threads needed. We roll up the threads with that big drum, which fixes both the number and the length of threads. We must have special skills to sustain the same tension of the rolls of thread; otherwise, the completed woven cloth would be inconsistent in its texture. It takes at least two years to learn the skills of our trade.

I am not married. I live alone. There are many single weavers, because they are not exposed to the larger society outside their job and most women really do not want to marry weavers. Just like this lady [pointing to an employee], weavers' wives have to do many things. Since we are paid for our product, rather than as individuals, wives cannot help but work with their husbands. There are many workers in Nishijin who are not married. Most of them work all day long in their homes without going out, so they have very little chance to meet women.

I grew up in Nishijin in the house where my parents are living now. This [where the interview took place] is only the workshop. I am living in Hakubaicho [a district west of Nishijin]. My family has been doing warping for three generations. My father and brother used to do this before I started. I began this job at the age of thirty-five, but it took me only one year to master the skills. I worked very hard to make a living, and I used to see this work in my childhood. Until the age of thirty-five, I was a car dealer. I got involved with labor union problems, so I quit that job. I am the third son, and I was not interested in this work. I consciously avoided this work because of the bad labor conditions, because of working hours, and because of our inability to negotiate with the manufacturers who order the warp. We cannot depend on the labor union very much, and we have to negotiate with the manufacturers individually. I negotiated with the manufacturer's department of warping *[seikei]*. The pay has not changed for the past seven or eight years. We are not employed by the manufacturer; rather, he subcontracts with us. We deal with five manufacturers, each of whom provides me with a different amount of work.

My father was doing warping, but my grandfather was weaving plain cloth for *kimono [o-meshi]*; he was a cottage weaver. My father started weaving *obi* and he lived on weaving alone. He once tried to be a manufacturer, but his business failed. This happened when I was an elementary school student, about twenty-five years ago. Maybe his capital was too small to run the business well. After World War II, they had the *gachaman* prosperity.[1] Manufacturers who started at that time were

---

1. *Gachaman* is the nickname for the prosperity of Nishijin weavers following the post–World War II recovery. Literally, it means that a weaver was making ten thousand *yen* every time the shuttle went through the warp.

strong enough to survive the depression that followed, during the Korean War. But my father was wounded in the war and he started his business rather late, so he could not survive. We have to ride the tide of business to be successful. My father had tough luck. He started warping to support his family after the failure of his weaving business. My father started this job in 1966. He was a cottage weaver. We actually have two types of production in this house: weaving and warping.

Warping is a really small business, so we have to compete in order to survive. The manufacturer pays us monthly by the piece. We go to the manufacturer to deliver finished work and to collect new work. We are independent, so we can select the manufacturers to work with; but being such a small business, we do not have that much freedom in selection. We have to find jobs first of all. Plus we have been working for the same manufacturers for generations, so we cannot change them too easily. I inherited some of the manufacturers from my father. But the sons of the manufacturers have different policies; then we may have to switch to other manufacturers. For our survival, we have to keep trying very hard to find new manufacturers.

In Nishijin, it is very difficult to organize unions. People are afraid of rumors. This is a conservative society. We are very dependent on human relations. The relationship between employer and employee is like that between a parent and a son. Many employees want to be employers some day, so the union does not make any sense to them. The employees feel they do not need the union. Unlike workers in ordinary factories, they do not have the consciousness of laborers. They want to be manufacturers some day.

I am paid by my brother, because I am working for him. I do not weave, but I deliver his finished products to the manufacturer. My brother does the main job. He pays me a fixed amount monthly. I am not paid by the piece. I am paid even when we have no orders. But when I think about the growth of our business, I am happy when we have more orders; that enables us to save money. We get the grand total of sales every year. Accordingly, we decide how much each of us should be paid. My brother does warping as well as management. We have no regulation of working hours. We sometimes work till 11:00 P.M. or 12:00 midnight, and some other times we finish at 6:00 P.M. There are no workers besides us, except one spinner.

Yes, it is difficult to work together with my brother. If I were working with a stranger, I could count it as business. In our case, we have to be very thoughtful to each other in every respect. We share the same vision of enlarging our family business, though. I do not get any extra profits from this business. We have to save all profits in this time of growth in our business. In the economic boom of the '60s, many old families changed their business systems. They reorganized their companies according to new laws and recruited labor from other localities. Individual businesses became incorporated then. From Shōwa 39 to 41 [1964–1966], many weavers quit their jobs as a family industry. The whole country began having nuclear families at that time. Those two developments happened in Nishijin at the same time.

In my opinion, people who keep doing small family businesses in Nishijin seem to survive in this depression. Many large incorporated businesses fail. Small-scale business is strong in situations when the demand is low. The demand for *kimono* will never increase from now on. People now wear Western clothes even in weddings. Yes, I sometimes think of changing to another job, in particular when I am put under the pressure of paying many bills and when I have to hurry up to meet the order of the manufacturer. The amount of orders is irregular, though. We are at a disadvantage because we do not have steady work.

Nishijin manufacturers have employed cottage weavers in Tango since about the 1970s. Even worse, they order *obi* weaving from weavers in Korea and Taiwan, and they do not know who works for them at all. They do not announce in public the fact that Nishijin *obi* is also produced in other countries. They can get much cheaper silk thread in those countries.

We have not had any decrease in orders yet. We just hear the rumor about the depression, but we are not affected by it directly. We do not feel it. This is good for us. It is very risky for us to have this business at this time, though. We may not have any jobs tomorrow. We have not had any preparation for such difficult conditions. We would have to respond to the crisis after it occurred, without any preparation. Since we belong to the Greater Nishijin Labor Union, we are also covered by social security *[kōsei-nenkin]*.

We also have another union, only for owners of warping companies. It is open for both owners and employees. My brother is the owner and I am his employee. In that way, we can be covered by insurance. We belong to the Nishijin Textile Industrial Association, but not to the Union of Warpers. My brother is qualified to belong to this association, under which our employees are also covered by the benefits of the union.

Human relations have changed in Nishijin. They have become more business-like. The manufacturers now lack thoughtfulness. In the old days, they took it as their responsibility to support their employees' families. Now they cut off relations with employees easily when their business does not go well. Office workers change their positions very often. So we have to contact new people when we deliver our work to the manufacturers. In the old days, we were dealing with the same managers *[bantō-san]* in the manufacturers' headquarters and we maintained contact with them for many years. Employers and employees are interdependent, but in the present system we have poor communications.

In dealing with us and with subcontractors, the manufacturer likes to stay at the center of the process. After sending the product to be dyed, he wants to check the colors himself. Dye is something very subtle. He also wants to limit contacts among various craftspeople with whom he has subcontracts, in order to keep their business attached to him. He does not want the subcontractors of dyeing *[ito-zome]*, warping *[seikei]*, or harness making *[soko]* to contact each other. This is a traditional strategy of Nishijin manufacturers. Even though my brother deals with several manufacturers, each manufacturer guards his business secrets and protects his business from any leakage. We know what colors the manufacturers use, but we do not know how they use them in their designs. Some weavers make use of secret information from their manufacturer in order to get better positions with other manufacturers.

Traditionally, successful people in Nishijin started their career from warping. Warpers have become manufacturers, more so than dyers or pattern makers. The senior employees of manufacturers *[bantō]* have the best opportunity to become manufacturers, of course. They just try to be independent without any support from their former employers. My brother can be described that way. He had to develop his own business by himself. He is now forty-seven years old—four years older than me.

We have some social activities among Nishijin workers. We go to picnics for recreation sometimes. The senior workers *[bantō]* in warping, in dyeing, and in the manufacturer's office get together on those occasions. This is something new in Nishijin. Recently workers in different fields have had chances to get together. We have fewer work hours, compared to the old days. We are exposed to leisure time much more than the old workers were. The whole family joins the picnic on those occasions. They go to the countryside to have fun.

Mrs. Uebayashi

*Cottage Weaver on the Tango Peninsula
on the Japan Sea*

---

*Mr. Uebayashi Akira and Mrs. Uebayashi Chiyoko, his wife, live on the
Tango Peninsula in one of the four fishing villages of Ine Chō that surround
a bay at the the foot of steep mountains. The narrow stretch of land between
the mountains and the sea is only wide enough for a road, flanked on one side
by the dwellings at the foot of the mountain and on the other side by the boat-
and fish-houses skirting the sea. These boathouses, called funaya, are unique
in Japan. Each family has a fish-house combined with a boathouse directly
across the street from the family home. It reaches out over the water, so that a
fishing boat can be stored directly on the water under the floor. The second
floors of these buildings are now used for guest quarters, as retirement flats for
elderly parents, or for an unmarried adult son, like Mr. Uebayashi's son.*

Mrs. Uebayashi started weaving obi *for Kyoto manufacturers when* obi
*weaving was introduced to Tango in the 1970s. Her husband has continued
to work as a fisherman. Like the other women in the village, Mrs. Uebayashi
also does farming on her little family plot on the slope of the mountain. The
Uebayashi family lives in a spacious new wooden house, built in the traditional
style with ornate traditional wood carvings. When we came for the interview,
we were received by Mr. Uebayashi while his wife was still washing dishes after
dinner. He brought out the special low table used for guests into the spacious
tatami room reserved for formal occasions. He then assembled zabuton [cush-
ions for sitting on the floor] around it. Then he called his wife in and both of
them sat down. Since his wife was the weaver—I had specifically requested an
interview concerning weaving—he fulfilled the role that the hostess would normally do and took a secondary role in the interview.*

Mr. U. = Mr. Uebayashi

Mrs. U. = Mrs. Uebayashi

MRS. U.: I began weaving *obi* in May of Shōwa 48 [1973]. I started to supplement my husband's income, which was not enough for us to have any savings. Weaving was just a part-time job then, but now it has become a full-time job for me. When the manufacturer *[oyakata]* required me to achieve a higher production quota, I started to work from 7:00 A.M. until 7:00 P.M.[1] Yes, I feel overburdened. I also wake up at 3:30 or 4:00 A.M. to see my husband off when he goes fishing. I have to help him load many things on the boat. I cannot feel relaxed unless I see him off each morning, so if something happens to him on the boat I know that at least I did my best. Yes, I have been doing it that way since I got married. It does not mean any superstition or good-luck sign. He is supposed to leave the shore together with all the other boats, so I have to help him prepare everything so that he can leave on time. Each fisherman can fish as much as he likes, but all of the boats have to leave together. Well, sometimes I may go back to bed again; but I wake up at 4:30 A.M., so it is just a half-hour nap. In the winter, fishing stops from January to March. Then I get up at 5:30 A.M.

I start weaving at 7:00 A.M. About thirteen years ago, it became impossible for *obā-san* [husband's mother] to work. No, she cannot even work in the garden. Each morning I clean house and do the laundry and cooking and other chores before I begin weaving. After I finish weaving, I have to prepare dinner. No, my husband does not help me in the household. He is a fisherman. He leaves home at 4:00 A.M. and comes back at noon. He goes to get bait for fishing at 5:00 P.M. That is all he does. He also fixes the hooks in the fishing net every day. My husband has to prepare for spring fishing even during the winter, so he does not have time to help with housekeeping. We have time to talk with each other after dinner. And when there is a storm, he stays home and we talk a lot while I weave.

I have an hour for my lunch break. It is nonstop work. I do not feel the day is long at all. I feel it is short; I wish I could have more time to work. I cannot achieve what I expect each day. The manufacturer *[oyakata]* does not order a specific number of *obi,* but somebody [middle-

---

1. She uses the old-fashioned term for manufacturer, *oyakata,* meaning "father."

man] comes to pick up what I weave every day. Yes, depending on the kind of *obi* I am weaving, I can make one or two *obi* a day, or one *obi* in two days. The manufacturer tells us when to change the punch cards for the design for the jacquard. If the design is popular, he tells me to use it for one month.

I call two women experts to come here to do the tying of the warp [*tate-tsunagi*].[2] I pay them from my own income. I call them in the morning to come at noon, so that I will be prepared just when the current thread ends. They have a tight schedule. If they can't make it, they call me so that I can ask others. If I am not ready by noon, I call them and ask them to come a little later. I cannot let them wait for me here. Though I cannot do it, some people tie the warp by themselves. They do not have to spend money for it. It is due to my own inability that I have to pay others. I have not had any trouble with the *tate-tsunagi* women. I can estimate how long it will take me to use up the thread before I need them to come.

I have a middleman [*daikō-ten*] who works for the manufacturer. Of course, the manufacturer pays the middleman [a certain percentage]. I have been working with the same middleman for the past thirteen years. I have not had any troubles with him over these years. In the depression, the middleman is often stricter and points out the defects in our work. So many other weavers keep changing their middleman. But I never changed mine. I do not have any intention of changing to another one, even in the future. I do not think I receive any unusual support from my middleman, but if I have trouble with the looms I can call him to fix them. He does not urge me to work more and he does not rush me. He does not say to me, "Produce less," even during this depression. Except about five years ago, I also experienced something like a depression in Nishijin. At that time, I was told to produce less. I have been working on the same pattern from 7:00 A.M. to 7:00 P.M. each day since I began weaving. Even if I was told to produce less, I was given more complicated work to do in order to sustain the same income, such as 150,000 *yen* a month. I was working on complicated pieces that took the same length of time, even though I produced fewer pieces. We do not talk with other weavers about our income.

2. *Tate-tsugi*, connecting the new warp to the jacquard mechanism, is a delicate operation requiring a high skill level. It is done by retired older women weavers [*tate-tsunagi*], who go around in pairs when called to a weaver's house to perform this procedure. They usually carry a bamboo rod, which they use to separate the threads.

If I find any defect, I mend it by myself. Yes, I want to produce perfect work, even if I can make ten thousand *yen*. If there were defects, they would pay me just eight thousand *yen*. I check my work carefully before I give it to the middleman. If I find a defect that cannot be repaired, I pin a red thread over it and tell the middleman. If the defect is repairable, they do not deduct anything. But if it cannot be repaired, they deduct one or two thousand *yen*. Yes, I mostly weave *hikibaku* by hand [a technique of pulling the gold thread through as the shuttle moves the weft across the warp]. I cannot afford a new loom which can do *hikibaku* with just one push of a button. Such a loom costs 1.5 million *yen*. Pulling through the gold thread *[haku]* by hand is most difficult, because the gold thread is very thin.[3]

No, I do not have any pain in my hands, but the backs of my feet hurt sometimes. I stand up all the time when I work. No, I cannot work sitting down. I have to keep standing to check defects. In my household work, I also stand up, but the change of tasks relieves my tiredness. The change from weaving to household work is sort of a rest for me. Yes, I watch television from 8:30 to 10:00 P.M. I go to bed at 10:00 P.M. exactly.

I usually do not work on Sundays. I have to make three *obi* per week, so I have to sustain the amount of work. No, I do not have any hobby right now. I used to play softball on Sunday afternoon with other women in the women's association *[fujin-kai]*. I stopped it because I reached age fifty. Yes, I go to our vegetable fields on Sunday. We have a *dandan-batake* [ladder-like garden, meaning terraced fields on the mountain slope] where I raise onions, potatoes, and so forth. Yes, I climb the steep slope, but it is nearby, only a ten minutes' walk. On Sunday, I go to the fields and take care of the flowers and vegetables. I go there to pick flowers each Sunday morning and I arrange them at home. No, my husband does not work in the fields, but he is devoted to fishing. When he can get three days off, he sometimes helps me with farming. If he has one or two days off, he has to fix the fishing tools. Yes, he has to repair the fishing nets. This usually takes an hour and a half. He has many other things to fix on his boat. He runs his fishing

---

3. *Haku* is the gold thread that has traditionally been pulled through by hand, rather than by shuttle. The new *hikibaku* machine has an attachment that looks like the hand of a robot. It moves back and forth and pulls through the gold thread, rather than the weaver having to do it.

business by himself, so he has no age limit for retirement. He does not belong to the Union of Fishermen.

We do not travel at all. No, we have not been to Kyoto together. But I go there once a year for the meeting of the women's group *[fujin-kai]*. I rarely leave home. I belong to the group of fishermen's wives. There is a group of women weavers that I also belong to. We share our troubles and discuss them. We talk about how to fix looms and repair defects in our work. Many people have troubles with their middleman; we discuss that issue, too. Yes, it is only a women's meeting. The leader's husband is the head of the whole Tango Union of Weavers *[Tango Ori Rōdo-Kumiai]*. Our group is formally called *ito-guruma*, but we call it informally a "chatting meeting." We meet at least once a year to have dinner together. We have occasional lectures, but not very many people come. Yes, I value this group where I can learn from other people. Among weavers, I am the newest one—even after thirteen years of weaving.

We have a trip once every three years with other weavers and once a year with the members of the women's association. They are mostly one-night trips. The group of weavers is very interesting for me, since we can talk about the same job. The middleman arranges a trip for us with other weavers. He invites weavers from other areas. We save one thousand *yen* each month for this trip. I think the middleman shares half the cost of the trip. The fee for this trip is automatically drawn from our monthly payment. If we do not join the trip, he returns half of the savings. Some middlemen do not do this kind of thing at all. When we went to Kyushu, we had many things to talk about with fellow weavers who worked for the same middleman. Each time we take a trip, we visit at least one place related to weaving. Besides Hakata [in Kyushu], we went to Nishijin. We had a tour of Nishijin. Yes, I have been to my manufacturer in Nishijin three times.

MR. U.: Weavers in this area do weaving as a side job. But weavers in other areas, such as Amino Chō [the main weaving town in Tango], do weaving as their main job. So they start weaving even before 7:00 A.M. They work long hours because they compete to weave as much as possible.

MRS. U.: That is right, but what I do is heavier than most full-time jobs for women.

MR. U.: What I meant as a "side job" is that weaving is a side income for the whole family. Of course, it is a full-time job for her [wife]. I take a half-hour or hour nap after lunch, but I do not mind the weaving noises.

MRS. U.: Well . . . [laugh], I like it best when I am almost finishing a whole *obi*. I feel satisfied after the long hours of weaving. I finish one *obi* in two days. I am now working on complicated patterns. I have a preference for certain designs and colors. It takes longer to weave designs and colors that are not my favorites. Too complicated a design, which necessitates the frequent cutting of the thread, makes me feel not so nice. I do not feel like a laborer. I feel like a craftsman. Why? If I were a laborer, I would work punctually and mechanically from 7:00 A.M. to 7:00 P.M. without any particular consciousness. But I am very responsible and mindful of what I am making. Yes, I believe that there is a difference between laborers and craftsmen *[shokunin]*. A craftsman is conscious of his unique skill to make something of his own.

If I had to do something in the daytime, I would have to keep working even after 7:00 P.M. to make up for lost time. The weavers' union made this regulation that we should work from 7:00 A.M. to 7:00 P.M. Yes, we are allowed to work for twelve hours a day. If somebody wants to stop at 5:00 P.M., it is all right to stop. In principle, we are supposed to work from 7:00 A.M. to 7:00 P.M. [By this, she means weavers should not start any earlier or work any later in order not to disturb neighbors.][4]

MR. U.: About labor hours, the Tango Association of Textile Manufacturers *[Tango Ori Kōgyō Kumiai]* decided on these hours.[5] The market of Tango *chirimen* is in a depression.[6] Weavers are supposed to follow the regulations, but some of them work more than that. Weavers are allowed to work longer than eight hours because weaving is a family production. Even small stores in town are like that. They cannot stick to eight hours. If the weaving is organized as an official company [corporation], they have to follow the law. If they have to work longer than twelve hours, they set up shifts dividing the working hours into two sections.

4. The eight-hour law, which was introduced in Nishijin in accordance with the Fair Labor Standards Act, did not apply to Tango.

5. The *Tango Ori Kōgyō Kumiai* is the union of the *oyakata* [manufacturers] of weaving. Cottage weavers belong instead to the Tango Union of Weavers.

6. Tango *chirimen* is white, textured silk cloth for *kimono*, which is dyed after it is woven. This was the product for which Tango was famous. The weaving of *obi* that Mrs. Uebayashi and the other weavers in Tango are doing gradually replaced the weaving of *chirimen* after its markets declined.

MRS. U.: If they employ people for weaving, they have to keep the regulations. For us, it is a household industry.

MR. U.: For example, if one *obi* requires twenty hours to be finished, my wife will spend twelve hours each day on it, rather than just eight hours, because she is paid by the piece. Twelve hours is the maximum, but if we want to, we can work less, too. Twelve hours is the limit, not the requirement.

MRS. U.: I heard that twenty years ago cottage weavers would even work through the night. Nobody wants to weave now, because this is a difficult job. No young people are weaving here now. There was an increase in the number of weavers, but the present weavers quit one by one with this depression. Recently, Kura Shoji-san quit, too. He was a good weaver, so I do not know why he quit. Maybe because of the depression . . . maybe because he can make more money in *minshuku* [family-run guest house]. There are many other people who quit weaving recently. We have a depression and the middlemen want us to produce perfect work. They often complain of defects and the weavers get upset. Because of the depression, the middlemen got really fussy. They want to keep only the weavers who do better work.

MR. U.: Oh, this house is just three years old. Since our oldest son decided to come back from Kyoto after he finished college, we renovated this house. He is a fisherman. No, I was not surprised when he agreed to succeed to my job, because I expected him to. When he left for college in Kyoto, I told him to come back later. He is working hard and seems to like it. Many of the oldest sons in the families of this town have come back to be fishermen after working in big cities for three or four years. Most of the oldest sons are conscious of their responsibility to be successors to their family businesses. They did not fail in their jobs in the cities. They came back to take on their responsibilities here. This is sort of a tradition. I do not think that their parents urged them to come back, but the oldest sons were responsible enough to follow their roles.

Well, about marriage, fewer sons bring back fiancées from the cities. They are given freedom in their college age. The parents try not to interfere with what their sons are doing. But once the sons decide to come back to succeed their fathers, they take marriage very seriously. Our son is not yet married. He is twenty-six years old. That is not something unusual. There are many men older than thirty who are single in this town. Modern young women do not want to marry fishermen and farmers very much. Many families are encountering difficulties in finding young wives.

MRS. U.: Yes, young women would like to marry salary men, but not fishermen. When I was young, things were not like that. We did not care about this. Young people today hate hard work. They do not want to weave from 7:00 A.M. to 7:00 P.M. I am a bundle of ambition; that keeps me working [laugh].

MR. U.: Young girls dream of marrying someone who will establish a residence apart from his parents. They want to have an easy time at home after their husbands leave for work. They dream romantic dreams. Yes, many urban women want to work outside the home, but once they get married, they prefer staying home. Later some of them may want to return to work when they experience financial problems in their homes, though.

MRS. U.: For instance, most young women of Ine Chō do not have particular skills in their work. They just do simple office work. So once they get married, they give up their jobs. But our daughter has been married for five years. She keeps working outside, because she does not have a child. She is living in Mie Prefecture. Even though she got a certificate for kindergarten teaching from a community college in Osaka, she is working as a clerk of financial management in a dentist's office. When I began weaving, she was already a high school student. I did not have a problem raising babies while weaving.

MR. U.: The history of weaving in Ine Chō is not very long. The longest weaving career would be twenty years at the most. So most weavers are older than fifty-five. Their children do not have to be taken care of by their parents. Rather, children may help their mothers by going shopping or doing the laundry. Even if some of the weavers have small children, they have an advantage in the family structure in the countryside. Unlike in urban families, grandparents can take care of young children.

MRS. U.: I came from Miyazu City. My parents were working half as fishermen, half as farmers [hangyo hannō]. They did not weave at all. I did not hesitate to marry a fisherman. We had to change our lifestyle to some extent due to my weaving. For example, I try not to stop weaving in the middle of the day. Once I start to work at 7:00 A.M., I prefer not to stop. So I have to ask a favor of our grandmother [husband's mother] to take care of some housekeeping. She sometimes complains about that. We have been living together with my husband's parents. My husband's father died three years ago. He was also a fisherman.

MR. U.: As far as I could learn through the record in the temple of this village, I am the sixth generation of fishermen. We have been in this Ine Chō village all the time. I do not know anything about the origins of our family. The past record of the family in the temple is the only way for me to look up the history of several generations.

Mr. and Mrs. Nagahama

Cottage Weavers of Wedding Kimono
on the Tango Peninsula

Mr. Nagahama Jouichi and Mrs. Nagahama Minako, his wife, live in Ta-
kanashi, one of the four fishing villages in the Ine Chō area on the Tango
Peninsula. Mr. Nagahama is from an old family of fishermen. He and his
family live with Mr. Nagahama's parents in the original family home on the
narrow strip of land between the mountain and the sea. Their weaving shed
is across the street from their home on the edge of the sea, in what used to be
their fish-house. The Nagahama home is one of the most elaborate traditional
houses in the village, consistent with the family's high status in the fishing
industry in the past as well as with their leadership in the community. The
house still serves as the headquarters for the childrens' and teenagers' teams
that perform ritual dances during the Ine Festival, which takes place once a
year in July (see fig. 29).

Mr. and Mrs. Nagahama weave uchikake — the magnificent brocade wedding coats worn by brides over kimono. The technique for weaving uchikake
is similar to that of obi. It differs, however, in the complexity of the designs
and the colors. The biggest difficulty is in the requirement to weave the design
symmetrically, so that two halves of each design line up exactly in front where
the two parts of the coat meet. If the design fails to line up, the entire length
of cloth is wasted.

Mrs. Nagahama does most of the weaving. Her husband weaves occasionally and helps with the preparatory work. They have five children. The oldest
was a student at Kyoto University at the time of the interview. It is a very
unusual achievement for a fisherman's family in Ine Chō to have a son study
at Kyoto University. Mrs. Nagahama is a Christian; she was educated in the
Catholic girls' school in Miazu (30 km away). Once a month, the itinerant

FIGURE 29. Village of Tateishi in Ine Chō on the Tango Peninsula, during the major fisher-men's festival, *Ine Matsuri*. A boat carrying a shrine is moored in front of the traditional houses [*funaya*]. Photograph by Tamara Hareven.

priest comes from Miazu to celebrate Mass in Mrs. Nagahama's house. Several
other Catholic women who live in Ine Chō assemble in her house for the Mass.

Mr. N. = Mr. Nagahama

Mrs. N. = Mrs. Nagahama

MRS. N.: I have been weaving since the age of nineteen. This was not
necessarily common at that time. I am the daughter of weavers, but I
had never entered my parents' workshop till I graduated from high
school. Yes, I helped some after school. I swept the floor. But I began
weaving with my parents after I graduated from high school. When I
started weaving for the first time, I found that tying the warp was extremely difficult for me. I had a hard time till I could master the skill of
connecting the threads. Most of our relatives were weavers, and they
helped me weave. I am the oldest daughter in our family. My sisters
were not interested in weaving. They worked outside. When I graduated
from high school, my parents did not have any employees, so I just
began helping my parents weave. I have a younger brother who also
used to weave at home. He came back to weave *chirimen* [textured white
silk for *kimono*], but since the Oil Shock, the market for *chirimen* has
become pretty bad. So he is now weaving *obi* together with his wife.
My parents wanted him to help them. When I got married, I did not
imagine that I would have to keep weaving. But I could not help weaving even after my marriage. Yes, I like this job; it seems like the best
type of work for women. People want to marry partners from somewhere else. I came from Miazu, the neighboring town. It is just fifteen
minutes from here by car.

MR. N.: After our marriage, I worked for a while on *dekasegi* — that is a
seasonal side job for which workers leave their home community and
work somewhere else. I worked on the construction of the road that
runs on top of the high cliffs on the tip of the Tango Peninsula.

MRS. N.: I heard that he risked his life many times in the construction
of that road. So it is better that he became a weaver.

MR. N.: We started weaving twenty years ago. My parents were never
engaged in weaving.

MRS. N.: They [husband's parents] say our work is beautiful, but I do not think that they wanted to do this kind of work. They do not help us weave, but they help in housekeeping. They do not come to our weaving workshop. Technically, it is difficult for them to help us out.

MR. N.: If they make a mistake, it is a big damage for us; it will be deducted from our income.

MRS. N.: After my marriage, I was weaving all day. The grandparents [Mr. Nagahama's parents] took care of our children a great deal. Grandmother did the household work, including cooking. When we began weaving, I used to work from 6:00 A.M. to 7:00 P.M. No matter how small the children were, I worked all those hours. Nowadays, I go to weave after all the children leave for school. I even work after supper till 8:30 P.M. I have very little time to be with our children. I talk with them before they leave for school or over dinner. On Sundays, too, we work unless we have something very special.

MR. N.: It would be very nice to work less, if only we could survive. We have five children. The youngest girl goes to elementary school. The oldest son will go to college.[1] He failed his entrance exam to the university this year. He wants to go to Kyoto University next year, so he goes to a "cramming school" in Kyoto.[2] My wife and I work for two different manufacturers [oyakata]. Had we worked for the same oyakata, we would be paid as a family. They calculate the pay for each of our looms, but they pay the total for the family. Now we are paid separately, each by our own oyakata.[3]

MRS. N.: If we become subject to the labor law [Fair Labor Standards Act] and are limited to work no more than eight hours a day, we would have to starve.

1. During the first interview, college was only part of the plan. Subsequently, the son was admitted.

2. A "cramming school" is a special tutorial school that prepares students for entrance exams. The following year, the son was admitted to Kyoto University—one of the two most difficult national universities to gain admission to.

3. Having each household member work for a different manufacturer was exceptional in Nishijin. It was not problematic in Tango, because the remoteness of Tango villages made it less likely that manufacturers could steal designs.

MR. N.: Most individual weavers cannot afford such a system. The minimum pay for labor is very different between Nishijin and Tango. The manufacturers are very pragmatic to employ us for cheaper pay than the Kyoto weavers. They have to pay much more to the Kyoto weavers. It is the system of Nishijin. The company we work for is considerate. When we have to wait for the company to settle the claim, we are paid for these hours to some extent, but they do not pay as much as we expect. In the case of wedding coats *[uchi-kake]*, we cannot afford to make the slightest mistake with colors. For instance, when we weave this phoenix design, we have to use the same color to the very end of the phoenix's tail. If the color changes, the whole *uchi-kake* cannot be sold at all. Even silk threads with the same color identification code usually differ in the finer nuances of the color each time, because the solution with the dye in the boiling kettle is changed quite often. It is something very delicate. There will never be the same color twice on this earth. When we get new threads, they may look slightly different from the previous ones; once we finish weaving, the colors look really different. If the color looks uneven, we have to pay for it.

MRS. N.: We have to blend the older thread with the new one to avoid a conspicuous change of color. Of course, people in Kyoto [manufacturer's office] tell us what colors to use. For example, they tell us to make this pine design in purple. We cannot do anything according to our own choice. In the case of *obi*, the weavers can be careful not to repeat the same mistake for the next one. In our case, one mistake and that's it. In *uchi-kake* weaving, no mistake is allowed. First we have to weave the whole sample. Then, after we have completed the sample, they [middlemen] tell us that we have to change the colors.[4] The manufacturers provide technical instructions to weavers. But they do not give sufficient information about how to do our order right. The sample pictures often come out differently in the completed weaving. One cannot say anything until one really sees the finished product.

We now have a dispute with our company. I received no instructions as to what colors to use for this *uchi-kake*, so I just started weaving it the way I believed the colors should be. I stopped doing it soon after, because the way I wove appeared to be strange. Usually the manufacturer's office puts notes with instructions about the colors with the

4. The basic design is generally produced in different color combinations. The weaver receives from the manufacturer both the design and color instructions.

roll of raw material. If the design is simple, I could ask them on the phone what colors I should use. But this was too complicated to discuss on the phone, so I put another sample beside it and I completed the other one while guessing on my own. Later they sent the product back to me and I did it again. This is the third time I have woven for the same order since I first received the punch cards for the jacquard [mon-gami] for this roll. They did not return my weaving. They could not sell it, either. I hope that they will pay me. I have not yet gotten paid.

MR. N.: We are waiting for the next order without being paid for the previous one. If we turned in our work today, it would reach the man-ufacturer tomorrow. Then the manufacturer would say something about it tomorrow night. His comment would then come back to us the day after tomorrow. We have to waste two or three days each time. We wasted one week for this work, because we were requested to redo it three times.

MRS. N.: We spent half the month waiting.

MR. N.: Since they [manufacturers] know that this was their fault, I hope they will compensate us for our lost time, to some extent. We had to prepare the looms [hatagoshirae] for three days before we started weaving this order, because we had to switch from the previous design to this one. Changing the weaving method [shikuchigae] is something fatal for weavers. When it occurs too often, we suffer great damage from it. In this case, we had to change the design due to the manufacturer's fault and we expect them to pay for our labor. Of course, if the pay is too low, we could complain through the middleman [daikō-ten]. We can also contact the manufacturer directly. I do not know if they could listen to us, though. There is also the Tango Ori Kōgyō Kumiai [Tango As-sociation of Textile Manufacturers], which has a local branch for each district. The weavers' union is not strong enough to help us. The union stands on our side, but they do not have any full-time workers who can negotiate with the manufacturer. It consists of part-time weavers.

This wedding coat [uchi-kake] is much more expensive than what we were weaving the last time you visited. Only two pieces of this type can be produced per month. We are usually expected to repeat the same design at least ten times. We can keep weaving in the same way for half a year, unless the design and color change. This one is much more com-plicated. We had to spend, therefore, much more time on this. We used twenty-six colors for this one. We used about twenty colors for the other one.

MRS. N.: I hope we are paid more for this one. We can make four rolls of the previous one in the same time that we make just two of the present one. So we should be paid better for this one. We barely get used to the new design when we are told to change again to another one. They [manufacturers] are clever in this way to save money. They are in a hurry to get this type of weaving done as soon as possible [because it is for weddings]. So I do not think they would let us wait for the next job. In the case of *obi*, I know people have to wait sometimes for the next job, or they are often told to change colors in order to slow down their production. But we do not suffer from that kind of thing. This is the first time they have told us to change the colors of *uchi-kake*.

MR. N.: The production of *uchi-kake* has not declined yet, because even in the depression people have weddings. I heard that the same manufacturer for whom I work has reduced 20 percent of production of *obi* in the summer this year. But they encourage us to produce more *uchi-kake*.

MRS. N.: I do not care very much about their choice of colors. What I am concerned about is the payment. I heard that the manufacturer is struggling to find original color arrangements because the patterns for *uchi-kake* are generally similar.

MR. N.: In general, they like conspicuous, colorful designs for wedding wear.

MRS. N.: We never thought of switching to handlooms, because we spent much money buying powerlooms when we started this job. When we started weaving, everybody was using powerlooms. The handloom was introduced here in Tango later. There are two or three people working with handlooms in Ine Chō, but they are doing specialized work for special orders.

MR. N.: Ine Chō is a town of fishermen. Men cannot be involved with weaving. Fishing is more important for them. So here most of the weavers are women.

MRS. N.: Unless we are educated, we cannot do anything other than weaving. Yes, if our children would weave with us, we would be very happy. But I do not think it will happen. If they could work with us at home, it would be very nice. If they say they will work with us, we would have to buy extra looms. Yes, I have asked our children whether they would succeed us, but they did not show any interest. Weaving is lonely work; just facing a loom all day long is very lonely.

Conclusion

The Nishijin Experience in Comparative Perspective

The questions addressed in this study are central to an understanding of the relationship between individuals and the process of social change in various parts of the world, past and present. Even though the Nishijin experience has many aspects unique to Japanese society and culture, it also parallels developments that followed the industrial revolution in Western Europe and the United States in the nineteenth century. The textile industry, in this respect, is a good case in point. In Europe and the United States, the replacement of a traditional craft by a rapidly advancing industrial technology led to redefinition of the craftspeople's status and skill and to the restructuring of work roles within the family.

On the other hand, the historical circumstances in Nishijin differ in many respects from those in the West. While in the West powerlooms almost entirely replaced handlooms, in Nishijin the two have coexisted as two different forms of technology within the same craft, making the same product, often in the same establishment or in the same family. Another difference lies in the historic period of industrial development when powerlooms were introduced. In Japan, these changes have been taking place in the midst of an industrialized society. In Western Europe and the United States, the entire society was undergoing industrialization in varying degrees during the nineteenth century.

An important contrast between Nishijin and England concerns the introduction of the powerloom. In a discussion that describes conditions similar to those of contemporary Nishijin, E. P. Thompson argued that in Britain in the 1830s, the main cause of the decline in the status and earning of the weavers was not the powerloom. Rather, the pow-

303

erloom was used as an explanation that obscured more complex factors, including "[f]irst, the breakdown of both custom and trade union protection; second, the total exposure of the weavers to the worst forms of wage cutting; third, the overstocking of the trade by unemployed people. . . ." The spread of the powerloom in Nishijin was not the major cause of the decline in the weavers' status in Nishijin, either, although some of the weavers attributed Nishijin's problems to the powerloom. Nishijin male weavers' main concern about the powerloom was that it led to weaving being taken over by women, which they perceived as a decline in skills. Most Nishijin weavers are painfully aware, however, that the source of the decline of their craft and status emanates not from the powerloom but from the weakness of the labor union and from what they consider the manufacturers' unfair payment practices and manipulative ways of curtailing production.

The experiences and statements of Nishijin weavers suggest comparison with patterns in the textile industry in Europe and the United States. The Nishijin cottage weavers' perception of themselves as craftspeople, rather than as industrial workers, brings to mind Thompson's depiction of the mentality of English handloom weavers who were working in household production, which differed from that of factory workers. As mentioned earlier, Nishijin cottage weavers cherished the privilege of determining their own time schedules and control over what Thompson coined as "rhythms of work and leisure" (Thompson 1964). Nishijin weavers became frustrated when legislation or pressure from neighbors intruded upon this freedom. As Mrs. Uebayashi, a weaver in Ine Chō in Tango, put it:

I do not feel like a laborer. I feel like a craftsman. Why? If I were a laborer, I would work punctually and mechanically from 7:00 A.M. to 7:00 P.M. without any particular consciousness. But I am very responsible and mindful of what I am making. Yes, I believe that there is a difference between laborers and craftsmen [shokunin]. A craftsman is conscious of his unique skill to make something of his own. If I had to do something in the daytime, I would have to keep working even after 7:00 P.M. to make up for lost time. The weavers' union made this regulation that we should work from 7:00 A.M. to 7:00 P.M. Yes, we are allowed to work for twelve hours a day. If somebody wants to stop at 5:00 P.M., it is all right to stop. In principle, we are supposed to work from 7:00 A.M. to 7:00 P.M.

By this, she means weavers should not start any earlier or work any later in order not to disturb neighbors.

Thompson described similar preferences for flexibility on the part of English weavers early in the nineteenth century. He quoted the son of a weaver from the Heptonstall district in England who recalled that, during his childhood in the 1820s, the weavers "had their good times," most importantly because there "was no bell to ring them up at four or five o'clock . . . there was freedom to start and to stay away as they cared. . . . " Another weaver, a factory child laborer from Keighley, testified that he preferred handloom weaving to working in the mill "a great deal." He explained, "I have more relaxation; I can look about me, and go and refresh myself a little" (Thompson 1964, 291). It is important to remember that in Nishijin, the preference for weaving at home and maintaining flexible schedules was mainly that of male weavers. Nishijin women preferred the factory, because it freed them from interruptions at home and because of the sociability of the workplace. In this respect, the Nishijin women shared a common attitude with women weavers in twentieth-century New England and Western Europe (Hareven 1982).

While Nishijin craftspeople held a great deal in common with handloom weavers in early-nineteenth-century England, striking similarities have also emerged from the comparison of the experiences of the former Amoskeag workers in the twentieth century with those of the Nishijin weavers. The similarities in their perceptions appear despite the fact that the Amoskeag Mills were the world's largest textile plant making mass-produced fabrics and Nishijin is a traditional industry producing high-quality luxury weavings. Although there are profound differences between the United States and Japan, the weavers' experiences were so similar, in some respects, that some of my questions, deriving from my American textile research, struck a familiar chord among the Japanese people interviewed. In fact, early in the interview process some Nishijin weavers asked me, "How do you know to ask these questions?"

Similarities emerging from the reconstruction of life histories of Amoskeag and Nishijin workers are expressed in their self-perceptions of their role as craftspeople, their identity as textile workers, their relationships to their employers, and the roles of women weavers in the family. Both Amoskeag and Nishijin workers expressed a strong sense of belonging to their respective industries and to their working and living places. But they also viewed their involvement with their industry as the unavoidable result of having been born and raised in those settings. This inevitable sense of belonging also made them feel vulnerable when their industries declined or shut down. As Raymond Dubois, a former Amoskeag worker, put it:

I was brought up in the area of the mill. All our people were mill people, and we didn't know anything else but mills. We didn't know anything else existed, really . . . the only people we knew were mill people. We lived near the mills, we carried dinners for our parents, and we just were accustomed to the mills. It seemed like this was where we would fall in when we got old enough. I went in a few months after I became sixteen. (Hareven and Langenbach 1978, 152)

This statement is very similar to those of Mr. Nishitani, Mrs. Fujiwara, and the senior Mr. Shibagaki, who emphasized that they were born into the Nishijin industry and that they never knew another world. (See their interviews.)

Another experience that Nishijin weavers and Amoskeag workers held in common was the cross-stitched and "disorderly" character of the Nishijin weavers' work careers, resulting from fluctuations in the market, business cycles, and changing production policies. This is a characteristic shared in general by textile workers in historic Europe and in the United States. The workers in the Amoskeag Mills experienced "disorderly careers" as a regular condition of their employment patterns. They structured their work, migration, and family lives around these uncertainties. Despite the instability of the workers' careers, both Nishijin and Amoskeag workers repeatedly expressed a sense of continuity and a strong identification with the companies they worked for, and most notably with the products they made. Like the Nishijin artisans, the industrial workers in Manchester had a strong commitment to their work, along with an identification with the Amoskeag Mills' fame and the special quality of the cloth they were producing. Former Amoskeag workers were proud of the fact that the Amoskeag Mills had been the world's largest textile factory, and that the quantity of cloth it produced in one day was enough to "wrap around the world." This was true even for unskilled or semi-skilled Amoskeag workers who operated power-looms to weave mass-produced textiles. Unlike the Nishijin weavers, the Amoskeag workers did not describe their quest for perfection as a "spiritual exercise." They did use powerful language, however, to describe their commitment to quality. Omer Proulx, a French-Canadian weaver in the Amoskeag Mills who later became a loom fixer, was articulate about his continuing quest for perfection:

Fifty years ago, when I worked in the mills, it was to try out new things more than anything else. Weaving cotton was just a small part of it. . . . You have to like to do something before you can do it well. . . . It has to be in you to do something well. You have to love it.

Marie, Omer's wife, added:

You have to want it [your work]. Amoskeag was serious about perfection. It had men to see to the bottom of things. . . . It was a joy, it was a joy to go to work. (Hareven and Langenbach 1978, 70)

This type of identification with the product and the high standards of perfection are characteristic of textile mill workers at large. The fact that weavers produce a visibly whole product, rather than a segment on an assembly line, partly explains this. For that reason, even semi-skilled or low-skilled textile workers in the United States spoke about their product with a sense of pride and identification, similar to that of the highly specialized artisans in Kyoto.

Similarly to the women weavers in Kyoto, former Amoskeag women weavers expressed a strong sense of pride in their skills and a connectedness to their work. Criticizing some women weavers who worked for the money only, Cora Pellerine, a former weaver in the Amoskeag Mills, emphasized her own dedication to her craft, even though she admitted that money was also a major consideration for her:

Some weavers weave all their lives and never get the hang of it. Some women, especially, they just weave because they have to earn money; they never apply themselves to it. They were housekeepers. . . .

But as far as Cora was concerned, "I loved my work; it was my life" (Hareven and Langenbach 1978, 206).

Bette Skrzyszowski, a former battery hand about one generation younger than Cora Pellerine, was in her early fifties when we interviewed her. Bette mourned the loss of her world of work when the last textile mill shut down in Manchester in 1975:

After you put that many years into a place, it's like a second home. You go every day, you know how much time it's going to take you, and you come home at a certain time. Just a nice routine. You knew what to do and how to do it, and you knew how long it would take you. Nobody bothered you. You knew you had a job to go to. It was a good feeling. Now you know your time has come, and you feel lost. You just have no place to turn. . . . There's no more weaving. . . . I don't know how to explain it. But you're connected with the machinery. It's part of you; it's your life. I love the mills, I love to work, I loved being a battery hand. I always liked it. . . . I'll miss the people I worked with; I'll miss the mill itself. The day they close will be the saddest day I've ever seen. (Hareven and Langenbach 1978, 381–384)

Despite their commitment to their craft and industry, both Amoskeag and Nishijin workers expressed ambiguities in their self-perceptions as workers. Neither the Nishijin weavers nor the Amoskeag workers considered themselves permanent members of their class. Nishijin weavers working in their own household production viewed themselves as craftspeople as well as aspiring small entrepreneurs. Similarly, Amoskeag factory workers did not perceive themselves as permanent members of the working class. Their aspirations were to eventually escape factory work and join the middle class. Marie Proulx reported her husband harbored such hopes early in his life: "When Omer wasn't any older than fifteen, he was saying, 'I'm going to have a white collar some day'" (Hareven and Langenbach 1978, 69). The implications of these self-images and aspirations of Nishijin craftspeople and Amoskeag workers had similar, significant implications for union membership in both communities. The weakness of the labor unions in Nishijin and the tardiness of their appearance in Amoskeag partly resulted from both groups of workers' lack of a sense of collective identification as members of a working class.

The ambivalence and the sense of betrayal that Nishijin weavers have experienced during the precipitous decline of their industry in the 1980s and 1990s was matched by a similar sentiment that the Amoskeag workers expressed when the manufacturing company in which they had invested their energies let them down during its decline and final shutdown in 1936. The stronger the sense of identification with an industry, the more intense the feeling of betrayal. While both Nishijin weavers and former Amoskeag workers were bitter when their livelihood was endangered by declines in employment security and in wages, what they resented most was the apparent lack of concerted effort by their employers to find constructive solutions that would save the world of work to which they had committed their loyalty.

The strong integration of individuals with the family's collective identity and economy was another characteristic of both Nishijin craftspeople and Amoskeag workers. This integration was prevalent among Amoskeag workers, even though they worked in a factory rather than in household production. It is precisely this strong involvement of individual careers with the family's collective goals that led to the ambiguity in the roles of women weavers. As in Nishijin, women in the Amoskeag Mills who worked in jobs similar to those of men viewed their work as an integral part of their domestic activities, rather than as individual careers. Like the senior Mrs. Shibagaki in Kyoto, Maria LaCasse, an eighty-year-old former weaver in the Amoskeag Mills who had raised nine children, viewed her paid work in the factory, her housekeeping, and her various money-generating projects at home (such as taking in boarders) as part of a continuing effort to sustain her family:

My husband never stopped me from going to work when we needed the money. I had to make all the clothes, even the pants for the little boys. I used to sell sandwiches to the girls in the mill if they didn't bring their lunch. My husband was just across the street, and he used to whistle from the millyard and tell me how many sandwiches he wanted. My husband always wanted his meal hot, so I would send him something hot in a pail. (Hareven and Langenbach 1978, 261)

Maria's daughter, contrary to her mother's interpretation, claimed that her father did not want her mother to work in the mills and emphasized her mother's various domestic contributions to the family economy, but admitted that her mother worked sporadically in the mills despite her father's resistance:

After my parents got married, my mother just worked periodically, for two or three months at a time, when things would get too hard and my father didn't have any money. My father didn't really want her to work. That was a big issue because she always wanted to go in and earn a little money. But the minute she said she wanted to work, there would be a big fight. He'd say, "No, you're not going to work. You're going to stay home." And that's why she did other things. She'd make clothes for him, take in boarders, rent rooms. She used to rent one or two rooms for $12.00 a week to people who worked in the mills. Sometimes she'd also work little stretches at night, from six to nine, because we lived right in front of the mills. When there were big orders, the mills were always looking for people to work. But my father didn't want to keep the children. That was women's work; his work was outside. (Hareven and Langenbach 1978, 255)

Despite the dramatic differences in the organization of production, the types of cloth woven, and the organization of the family and gender roles, there were significant similarities between Manchester and Kyoto. Even though the Nishijin weavers were highly skilled artisans, they held many attitudes and self-perceptions in common with the industrial workers in the Amoskeag Mills. Their experience in the production of textiles and the "textile language" they spoke in some respects transcended the cultural differences between Japan and the United States. The commonality of the experience of producing textiles and of being skilled weavers, active in highly recognized industrial enterprises, cut across the two cultures.

Textile workers in these two societies obviously shared common ways of life, customs, and cultural beliefs with members of other occupations and social classes in their respective societies. But where their sense of expertise and pride in textile production, the integration of family and work in their lives, and the roles of women as textile workers were concerned; in some respects Nishijin and Amoskeag workers held more in common with each other than with other groups in their respective societies.

The question that needs to be raised now is: How do the textile workers' identities, which are so deeply rooted in their work, interact with the other aspects of their respective cultures in shaping their views of themselves and their worlds? Answers to this question require an entire book. It is clear that despite the commonality in experiences and attitudes between the Nishijin weavers and British and American textile workers, Nishijin weavers were Japanese and conformed to Japanese customs, mores, and ways of life in their own society.

Even though their work schedules, their sense of themselves as crafts-people, and the role of women as weavers have differed from those of factory workers and salary men in Japan, they share the strong Japanese conformity to the outside world—in the neighborhood, on the street, and in other public places. The concept of "inside" and "outside" is very powerful in Japan. The slatted door of the house and the *noren* [split curtain with the sign of the shop] separate the outside world from the inside. Japanese people respect this separation, which is much more powerful than privacy in the West. While Nishijin people are living different kinds of lives than Japanese factory workers and salary men, they adhere to this customary division. This is clearly evident in the example drawn from the lives of Mr. and Mrs. Konishi. Although Mr. Konishi helped his wife carry the grocery bags when they were not seen by their neighbors, he did not feel comfortable doing so in their own neighborhood.

Gender role division and segregation are far more powerful in Japan than in the United States. Even though these divisions are some-what modified among Nishijin weavers, because of the wives' high skills and productivity in the craft, conformity to social rules govern-ing gender in Japanese society has been entrenched and preserved in Nishijin as well. This is expressed in the fact that Nishijin women weavers work a "three-shift" day. In addition to their weaving, they have a responsibility to housework and child-rearing. This pattern dif-fered only in degree from American working-class experiences. As explained earlier, both Nishijin women weavers and American women textile workers viewed their craft as inseparable from their overall contribution to their household economy and family survival. The major contrast between the Nishijin weavers and their twentieth-century counterparts in the United States was in styles of sociability. Nishijin men conformed to the customs of their culture by socializing, drinking, and gambling with other men in the evenings. These gender-segregated activities are also characteristic of members of the American working class (Gans 1962; Hareven 1982). There is, however, a difference in the degree of social segregation along gender lines in Japan. Similarly to salary men and other Japanese workers, most Nishijin men spend their evenings with other Nishijin men. Although family members work together in Nishijin, husbands and wives are segregated in their social activities.

Generational relations among Nishijin workers also conform much more closely to Japanese family relations than to American styles. The expectations about how adult children should relate to their aging parents and about the relationships between mothers-in-law and daughters-in-law resemble those of other groups and social classes in Japan. If the older generation resides in the same household with adult children, they contribute to the household production effort. Grandmothers usually help care for their grandchildren while the mother is weaving, even if they do not live in the same household. Similarly to other groups in Japan, Nishijin weavers maintain more formal relationships with the older generation than the Amoskeag workers did. This kind of formality is embedded in various aspects of Japanese culture, and can also generate tension. Because of the Japanese concern for harmony, however, open confrontations are rare. The Japanese quest for harmony requires that conflicts be suppressed and that individuals sacrifice their preferences and priorities to the common good and to the continuity and success of the house, the lineage, and the community.

Despite the similarities emphasized here in the relationship between family and work, and the mentality inherent in the common experience of producing textiles among the American and Japanese laborers, one cannot stress strongly enough that the Nishijin weavers and manufacturers *are* Japanese. They live in a very different world than that of the American immigrant workers in Manchester, New Hampshire. They function in a different culture; they use a different language. Despite all the modern technological implements they employ in their homes, they follow traditional Japanese customs and are strongly integrated with their own culture. Even the textiles they produce carry a special cultural symbolism and meaning. These vast cultural differences make it all the more striking that Nishijin weavers asked me, an American researcher whose questions touched on their inner experiences unbeknownst to me, "How do you know to ask these questions?"

Appendix

The Subjective Reconstruction of Life History

Oral history and life history are important components of this book. Therefore we need to understand their creation and their role as sources. Oral history has inspired enthusiasm for its unique role in recovering the experiences of anonymous people. At the same time, oral history has been criticized as a historical tool because of its distance in time from the events recalled. Hindsight, clearly the source of its strength, is also a potential source of weakness. When using oral history to reconstruct historical experiences, it must be remembered that the people interviewed are survivors. Only people who can be tracked down and who are willing to share their memories can be interviewed. Thus, by its nature, oral history raises questions of representativeness.

As a research tool, oral history emerges from several distinct areas of research, including the anthropological study of folk cultures and the psychological study of lives through interviews and personal documents, developed by John Dollard, Gordon Allport, and others in the 1930s and 1940s. More recently, Oscar Lewis and Robert Coles have demonstrated in their respective works the power of this method when applied to the reconstruction of the lives of Puerto Rican and Mexican families, the urban poor, and the children of migrant workers and sharecroppers.

The widespread use of the cassette tape-recording machine over the past three decades has contributed considerably to the popularization of oral history interviewing. Like the computer, the recorder has facilitated the gathering and preservation of data, and has also generated a mystique of authenticity that is attributed to technological means. In the preface to one of his books, Oscar Lewis somewhat glorified the role of the tape recorder:

This appendix has been adapted from the appendix to my book, *Family Time and Industrial Time* (Hareven 1982), which is called "The Subjective Reconstruction of Past Lives."

The tape recorder used in taking down the life stories in this book has made possible the beginning of a new kind of literature of social realism. With the aid of the tape recorder, unskilled, uneducated and even illiterate persons can talk about themselves and relate their observations and experiences in an uninhibited, spontaneous and natural manner.

People who employ the tape recorder, like those who use the computer, quickly discover that it does not have intrinsic magic. Without a historical and sociological imagination to guide the process, only hours of meaningless information are obtained.

Oral history is not strictly a means for retrieving information but rather a process for generating knowledge. An oral history narrative is the product of an interaction between interviewer and interviewee. It is a process of life review. With the stimulation and assistance of the interviewer, people relive their past lives. The interviewer is like a medium, conjuring memories through his or her own presence, interest, and questions. The process can be intrusive, even when the interviewer tries to remain inconspicuous.

Oral history is a subjective process. It provides insight into how people think about their lives, as well as about outside events, and how they perceive their role in the course of historical events. More than being a source of factual evidence (a reconstruction of reality), oral history re-creates people's memories and perceptions — it teaches us what people remember, why they remember it, and how they remember. Sometimes the subjectivity of oral history is individual in nature and at other times it is collective, depending on whether the people interviewed are several members of the same family or several participants in the same event. In both cases, however, it is a result both of an individual's personal attitude and of the set of cultural values and collective ideology that guides his or her life.

Historians have long been accustomed to employing such subjective documents as diaries, letters, and investigative reports in the reconstruction of past events. In this respect, oral history fits into a wider context, namely the use of personal documents for historical and sociological research. An oral history account is essentially a subjective, personal document. In a systematic scrutiny of the reliability of using personal documents in psychological research, Gordon Allport defined personal documents as

[a]ny self-revealing record that intentionally or unintentionally yields information regarding the structure, dynamics, and functioning of the author's mental life. It may record the participant's view of experiences in which he has been involved, it may devote itself deliberately to self-scrutiny and self-description; or it may be only incidentally and unwittingly self-revealing. (Allport 1942, xii)

Oral history is an expression of the personality of the people interviewed, their cultural values, and the historical circumstances that shaped their outlook. Indeed, this subjectivity is its great value. Diaries and personal letters are also highly subjective, though their bias is of a different nature. A diary or a letter reflects a person's individual experiences or observation, whereas an oral history account consists of the individual's past experiences as evoked by an interviewer who has an influence on what is remembered and the way in which it is recounted. This is a result of the interviewer's intervention, as well as of the sense of communication that the person interviewed has with posterity through the interview process. Diaries and letters are acutely connected to the specific event that generated them. Oral history can be both handicapped and enriched by its distance in time from the event recounted. The accuracy of the account could be limited by faulty memory or changed by people's own perceptions of their lives. Ironically, this handicap is also a source of strength. It offers the advantage of reconstructing past events from a larger vantage point and interpreting earlier events in the context of subsequent developments. The perspective on time gained through oral history creates a different scale of importance by which to judge past events in the light of changes in one's own point of view. The careful listener gains insight into how people reconstruct their life histories, how they order events of their past lives, and how they articulate meaning in their lives.

Thus oral history offers a glimpse into the sequence of events in people's lives as well as insight into how, in the speakers' search for patterns, their memories are reassembled and disassembled as in a kaleidoscope, losing meaning, changing meaning, disappearing, and reappearing in different configurations at different points in time. A great difficulty in the interview process lies in the listener's inability to discern the specific meaning that an event held earlier as opposed to the significance that the interviewee subsequently attributes to it. Certain occurrences that seem valuable to the historian may be forgotten because their original meaning has been lost for the actor, whereas other events are often elevated out of proportion to their past significance in people's lives because subsequent events have placed them in a new perspective.

The dynamic interplay between past and present in an individual's reminiscences takes different forms. At times, people interviewed temporarily immerse themselves in a past episode as they recount it. This is especially true for childhood memories. On such occasions, the individual slips back into the past and vibrantly recounts earlier episodes without any consciousness of the present. The person interviewed becomes an actor playing a past role. For example, in recounting a specific scene of conflict with a boss, interviewees often reenacted the scene without any self-consciousness, staging a dialogue with the other characters involved, mimicking themselves and the other person as they might have been in the past. To re-create the scene, elderly people interviewed even left their seats, sometimes pacing back and forth and sometimes standing in one place. When people interviewed were asked to describe their jobs, their detailed descriptions were often accompanied by reenactments of the specific operations involved in handling the machinery. On most occasions, the people interviewed retained a conscious separation between the historical account and the present and offered a contemporary perspective on past experience.

Sometimes people just forgot experiences, or they chose to forget; or if they remembered, they did not want to talk about them. According to Gunhild Hagestadt, in many families there are forbidden zones, avoided as if by unspoken agreement (personal communication 1979). Although people interviewed can often sense the invisible fences when approaching such areas, they can do little about them. Actual events or situations are sometimes misrepresented or reinterpreted because of a faulty memory or a repression of difficult experiences. Traumatic experiences, in particular, can lead to the repression or reinterpretation of events.

In assessing the reliability of oral history, one needs to distinguish between faulty memory and lack of perspective. People who forget certain experiences or events do not necessarily suffer from a lack of perspective or hindsight on the events they do remember. The memory of early life events, although limited by distance in time or colored by fantasy, can still be remarkably clear in old age. Older people interviewed for this study, such as Mr. Nishitani and Mr. Shibagaki, remembered earlier life events with great clarity and elaborate detail. Actually, most of the people interviewed had clear senses of their own lives and were able to place their past in perspective, observing how they interpreted certain events at the time of their occurrence and how they changed their point of view as the years passed.

Do these retrospective characteristics of oral history render it useless to historians? Most historical information drawn from traditional written sources is also fragmented and biased. The most elaborate letter, diary, or court record still represents only a small fragment of reality, colored by people's perceptions at one point in time. Even quantitative data, frequently hailed as scientific or objective, are biased. As historians frequently point out, the census itself is a record of perceptions—those of an individual or family group defining its household status, occupational status, literacy, ethnic origin, family relationships, and many other characteristics. The census may even represent the census-taker's personal perceptions, rather than those of the individuals being counted.

Beyond doubt, oral history is a record of perceptions. It is not a re-creation of historical events. It can be employed as a factual source only if corroborated. The necessity of cross-checking information does not detract, however, from the value of oral history in understanding perceptions and recovering levels of experiences not normally available to historians.

Through oral history, the student can better understand how people construct meaning for their lives and, most important, how they interpret their past lives in the context of their own culture. As Everett Hughes put it, life history involves the "moving perspective in which a person sees his life as a whole and interprets the meaning of his various attributes, actions and the things which happen to him" (1971). Such a "moving perspective" is derived not only from a person's individual experience but also from a person's own culture. Because memory is selective, people remember events and experiences only when they are significant, by virtue either of their intrinsic value in people's lives or of the external historical circumstances associated with them and the cultural attributes that give them meaning.

By its nature, the oral history interview allows the development of two levels of meaning. The people interviewed are able to reconstruct their past lives and assess their meaning. The interviewer is permitted to study both the narrative itself and the meaning attributed to it. Although interrelated, these two levels of meaning are not always identical. Aspects that are significant to the person interviewed are often less important to the interviewer, and vice versa. The interview sometimes provides both an opportunity to recall the past and a chance to view one's life in light of the present. Thus an interview may become an occasion for squaring accounts with the past, for clearing up earlier misunderstandings, and, at times, for self-justification.

In summary, oral history is a powerful, indispensable source. It provides a depth of insight that can rarely be retrieved from other sources. It is unique in offering the opportunity for subjective reconstruction of past lives. Like surveys, it calls up attitudes and perceptions. Unlike surveys, it places these perceptions in the context of an individual's and a family's life history. These perceptions are exceptionally valuable, not as individual case histories but as historical, cultural testimonies. Each interview reflects the common cultural frame of reference that shapes the reconstruction of individual lives — that is, individual lives gain their sense and meaning from the collective culture or the subculture. As Robert LeVine put it, "The subjective career can be dealt with in both collective and individual representations and individual representations of it are permeated with cultural meanings" (LeVine 1978). This is where a strong link lies between oral history and life history.

Glossary of Japanese Words

aizome	indigo-dyed
arubaito	work part-time; derives from German word "arbeit"
bantō, bantō-san	head clerk
bata	see *hata*
bentō	lunch; lunch box
bijutsu-hin	works of art
bokashi	complexly colored weaving design, with gradations of color like in an impressionistic painting
bungyō	division of labor
bunke	branch family, or branch family business
chin	hire
chinbata	"hiring of the loom"; cottage weavers who rent their looms from the manufacturer; used interchangeably with *debata* in this book
chirimen	white textured silk for *kimono* that is dyed after it is woven; silk crepe
chōnin	city dwellers and tradesmen
chōsei-hō	regulation or adjustment of pace of production
daikō-ten	middleman between Nishijin manufacturers and Tango weavers
Dai Niji Sekai Taisen	World War II

Dai-Tōa Senso	Greater East Asian War, started in 1941; term used at the time within Japan to describe the Asian conflict of World War II
dandan-batake	"ladder-like garden"; a terraced garden or farm on the slope of a hill
date-maki	rolls of cloth
debata	cottage weavers who own their own looms; used interchangeably with *chinbata* in this book
dekasegi	a seasonal side job for which workers leave their home communities and work somewhere else
deki-daka	piece-rate pay system
deki-daka-barai	pay by piece-rate
Dentō Kōgei	certificate of master for the traditional arts
dentō sangyō	traditional industry
detchi	apprentice, or the lowest-ranking employees in a company
donchō	big curtain for theater
Edo	old name for Tokyo; see Tokugawa
endai	porch extending toward the garden
enka	popular ballads sung by street singers in Japan during the period from 1900 to 1930
fujin-kai	women's association
fukkō keiki	market comeback or market boom
fukuro-obi	a special style of *obi*
funa-ya	boathouses that reach out over the water, so boats can be stored under them
futon	folding quilted mattress used for sleeping on the *tatami* mat
fuyu-mono	winter clothing
gacha	the clattering of the shuttle on the loom
gachaman	nickname given to Nishijin weavers by Kyoto residents, meaning each time the shuttle clicked when it moved across the warp, a weaver earned a *man* [ten thousand *yen*]
geisha, geisha-san	a professional beauty and entertainer
genshi	original design paper
geta	sandals
getsumatsu-barai	payments at the end of each month
gijutsusha	a person with an artistic technique

go	the national board game of Japan
go-chisō	a feast; a dinner; a banquet
gofuku-ya	*kimono* retail store
gokudō	a very bad guy; often used to refer to gangsters
gunju sangyō	industry for war supplies
gunzoku	civilian employee in the military for war industries
gyokusai	"death-for-honor" strategy
haku	gold thread
haku-naishō	cataract
hana-fuda	Japanese playing cards
hana-o	sandal straps
hangyo hannō	half fisherman, half farmer
happosai	a Chinese dish, meaning "eight vegetables"
hata	loom; when connected to another word preceding it, *hata* becomes *bata*
hatagoshirae	prepare the looms
hata-ya	weaver, or weaving shop
hatazao	equipment of the loom
Heisei period	from 1989 to the present
hikibaku	technique for pulling the gold thread through the warp
hōkō	apprentice
honke	main or head-family house or business
hoshō	guaranteed payments
ichinin-mae	independent; self-supporting
iro awase	color matching
ito	thread
ito-guruma	spinning wheel
ito-kuri	twisting the thread
ito-ya	wholesaler of thread
itozome	dyeing the thread
jaku	measurement of length equal to about thirty centimeters; same as *shaku*
jiei	independent business; self-employed
jimae	small-scale manufacturer
jinrikisha	cart pulled by a human
jitsudō	actual working hours

jukuren-kō	skilled workers
kabushiki-gaisha	a joint-stock company
kagikko	"latchkey kids"
kake-jiku	a long, vertically hanging scroll picture
kanai kōgyō	cottage industry system
Kantō	Tokyo and surrounding prefectures in eastern Japan
Kantō Daishinsai	Great Tokyo Earthquake of 1923
kanzome	intuitive dyeing
kawaraya-san	roof tilers
kazoku	family
kenkō-hoken	health insurance as part of a public pension system
kiito	raw silk thread
ki-jaku	plain cloth for *kimono*
kiki	crisis
ki-nagashi	informal clothes, worn mostly in the summer
kinran	gold brocade
kiori-ya, kiori-ya-san	powerloom weaver
kōchin	wages
Kōjin-san	a guardian deity of a house site, or a festival for that deity
kokata	"child"; paternalistic term for weaver in historic Nishijin
kōsei-nenkin	a variety of contributory pension
koshi	movement of weaving; position of weft; used to calculate payment to weaver
kotatsu	low table with a foot-warming heater underneath
kōtō-shōgakkō	higher elementary (grade) school through seventh and eighth grades in the pre-war school system
kō-zukai	pocket money given to parents by their grown children as a gift; customary in Japan
kuchiberashi	"get rid of extra mouths to feed"
kuchi o azukeru	"keep your mouth over there," or eat away from your family
kumiai	union or association

kuri-ya	twisters or winders
Kurume *kasuri*	hand-dyed indigo cloth, following a technique similar to *ikat*, with a splashed pattern; from Kurume City in Kyushu
kuzu kiito	"junk" silk thread
kyubata	resting the looms
kyuki	interruption in textile production
kyūtei	Imperial Court
machi	adding excess cloth
machi-ya	townhouse
maki-e	paintings on lacquer
man	ten thousand *yen*
maru-obi	wide *obi*
mawata	silk floss
Meiji Period	reign of the Meiji Emperor, 1868–1912; sometimes broken into an early period (c. 1868–89) and a late period (c. 1890–1912)
Meiji Restoration	military overthrow of the Tokugawa shogun and subsequent modernization reforms
meshi-ya	a small eating house
miai	arranged marriage
mikomi seisan	estimates and calculations for future production
minarai	training
Ming *tsuzure*	figured brocade with a sculptured effect; weaving technique originally from China
minshuku	family-run guest house
miya-daiku	carpenter for the Imperial Palace and for shrines and temples
mizu-nomi byakushō	"drinking-water peasant," meaning a poor peasant
mongami	punch cards with the design for the jacquard
mongen	curfew, closing time
mon-ori	brilliant weavings textured with motifs in relief
mori-kiri	a single helping with no refills
muji	plain cloth
munen-musō	freedom from all thoughts and ideas
mura	village

Muromachi *don'ya*	Muromachi wholesalers
myoto	helper
naiju	domestic demands for goods
naishoku	a side job, usually for housewives
naka-gai	wholesaler, middleman (for kimono)
natsumero	once-popular sentimental songs that evoke nostalgia for one's youth or for particular periods
natsu-mono	summer cloth
nenki-bōkō	indentured apprenticeship
nenkin	retirement pension; an annuity
ni-gō	a concubine; mistress; one's secondary wife
ningen	human being
nippachi	literally means "two and eight"; in this case, it refers to February and August
Nishijin Ori Kōgyō Kumiai	Nishijin Textile Industrial Association
Nishijin Ori Kaikan	Nishijin Textile Center (Hall)
Nishijin Ori Rōdō-kumiai	Greater Nishijin Textile Labor Union
Nishijin Senshoku Kumiai	Nishijin Association of Thread Manufacturers and Dyers
Nisshin-sensō	Sino-Japanese War, 1894–95
noren	split curtain hanging over the entrance door as a shop sign
noren wake	status of an affiliate or branch shop
nuki-maki	winding the thread for the weft
nusumi-dori	to steal or acquire
obā-chan	very old woman; grandmother; *-chan* is an affectionate diminutive
oba-san	aunt
obā-san	very old woman; grandmother
obi	sash worn over *kimono*
Obon	Buddhist All Souls' Day, July 13–16 or August 13–16
ocha-ya	teahouse, usually a place for entertainment by *geisha*
ōdanna	elderly top master of house or business
ohina-san	set of dolls that are displayed during the Girls' Festival on March 3

o-jii, o-jii-san	grandfather; old man
o-kayu sawagi	depression known as the "rice gruel panic"
o-meshi	plain cloth for *kimono*
o-rei bōkō	free service after one has finished one's apprenticeship, to show thanks
ori	textile
oridaka-sei	the system of paying in accordance with the amount produced
oridema	amount of payment or cost of weaving operation
oriko	weaver; child; old-fashioned, paternalistic term for weavers
orimoto	a textile manufacturer
orite	weaver
ori-ya, ori-ya-san	textile manufacturer; another word for *orimoto*
ori-ya dachi	type of textile manufacturer's house in Nishijin
Oshima *tsumugi*	a roughly textured silk fabric woven in Amami Oshima, a southern island of Japan
ōte	major companies
otō-chan	"daddy"; the way a wife usually addresses her husband (*chan* is the affectionate term)
oyaji, oyaji-san	another word for "father" or older man
oyakata, oyakata-san	father; antiquated, paternalistic term for manufacturer
pachinko	slot machines
ren'ai-kekkon	marry for love
riki-shokki	powerloom
rōdō-kijun-hō	Fair Labor Standards Act
Rōdō-Kijun Kyoku	Bureau of Labor Standards
rōdō-sha	laborer
sakizome	silk threads dyed prior to weaving (*saki* means prior)
san	honorific word meaning Mr., Mrs., or Ms., but also used as a sign of respect when attached to other words
sanchi don'ya	local, intermediate wholesalers based in Nishijin
Seijin Shiki	adulthood ceremony
seikei	warping, preparing the warp

seisan chōsei	production adjustment
seken-no-sōba	a reasonable price, wage, or income, neither much above nor much under the level of compensation informally set by people concerned; average value for market
sensei	teacher, professor, master in an art or craft or the performing arts
sentō	public bathhouse
shachō, shachō-san	president; head of a tin
shaku	measurement of length equal to about thirty centimeters; same as *jaku*
shamisen	Japanese stringed instrument
shataku	company housing
shichi kinrei	an order prohibiting the use of gold or silver thread in Nishijin weaving during war times
shichirin	portable clay charcoal stove
shigoto	work
shikuchigae	change in the weaving method
shinkan	Shinto priest
shiro-kiji	plain white cloth
shishu	black cloth
shita	low
shitae	lining for *obi*
shita-machi	the traditional shopping and entertainment districts of a city, usually geographically low-lying
shita-shigoto	subsidiary tasks involving preparation and clean-up; low-status work
shita-uke	subcontracting of services
shizoku	gentility
shō	measurement of rice; approximately 1.4 kilograms
shōgi	Japanese chess
shōgi	commercial prostitutes
shokki	looms
shokkō	live-in weaver
shokugyō-anteisho	government employment office for people who have lost their jobs

shokunin	craftsmen, craftspeople
Shōwa Period	reign of the Shōwa emperor; 1926–89; often divided into an early period (1926–37), a wartime period (1937–45), and a post-war period (1946–89)
shūdan-shūshoku	boys and girls employed in a group after graduation from junior high school
shūgi	a congratulatory gift in cash during celebrations and festivities
shushi	the thrust of one's argument
shushoku	rice; the staple food
soko	preparing harnessess and treadles for controlling the warp on the loom
some-ya	dyeing workshops
sonohi-gurashi	hand-to-mouth existence
sorabiki-bata	the "human jacquard," a loom where the warp was manipulated by hand for the design, before the introduction of the jacquard
Taishō Period	reign of the Taishō emperor; 1912–26; period of the extension of democracy and mass culture
taishoku-kin	a retirement grant, usually but not always in the form of a lump sum
takahata	double-tiered handloom with "human jacquard"
tan	rolls of *obi* or cloth
Tango *chirimen*	white textured silk for *kimono* that is dyed after it is woven; silk crepe, woven in Tango's traditional cottage industry
Tango Ori Kōgyō Kumiai	Tango Association of Textile Manufacturers
Tango Ori Rōdo-Umiai	Tango Labor Union of Weavers
tanka	price per piece
tansu	chest of drawers
tatami	mat(s) used to cover the floors of rooms
tate-ito	warp
tate-tsugi	tying the threads of the new warp to the loom frame
tebata	handloom
tegata	promissory note
teori	handweaving

Tokugawa Period	period of Tokugawa house rule, 1600–1867; also referred to as the Edo Period
tonari-gumi	neighborhood group or association
ton'ya	wholesalers of *kimono* wear; also defined as "middlemen"
totei	historic apprentice system
tsumugi	see Oshima *tsumugi*
tsuzure	figured brocade with a sculptured effect; weaving technique originally from China
uchibata	weavers in factories
uchikake	brocade wedding coats worn by brides over *kimono*
udon-ya	noodle shop
ukeoi seido	contracting system
unagi-no-ne-doko	"sleeping place of the eel"; nickname for the traditional wooden houses in Nishijin
urushi	lacquer work
usakizome	natural dye, vegetable dye, from ash
yabu-iri	July 15 and 16; summer holiday
yami	weave secretly; "hidden weavers"; black market; dye threads secretly
yasumi	holidays, breaks
yonabe	night work
yonabe-suru	worked at night
yojin	outsiders
yūkaku	licensed prostitution quarters
yukata	summer cotton *kimono*
yūkyū-kyūka	paid vacation; holiday with guaranteed pay
yūzen	a technique of dyeing *kimono*, using a paste resist or stencil
zabuton	cushion(s) for sitting or kneeling on the floor
zenzai	thick, sweet, bean-meal soup with rice-cake

Bibliography

Allport, Gordon. 1942. *The Use of Personal Documents in Psychological Science*. New York: Social Science Research Council.

Chujo, Takeshi. 1965. *Keiei Rōmū no Kindaika: Nishijin no Kindaika ni Yosete* (Modernization of Management and Labor: Modernization of Nishijin). Kyoto: Sanwa Shobō.

———. 1984. *Nishijin no Chinbata Rōdō to Seni Kōzō Taisaku* (Nishijin Chinbata Workers and Solutions of Fabric Structures). Kyoto: Sanwa Shobō.

Demos, John. 1970. *A Little Commonwealth: Family Life in Plymouth Colony*. New York: Oxford University Press.

Elder, Glen. 1978. "Family History and the Life Course." In *Transitions: The Family and the Life Courses in Historical Perspective*, edited by Tamara K. Hareven, 17–64. New York: Academic Press.

Fowler, Edward. 1996. *San'yo Blues: Laboring Life in Contemporary Tokyo*. Ithaca, New York: Cornell University Press.

Furumai, Toshio. 1965. "Nishijin Kigyō no Daiyoji Chōsa ni Motozuku Rōdō Tōkei Shiryō" (Statistics of Labor Conditions in Nishijin Industry). *Doshisha Keizai-gaku Ronsō* 14, no. 5.

———. 1965. "Nishijin Orimonogyō to Hito-de Busoku" (Nishijin Silk Weaving Industry and Shortage of Workers). *Kyoto Shōkō Jōhō* 62: 4–14.

Gans, Herbert. 1962. *The Urban Villagers: Group and Class in the Life of Italian-Americans*. New York: Free Press.

Gutmann, Myron, and René Leboutte. 1984. "Rethinking Protoindustrialization and Family." *Journal of Interdisciplinary History* 14: 587–607.

Haak, Ronald. 1975. "The Zesty Structured World of a Weaver." In *Adult Episodes in Japan*, edited by David Plath, 45–50. Leiden: E. J. Brill.

Hareven, Tamara K. 1978. "The Dynamics of Kin in an Industrial Community." *American Journal of Sociology* 84: S151–82.

———. 1982. *Family Time and Industrial Time: The Relationship between the Family and Work in a Planned Industrial Community*. New York: Cambridge University Press.

———. 1985. "Nishijin no Jirenma" (The Nishijin Dilemma). *Kyoto Prefecture Labor Institute Publication* no. 85 (October): 24–28.

———. 1988. "Kazoku Rōdō ni Oyobosu Gijutsu Keizaiteki Henka no Eikyō" (The Impact of Technological and Economic Change on Family and Work in the Nishijin Silk Weaving Industry). Translated by Sumizawa-Himeoka Toshiko. *Shisō* 6: 97–122.

———. 1992. "Between Craft and Industry: The Subjective Reconstruction of the Life Course of Kyoto's Traditional Weavers." In *Japanese Biographies: Life Cycles and Life Stages*, edited by Susanne Formanek and Sepp Linhart. Vienna: Östereicheische Akademie der Wissenschaften: 179–207.

———. 1992. "From Amoskeag to Nishijin: Reflections on Life History Interviewing in Two Cultures." In *International Annual of Oral History, 1990: Subjectivity and Multiculturalism in Oral History*, edited by Ronald J. Grele. Westport, Connecticut: Greenwood Press: 9–42.

Hareven, Tamara K., and Randolph Langenbach. 1978. *Amoskeag: Life and Work in an American Factory City*. New York: Pantheon Books.

Hareven, Tamara K., and Masaoka Kanji. 1988. "Turning Points and Transitions: Perceptions of the Life Course." *Journal of Family History* 13, no. 3: 271–89.

Hattori, Shiso. 1948. *Nishijin Kigyō ni Okeru Genseiteki Sangyō Kakumei no Tenkai* (Development of a Primary Industrial Revolution in Nishijin Industry). Kyoto: Takakiri-Shoin.

Hōkōi, Akimasa. 1961. *Nishijin Kigyō to Rōdōsha* (Nishijin Industry and Its Workers). Kyoto: Rōdō Geppō.

———. 1963. *Nishijin Kigyō Rōdōsha to Chiiki no Soshiki ni Kansuru Chōsa Hōkoku* (Report on Nishijin Workers and Local Organizations). Kyoto: Nishijin Kai.

———. 1968. "Nishijin Kigyō no Rōdō Keizai Jijyō" (Labor Conditions in Nishijin Industry). *Kikan Rōdō to Keizai* 17: 28–35.

Honjo, Ejiro. 1930. *Nishijin Kenkyū* (Research on Nishijin). Kyoto: Kaizosha.

Hughes, Everett. 1971. *The Sociological Eye: Selected Papers*. Chicago: Aldine-Atherton.

Japan Statistics Bureau. 1920. *National Census Report*. Japan: Statistics Bureau, Management and Coordination Agency.

Kawabata, Yasunari. 1962. *The Old Capital*. Translated by J. Martin Holman. San Francisco: North Point Press, 1987.

Kleinberg, Jill. 1983. "Where Work and Family Are Almost One: The Lives of Folkcraft Potters." In *Work and Lifecourse in Japan*, edited by David W. Plath, 215–47. Albany: State University of New York Press.

Kondo, Dorinne K. 1990. *Crafting Selves: Power, Gender, and Discourses of Identity in a Japanese Workplace*. Chicago: University of Chicago Press.

Kuromatsu, Iwao. 1969. "Nishijin Kigyō no Dōkō to Sono Sho Mondai" (Problems in Nishijin's Industry). *Keiei-gaku Ronsō* 18, no. 1–3: 1–48.

Kuromatsu, Iwao, ed. 1965. *Nishijin Kigyō no Kenkyū* (Research of Nishijin Industry). Kyoto: Mineruba Shobō.

Kyoto Women's Problems Research Committee. 1969. *Life and Labor of Housewives in Nishijin*. Kyoto: Kyoto Women's Problems Research Committee.

Kyoto-fu, Gakumu-bu, Shakai-ka. 1934. *Nishijin Chin'ori Gyōsha ni Kansuru Chōsa* (Research on Nishijin Pieceworkers). Kyoto: Kyoto-fu, Gakumu-bu, Shakai-ka.

Kyoto-fu, Shakai-ka. 1938. *Bukka Tōki no Shomin Seikatsu ni Oyoboseru Eikyō Chōsa* (The Impact of Rapid Rise in Prices on Common People). Kyoto: Kyoto-fu, Shakai-ka.

Kyoto-fu, Shōkō-bu. 1973. *Nishijin Kigyō no Chinbata ni Kansuru Genjō to Mondaiten* (The Situation and Problems of Cottage Weavers in Nishijin Industry). Kyoto: Kyoto-fu, Shoko-bu.

Kyoto-shi, Keizai-kyoku. 1968. *Nishijin Kigyō Chiku no Saikaihatsu ni Kansuru Chōsa* (Research on Redevelopment in Nishijin Industrial Area). Kyoto: Kyoto-shi, Keizai-kyoku.

Kyoto-shi, Kikaku Shingi-shitsu. 1951. *Nishijin Kigyō Jittai Chōsasho* (Report of Research and Realities of Nishijin Enterprises). Kyoto: Kyoto-shi, Kikaku Shingi-shitsu.

Kyoto-shi, Shakai-ka. 1948. *Nishijin Kigyō ni Kansuru Chōsa* (Research on Nishijin Industry). Kyoto: Kyoto-shi, Shakai-ka.

LeVine, Robert A. 1978. "Comparative Notes on the Life Course." In *Transitions: The Family and the Life Course in Historical Perspective*, edited by Tamara K. Hareven. New York: Academic Press.

Matsumoto, Michiharu. 1968. "Nishijin Kigyōsha no Chiiki Seikatsu: Toku-ni Nishijin Kigyō o Kiteisuru Chiiki Seikatsu no Tokushitsu ni Tsuite" (Lifestyle of Nishijin Workers: Especially about Characteristics of Lifestyle, Which Regulates Nishijin Industry). *Jinbun-gaku Doshisa Daigaku* 109: 1–31.

Matsuo, Hiroko. 1999. *Kyō Nishijin*. Kyoto: Tankosha.

Medick, Hans. 1976. "The Proto-Industrial Family Economy: The Structural Function of Household and Family During the Transition From Peasant Society to Industrial Capitalism." *Social History* 1–2 (October): 291–315.

———. 1981. "The Proto-Industrial Family Economy." In *Industrialization before Industrialization: Rural Industry in the Genesis of Capitalism*, edited by Peter Kriedte, Hans Medick, and Jürgen Schlumbohm, 38–73. Cambridge: Cambridge University Press.

Mendels, Franklin. 1972. "Proto-Industrialization: The First Phase of the Industrialization Process." *Journal of Economic History* 32: 241–61.

Mitsuka, Takeo. 1968. "Nishijin Kigyō ni Okeru Chinbata Rōdōsha no Seikatsu to Sono Jittai" (Characteristics of Chinbata Workers in Nishijin Today). *Jinbun-gaku Doshisa Daigaku* 109: 32–72.

Mitterauer, Michael. 1992. "Peasant and Non-Peasant Family Forms in Relation to the Physical Environment and the Local Economy." *Journal of Family History* 17, no. 2: 139–59.

Morris-Suzuki, Tessa. 1994. *The Technological Transformation of Japan: From the*

Seventeenth to the Twenty-first Century. Cambridge: Cambridge University Press.

Mosk, Carl. 2001. *Japanese Industrial History: Technology, Urbanization and Economic Growth*. Armonk, New York: M. E. Sharpe.

Nishijin Ori Kōgyō Kumiai. 1980. *Nishijin Orimonogyō Sanchi Shinkō Keikaku* (Plans for Developing the Area of Nishijin Weaving). Kyoto: Nishijin Ori Kōgyō Kumiai.

———. 1981. *Nishijin Seisan Gaikyō* (Report on Nishijin Production). Kyoto: Nishijin Ori Kōgyō Kumiai.

Ochiai, Emiko. 1997. *The Japanese Family System in Transition: A Sociological Analysis of Family Change in Postwar Japan*. Tokyo: LTCB International Library Foundation.

Plath, David W. 1980. *Long Engagements: Maturity in Modern Japan*. Stanford: Stanford University Press.

Reischauer, Edwin O. 1989. *Japan: The Story of a Nation*. 4th ed. New York: Alfred A. Knopf.

Saito, Osamu. 1983. "Population and the Peasant Family Economy in Proto-Industrial Japan." *Journal of Family History* 8, no. 1: 30–54.

Sanpei, Koko. 1961. *Nihon Kigyō Shi* (The History of the Japanese Weaving Industry). Tokyo: Yūsankaku.

Smith, Robert J. 1983. "Making Village Women into 'Good Wives and Wise Mothers' in Prewar Japan." *Journal of Family History* 8, no. 1: 70–84.

Thompson, Edward P. 1964. *The Making of the English Working Class*. New York: Pantheon Books.

Tilly, Louise, and Joan Scott. 1978. *Women, Work and the Family*. New York: Holt, Reinhart and Winston.

Toda, Teiza. 1937. *Kazoku Kōsei* (Family Composition). Tokyo: Kōbundō.

Vlastos, Stephen. 1998. *Mirror of Modernity: Invented Traditions of Modern Japan*. Berkeley: University of California Press.

Vogel, Ezra. 1979. *Japan as Number One: Lessons for America*. Cambridge, Massachusetts: Harvard University Press.

Wilensky, Harold. 1961. "Orderly Careers and Social Participation: The Impact of Work History in the Middle Mass." *American Sociological Review* 26.

Yamashita, Takayuki. 1961. "Nishijin Kigyō ni Okeru Uchibata Uibā no Seikaku to Rōdō Jōken" (Characteristics and Movement of Uchibata Workers in Nishijin Industry). Kyoto: Kyoto Shi Deizai Kyoku.

Yasuoka, Shigeaki. 1977. "Edo Kōki Meiji Zenki no Nishijin Kigyō no Dōkō" (Movement of Nishijin Industry in the Late Edo Period and the Early Meiji Period). *Shakai Kagaku* 23: 1–23.

Index

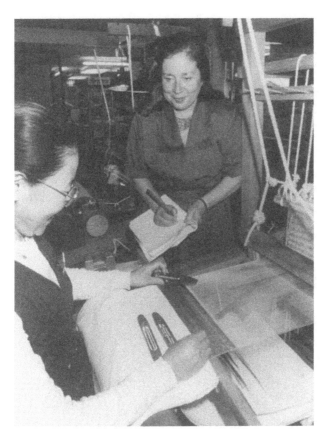

Tamara Hareven interviewing Mrs. Shibagaki. Photograph
courtesy of *Kyoto Shimbun* newspaper.

Compositor:	Binghamton Valley Composition, LLC
Text:	11/13 Galliard
Display:	Galliard
Printer and Binder:	Friesens Corporation